The Cover: Nestled comfortably into a hillside in western North Carolina is "My MOTHER's House", the full-scale energy-efficient dwelling designed and built at MOTHER's Eco-Village as an alternative energy research project. See chapter III for the complete story.

by the editors and staff of
THE MOTHER EARTH NEWS
Project Editor: Robert G. Miner
Art Director-Illustrator: Wendy Simons

THE MOTHER EARTH NEWS, Inc,
Hendersonville, North Carolina

Published 1983
Printed in the United States of America
THE MOTHER EARTH NEWS, Inc.
105 Stoney Mountain Road,
Hendersonville, North Carolina 28791

Library of Congress Catalog Card Number 83-61937

ISBN 0-938-432-03-6

THE MOTHER EARTH NEWS magazine is published at 105 Stoney Mountain Road, Hendersonville, North Carolina 28791. It is the bi-monthly publication edited by, and for, today's turned-on people of all ages . . . the creative ones, the doers, the folks who make it all happen. All material in MOTHER's HOMEBUILDING & SHELTER GUIDE has previously appeared in, or has been adapted from, THE MOTHER EARTH NEWS magazine or a related publication. Not all facts and figures are necessarily current.

INTRODUCTION

I EARTH-SHELTERED HOMES

II SOLAR ENERGY HOMES

III ALTERNATIVES COMBINE IN A TEST HOUSE

The desire to build your own home is a dream that incorporates more than a mere saving of dollars. That dream—once realized—becomes a permanent reflection of your lifestyle . . . one that blends the basic needs of food, water, and shelter with the soul-satisfaction that comes from an appreciation of what's natural, beautiful, and environmentally sound. As the saying goes, "It takes a lot of lovin' to make a house a home." So, with that in mind . . .

Before You Dig . . .

For most of us, the house we build (or purchase) will be the single largest investment we ever make. And for the owner-builder, that investment is far more than monetary. It involves time, effort, labor, and a great deal of thought . . . which all add up to an extraordinary outpouring of energy. No matter what you build or how you build it, the sum total of your efforts is bound to be impressive . . . however, the *product* of those efforts may not be. For instance, most of us have seen tract houses that go up—from footers to finish—in three weeks. Now that's impressive! But often it's difficult to determine which will last longer: the house or its mortgage. Therefore, keep in mind that a worthwhile product depends on more than a frantic display of effort. It requires a certain mind-set that realizes the importance and the sheer magnitude of the undertaking. It also demands a directed, detailed, and fully *conscious* effort to produce a solid structure that will stand for generations to come.

MAKE A SOUND INVESTMENT

A house is composed of thousands of different pieces, and an even greater number of joints and fittings. They don't all have to be perfect, but they do have to work. And with due respect to the environment that sustains us, they ought to work for a long, long time. A well-planned effort can result in the difference between an annual heating bill of $30, and one of $3,000 . . . between an earthquake-proof foundation and a cracked retaining wall . . . or between a balanced budget and a $10,000 cost overrun. So to give your house-building experience the respect it deserves . . . take your time, and do some homework.

THE EFFICIENCY CONCEPT

Just why is everyone so excited about the latest trends in home design? And what exactly *is* an energy-efficient house, anyway? When compared with the uninsulated homes of the 1920's and 30's, the residences of the 1960's were marvels of efficiency. Yet compared with the alternative building designs that have been available for well over a thousand years, those 60's structures leave a lot to be desired.

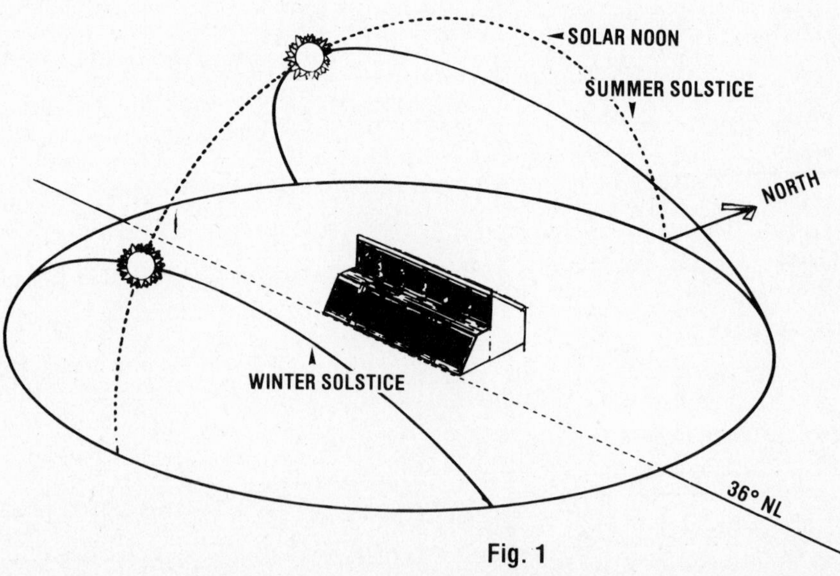

Fig. 1

There's no reason why a building can't furnish at least 40% of its own thermal (warming *and* cooling) requirements through conscientious design and building practices. And—given the right combination of techniques—it's entirely possible to achieve a 70, 80, or even 90% heating fraction. The secret to this success lies in three key concepts: *conservation*, *insolation*, and *heat storage*. They are the backbone and—to a certain extent—the focus of this entire book.

CONSERVATION

The root of any energy-efficient building is minimized heat loss. Without this key design element, you'll forever be indebted to the power companies. The principle components of conservation are *insulation* and *controlled infiltration*. Even the most shaded building—or sun-baked desert dwelling—can be made more efficient through the appropriate use of conservation techniques.

For example, no matter how much solar gain you've provided for your house, if the cold winter wind is able to blow right through it, you'll find yourself shivering on a cool day. Likewise, let's suppose it's a hot summer day, and all the shades are drawn. If the air in your home is stagnant, you're surely going to swelter . . . even without feeling the effects of direct sunlight. In both situations one element of the outside environment is controlled to maximum advantage (i.e., winter sun in . . . summer sun out), but because that control wasn't refined to incorporate another variable (airflow), you'd be uncomfortable in either situation.

AN OUNCE OF PREVENTION IS WORTH A BARREL OF OIL

Isolating the interior of a house requires plenty of insulation and careful workmanship. The advantages of insulating are well known. You simply can't expect a low fuel bill without the benefit of materials such as fiberglass, cellulose, and polystyrene. Each particular type of insulation has its strong and weak points, of course, and different varieties suit different designs. One example is fiberglass, which seems tailor-made for a wood-frame house but wouldn't be at all suitable in an underground dwelling. For a good discussion on the different types and applications of insulation, read *The Complete Book of Insulating*, edited by Larry Gay (The Stephen Greene Press).

The importance of good workmanship in framing and finishing a house is a bit harder to qualify. However, it's the single most important aspect of the conservation process . . . there's nothing colder than a drafty house. The constant loss of heat from the exchange of warm interior air for colder exterior air is called *infiltration*. And the rate at which infiltration occurs is referred to as the number of *air changes* per hour. In other words, it's the number of times in one hour that the volume of air contained in your house is replaced with an equivalent volume of outside air.

Naturally, the greater the number of air changes per hour, the more you'll need to stoke your stove. A high rate of infiltration—for instance, two, three, or four air changes per hour—will result in a staggering heat loss. What's more, all that insulation you've piled up in the attic is virtually useless when cold air is whistling around it in a leaky house.

This is where good workmanship counts most. Make certain that all doors and windows are tightly sealed. Insulate sill plates, electrical outlets, and all siding and sheathing. Finally, remember to caulk, caulk, caulk! Builders who are conscientious in this area are worth far more than their weight in oil.

A well-built aboveground home will average about three-fourths of an air change per hour. But, a super-tight house can achieve a rate of one-half change per hour or less. Dwellings that are built with these low change rates—such as earth-sheltered, underground, and superinsulated homes—should usually have a controlled heat exchange system that allows incoming fresh, cold air to be warmed by outgoing interior air.

INSOLATION

Insolation—the second concept mentioned earlier—is merely another word for solar gain. And solar gain can be defined simply as the amount of solar energy entering your house.

Modern passive solar structures most often use glass or plastic to provide a one-way portal for thermal energy. The trick is to let it in and keep it in, and windows—used in combination with energy-saving, movable insulation during the night—provide a reasonably efficient method of controlling energy flow. (The word "reasonably" is used because, in comparison with the insulating properties of a six-inch-thick, fiberglass-insulated wall, even a double-glazed window with insulating curtains has a relatively low R-value.)

But the success of a solar design is not measured by glass alone. Needless to say, an all-glass house is hardly energy-efficient. Once again, then, a proper balance is essential: You want a system which yields optimum solar gain with minimum heat loss for winter heating, and minimum solar gain with maximum heat loss for summer cooling. And therein lies a major reason that passive solar design is being lauded by home builders: In a properly designed solar building, the sun does all the balancing . . . with the exception of the opening and closing of windows or vents now and then.

IT'S ALL IN THE ANGLES

The way the sun positions itself throughout the seasons is truly a cosmic convenience. We're all aware that summer days are longer than winter ones . . . and that the sun sits higher in the sky during the warmer months. Of course, the opposite is true in the winter. The net effect of this varied trek across the sky is that in winter, when the sun's angle is low to the horizon, its rays can penetrate deeply into rooms with south-facing glass. (Naturally, residents of the southern hemisphere receive their sunshine from the northern exposure.) In the summer, however, when the sun is high overhead, hot solar rays are effectively blocked by the tops of the windows, the roof, and other appropriate overhangs. (See Figs. 1 & 2.)

Furthermore, other natural processes can be utilized for cooling a home. By capitalizing on the fact that warm air rises (known as *thermosiphoning*), a designer can take advantage of excess heat while getting rid of it. If vents or windows are placed at the highest points in the structure and low against the north wall, the warm air will rise and escape . . . which will draw in cooler air from the shaded north side of the building. *Voilá* . . . a summer breeze wafts through the house! What's more, the cooling effect can be augmented by pulling air into the dwelling through pipes buried in the ground, where temperatures remain relatively cool throughout the summer.

THERMAL STORAGE

But conservation practices and harnessing the sun's power for both heating and cooling are just part of the task. A method for storing the acquired energy is needed. Because significant solar gain occurs an average of only six hours a day in winter, it's advantageous to be able to take in a surplus of heat during that period. But without some way of storing the energy, a house would simply overheat.

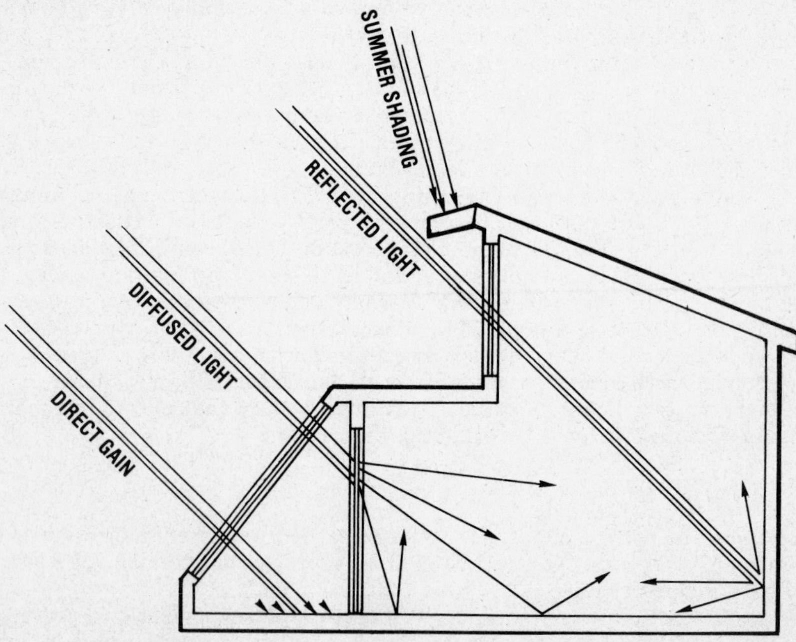

Fig. 2

Fortunately, it's possible to save up heat by allowing it to be absorbed in *thermal mass*. Nature provides us with several good examples of the principle. If you leave a rock out in the sun, you'll discover that it remains warm for several hours after dark. Likewise, you've probably taken a quick evening dip in a lake that's substantially warmer than the surrounding air. In both cases the material (rock or water) has the ability to absorb warmth and dissipate it slowly once the surrounding air becomes cooler. The same substances are often used in solar design.

Because of a basic thermodynamic principle (that heat will migrate to cooler substances to establish thermal balance), mass can work for us in several ways. In winter, a thermal mass can absorb excess heat during the day, releasing it at night to help keep us warm. During the summer this ability to absorb heat can be used to help cool the house. Therefore, houses with substantial amounts of mass (which include earth shelters, where the earth around the building acts as mass) maintain relatively stable temperatures.

As a matter of fact, mass is the main reason that earth sheltering is so effective. The surrounding ground becomes a portion of the effective mass of the building, thereby absorbing major fluctuations in temperature. But there's another functional aspect to the earth cover: Because warmth diminishes very slowly outward from an earth shelter's wall, the difference between outside and inside temperatures is relatively small.

Since heat loss from a building is a function of that temperature differential, an underground dwelling starts out with a built-in advantage. While an aboveground house may be asked to achieve 65°F indoors when the outdoor mercury has plunged to below zero, the inside temperature of a subterranean structure will have to be raised only from ground temperature (which is generally considered to be equal to that of ground water and is likely to be between 45 and 60°F).

DOING MASS WITH LESS

The expense of including mass in your home can be somewhat offset by using the material as part of the structural support system. One prevalent practice is to construct one of the main interior load-bearing walls out of a mass-intensive material such as concrete, rock, or filled block. Concrete floors are another way of using mass in both a thermal and a structural capacity. What's more, this mass can be located anywhere from only inches behind south-facing glazing (as in the Trombe wall system) to an insulated north wall. It's not even necessary for the thermal mass to be placed in direct sunlight, since such materials can absorb heat from reflected or diffused sunlight as well as from warm air as it circulates. (See Fig. 2.)

FINE DESIGN

Thermal efficiency is but one aspect of a functional, livable home. Good architectural design cannot be over emphasized. Space, movement, light, aesthetics, and many other elements must be effectively coordinated to make the building environmentally pleasing. The possibilities are limitless and present an opportunity to create a house that is a singular reflection of the family members' personalities.

The following questions concern only a few things you should look for as you visualize various sample designs on paper: Do the movement patterns in the house flow . . . or do they appear chopped and stilted? Do the open spaces allow varying levels of intimacy with both the outside world and the other occupants? The nature of design is a subject area worth many hours of study and thought, and it's one that architects address on a daily basis. So don't be afraid to consult a professional. As a consultant, he or she can be a valuable asset to the owner-builder. Even if you're developing your own design, a good architect can help save you time and money while guiding you toward your building goals.

There's a book about environmental design that's recommended highly. *A Pattern Language* by Christopher Alexander, et al. (Oxford University Press) is fairly expensive, so you may want to borrow it from your local library during your planning stages.

LAND CONSIDERATIONS

You should have a specific piece of property in mind before you begin serious design work for a home. The site will be all-important in determining which approach will be the most energy- and dollar-efficient. Of course, the perfect site is a rare commodity. The best most of us can do is to evaluate

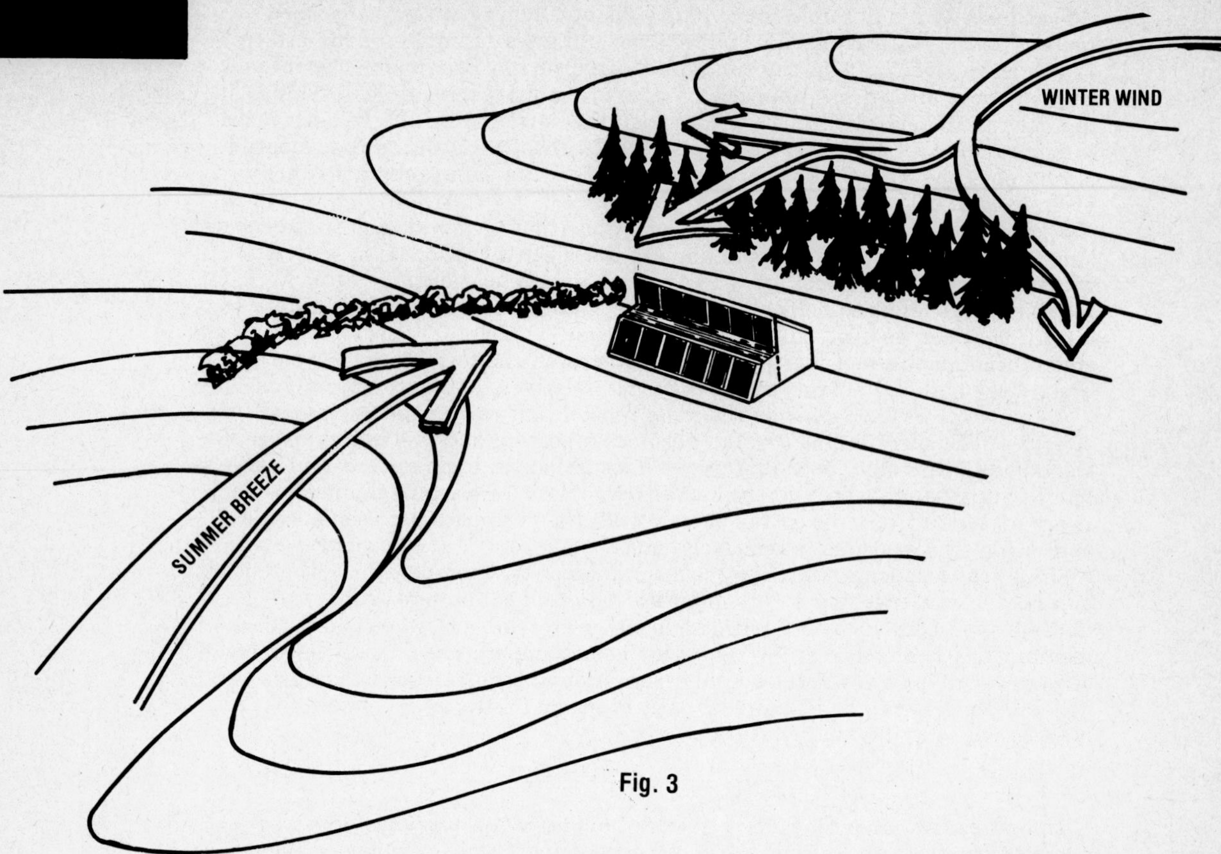

Fig. 3

carefully our priorities and then make necessary compromises in our choice of land . . . while keeping in mind that it's possible to develop and improve a parcel without destroying its character.

If you're primarily interested in a solar design, the plot's *exposure* is the most important aspect to consider. A parcel that never sees the winter sun just won't do. North-facing, sloping land will often be shaded in the winter, as a result of the low angle of the sun. And a steeper slope corresponds to more months of shading. Therefore, the ideal site will have a gently sloped southern exposure.

Of course, rating a site for solar input isn't generally a "cut and dried" procedure. Let's suppose you find a site that has a gently rising ridge to the south . . . a steep down-slope to the east . . . and no slope at all to the west. How can you determine the land's suitability? Because it's so important to establish exposure and get a good estimate of solar gain for determining the home's orientation and for designing such features as windows, it's a good idea to create a see-through chart on which you can plot the sun's path in different seasons and locate any surrounding obstacles (topography, buildings, trees, etc.) which might shade your future home. Without a chart, you'll be burdened with actually visiting the site on a regular basis to record this information. There are a number of ways to prepare such a chart, but *The Passive Solar Energy Book* by Edward Mazria (Rodale Press) provides an exceptionally good set of graphs, along with instructions on how to make a sun chart.

Solar access is the second most important consideration in site selection, and it's quite apart from the concept of exposure. One good definition of this access is "the legal right to the sun". The most perfect solar exposure will become totally useless if someone constructs a high-rise building to the south of you after you complete your home. For solar gain, such a situation is no different from building on the north side of Mt. Everest!

Access is a more serious consideration in the city or suburbs where lots are often small and tightly spaced. But even rural property is not exempt: A phenomenon as natural as your neighbor's rapidly growing spruce could be just as big a headache.

If a particular site meets the two major considerations already mentioned, you can then begin to evaluate the physical characteristics that will affect your design . . . such as drainage, geology, topography, and vegetation.

DRAINAGE

Adequate drainage is extremely important if earth sheltering is your goal. Waterproofing is a very difficult task at best, and the results are never guaranteed. Always consider waterproofing to be a second line of defense . . . and make *controlled drainage* the first. If at all possible, examine the site in its dry and wet seasons in order to determine its hydrology. Certain water problems are surmountable with reasonable effort and expenditure, and others can make your proposed project an economic bust. Most good books on earth-sheltered design contain chapters on waterproofing and drainage.

GEOLOGY AND TOPOGRAPHY

Surface inspection—along with soil and core samples—is a most important part of planning an earth-sheltered home. An unexpected layer of solid rock can thwart the best-laid plans . . . since blasting large areas of rock is not only very expensive, but also usually futile.

Check the characteristics of the soil closely. Expansive clay isn't suitable for underground dwellings, as the swelling of this type of soil when it's wet creates great pressures against the floors and walls. Again, seek help from professional consultants and/or the library whenever a question regarding soil suitability arises.

Solar exposure is just one of many factors influenced by topography. For instance, we're seeing more and more residences being built on steep ground, as the ideal locations become increasingly rare. This can be a major plus as far as energy is concerned. However, the design of foundation and retaining walls to hold back the uphill earth becomes a much more critical factor than corresponding designs for homes constructed on flatter land. Wind flow is also affected by the site's topography. By learning the seasonally prevailing wind directions, you will be able to determine how the landforms will affect the heating *and* cooling of your homesite. It's advantageous to situate your house so that rises will block the prevailing winter winds, while the area from which summer air currents come should be relatively clear.

VEGETATION

An optimal site will have the ability to seasonally augment a building's energy needs. Deciduous trees are one example. In the summer their leafy fullness provides ample shade, yet when winter arrives, their limbs stand bare to allow solar access. Cold north winds can be blocked by evergreens in the winter, while during the summer months these trees can help to direct a cooling western breeze through a properly designed and landscaped home. (See Fig. 3.)

Energy conservation is not the only reason for considering landscaping. Proper topography and vegetation will establish varying levels of privacy on your property . . . which can be especially important in urban and suburban areas. A house with no separation between street and yard will always be strongly—and sometimes adversely—influenced by traffic, pedestrians, service crews, and more. Yet it's also possible to be *too* secluded. A house completely walled off from its surrounding environment totally isolates the residents from the community . . . and this can have a negative impact. But if you are careful to blend the land and the home so that they offer varying levels of interaction with the outside world, the human needs of communication and privacy can *both* be met.

One example of lack of site planning is the large front yards typically found in modern neighborhoods. They are, in most cases, just wasted space. Most families prefer to carry on their recreational activities in the back or side yard . . . no matter how comparatively small those areas are. What's more, large front yards actually hinder interfamily communication. For these reasons, it may be worth considering moving homes closer to the street. The available space for a back yard would be increased, and people would have a better chance of getting to know their neighbors.

However, the need to buffer the transition from busy street to quiet haven still exists. One solution is a front porch, which can act as a bridge between two worlds. The security and privacy of the inner home won't be breached by a visitor on the porch. Perhaps trees and shrubs could be used to establish private areas in the yard, while plants and flowers would draw passers-by to the porch area. Obviously, there are as many different possibilities as there are people to create them. As you delve further into the pages of this book, notice how each of the different homes featured has solved problems and balanced the various elements of design. Once you've read these pages and have reviewed several of the recommended books, you should be prepared to design the right house for yourself and your family.

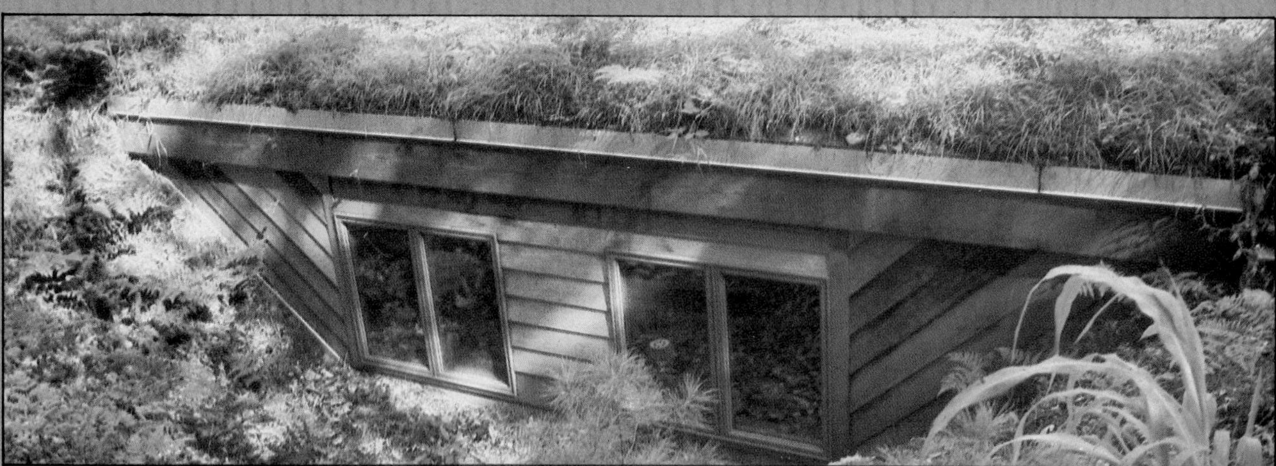

EARTH-SHELTERED HOMES

Although humans in "primitive" societies recognized long before the dawn of recorded history that the earth itself could shelter them and provide relative year-round comfort and protection from the elements, people in modern times drifted into an easy romance with fossil fuels using nonrenewable sources of energy to heat and cool inefficient dwellings. Today, however, with nonrenewable energy sources becoming scarcer and dearer, many people are forsaking oil, gas, coal, and electricity to temper the environments inside their homes . . . and are turning instead to energy-efficient, earth-sheltered houses, in which age-old principles are being applied in innovative and often ingenious ways.

"DUG IN" TO SAVE MONEY

You've heard tales about eccentrics who bury their money in the back yard. Well, Daniel Rinker, a retired tool-and-die maker from Michigan, went a step further . . . and buried his daughter, too! The story isn't at all gruesome, however, because the "back yard" is 4-1/2 acres of forested sand hills in Michigan . . . and Joyce, his daughter, is happily "dug in" there in a modern three-bedroom, earth-sheltered home with an attached two-car garage.

Joyce had read about an underground dwelling constructed in Massachusetts, and she liked the idea and told her parents about it. Daniel agreed that it sounded sensible, and —since he and Mrs. Rinker were about to take off on a tour around the country—they investigated all of the earth-sheltered structures they could find. They visited the library at Hendrix College in Conway, Arkansas, an underground elementary school in New Mexico, and a number of other partially or completely subterranean homes and institutions. They talked with homeowners, realtors (to see how these buildings affected area property values), janitors, and principals in the belowground schools . . . in short, just about anyone who could answer their many questions.

Upon arriving back in Michigan, Mr. and Mrs. Rinker volunteered to put all of their new-found knowledge to work to help Joyce in her project. They engaged the services of Tom Halberg, a local architect, who agreed to check building codes, design the house (with some "back-seat drafting" from Daniel), *and* build it.

When Halberg suggested all-weather, pressure-treated wood construction rather than concrete or cement blocks, Daniel did some research and found that an Indiana firm had built more than 60 homes with all-weather, wood basements. He learned that the cellars stayed dry despite having the typically wet Indiana clay around them, and that convinced him that Halberg had a good idea.

The construction material chosen was southern pine—pressure treated at 50 to 60 pounds per square inch—because it's water-repellent, resists fungus and rot, and doesn't appeal to termites and other insects. Daniel figured the stress loads and angles with the help of his trusty machinist's handbook. Although he maintains that most folks could run these calculations for themselves, his 38 years as a tool-and-die maker did make the job especially easy for him.

Just to be on the safe side, they added a 6-mil layer of black polyethylene waterproofing—between the wood and sand—to all of the building's earth-facing surfaces. The plastic sheet should last at least 50 years in that application.

All the dwelling's walls were built from 3/4" treated plywood and nailed—with hot zinc-dipped fasteners—to pressure-treated 2 X 6 studs arranged 12" on center to assure the strength of the structure. Then, to make these surfaces even more sturdy, all of the earth-covered walls were reinforced with diagonally braced sheets of 3/8" plywood before the sand was piled on.

The roof was constructed from treated plywood, too . . . nailed to 2 X 12 ceiling joists, also spaced 12" on center. This wood was then covered with five layers of felt applied with mopped-on hot plastic roofing cement . . . to reinforce and waterproof the top of Joyce's home. Over this fabric/glue mixture, they added two layers of the polyethylene and two inches of Styrofoam insulation, with a four-inch plastic drainpipe (which carries the roof water off to the surrounding soil) in between. This "layer cake" roof was covered with an average of eight inches of sand, black loam, and forest sod . . . just enough to support local vegetation and a patch of blueberries.

In only two years this underground haven, tucked unobtrusively into the forested sand hills of Michigan, saved its owner 67% of the heating and cooling expenses she would have incurred in a conventional home of the same size.

That topping of earth is, of course, a source of insulation. In addition, 12 inches of cellulose blown into the ceiling and six inches of fiberglass packed into the walls help hold temperatures stable. Andersen triple-glazed Windowalls let sun in without letting out too much heat. The insulation proved itself when the first snow on the roof melted at the same rate as the surrounding drifts!

In order to comply with the local building code—and because Joyce wanted windows in every room—the Rinkers left 22% of the house's outer surface exposed. These "naked" walls were dressed up nicely with redwood siding.

Joyce's "contemporary cavern" is heated with a single Ashley woodstove . . . and for backup she has electric baseboard heat, which neatly keeps her parakeet and guinea pig warm when she's away. The woodburner is centrally located on an eight-inch-high brick platform, and its vent and exhaust pipes push up through the roof . . . where they're disguised in hollow tree stumps.

The house and garage cost less to build than a comparable aboveground home in the area. Financing wasn't any trouble . . . mostly because the Rinkers' thorough, well-researched plans convinced the local banker that they knew their stuff!

After two years "underground", Joyce had fully tested the house's capabilities. During the first winter—a bitterly cold one—she burned 3-2/3 cords of "cut for free" wood, and only used the electric heat when she went away for two weeks that December. Furthermore, with the thermostat set at 70°F, and the air outside a chilly 10°F above zero, only 39 kilowatts a day were required to maintain the inside temperature. That works out to a heat loss of about 5,400 BTU per hour for 1,220 square feet of floor space.

During that winter, Joyce was pleasantly surprised to find that the woodstove performed so efficiently that the interior temperature never varied more than 4°F from one end of the building to the other. Even better, when she didn't light a fire—and the outside mercury plunged perilously to somewhere below zero—the temperature in her earth-sheltered home didn't drop more than a single degree every two to three hours.

WINTER TEMPERATURE RANGE

DATE	OUTSIDE	INSIDE	UNHEATED GARAGE
Nov. 26	26°F	70°F	44°F
Dec. 22	28°F	66°F	40°F
Jan. 12	−2°F	64°F	34°F
Jan. 30	22°F	68°F	38°F
Feb. 10	−8°F	65°F	32°F
Mar. 16	14°F	66°F	38°F
Mar. 31	26°F	66°F	40°F

Even the garage (which is insulated only by the surrounding soil) stayed warm enough all winter to melt any snow on the automobile when it was parked.

During Joyce's first summer, the northern Michigan temperature ranged from nighttime lows of around 40°F to daily highs that hovered around 100°F! During that period—with no fans or air conditioners in use—the air inside the home varied from 60°F (with all the windows open) to 76°F (on a very warm afternoon, while both the kitchen range and the washer were in use).

Carefully kept figures show that during her first two years of earth-sheltered living, Joyce saved at least 67% on her home heating and cooling costs . . . as compared to expenses in an equivalent-sized aboveground dwelling. The energy savings would have been even higher if earth covering had been used on more than 78% of the home's roof and wall areas. Such additional insulation, however, would have made it impossible to include windows in every room.

Many folks ask if the building is damp . . . and Joyce points to the pressure tank for the water pump, which has never even built up enough condensation to drip. There isn't any better proof of low humidity than that!

To people who ask about the possibility of burrowing animals damaging the walls, Joyce tells the story of a porcupine she watched amble up the treated wood in search of salt. A couple of nibbles convinced the porcupine that all it'd find was a bellyache, and it quickly sauntered away. If a porky turns it down, Joyce notes, it's just plain inedible!

Underground homes, Daniel Rinker is convinced, are more healthful to live in than conventional homes. He reports conversations with doctors in New Mexico who send children with respiratory problems to an earth-sheltered elementary school. The doctors believe being in such a building helps clear up their ailments. A chronic sinus sufferer, Daniel says his problems always seem to improve after he spends a day or two in Joyce's home.

Maybe the best feature of the home, at least to animal-loving Joyce Rinker, is the ringside seat it gives her for the daily local wildlife show. With the outside ground level just below the windows, Joyce can look out and, often as not, see a squirrel or raccoon peering back at her.

A single woodstove keeps the dwelling warm in subfreezing weather, and temperatures inside vary only a few degrees throughout the house.

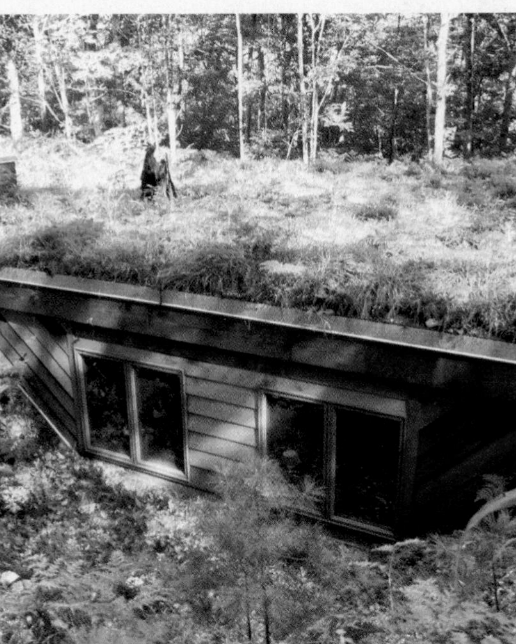

Ground-level windows at the ends of the house offer ringside viewing of the small wild creatures that share this woodland setting. So much a part of the landscape is this earth-sheltered home that the dwelling's vents are camouflaged as tree stumps.

THE HOBBITAT CUTS ENERGY COSTS

The energy of the sun and the orientation of the dwelling provide solar heating for the home, while the earth-bermed walls on the west end, the sod roof, and a bank protecting the bedroom help prevent the loss of heat and energy gained by the solar attic collector. The home is reached by a driveway that ends at a carport, partially protected by stacked firewood.

Until recently, it seemed that about the only people who bothered with underground structures were progressive architects, who overdesigned to suit their affluent clients, or truly adventurous folks who built their own shelters on a "learn as you go" basis.

Nowadays, however, the average citizen is able to build an underground abode—even if he or she needs professional help—and still find the process to be cost-effective.

One such person is Lloyd Remington, a professor of chemistry at the University of North Carolina's Asheville campus. Dr. Remington began building his pragmatically unconventional home in October 1977, and moved in the following May. His structure (he calls it "The Hobbitat") was never intended to be a public showplace or demonstration of the latest in gadgetry, but it clearly accomplished Lloyd's goals of affordability, security, and durability.

A SUCCESSFUL "EXPERIMENT"

Dr. Remington felt that "going underground" would be the simplest and least expensive way to achieve his aims. All told, the professor based his decision on four factors:

[1] The earth provides a stabilized energy "sink" to help buffer the extremes of seasonal climate.

[2] An "in-ground" dwelling affords the ultimate protection from what might be the least recognized variety of thermal drain . . . the windchill factor.

[3] Insurance premiums on an underground house are usually lower than those on a more orthodox residence, because there's less danger of damage from fires, storms, vandalism, or even falling trees. (Lloyd Remington's insurance company rates the risk "Triple A" . . . one of only two such ratings in his area.)

[4] An earth-covered structure affords a large degree of protection from radiation in the unlikely event of a nuclear crisis.

A LIVE-IN THERMOS BOTTLE

To keep his overall costs as low as possible, Dr. Remington acted as his own contractor . . . he chose, coordinated, and later paid his own subcontractors. A local architect provided the engineering and design skills necessary to produce a safe and aesthetically pleasing structure.

For the most part, the Remington home was constructed along lines common to *many* subsurface dwellings, but it has some interesting variations. The building site sloped toward the southwest, so the designer took advantage of the natural lay of the land and positioned the structure to face due south . . . eliminating the need for backfill berming except for that done on the west end of the dwelling. Then the main excavation was made to a maximum depth of 15 feet, and the driveway was graded to meet that level.

Rather than pour the foundation and footing as one, the builders chose to go with a "floating slab" design, in which the walls are supported on a stout perimetrical footing . . . and the foundation itself rests *within*, on top of a layer of gravel-over-polyethylene.

The 2' X 4' footing holds up block walls with filled, reinforced cores (except for those in the non-load-bearing rear wall, which have alternating poured and vermiculite-packed centers). The roof panels are prestressed concrete . . . laid east-to-west, half-lapped 1/4" and caulked at their lateral joints, and covered with a poured, 2" to 6" graded slab which is tied into the walls by means of 3/4" reinforcing bar all around. (All told, there are over *200 tons* of concrete in the structure!)

In order to guarantee a moisture-free environment, Dr. Remington enshrouded his house in a combination of rubber, Styrofoam, and a locally made foundation drainage material. First, the completed walls and roof were covered with a 1/10"-thick layer of cured-in-place butyl rubber waterproofing. Next, panels of 2" and 3" Styrofoam insulation were fastened to the structure's sides and top, respectively. Then Enkadrain foundation drainage matting was placed over all of the insulation board *and* the drainpipe which rests against the exterior face of the footing. Finally, the entire structure—and its insulated "raincoat"—was covered with earth, to a depth of 30" at the front and 48" at the rear.

PARTIALLY SOLAR-HEATED AND EARTH-COOLED, TOO

Because the Asheville area isn't known for its temperature extremes, Professor Remington chose an air-to-air heat pump to function as the backup system in his all-electric dwelling . . . partially because such a unit can be inexpensive to operate *if* used intelligently, but mainly because it included an ideal forced-air handling network that allows the distribution of *naturally* tempered currents.

The Tarheel Stater, you see, has incorporated a *solar attic* into the upper part of his home's south-facing wall and entranceway. Remington covered the exposed side of the attic with corrugated Filon glazing, framed out its lower surface with 1 X 6 "ribs" which support flat sheets of Kalwall, then tied the huge "hotbox" into his air handling system, using a thermostatically controlled fan. Not only does the massive collector provide a fair amount of heat—usually enough to supply the entire home during the daylight hours after 10:00 a.m. or so on a winter day—but it's also the source of plenty more-than-welcome light for the living area below.

Additionally, to supplement the other two heat sources, the Remington family uses a combination wood-and-coal stove . . . usually only when the outside temperature dips below 20°F, which is beyond the efficient operating range of the heat pump. Furthermore, a man-

With a low risk of damage from fires, storms, vandalism, or fallen trees, the home earned a "triple A" insurance rating.

Natural light enters the living area through glazing beneath the solar attic and through sliding glass doors, and a combination wood/coal stove provides supplemental heat to the dwelling's air-handling system through a damper.

While the solar attic provides both heat and light, an earth-cooled air duct can be used to temper the indoor climate in summer.

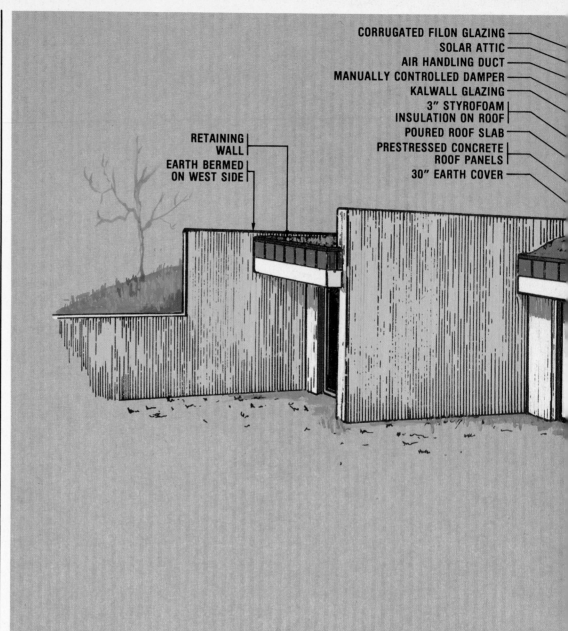

CORRUGATED FILON GLAZING
SOLAR ATTIC
AIR HANDLING DUCT
MANUALLY CONTROLLED DAMPER
KALWALL GLAZING
3" STYROFOAM INSULATION ON ROOF
POURED ROOF SLAB
PRESTRESSED CONCRETE ROOF PANELS
30" EARTH COVER
RETAINING WALL
EARTH BERMED ON WEST SIDE

Sunlight falling through the glazing beneath the solar collector reaches not only the back of the living room but the kitchen behind it as well.

ually controlled damper, built into the bottom of the air distribution duct and located at the top of a "channeling" shaft just above the woodburner, allows normally stagnant ceiling warmth to collect—for later use—in the insulated air supply chamber.

During the warmer months, Remington and his family usually enjoy a comfortable environment simply because they're essentially living "in the earth". . . . but, should temperatures within the home creep upward, a louvered fan installed at each end of the solar attic can "sweep" that area clean of heat (the blowers can also be left *closed*, and just the air delivery system of the heat pump activated, with the house windows open, an alternative that has proved to be reasonably cost-effective). But if the ambient air is uncomfortably warm, the Remingtons also have the option of utilizing an earth-cooled air duct (merely a 20-foot length of 18"-diameter culvert pipe buried in the soil), which feeds into the home's ventilation system to provide supplementary cooling.

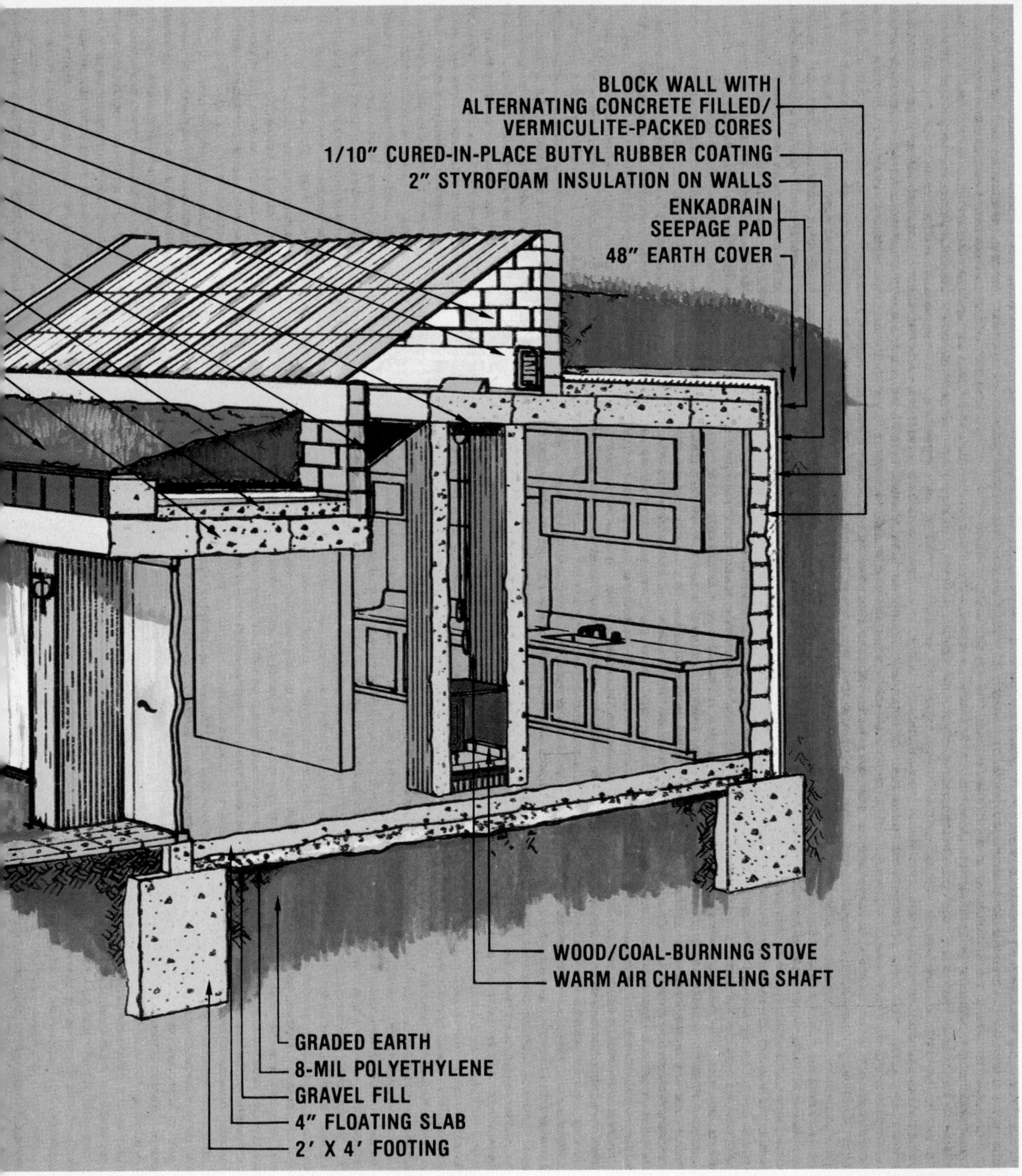

BLOCK WALL WITH ALTERNATING CONCRETE FILLED/ VERMICULITE-PACKED CORES
1/10" CURED-IN-PLACE BUTYL RUBBER COATING
2" STYROFOAM INSULATION ON WALLS
ENKADRAIN SEEPAGE PAD
48" EARTH COVER
WOOD/COAL-BURNING STOVE
WARM AIR CHANNELING SHAFT
GRADED EARTH
8-MIL POLYETHYLENE
GRAVEL FILL
4" FLOATING SLAB
2' X 4' FOOTING

Monthly savings on energy, maintenance, and insurance should make long-term ownership an attractive investment.

WELL WORTH THE INVESTMENT

It might be pretty hard for many folks to justify spending the amount of money that the Remingtons did ($80,000 or about $43 a square foot) . . . especially if the people had their sights set on a similar-sized *conventional* dwelling, which might cost one-half to two-thirds as much. But when you consider the energy savings to be had, it appears that the professor made a good investment. He has kept accurate records for most of the house's history, and calculates the minimum *total* power usage to be below 1,000 KWH per month, and the maximum 2,300 KWH. The average consumption for any "heated" or "cooled" month was about 1,500 KWH.

Thus the monthly savings—added to the reduced price of maintenance and insurance—could make the long-term ownership of such a subterranean dwelling quite attractive. If *you're* considering the construction of an earth-sheltered home, there probably isn't a better time to "get with it" than right now!

The kitchen, adjacent to the wood/coal stove, features modern, built-in appliances and custom cabinetry and is flooded by sunlight from the attic.

SIMPLY SOLAR AT LOW COST

David Schonberg's 35-acre organic truck farm provided his Minnesota family with a decent living, but it certainly didn't yield enough income to pay for a conventional structure suited to the needs of his family of seven. So David's thoughts turned to designing a house he *could* afford . . . and he began to plan his earth-sheltered, solar house, concentrating on cutting every dollar he possibly could from its potential cost.

The home he planned and built is comfortable, energy-efficient, large enough for the family, *and* very attractive. David is sure people with plenty of money could have found ways to sink much more into the design, but he's happy with his 1,800-square-foot, four-bedroom dwelling, which cost about 40% as much per square foot as the typical conventional home in his area.

EARTH SHELTERING

Three walls of the Schonberg home are built into the earth, and even the south side sports a 3-1/2-foot berm. The bulkheads are 8″-thick reinforced poured concrete, insulated on the outside with 2″-thick polystyrene. The wall-setting went quickly . . . they excavated one day, set the forms and poured the footings on the second, then formed up and poured the walls on the third.

Only the south side of the building has windows . . . and that simplified the construction, although it meant that the four bedrooms and the utility room are windowless.

The lack of glazing presented both advantages and problems. On the positive side, the rooms have no energy-wasting glass, and a bundle of money was saved on materials . . . as anyone who has priced windows can imagine. But on the *negative* side, the problem of lighting the back rooms had to be solved without depending upon costly electricity. Skylights were ruled out because they are expensive, leak-prone devices. And the Schonbergs weren't interested in shoveling snow from the roof-mounted glazing in the winter . . . or baking beneath it in the summer.

The solution was to install light-diffusing, translucent plastic panels (in the form of fluorescent-light covers) in the walls between the dark, windowless rooms and the *very* bright front chamber. The panels are breakable (the Schonbergs fully expect a runaway toy to go crashing through one some day) . . . so they were installed in a way that they can easily be replaced. (As an added benefit, a person could—in an emergency—break through the plastic, giving each room an additional fire exit.)

Just how successfully do the panels function? Well, even the bedrooms *twice removed* from the south windows are nearly as bright as would be a conventional north room with a curtained opening, while the rooms immediately adjacent to the south living area are very well lighted indeed. It's a simple idea, and it works!

SOLAR HEATING

Capturing heat from the sun is easy. Simply put enough windows on the south side of a well-insulated building, and it gets toasty even during subzero weather. The real challenge is to provide the right amount of heat storage and air circulation to prevent overheating during the day and to keep the building warm at night.

Guided by their stringent budget—and following the very rudimentary principle that warm air rises—the Schonbergs designed a passive circulation/storage system that is both simple and inexpensive. It performs so well that standby plans, which included the addition of

Both light and heat for the 1,800 square feet of living space come almost entirely through the 200 square feet of south-facing glass, which constitutes the only window area in the dwelling. The kitchen at the east end of the building shares the open sunspace with the living room and dining area.

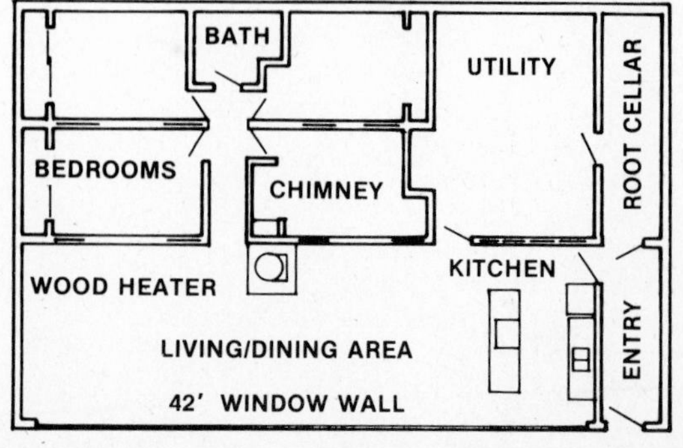

an active system incorporating fans and thermostats, were dropped.

Openings were left in the east-west partitions to assure that air rising to the ceiling of the sun room would move back into the northern rooms. Of course, a room—like a bottle—can take in air only if there's a way for the old air to escape. Therefore, to give the cooler, heavier air an exit, a vent was made in the floor along the entire north wall. That cooler (but still warm) air falls beneath the floor and moves back to the south, passing underfoot. A vent under the south wall completes the loop.

Concrete walls (56 tons' worth in this house) provide a good deal of heat storage capability, but the design doesn't stop there. Air paths were constructed *under the floors* through the use of 900 concrete blocks arranged in east-west rows on 16-inch centers, providing air channels, thermal mass, and floor joists.

The cavities in the blocks are lined up north to south and provide the channels through which air moves, entering and exiting through 2-1/2-inch vents all along the north and south walls. The rows of blocks rest on a 2" layer of pea gravel, which, in turn, sits on a sandwich of cardboard, 0.006" polyethylene, and more cardboard. Nailers—simply 2 X 4's set on their sides—are laid directly on the block joists and support a 3/4" plywood floor.

The technique was several hundred dollars less expensive than a conventional flooring system would have been, and the family reduced the cost even further by purchasing chipped and cracked blocks.

Naturally, the Schonbergs could hardly wait until the construction process was far enough along to allow a *test* of the circulation/storage system. And once the east-west partition walls were completed, the setup's effect immediately became obvious. As soon as the front room—heated by the sun—became warmer than the bedrooms and utility room, the air began to circulate. And, as the temperature difference between the south room and the north rooms built, the rate increased. The Schonbergs have found that once a 10°F disparity is reached, the movement from the south wall vent can be strong enough to hold a single-ply tissue straight out and flapping like a flag!

Thus, as you'd imagine, it doesn't take long for the rear rooms to warm up. And then an interesting thing happens: The temperature in the front room seems to stop rising, and the temperature difference between the front and rear portions of the house stabilizes. Apparently, as the solar gain increases, the air in the thermal loop just moves more rapidly . . . depositing excess heat in the 900 concrete blocks below the floor. The front room's temperature levels off at about 75°F on sunny days, no matter whether it's plus or minus 30°F outside. And at night—because the living room loses heat through the south-facing glass—the direction of the airflow reverses, and the block-stored warmth is delivered to the bedrooms.

In short, not even insulating drapes have been needed to keep the home's interior temperature comfortable. On even the coldest sunny days in winter, no more than an armload or two of wood was burned in the heater in the evening. A load of kindling was all that was required on cold mornings to take off the early morning chill.

Someone asked Mrs. Schonberg what she *didn't* like about her new home, and upon reflection, she admitted that there *are* a few drawbacks to this sort of residence.

Because of the large south room and the openings above the partitions, noise does carry more easily than it would in a building with smaller, soundproof rooms. In addition, without a basement or crawl space, it's necessary to remove a floor panel to service the plumbing . . . an eventuality provided for by screwing, not nailing, the panels above the pipes to the 2 X 4 nailers below.

The building's soil-level roofline has presented a couple of small problems, as well. For one, the family's dog can be heard *inside* the house when he decides to take a rooftop romp. Also, the northwest storm wind sweeps unobstructed across the roof, sometimes depositing a large snow drift in front of the south window. However, both annoyances can easily be corrected with the addition of appropriate fencing.

With three sides of the home surrounded by the earth, maintenance should be minimal and heating costs next to nothing.

Not even insulating drapes are needed to maintain a comfortable temperature . . . even on the coldest nights.

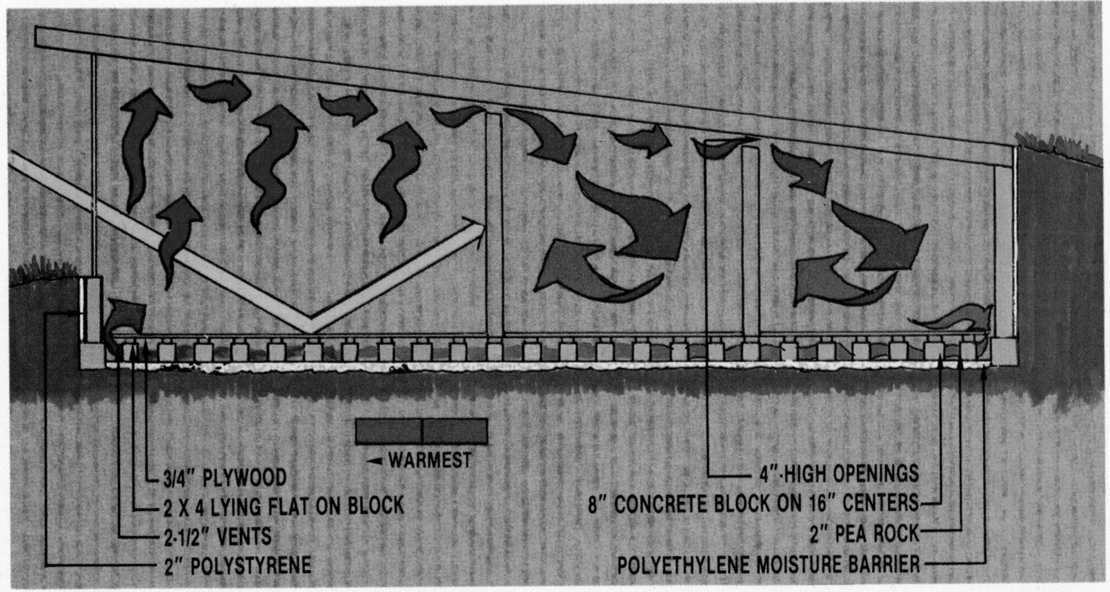

The utility room behind the kitchen and the bedrooms, which also are placed at the back of the house, receive natural daytime lighting through translucent panels in the major east-west wall.

THE HOUSE IN A HOLE

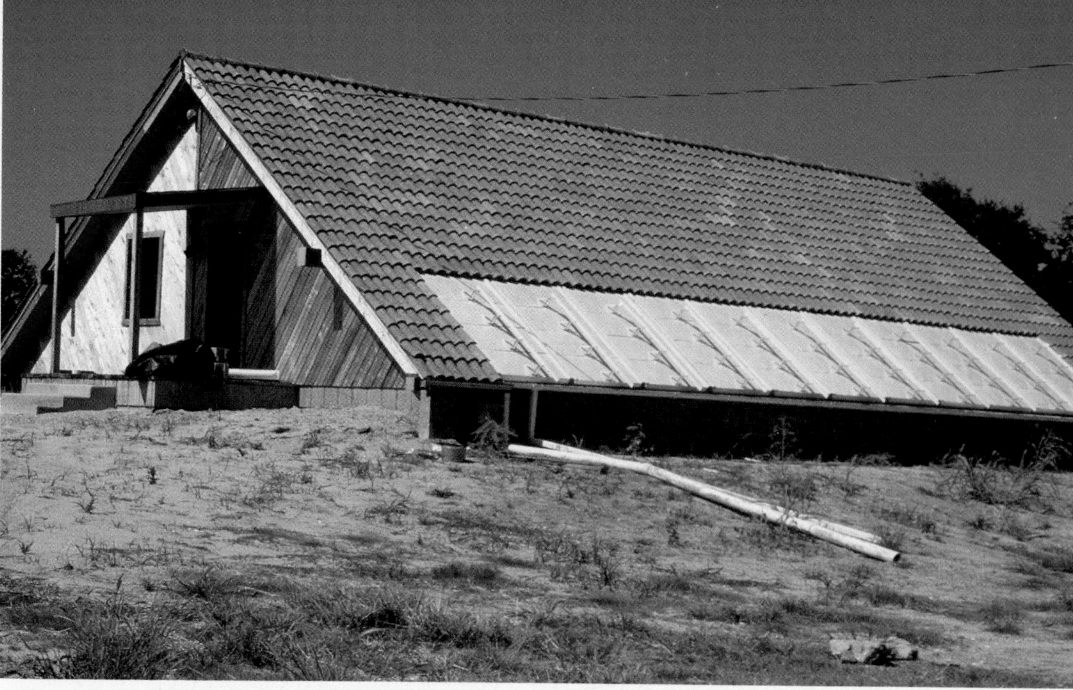

The energy efficiency of most underground homes makes this sort of dwelling very attractive in these days of skyrocketing utility bills, but many would-be owner-builders are discouraged by the difficulty of designing and building the heavily reinforced walls and roof that are necessary to withstand the pressures exerted by the earth-mass surrounding the structure. Then there's the problem of adequately waterproofing the building's envelope. Doing these things right can be expensive . . . but doing them *wrong* can spell disaster. Therefore, the extra costs often involved in underground construction have caused many budget-conscious builders to look for other answers to their housing needs . . . and the Vertical Crawl-Space Home (VCSH) may be one such solution.

Basically, the VCSH is a concept developed by Rod Rylander, a designer and contractor who has built a half-dozen VCSH's.

ABC's

To build a VCSH you just: [1] Dig a hole with sloping sides, [2] build whatever type of house you desire in the hole, and [3] cover the hole with a roof or second floor that extends out past the excavation's sides and which is tied into a footing.

Of course, it's not really that simple. It's important to do some preliminary site testing before calling in the backhoe! Test holes should be bored to determine the soil composition (if you hit a large section of solid rock you might want to choose another location . . . since blasting is expensive) and the level of the water table. Be sure that the latter is *well below* the depth of your planned excavation (Rod's designs call for a hole that's eight feet deep), and don't forget to take into account seasonal variations in the water table which might be caused by heavy rains.

Because the excavation must be cut very accurately—to conform with your housing plan and to insure the uniformity and stability of the sloping sides—Rod suggests that a large backhoe (*not* a bulldozer) be used. The sides of the hole should begin about three feet away from the bottom of the planned house walls, and the angle of the slope should be uniform. His designs for Texas conditions call for a slope of 60 degrees. (The desirable angle of slope will vary depending on soil composition and stability. Some builders recommend slopes as shallow as 34 degrees.)

When the hole is completed, a French drain (or perforated pipe) with a sump pump is installed to dispose of any moisture which may accumulate in the hole during or after construc-

All we see is the roof with shuttered windows that can be opened to admit light to the subterranean house . . . the drawings illustrate the variety of structures that can be incorporated into the low-cost Vertical Crawl-Space type of construction.

PHOTOS BY ROD RYLANDER

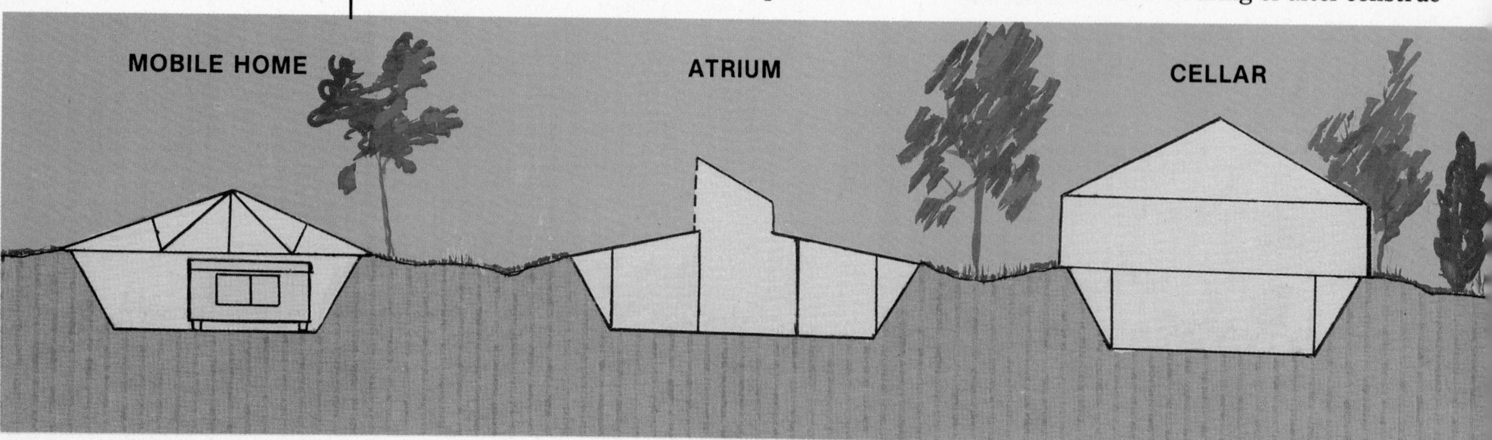

tion. This stage in the building process is also a good time to dig a septic tank (if you plan to use one) or to install "cool tubes" for earth-tempered cooling of air.

Rod uses cool tubes in his VCSH contructions and recommends them as a good way to circulate air through the crawl space in order to lower humidity. This air can be drawn through the house and exhausted through an attic fan or solar chimney.

CONSTRUCTION TECHNIQUES

It's possible to build just about any kind of home you want with a VCSH design. The foundation may consist of a poured slab, piers and beams, or footings . . . and the walls may be wood frame, concrete block, or you-name-it. Because the structure doesn't have to resist the pressure of the earth (as is the case with other underground designs), it doesn't have to be any stronger than does a conventional house. And since there's no reason to finish the exterior walls, there's a significant construction cost saving.

Another advantage can be realized by designing the plumbing so it's located on the outside of the walls. By doing so, you'll make installation easier and faster (and therefore less expensive), and the pipes will be immediately accessible should there ever be a problem.

In areas where summer cooling is a significant consideration, placing the water heater and other heat-generating devices in the crawl space can also save energy. In fact, the only disadvantage of the design in regard to plumbing is the possibility that your sewer line or septic tank may be sited at a level which is above that of your fixtures. If so, a sump pump will be a necessary addition to your plan.

In the Sunbelt the below-ground-level walls need not be insulated, since the air envelope around the house and the stable temperature of the earth provide sufficient protection against the cold. In colder climates, though, varying degrees of insulation may be needed . . . and in Alaska, the walls must be heavily insulated in order to prevent the permafrost in the surrounding soil from being melted by heat from the house. (In this case, all exposed plumbing should be insulated as well.) All of this is just a reminder that before you build a house—any house—you should be in touch with your environment.

A number of roof styles may be used to cover your house-in-a-hole. Flat, slanted, and conventional peaked roofs have all been used successfully . . . as have A-frames (where the upstairs space can be used as a conventionally heated living area or for storage). The roof must, of course, be designed to extend out over the edges of the excavation, but it can be anchored in several ways. If the roof's weight is supported by the house walls, for example, then a footing should be poured around the hole, and the eaves should be tied to it. When beams span the hole to support the roof, they should rest on piers . . . which, in turn, should be connected to each other by enclosure beams fitted with metal skirts. It's also important for the roof to have an effective rain gutter system, and the ground should slope away from the footing to insure proper drainage. In addition, an insulated water barrier (such as extruded polystyrene board) should be laid about a foot beneath the surface of the surrounding earth, sloping away and extending about four feet from the footing to protect against seepage.

It's possible to incorporate many passive solar features in a VCSH design. Rod likes to use windows (with shutters) on the roof . . . to flood the house with light and to capture solar heat in the winter. You can also set skylights into the overhanging portion of roof, and then landscape part of the crawl space or use it as a garden.

The VCSH concept means that an underground home no longer has to be more expensive to build than a basement-equipped, aboveground dwelling. Once the hole has been dug and properly protected against seepage, conventional construction techniques can be used to build a long-lasting, energy-conserving underground home. Vertical crawl-space construction techniques are also admirably suited to farm buildings or large commercial or industrial complexes. In fact, VCSH is a useful alternative for just about anyone who wants to save money in building, as well as in owning!

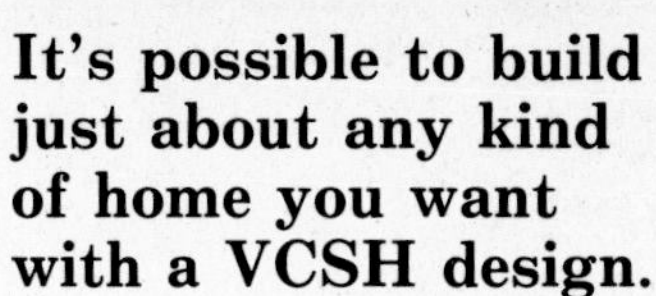

1. VENT
2. THERMAL TOWER
3. SOLAR WINDOWS
4. PIERS
5. INSULATION
6. GUTTER
7. DRY WELL
8. COOL TUBE
9. WOODSTOVE
10. VERTICAL CRAWL SPACE
11. DRAIN

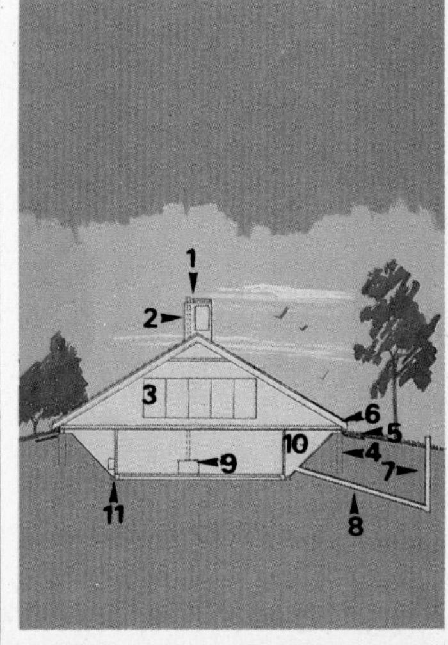

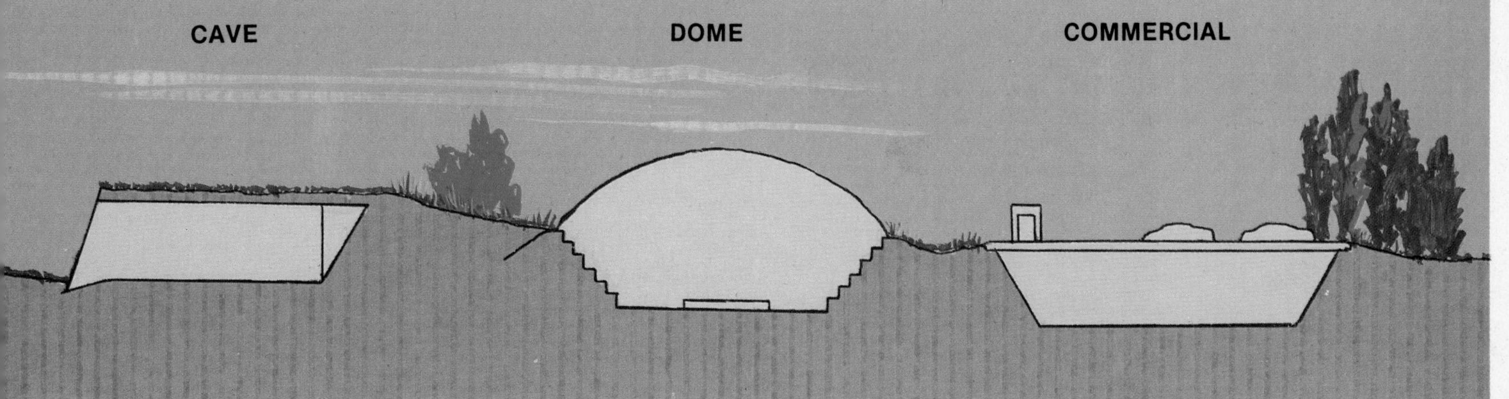

IN ACCORD WITH NATURE

In designing their home to take advantage of environmental conditions, the Yamberts have created an ecologically sound dwelling that matches their philosophy of living *with* nature instead of in opposition to it. Below is the entry to the wood storage room, which has a door to the inside of the house.

PHOTOS BY JIM MURPHY

When Carla and Paul Yambert moved into their solar- and wood-heated, earth-bermed home, they regarded the event as yet another stage in a lifestyle that has—through the years—increasingly translated the couple's eco-*philosophy* into actual *living* in accord with nature.

The Yamberts have always been lovers of the outdoors (Paul's an environmental studies professor at Southern Illinois University), and they raised their family in the woodsy setting of Shawnee National Forest, which runs across Illinois' southern tip. Though the couple found the *locale* to be ideal, their original dwelling was fairly conventional . . . so when the youngest child left home, the senior Yamberts began building the smaller, tighter, more ecologically sound, and more self-sufficient nest they'd been planning for years.

Perhaps the most fascinating (and instructive) feature of the Yamberts' new home is the manner in which it combines a *variety* of existing technologies and materials to provide both efficiency and comfort. Nestled into a south-facing hillside for natural insulation, the house also makes good use of passive solar techniques, relying—for storage—upon the thermal mass supplied by a huge stone fireplace that receives the winter sun's rays streaming through an expanse of glass, and also, of course, stores heat from the wood fires burned there.

In addition to the earth sheltering and the fireplace, extensive insulation, a solar greenhouse, and two heat-lock vestibules help the sun-wood combination provide *all* the building's space heating. And other systems—including a cistern and a composting toilet—allow the couple to further reduce the burden they place upon nature.

QUALITY CONSTRUCTION

The rectangular house—which has a shed-style roof—is a sturdy structure containing 1,360 square feet of floor space . . . including the loft. Its quality of construction far exceeds that of today's average frame building: Consider, for example, that the exterior walls were built from 2 X 6 lumber on 16-inch centers . . . or that the main floor is slate (a material which doubles as a second heat sink) . . . and that rough-sawed cedar siding is used extensively inside and out.

The way in which the building is insulated also sets it apart from most conventional structures. On the north (uphill) side, the house is set into the earth nearly to its roof line. The side walls, however, are made of con-

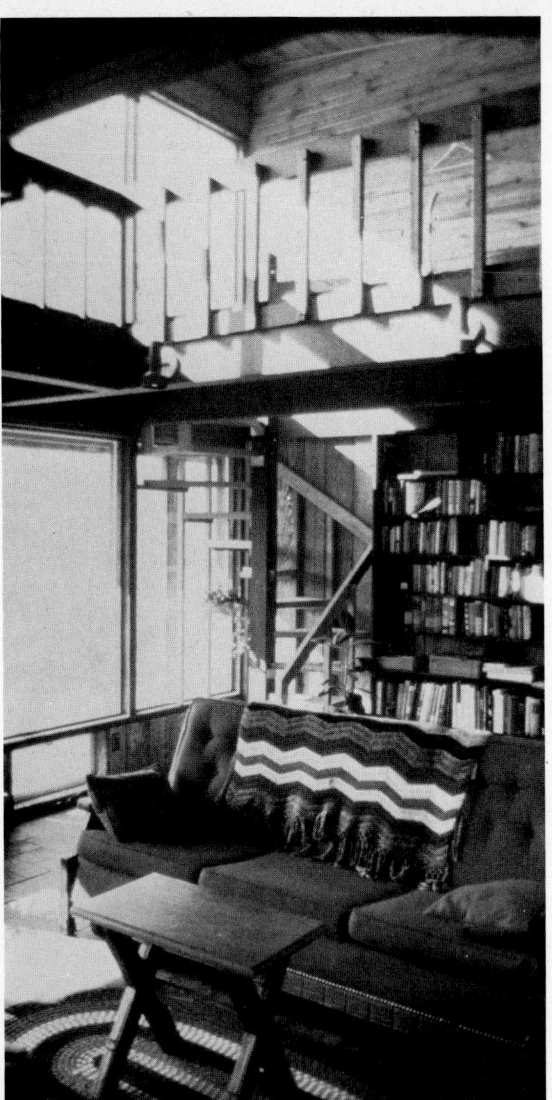

Sunlight streaming into the Yamberts' living room from two stories provides a cheerful setting . . . as well as plenty of solar heat for winter months. Mylar shades have been installed and can be lowered as needed to regulate the amount of light coming in. Stairs leading to the balcony can be seen to the left of the bookshelves.

crete blocks filled with vermiculite, which are—in turn—backed with 2″ of polyurethane on the outside and 2″ of fiberglass insulation on the inside . . . for a total R-value of about 24. Furthermore, the wooden walls have 6″ and the ceiling has 12″ of batt (with even *thicker* insulation in the critical heat-retention area above the fireplace).

The Yamberts employed a conventional builder to undertake what they considered to be the *basic* elements of the home's construction, but wound up doing much of the work themselves anyway. Looking back, they realize that the preconceptions held by the average contractor can be a significant disadvantage to folks who are trying to build in a more ecologically sound fashion. As Paul aptly put it, "The professional isn't sure whether your variations on standard techniques are the result of cleverness or stupidity, so he or she tries to change them back to comply with the rules of normal procedure . . . and then—to avoid embarrassing you—doesn't *tell* you what was changed."

Such an incident almost occurred during construction of the Yamberts' bathroom. Because standard building practice is to put the toilet between the bathtub and the sink, the contractor took it upon himself to change the locations that the couple had specified for the water supply, *and* for the "stool's" vent pipes. However, the composting toilet *needed* to be placed directly over the huge decomposition unit that had *already been built* under the house. (And for that matter, a "fermenting potty" doesn't require any water supply lines to begin with!)

Fortunately, the owners caught the mistake in time to correct it, but they found it necessary to keep a constant eye on the builder to avoid having their *innovations* replaced by the exact outmoded procedures they were trying to get away from!

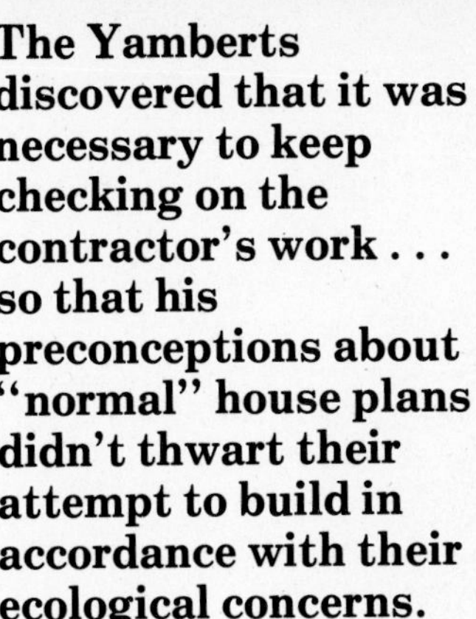

The Yamberts discovered that it was necessary to keep checking on the contractor's work . . . so that his preconceptions about "normal" house plans didn't thwart their attempt to build in accordance with their ecological concerns.

ENERGY CENTER

The fireplace's huge column of rock—located in the middle of the structure—is the main component of the home's heating system. Outside air, for combustion, is drawn into the unit through ducts in the floor, and the firebox is equipped with glass doors and a special thermal grate—a Martin Octotherm—which pumps the warmed air back *into* the room.

Additionally, the heat that rises through the large flue is captured and piped down into a 2-1/2-foot-deep rock storage area located beneath the building's 6″ concrete foundation. A 6″-diameter pipe transmits the air in the flue, and 4″ ducts carry the warmth to the stones beneath the floor.

At present the system is operated by means of a 1/24-HP blower, but the Yamberts have discovered that their system is both undersized and underpowered. "We didn't adequately estimate how *buoyant* the hot air would be . . . how much it would resist being pulled down," Paul says. Consequently, the owner/designer now recommends that anyone duplicating the idea use 12″ pipe in the flue, 6″ ducts in the floor, and a 1/2-HP fan.

The Yamberts realized, from the beginning, that their fireplace wouldn't be quite as *efficient* as a stove, but they wanted to be able to sit before the open hearth. Now, however, Paul concedes that a fireplace insert would be a good idea. It's not that the system has failed to keep them warm . . . but that he feels he's had to cut too much wood to maintain a comfortable temperature even during the mild winters.

Of course, in addition to providing a cheery blaze in the main room, the fireplace also furnishes heat to the building's water heater. During the wood-heating months, the setup has proved itself more than capable of supplying almost all the household's hot water needs, and the backup electric unit seldom comes into play. The system is further enhanced by solar collectors which provide electricity-free hot water during warm weather.

The south wall of the home is made up of an expanse of double-insulated glass which allows the winter sun to shine deep into the house and bake into the stone fireplace. Paul and Carla got a bargain on their glazing by locating factory-sealed double panes *without* any casements, and fabricating their own frames.

The home's location (and the placement of its porch and eaves) was planned to *capture* the winter sun and *reject* the summer rays. Specifically, the Yamberts designed their

From start to finish, the Yamberts did what they could to make their home an integral part of its environment.

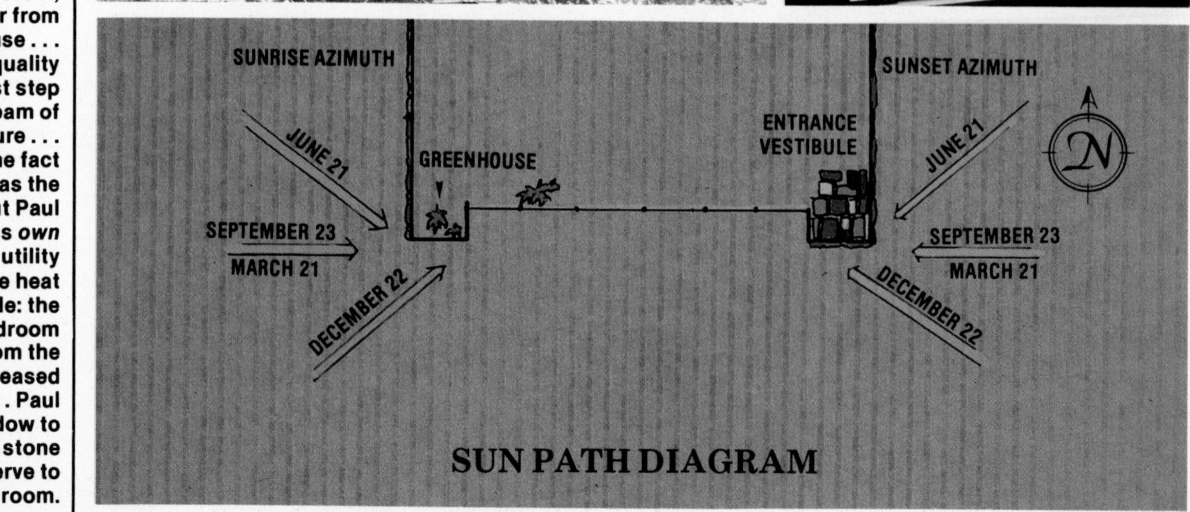

Instead of drilling a water well, they decided to install a cistern, which collects rainwater from the roof of their house . . . careful planning and quality construction was the first step toward realizing their dream of living in harmony with nature . . . the wood pile attests to the fact that it takes work to live as the Yamberts choose to do, but Paul would rather rely on his *own* energy than that of the utility company . . . more heat collection, solar style: the rocks around the bedroom window store warmth from the sun's rays, to be released slowly into the room . . . Paul opens the bedroom window to admit heat collected in the stone "well". The rocks also serve to reflect some light into the room.

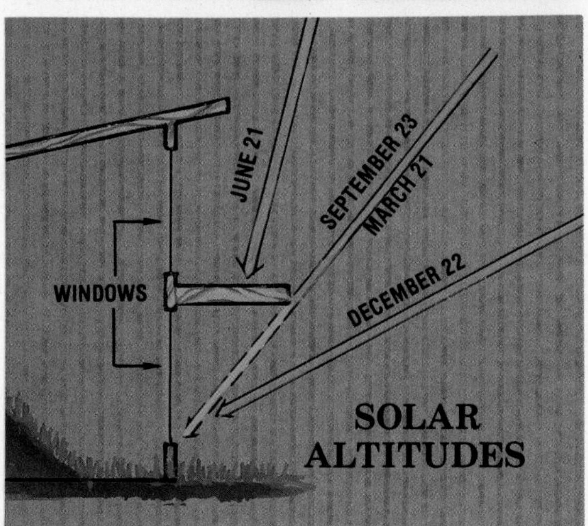

structure to take full advantage of solar heat from one week before the fall equinox to one week after the spring equinox. The eaves provide midday shading when the summer sun is high, and the entrance vestibule (east) and the greenhouse (west) were positioned to protrude from the front of the building for extended early morning and late afternoon sunshine control.

And, in day-to-day use, the siting of the structure has been even more effective than Paul and Carla had expected. In fact, they were surprised to find that they were often getting more solar heat than they needed. So, halfway through the first cold season, they installed reflective Mylar-faced fiberglass shades, which can be pulled down as needed to regulate the amount of light entering the house.

With the sun warming the outside of the rock and the fire heating it inside, the thermal storage of the fireplace "core" keeps the interior of the Yamberts' home cozy *throughout* the winter . . . despite temperatures that nudge zero on occasion.

WATER AND SEWAGE HANDLING

The Yamberts were particularly concerned —while planning their home—with the problems involved in gathering and disposing of water. Rather than go to the expense of drilling a well, they opted for a cistern, which is fed by the entire expanse of the structure's roof. And the system has provided the couple with *plenty* of domestic water, largely because their Clivus Multrum composting toilet greatly reduces their demand for the precious liquid.

The local health inspector agreed to the installation of the toilet, but initially demanded that a septic system be installed to treat the "gray water" from the bathroom and kitchen . . . despite the fact that all solid garbage would go into the composter. The Yamberts talked with the official for several months (during which time "the man educated himself", as Paul puts it) and eventually got him to agree to a gray-water system consisting of two 50-foot lengths of drainage pipe, surrounded above and below by a foot of gravel and covered by topsoil. The ditches—dug ten feet apart—have proved more than adequate for returning soapy liquid to its pure state and have done so at low cost *and* with minimal impact on the environment.

Though the Yamberts are not displeased with the *economic* benefits provided by their new home, they still like to touch back on their *philosophical* intentions behind the project. The couple often talk about adapting to nature, rather than forcing the environment to bend to their whims.

Sure, they could have made the house *easier* to live in: Each day they open and close shades in cycle with the sun . . . and chopping and toting wood are regular chores. But, by constructing their house without a backup heating system, the two people have *intentionally* tied themselves intimately to nature. "That underlying philosophy is very important to us," says Paul. "We want to make our own bargain with the environment . . . our own private arrangement."

The fireplace's huge column of rock is the main component of the structure's heating system.

View of the south side of the Yamberts' earth-sheltered, solar- and wood-heated house. Ample use of glass and stone makes the place easy to heat. Reflective shades, seen here pulled down over the top windows, allow control of light and solar heat . . . looking from the sunny balcony down at the massive stone fireplace, which also doubles as a solar heat collector, absorbing warmth from both stories of windows.

BUILT INTO A KANSAS HILL

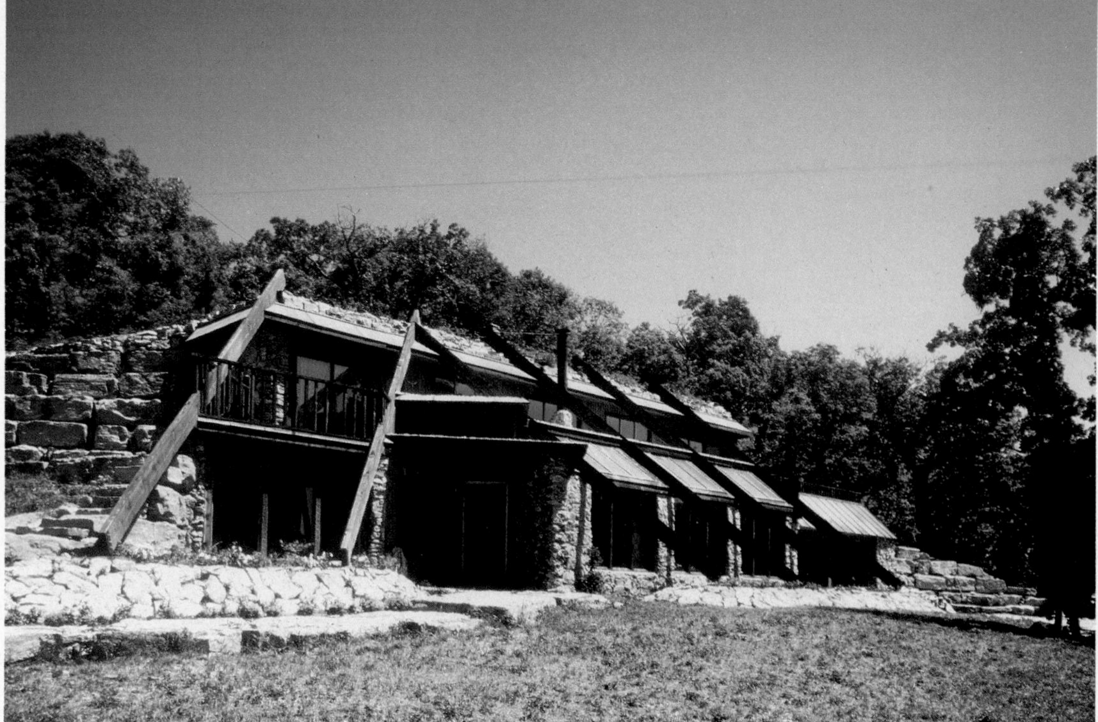

Massive angled beams at the front of the house support the exposed edge of the roof. The fountain inside is more than just an aesthetic touch . . . it humidifies the home's interior.

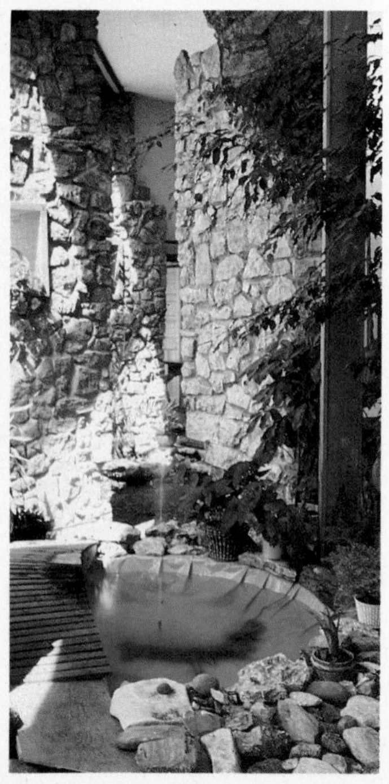

The Knapp family (Evelyn, Gifford, and their son Kenneth) began to work toward self-sufficiency almost 20 years ago . . . long before solar energy became a common topic of conversation. They've pursued their dream of self-reliance by planting gardens, digging fish ponds, maintaining timber lots, and researching wind and water power. And the Kansans learned early that the *foundation* of their pursuit would have to be a home that demanded an absolute minimum of energy from external sources.

In the beginning Gifford and Kenneth were most intrigued by *active* solar systems, but—after researching the matter closely—they became convinced that intensive solar collection didn't suit their situation. First of all, the Sunflower Staters reasoned, active collectors really didn't provide many BTU per dollar invested. And the complexity of such devices was bound to lead to extensive maintenance sooner or later.

The concept that the Knapps' years of analysis led them to favor was a marriage of earth-sheltering and passive solar features. So, with a vision in mind, the family began searching for a piece of property that would fit their plans perfectly. As you can imagine, it wasn't easy to find the ideal site, but they managed to purchase 12 acres—on the outskirts of Kansas City—which had a south-facing hillside (unobstructed by topography or trees), a three-acre pond, flat garden sites, and a good stand of timber. Because they were *so* well prepared (as a result of their decade and a half of research), Mr. Knapp and Kenneth had little difficulty getting the appropriate permits and financing.

Both Kenneth and his father are experienced earth-movers and have worked in contracting, so they elected to rent a bulldozer and do their *own* site preparation. With the forethought that's typical of their efforts, they dug the two-story-deep hole in the hillside a *full year* before they intended to start building . . . to permit the earth to settle *and* allow time to be very sure that any wet-weather springs had been identified and dealt with.

POST AND BEAM

Earth-sheltering puts unusually high loads on a building . . . as a result of the dirt's weight pressing against the roof and walls. Consequently, the heavy-duty construction required by "going underground" *can* be the source of more than conventional expense. However, the Knapps determined that a steel beam and concrete assembly approach could save them a great deal of money. ("Post and beam" construction, as it's called, has been used for centuries in wooden homes, but it's primarily employed in large commercial buildings today.)

The father-and-son team started by constructing a 12-inch-thick reinforced retaining wall against the back of the excavation. A monolithic pour was used to avoid the contact surfaces (called cold seams) which result from multiple stage pouring . . . and the concrete was pumped to eliminate bubbles. At the top of the first story, the builders capped the wall with cement—leaving pockets, spaced four feet apart, for beams—and then continued with an eight-inch-wide pour. At the roof line, they capped the wall again and added more recesses for girders.

With that done, 12-inch-thick side walls were added (which buttress the rear retaining wall and provide support for additional horizontal struts). The network of steel I-beams was then set into position—with vertical posts spaced no more than 12 feet apart to provide support—and the concrete second floor and roof were poured directly onto corrugated steel panels . . . which function as both forms *and* reinforcement.

WATERPROOFING

In keeping with their "better safe than sorry" approach to building the energy-efficient

This house features a centuries-old building technique that cut construction cost.

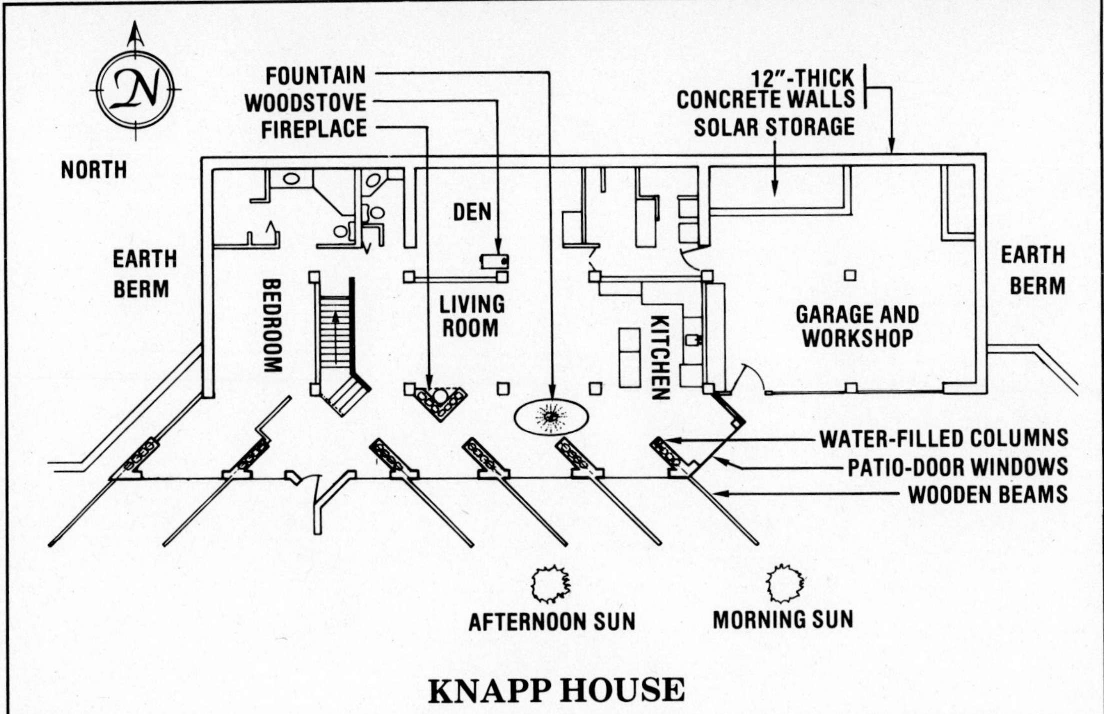

structure, the Knapps took every possible waterproofing precaution . . . and added some inventions of their own for *extra* insurance. They first coated the exterior walls and roof with polyurethane sealant and then covered the carefully applied water barrier with hardboard . . . to protect it from any rocks that might settle out of the 36-inch earth covering. (One-inch extruded foam insulation was also added to the roof, and to the upper five feet of the walls, at this point.)

Next, Gifford and Kenneth devised a system to keep the load on the waterproofing as light as possible. Tiles—placed in gravel beds—were set at the fill-dirt line, against the base of the foundation *and* underneath the 4-inch-thick floating slab.

PASSIVE SOLAR

To maximize the amount of light entering the structure, the family invested in a massive expanse of glass to cover the building's southern exposure. They also included a row of plexiglass windows, angled at 45° to help light penetrate *deeply* into their earth-sided solar home.

With such a large amount of glazing, the Knapps knew they *could* have difficulties with overheating during sunny spells, so they devised a method to take some of the excess solar warmth and store it away for the evenings. Stone columns—each filled with 150 gallons of water in glass jars—were set to face 45° west of south . . . allowing sunlight to beam directly into the house in the morning, but shading the interior (while absorbing the sun's heat) in the afternoon. The columns, as well as a water-filled stone fireplace (which also has a built-in convective air current channel), were all constructed from rock that was quarried on the Knapps' property.

A number of other features help to maintain a comfortable environment in this earth-sheltered, passive solar home. A fountain and a kitchen exhaust fan were installed to help maintain the desired humidity level inside the dwelling. And the building's air is tempered by a 22-inch-diameter, 200-foot-long intake tunnel fitted with radiators which circulate pond water. Plus, for those really hot spells, panels of Sunscreen solar shade can be pulled across the plexiglass windows to shield the interior.

HOW WELL DOES IT WORK?

The union of earth-sheltering and passive solar techniques has proved to be so successful that the house is now virtually heating and cooling self-sufficient. The chill of winter has forced the family to light their fireplace just six times, and their backup woodstove has yet to be used. In fact, when the Knapps once went away for six days during near 0°F weather, the temperature inside the dwelling dropped only to 57°F. And the home's warmest interior reading has been 86°F . . . during an exceptional summer heat wave.

MOST OF THE WAY THERE

Total energy independence is right around the corner for the Knapps. Their house is complete, many of the components that will make up their hydropower plant are already built, and their own homemade windplant is about to come off the drawing board.

When one views the Knapps' already considerable achievement—and the plans they have in the works—it becomes obvious that their dream of self-sufficiency can't be far away. As Mr. Knapp has said, "Most people say that being really independent is impossible without jeopardizing your lifestyle. Well, we set out to prove that a person *can* heat with the sun and cool with the earth. And we set out to prove that an earth-sheltered home can be beautiful. What's more, we set out to prove that such a lovely, efficient dwelling can be built for the same cost as a conventional house . . . or *less*." So far, the Knapps are batting 1,000!

Light from clerestory windows brightens the living room . . . the fireplace has a water-pipe grate that feeds hot water to a 40-gallon storage tank.

LIVING IN A LOG-END CAVE

Dug into the south face of a hill, the roof line of the Roys' "cavern home" follows closely the natural slope of the terrain on the couple's homestead. The natural materials used in the dwelling repeat the theme of the wood and stone found on the land itself.

Rob and Jaki Roy—after living in a stackwood cabin for more than two years—decided to build a new, larger dwelling . . . but, being "totally enamored" (as they put it) of the warm and beautiful appearance of log-end-paneled walls, the couple felt they couldn't plan a new home-building project without including cordwood in the structure, despite the fact that their intended home would be earth-sheltered. Completed in February 1978 after about a year's building, the dwelling is called, with affection, the Log-End Cave.

Though the first little cottage hadn't been difficult to heat, Rob and Jaki knew from research and experience that they could build a *roomier* house that would be *more* energy efficient. Their goal was to go from heating 700 square feet on *seven* cords of wood a year to warming their proposed structure of 924 square feet (1,050 square feet gross) on *three* cords. Since they planned to homestead on their land for a long time to come, the potential saving of four cords every year could mean the elimination of a lot of work over several years . . . and even eventually provide an income from the sale of the "surplus" firewood.

When the couple began the construction of their earth-sheltered dwelling, there wasn't much literature available on underground buildings. They recognized, however, that there were three obvious major considerations in planning earth-sheltered housing: structural strength (to support the heavy roof load and pressure on the walls), waterproofing, and livability.

The Roys' friends feared that underground living would be dark, damp, and likely to induce claustrophobia . . . but, in truth, the finished "cavern" is much brighter inside than their earlier aboveground cottage, and—thanks to careful site selection—it has a better view *and* allows the couple to feel closer to the natural world around them.

BUILD FOR STRENGTH

Any structure should be built to withstand the worst possible conditions that can be anticipated. Suppose, for example, that March finds a four-foot snow accumulation on a 6"-thick sod roof. Then a warm spring rain pours for two days . . . the snow compresses . . . and the sod becomes soaked. Under such a circumstance, Rob estimated that the load on the roof of his home could approach *120 pounds per square foot* . . . so normal framing, which is designed to handle only 40 pounds per square foot, wouldn't come near doing the job. The choices were to go with a reinforced concrete roof (an option not especially suited to an owner/builder on a low budget) or a heavy post-and-beam framework combined with a plank-and-beam roof.

The couple chose the latter type of roofing system, and the way they implemented it turned out to be incredibly strong. The planking is 2 X 6 hemlock (a particularly sturdy wood) on full-sized 4 X 8 hemlock rafters spaced on 32" centers. The rafters, in turn, are carried by three massive 10 X 10, 30-foot-long barn beams. These huge timbers are, themselves, well supported by 8 X 8 and 10 X 10 posts.

Span is very important, and Rob admits to building overcautiously in this regard. For example, his 18-foot-long 4 X 8's are supported at each end *and* in the middle, for spans of about 8 feet. The greatest span for the 10 X 10's is slightly less than ten feet. The completed framework is sufficient to support 6 to 8 inches of sod . . . even in a heavy-snow climate.

Rob does not advise that anyone use an earth roof more than 12 inches thick in combination with timber framing. If such a heavy earth cover is required, it's best to use a reinforced concrete—or concrete plank—roof. In doing so, though, one loses the beauty of an exposed wooden ceiling . . . not to mention the ease of construction and the advantage of lower cost.

The key is to give water a path away from below-ground walls.

In short, the trade-offs involved with a super-heavy roof are—he feels—simply not favorable.

Besides having a strong roof, an earth-sheltered structure must be built so it will be able to withstand the lateral pressure against its side walls. The Roys selected bonded 12″ concrete (not cinder) blocks . . . which resulted in the strongest wall possible, short of poured and reinforced concrete. Block construction is relatively inexpensive and easy for the owner-builder to deal with . . . especially when used in conjunction with surface bonding, which produces a block wall about six times stronger than does conventional block-and-mortar construction.

This bonding technique consists of applying a 1/8″ coating of cement and fiberglass material to *both* sides of a wall of dry-stacked blocks. (Only the first layer is mortared . . . to establish a good, level surface for succeeding courses.)

MAKE IT WATERPROOF

Despite the fact that, in their first cottage, the Roys had used two coats of Thoroseal waterproofing compound and installed footing drains according to the best specifications they could find, the structure's basement wall still cracked along a mortar joint as a result of the second winter's frost heaves. They'd had an inch of water on the floor . . . which wasn't *overly* upsetting in a basement, perhaps, but Rob and Jaki wanted to make sure the same thing wouldn't happen in their underground living space.

Footing drains are only as good as is the percolation capability of the earth above them, and the mistake in the couple's first cottage was in backfilling with the liquid-trapping claylike soil that came out of the excavation. (All the sealing in the world will do little good if the water is allowed to collect—and freeze—against a below grade wall.) The key, then, is to give the liquid an easy path *away* from the walls . . . in other words, to provide good drainage. Sand and gravel have the percolation qualities necessary to carry surface water to footing drains efficiently. Therefore, when building their underground house, the Roys brought in 25 loads of sand for backfill.

Surface bonding supplies some waterproofing, too, since it offers a greater resistance to seepage than does a mortared wall. (In fact, according to a USDA bulletin: "Mortar joints actually act as capillary wicks and draw moisture through the cracks between the mortar and the blocks.") But to make doubly sure of a dry home, Rob tarred the outside of the surface-bonded walls with black plastic roofing cement, and applied 6-mil black polyethylene over that.

The roof was sealed by first troweling on black roofing cement . . . then bedding a layer of 6-mil black polyethylene in the goop . . . and finally *repeating* the process.

Despite the fact that his finished roof is absolutely waterproof, Rob wouldn't wish the dirty work involved in the technique on anyone. He advises trying some other method instead, such as the application of a 1/16″ butyl or Bituthene protective membrane, or bentonite clay panels.

KEEP IT LIVABLE

Natural light and ventilation are the keys to an "open" atmosphere. Therefore, the Roys' home's south wall is only half underground, and features three 42″ X 84″ double-glazed win-

Log ends fill the space between the massive hemlock posts and beams in the south wall, where large windows let in sunlight and provide a view . . . both of which contribute to the open, airy feeling of the "cave". The chimney is one of the few "giveaways" showing from above that the house is even there!

Because of its low arc, the winter sun penetrates deep into the house.

dows. Because they face directly south, these inch-thick panes admit as much heat in the winter as they release . . . and the home's heat loss is further reduced by using insulated shutters on cold winter nights.

On the north side, four trapezoidal double-glazed windows are situated where the gables would be if the house were a surface structure. They're completely blanketed with snow most winters, and the two largest ones are shuttered with two inches of beadboard during the coldest months. As a result there's little heat loss—or winter light—on the north side. However, the winter sun (because of its low arc) penetrates deep into the house through the *south* windows, so little illumination is lost during the cold season. In the summer, though, the trapezoids bring soft north light into the back rooms.

In addition to the windows, three double-paned acrylic skylights let the sunshine into other parts of the house. They are of good quality and moderately expensive, but a skylight admits about five times more light than does a wall window of the same size.

To provide for ventilation, large beadboard-covered vents that can be adjusted to produce any cross-draft situation needed were installed in every room. The Roys' woodburning stoves get their combustion air from the outside via 4" under-floor vents.

The fact that there's an excellent view of the nearby forest from the south windows contributes to the house's airy atmosphere, as does the open plan for the living-dining-kitchen area. The chimney is centrally located to provide a "roomy" feeling, too, with one woodstove on each side of a massive stonemasonry heat sink. The perimeter chambers are separated by internal timber-framed walls, which keep the bedrooms four to eight degrees cooler than the living area . . . just right for sleeping.

CUT THE COST

An important factor that Rob and Jaki considered in designing their home—and one that's not peculiar to *underground* housing—was that of cost. Earth-sheltered homes have the reputation of being expensive, since contractors generally charge about 10% more to build a below-ground dwelling than they do for a surface home of the same size.

If the structure is *owner*-built, however, the cost can be kept down, depending upon the builder's resourcefulness and upon whether or not his or her area suffers from overly stringent building codes.

And just where, you may wonder, was stackwood masonry used in the underground structure? Well, it serves as infilling on the south wall and the north end gable, *and* as an interior design feature. The external walls consist of 10" cedar log ends laid within a heavy post-and-beam framework. Short 5" log ends were used to fill in the spaces where the 4 X 8's passed over the 10 X 10 barn beams.

In four years of experimentation, Rob found that "sawdust mortar" (consisting of 3 parts of sand, 3 of sawdust, 1 of Portland cement, and 1 of lime) is ideal for use with wood masonry. It seasons slowly, eliminating mortar shrinkage, and is extremely strong. An insulation space left between the external and internal joints helps reduce heat loss.

Bottles set in mortar between the large firewood-length "building blocks" in the gable of the front wall help provide light and create an interesting pattern. The Roys have decorated inside walls with shelves containing arts, crafts, and shells . . . and with other items. High trapezoidal windows in the section of the north wall that projects above ground level admit soft light during much of the year and help illuminate the back of the house, which is entered through an attractive wooden door beside one of the heavy stone retaining walls.

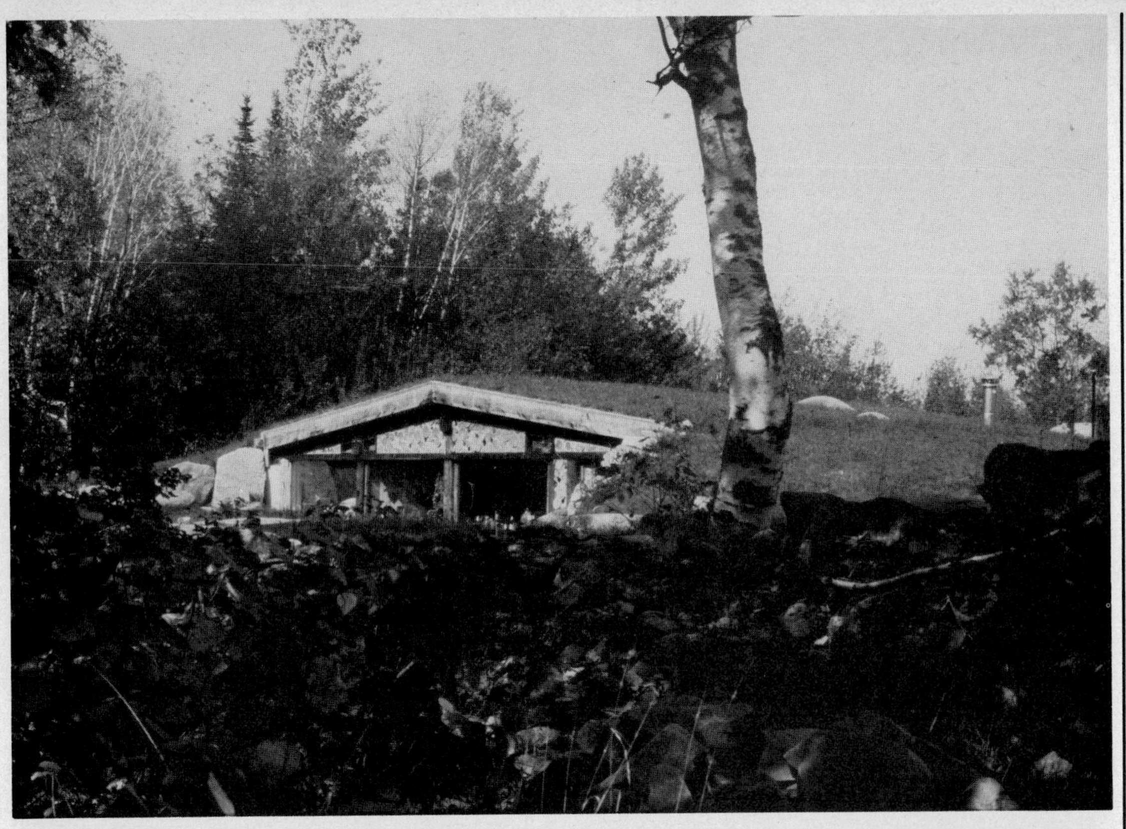

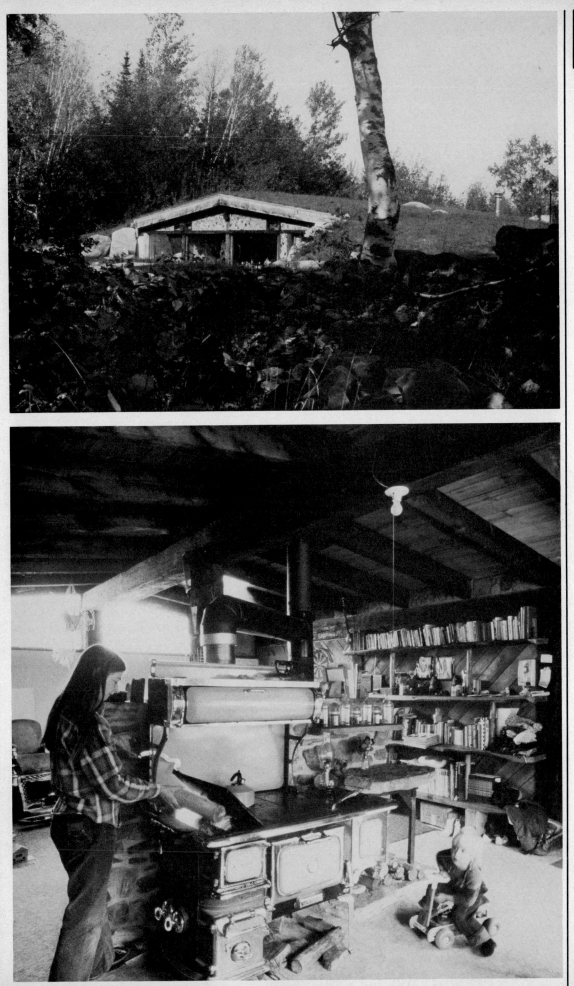

With the heavy load on the roof, the span of support timbers is very important.

Looking past one of the many birch and other deciduous trees that shade the cave in summer but allow solar energy free access to the home in winter, the cordwood wall can be seen basking in the sunlight. Inside, woodstoves fed by under-floor ducts to the outside provide both heat and a place for the Roy family to cook.

SOLAR ENERGY HOMES

Stand inside a sunny window on a winter day, and you'll feel the enormous heat delivered by the sun's rays. Then, walk to a shaded part of the same room, and you'll feel the warmth you absorbed at the window leaving your flesh.

A building acts just like your body . . . gaining heat when sunlight strikes it and releasing that stored energy at night.

Solar homes are planned and built to reduce the need for commercial energy for heating and cooling, by optimizing solar energy gain and minimizing the loss of stored warmth. To do this, an energy-efficient dwelling is oriented to make the best possible use of sunshine during both the winter and the summer and includes features intended to collect, store, and circulate heat . . . such as glazing and greenhouses, thermal mass walls and heat sinks, and active, passive, or hybrid—combined—air-transfer systems.

LIVING IN A DOUBLE SHELL

The beauty of the Smiths' house is matched by the efficiency of the thermal envelope design . . . and the woodburning stove can easily supply any additional needed warmth.

If you're contemplating building a solar home, one of your first considerations will be whether to make your heating system active or passive. Proponents of the latter system feel it's not practical to bother with pumps and pipes (which are not only expensive, but are also subject to periodic failure) when almost the same solar results can be obtained from a system that uses nothing but a well-planned design to achieve its goal.

Furthermore, "active" heating systems require a collector . . . something that [1] most likely will be commercially produced and expensive, [2] will probably detract from the beauty of the house, and [3] will usually necessitate additional engineering and construction considerations.

These factors helped Californian Tom Smith and his architectural advisor, Lee Butler of San Francisco, decide to go with a totally passive system. And—after 20 months of research and a full year of living in the house—Mr. Smith has no regrets. If anything, the structure's efficiency has *exceeded* his expectations . . . especially since the days are often overcast in his part of the Sierras, and even in bright weather the trees native to the area block much of the afternoon sun.

THE THERMAL ENVELOPE

The house is designed according to an "envelope" principle . . . that is, the living quarters are surrounded by an enveloping space of tempered air. In place of a collector, a 300-square-foot greenhouse—faced with 390 square feet of double-pane, tempered glass—is incorporated into the south-facing side of the house. Behind this solarium, the structure's interior (including three bedrooms and two living areas) is isolated from the north wall and roof of the house by an inner "shell" . . . which—in turn—is separated from the exterior by at least 12 inches of air space. This, combined with openings to the crawl space be-

In effect, the walls of this inner compartment act as both collector and storage medium.

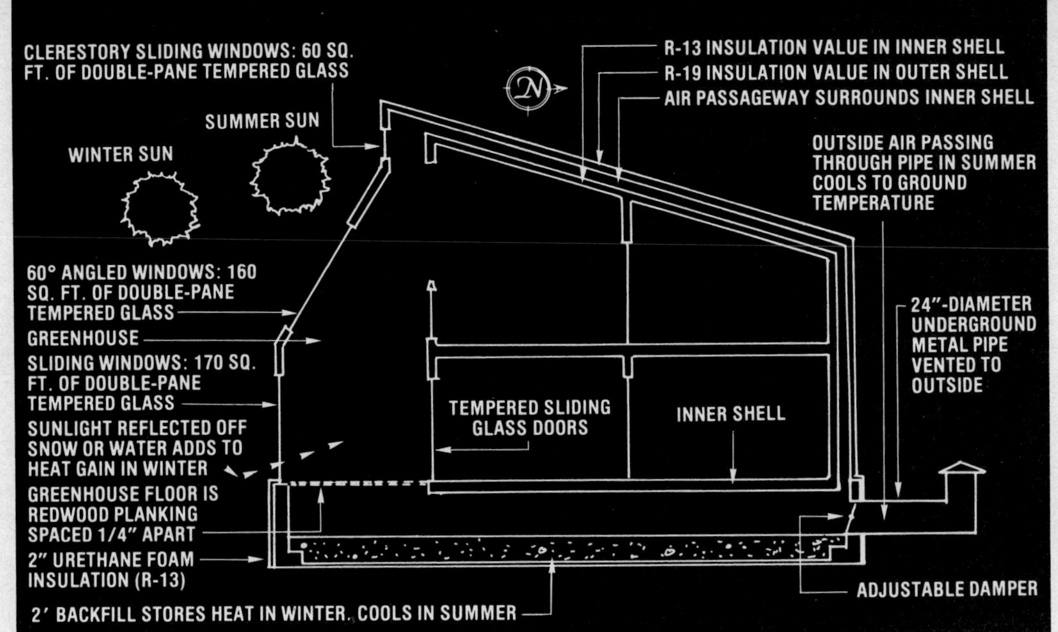

HOW THE "ENVELOPE" WORKS

The Smith house has two major parts: [1] the load-bearing outer shell, which incorporates a 300-square-foot greenhouse on its south side, and [2] the inner shell, which is separated from the exterior framework by a 12-inch air space (except on its east and west walls, which are shared with the "outside" structure).

As the low winter sun beats down on the building, its rays pass through the double-strength glass on the face of the greenhouse (a good deal of which is angled to catch more light), heating the air within. That warmed air rises, drawing behind it—through quarter-inch spaces between the planks of the greenhouse floor—cooler air from the crawl space below the house.

Then, when the heated air reaches the upper limits of the greenhouse, it's drawn through the air passageway between the roofs of the two structures, down through the same channel at the north wall of the house, and back into the crawl space . . . where it heats two feet of backfill spread atop the structure's well-insulated foundation.

This envelope, then, not only tempers the inner structure, but also warms the thermal mass beneath the house (which can maintain its warmth for up to three days). Additionally, the air space between the two shells serves as a "buffer zone" to the cold outside air.

At night, the cycle is reversed. As the air within the greenhouse loses its heat (mainly because of the large amount of glass on the structure's surface), it begins to fall, forcing the warm air in the crawl space to move *up* the passageway in the north wall and through the channel in the roof . . . where it eventually spills into the greenhouse to start the convective cycle all over again.

In the warmer months, the envelope works in a slightly different manner. The summer sun—now a good deal higher in the sky—can't feed as much heat into the house because of the angle at which it strikes the three rows of windows. Whatever heat does pass through the glass, however, rises and escapes out the clerestory transoms, which can be easily opened. In addition, there's an outside vent pipe—routed underground—which feeds into the crawl space at the north side of the house. A controllable damper on this pipe allows the desired amount of fresh outside air to be drawn through both the crawl space and the air channel between the shells . . . cooling the structure as it goes and finally exhausting from the clerestory windows.

neath the house, provides a passageway for the flow of warm air . . . not only creating a convective loop, but also maintaining the inner shell at a comfortable temperature (while still providing a "buffer zone" to the cooler outside shell).

So in effect, the walls of this inner compartment act as both collector and storage medium. And this system—coupled with the fact that there are two feet of backfill in the insulated crawl space—guarantees that heat gained during sunny periods (about 400,000 BTU on a typical January day in California's Olympic Valley) will be stored for up to 72 hours.

Naturally, Tom's envelope works just fine in the winter . . . but what about the summer? Well, during the warmer months, the "flow" cycle is reversed. When Smith opens the clerestory windows at the upper face of the house, the hot air gathered there is forced to evacuate, drawing behind it cooler air pulled from any open windows below. In addition, fresh outside air is drawn through an underground vent pipe at the north side of the building, and it passes above and below the shell of the inner structure, cooling the space within.

MORE (OR LESS) HEAT AS IT'S NEEDED

The basic design of the envelope house allows it to be about 80% energy self-sufficient in both winter and summer . . . an impressive figure considering the simplicity of the passive system. However, additional heat can be supplied by a woodburning stove, which more than makes up the remaining 20%. And, if an extended cold snap *should* happen along, the system is further backed up with baseboard electric heating . . . which is required by local building codes and lending institutions.

On the other side of the coin, summer cooling has presented no problem. However, if the

Tom and his son Taro enjoy the openness of the living room, which connects with the greenhouse and affords a feeling of being part of the outdoors.

Standard insulation for both shells is more effective than overabundant thermal protection.

When snow blankets the ground, the interior of the house stays comfortable . . . and if it's too cold outside for a boy to swing he can do so inside.

house were to be constructed in a hotter clime, simple adjustments (such as the installation of window shades, extra vents, or a roof overhang) would provide ideal cost-effective solutions.

INSULATION IS THE KEY

Unlike many other energy-efficient houses, the Smith dwelling doesn't require an overabundance of insulation. A standard resistance value of R-19 is achieved throughout the exterior shell with rigid insulation board, and the inner shell is insulated—in the same manner—to R-13. It's important to note that—although both shells *do* require insulation for the system to work properly—*excessive* thermal protection not only defeats the purpose of the dual-surface design, but wastes money . . . which could be more wisely spent on heavier glass for the interior wall of the greenhouse.

Tom also took full advantage of insulation when he designed the structure's foundation. Because it serves as a thermal storage area, the "base" of the dwelling was insulated (with two inches of urethane foam) to a value of R-13 . . . preventing heat within the mass from escaping to the outside.

The choice and placement of windows is every bit as important as insulation. Naturally, the south-facing windows are one major consideration, since they're at the "business end" of the house. Double-pane glass is used here (although single-pane glazing would cost less and admit more heat) because the loss of stored warmth through thinner material at night would exceed the slight gain reaped during the day. The east- and west-oriented windows are also double thick, and the north side of the house doesn't have "viewports" at all (though double- or triple-glazing could be installed if desired).

As a final precaution against the infiltration of cold outside air, everything "openable" was caulked or weatherstripped . . . including the two doors that constitute the double-lock entry, or vestibule. In this way, all drafts are eliminated, and the "air-lock seal" goes a long way toward keeping the house comfortable . . . especially when the outside temperature plummets to below freezing.

STANDARD CONSTRUCTION . . . AND REASONABLE COST

The construction techniques used in the house are conventional. Its foundation—aside from the insulation that shields it from the earth—is nothing more than block and poured concrete. And resting on this substructure is a network of piers which not only support the floor of the house, but also hold it several feet *above* the foundation . . . providing room for the necessary two feet of heat-storing backfill and circulation air space. This setup, then, is no different from a standard crawl space in any conventional dwelling.

Orthodox construction methods were used in the framing, too. The walls of the outer shell are 2 X 6 studs, and 2 X 12 rafters are

used in the roof (to support the heavy snow load). All windows and glass are standard commercial units, as are the prehung doors. The ceiling of the inner shell is merely fastened to the bottom of the 2 X 12 beams, and the north side of this interior structure is simply an extra 2 X 4 stud frame wall. Actually, then, the "inside layer" isn't load bearing, so it's no more difficult (or expensive) to construct than any other interior wall scheme.

Of course, there are those who will maintain that the cost of the additional materials required for this inner shell outweighs its advantages. Not so, claims Mr. Smith . . . he insists that the overall expense is *lower* because a large saving is realized by the elimination of expensive heating ductwork within the walls of the house.

Furthermore—since the structure *is* conventional—it fully complies with all local building codes (these differ from county to county) and can be financed through normal lending institutions. Best of all, the design is flexible enough to be adapted to whatever changes might be dictated by location, climate, building codes, or space requirements.

THE COMFORT FACTOR

It's difficult to explain the distinct feeling of satisfaction that this house provides. Unlike a conventionally heated home, which often seems "stuffy", the Smith residence has a natural "outdoor" feel to it . . . and this wholesome feeling is amplified by the fact that the entire south wall of the structure is open—at least visually—to the great out-of-doors.

In addition, there are no drafts or artificial convections inside the house. All air movement takes place within the "envelope" and heats the inner shell through absorption (with the exception of the greenhouse, which gets direct sunlight and is itself part of the "envelope" . . . by virtue of the fact that its floor planks are spaced 1/4 inch apart for airflow).

Of course, this enclosed current of air doesn't preserve a *constant* temperature throughout the home's interior, but a slight thermal variation from area to area is actually desirable, since it relieves "physiological boredom". Another benefit of Smith's design is that it keeps the relative humidity at an acceptable level (between 50 and 60%), rather than drying the air out as central heating units tend to do.

PROS, CONS, AND FUTURE PLANS

The "envelope" idea incorporated in this structure is a good one . . . it works as well in practice as it does in theory. However, there are disadvantages—though easy to live with—that should be noted. The first is that the passive system can store thermal energy for only two or three days, less than the typical active system. Also, the design is such that windows—especially those on the north side of the house—are difficult to install (or, at best, expensive) because of the double shell.

On the bright side, though, it can't be denied that the system is cost-effective . . . from the standpoint not only of initial investment but also of maintenance. And—once the house is built—heating is for the most part a "free ride".

Almost as important as the economy of the house is its overall flexibility of design. As long as there is an expanse of glass on the south-facing wall and a passageway around the inner shell for air to circulate, the layout of the rooms inside can be modified to suit personal tastes.

Now that Tom has been "living in an envelope" for a while, he's had time to evaluate his ideas on the basis of experience rather than theory . . . and he is more than pleased with the results. He does plan to add a work loft in the upper portion of the greenhouse and—if finances permit—a hot tub (warmed by the exhaust from the wood stove) set into the greenhouse floor. But, even without these "luxuries", the Smith "thermal envelope" house is a mighty pleasing package!

The owner found the design to be cost-effective both in initial investment and in maintenance.

Tom Smith enjoys a view of the greenhouse from his balcony . . . the light-filled master bedroom is another good place for plants in the "many-windowed" house.

HEATING AND COOLING WITH THE SUN

Ancient architectural methods and native building materials yielded a structure that blends well with the desert surroundings of Southern California's Imperial Valley.

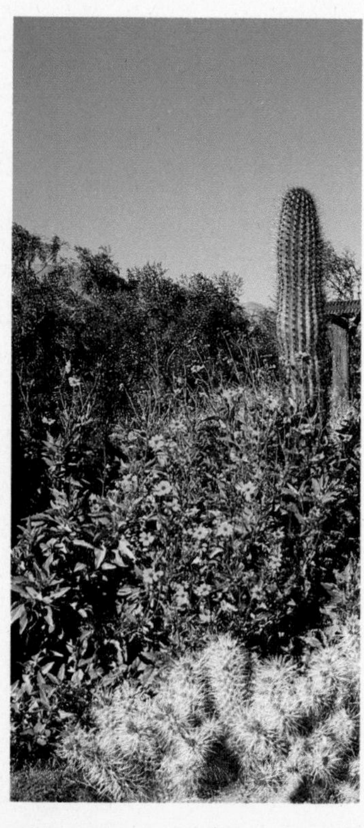

In the desert region of Southern California's Imperial Valley—just to the east of the urban sprawl of San Diego—the ambient temperature can seasonally fluctuate from a high of 130° to a low of 27°F, with humidity usually resting at a bone-drying 10%.

While most of the area's residents rely on power-eating air conditioners to cool their homes during the scorching summers, one particularly resourceful resident of this arid wilderness—university professor James Harmon—has chosen to abandon the "conventional" methods of climate control and let the desert environment *passively* temper his abode all year round!

In order to make his concept a working reality in the often-uncompromising desert, Jim really had to do his homework. The house he eventually designed [1] rests on a concrete slab foundation that's set about four feet below the desert floor to take advantage of the temperature-stabilizing effect of the earth, [2] incorporates a naturally convected ventilation system that serves to heat the home in winter and cool it in summer, [3] uses insulation to the utmost on both interior and exterior walls, and [4] takes advantage of desirable wintertime sunlight through the use of south-facing glass—much of which is shaded by roof overhangs in summer—both at ground level *and* within the roof's skylight "wall".

Mr. Harmon's plans included not only the construction of a practical, inexpensive, energy-efficient dwelling, but—on a more comprehensive level—the creation of a nearly (or *fully*) self-sufficient homestead. And, except for his modest needs for outside electrical power, Jim has pretty much accomplished his goal of independence. The house itself is only part of a master layout . . . which includes organic vegetable gardens and orchards (all of which are irrigated with underground watering systems), food drying bins, a workshop, a compost pile, a grape arbor, a greenhouse, and even a solar-heated outdoor hot tub!

Since construction of a dwelling was Jim's *primary* project (and because he scrounged much of his building material over a long period of time), the professor began to plan his structure long before he drove the first nail.

The design incorporates a bit of commonsense technology, some ancient architectural methods of the Middle East, and a smattering of southwestern American Indian building techniques. The result is a structure that's almost wholly passive, uses native building materials wherever possible, and leaves an almost indiscernible impression on the landscape.

AND IT WORKS LIKE A CHARM . . .

Exactly how does Jim's home achieve his goals? First, the concrete foundation was surrounded with a low block wall that rises up to ground level. The slab doesn't utilize a bed layer of insulation, because—being a thermal sink—it must be given the chance to absorb ground heat in the winter to help warm the structure and, by the same token, assimilate the home's excess interior heat in the summer

and transfer that warmth to the earth. Other factors were considered, too: The effect of occasional strong winds is minimized by the protective natural earth berming and the low profile of the dwelling. And, as an aesthetic plus, the line of sight to a nearby tarmac highway is conveniently interrupted.

But that's only part of the story . . . a natural ventilation system (adapted from Middle Eastern home design) is the *major* means of maintaining an acceptable comfort level in the house all year round. Eight unperforated, 4″-diameter, corrugated plastic drainage pipes are connected—using vent holes previously formed in the structure's foundation—near the edges of the octagonally shaped dwelling. From these openings underneath the house, the tubes curve around, then come together (a slight distance is maintained between them to assure proper thermal conductivity) within a broad underground channel, and run to a point about 100 feet away. Jim figures the depth of this ditch—40 inches—to be something of a compromise between a shallower trench (which wouldn't afford proper air tempering) and a much deeper chasm (which would be excessively labor-intensive for a relatively slight gain in efficiency).

The terminal point for the tubes—simply a 2′ X 2′ concrete block "manifold" extending from ground level to a depth of about four feet—is capped with a reworked kitchen exhaust fan that allows air to be drawn through even when the motor is off. (On rare occasions, use of the fan *is* required to force air through the system and into the house.)

Normally, though, the intensity of the sun (and, in part, the direction of the prevailing winds) is great enough to cause the ventilation cycle to operate perfectly. In addition to the underground tubes, Professor Harmon's design incorporates—in effect—*two* useful layers of roof on its windward side: the standard exterior surface, covered with tar and gravel, and an *interior* roof which is nothing more than pine tongue-and-groove finish board fastened to the lower face of the rafters. The upper surface of the inner roof is lined with builder's foil to form air passageways within the home's "cap". Jim provided inlets and outlets for the built-in ventilation channels by drilling a quantity of 1/2″ holes—in circular groups—through the soffits *outside* the house, and likewise by opening the ducts to the atmosphere at the apex of the roof, where he's built what he calls the "tower of power" (which is also open, through the use of small ducts, to the inside of the home).

IN THE SUMMER . . .

Hence, during the hot season, as the sun beats down on the structure's roof with a vengeance, it immediately heats the air within the ventilation channels. Naturally, this hot air begins to rise, moving upward with the slope of the roof. As the heated air flows out of the house by way of the tower, more air is drawn in from the outside eave vents . . . and the process continues, resulting in a steady flow through the roof passageways.

This rapidly moving air, in turn, creates a suction which pulls air directly from inside the house itself, through the ducts at the top of the tower. And, since a slight vacuum is created inside the dwelling, fresh outside air is pulled in from the only source possible: the underground ventilation tubes, which thermally condition the entering atmosphere by virtue of the constant 75–80°F ground temperature.

To help the cooling process during periods of intense summer heat, Jim also had the foresight to install *exterior* venetian blinds on the south-facing, leeward side of the house . . . which he closes to prevent the sun from beating in through the windows. Since these "light shutters" *are* external (and white, to boot), heat never has a chance to actually find its way into the house.

Another trick up Jim Harmon's "thermal" sleeve is the very convenient cooling effect of evaporation. During the hottest part of the year (when J.H.'s gardens need the *most* moisture anyway), the professor supplies the liquid by activating his buried sprinkling system. The sprinklers soak the ground, and as the water evaporates from the sandy soil, the temperature of the earth *decreases* considerably . . . which, in turn, helps to further cool the incoming air in the underground vent tubes!

Mr. Harmon can achieve still *more* indoor "air conditioning" by activating his "swamp cooler": a broad belt of thin foam pad, revolving in a shallow tub of water, through which forced air is passed. (Jim also has plans for an indoor hot tub . . . which could function year round to provide humidity and/or heat as required, depending on the season.)

The effect of occasional strong winds is minimized by the protective natural earth berming and the low profile of the dwelling.

Topping the house is the "tower of power", as Jim dubbed this vitally important part of the home's cooling system, designed to keep the heat out of the kitchen and other sections of the living area.

The design of the roof is important to proper ventilation.

AND IN THE WINTER

The same system that cools the air in summer also furnishes a temperate climate during the colder months. Since the sun is lower in the sky in wintertime (and because ol' Sol's effects are less intense then than in the summer), the heat buildup within the roof channels is not as great . . . and the airflow is likewise reduced just slightly. Fortunately, the home's roof was so designed that wind moving from the northwest, as it usually does in that locale, helps to draw air from inside the house—and thus through the tubes—by virtue of a suction effect as it passes over the peak. In case the flow is not sufficient to provide proper ventilation, Jim always has the option of activating the electric fan in order to *force* tempered air through the buried pipe network.

In addition, a considerable amount of winter heat is derived from direct insolation. Because the sun is low in the sky, its light can stream unhindered through the main south-facing windows and the vertical clerestory glazing at the peak of the roof. (Jim has installed freestanding redwood grape arbors above all the southern-exposed windows, to provide necessary summer shade *and* delicious fruit. Come cold weather, the vines dry up, so sunlight can pass *through* the arbors when it's most needed.) Good planning allows even desert dwellers some climate control.

HOW IT WORKS

Simply put, the Harmon house works on the principle of pressure differential caused by rapidly moving air. Here's how: In the summer, as the sun beats down on the surface of the roof, the air within the ceiling channel absorbs heat. Because the heated air has a much lower specific gravity than the ambient atmosphere, it tends to rise, flow upward along the channel between the inner and outer roof, and exhaust out the louvers in the "tower of power".

Naturally, with all this air escaping, a new supply must be brought in . . . and it enters by way of the groups of 1/2" holes drilled through the soffits under the outside eaves. So, what results is a constant—and sometimes downright *furious*—flow from the outdoors, through the roof channels, and outside again.

In order to take advantage of the air current, Jim Harmon has cut several small openings into the tower, at its highest point *inside* the house. As the heated air rushes past these holes, it actually entrains—or pulls—the air within the building right through the vents . . . in much the same way that an automobile's carburetor draws fuel out of its reservoir.

Of course, since air is then being drawn from the living area of the house itself, *it* must be replaced . . . and the only available sources of supply—as long as the home's doors and windows remain closed—are the eight ventilation tubes buried 40 inches beneath the surface of the earth . . . where temperature is maintained at about 75–80°F year round.

During the winter—when the path of the sun and its intensity result in lower temperatures within the roof channels—the system still functions, though not quite as efficiently as during the hot season. Fortunately, prevailing winds from the northwest, flowing over and around the outside of the "tower of power", boost the convection current through the chimney by pulling air out of the roof also. And, if this breeze effect is not sufficient to draw warmed air through the underground pipe network, the blower fan can always be activated.

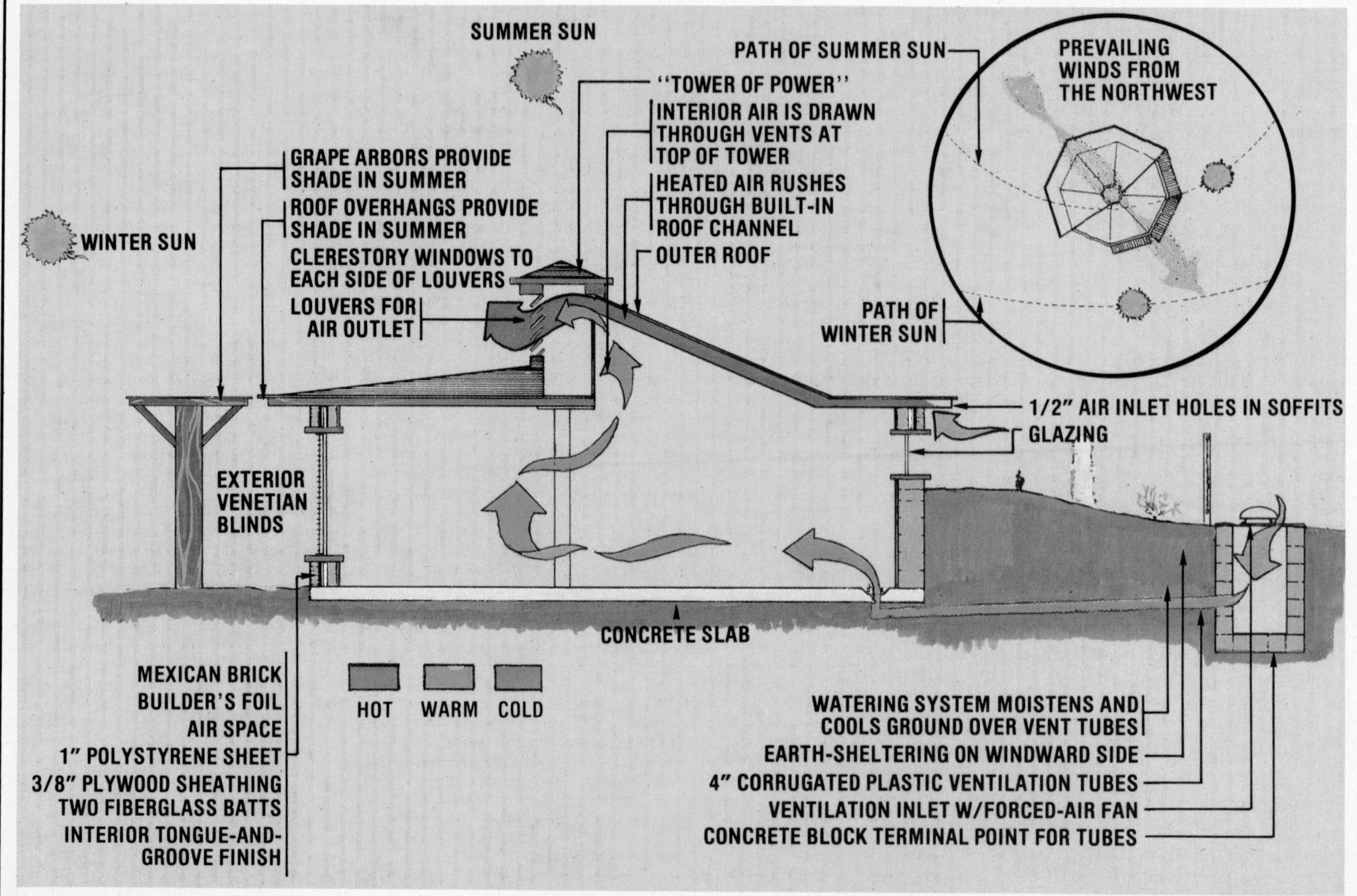

AN AIRTIGHT THERMOS BOTTLE

Of course, the home's unique ventilation system operates properly only if the doors and windows are closed and the walls are relatively airtight. But varying levels of comfort can be attained—at *any* time of the year—by opening the windows as desired.

Another factor which contributes to the success of the desert home design is the fact that Harmon has gone to great lengths to properly insulate the structure. The lower portion of his dwelling is, of course, earth-sheltered . . . and the upper part, framed with 2 X 6 studs, is also just about impervious to nearly any temperature fluctuation that may occur. Behind the tongue-and-groove interior sheathing are two batts of fiberglass insulation, then a layer of 3/8″ plywood. This surface is covered with 1″ polystyrene, which—in turn—is veneered with builder's foil.

The final covering is an exterior facade of *ladrillos*, or Mexican brick (similar in its thermal mass effects to the materials used in native American earthen shelters), which is set slightly *away* from the backing wall's foil-covered surface . . . to provide an air space through which excess heat—absorbed by the brick and reflected from the builder's foil—can escape into the roof channels. In addition to careful wall construction, the professor has fully insulated each thick exterior door.

Mr. Harmon believes that wood construction is a sound choice. "Framing a house with lumber remains a good way to go . . . mainly because, if you use the synthetics and other trash available on the market nowadays, you'll find such materials are just as expensive and provide *less* quality *and* longevity. I'd rather spend my money now and get it over with, and have the satisfaction of a well-done job."

Another reason Jim chose to go with wood (in conjunction with concrete and some of the native materials available in his area) was that he wanted his dwelling as impervious as he could make it to earthquakes . . . phenomena which are often problems in the Imperial Valley area. In order to assure his home's solidity, he designed the structure like a wagon wheel, with a central hub plate in the roof—acting as a pivot—from which the "spokes" (in this case surplus railroad trestle timbers) radiate and fasten to the eight corners formed by the walls of the house. In theory, this arrangement distributes both horizontal and vertical shocks evenly throughout the structure . . . with little or no damage to the framework. And Jim's design was given an acid test when a severe quake hit the area and did considerable damage to *several* local communities . . . while merely causing the Harmon home to creak slightly!

Framing a house with lumber remains a good way to go.

Vent holes in the soffits of the overhanging eaves and louvers in the "tower of power" combine to set up a convection current that draws hot air out of the house. South-facing windows admit the winter sun but are shaded in the summer by the grape arbor and exterior Venetian blinds. A "natural" fence stands as a windbreak.

AN AIR LOOP CUTS ENERGY COSTS

The south-facing roof of the Reeves' New England dwelling is angled to take maximum advantage of the winter sun and actually contains *more* glass than is needed for maximum efficiency. In contrast, the east (and other) walls are characterized by a minimum of window space. Viewed from the southwest the "open" front of the sunspace can be seen in the construction phase.

PHOTOS BY ROBERT REEVES

During a particularly long, cold winter, Robert Reeves and his wife watched their heating bills rise and toyed with the idea of building a solar home. Then, over the following two years, they drew up well over a dozen sets of plans, each based upon one or another of the then-current technologies. Among the possibilities they considered were Trombe walls and other masonry mass schemes . . . water and air collectors . . . water, rock, and phase-change storage . . . earth berms . . . and superinsulation, but—for a variety of reasons—none of the plans was satisfactory. Some required too much gadgetry. Others allowed too wide a variation in interior temperatures, required too much supplemental heat, or simply cost too much to build. So after two years, the couple felt they had gained a lot of knowledge but still lacked a design which suited their requirements.

Then they chanced upon a write-up of the Tom Smith double-shell house in the Sierras and sent for the book he had published about the home. After studying it and other related information, and drawing up another seven sets of plans, the couple finally arrived at a version of the double-shell house which promised to satisfy all their needs.

With their initial planning completed, the Reeves checked their design (especially the heat loss/gain calculations) with a solar engineer and made some revisions which reflected his suggestions. Next came a plan check with the local building inspector . . . and a few more changes. Finally, they contacted a contractor, who, though inexperienced in solar building, was enthusiastic and eager to learn. Construction began in early fall, and they moved into their new double-shell structure the next August . . . just in time to prepare for the winter to come. During that cold season the couple conducted extensive performance tests (designed to monitor the house's thermal efficiency and the degree to which it was fulfilling the goals which they had set), and they were happy to find at winter's end that the dwelling had surpassed their expectations.

THE HOUSE AND ITS SITUATION

The house is located in northwestern Connecticut, at latitude 41 degrees north (approximately) and at an elevation of 920 feet above sea level. The annual sunshine for the area averages 56%, and there are about 6,500 heating degree-days per year. The state building code mandates a design temperature of −10°F, to cope with the frigid New England winter.

The Reeves' house has a full first floor, a partial second story, and a full basement . . . and measures 40′ wide on the south-facing side by 39′4″ deep overall. On the south side, a 10′ X 40′ greenhouse rises to the full height of the roof, providing both light and greenery year round. The air envelope between the inner and outer shells runs full-width through the attic and then down the north side through a 12-inch space that's insulated on both faces. As a safety measure, spring-loaded, thermal-fused sheet-metal fire stops are set at the bottom of the north wall cavity. The air loop is completed by the full cellar and by slots in the floor of the greenhouse which allow air to return to the sunspace.

The greenhouse wall is vertical on the first floor, and then angles at 57 degrees from horizontal up to the roof peak. The north-facing roof slope is pitched 33 degrees from horizontal.

To allow it to blend in with the surrounding countryside, the house was sided with rough-sawed native pine board-and-batten over 1/2″ sheathing. The garage wing on the north side includes an air-lock vestibule, which allows people to enter and exit without letting much heat escape from the main structure.

Four inches of polystyrene, laid to the full depth of the foundation (and covered above grade by 1/4″ asbestos-cement board), was used to insulate the poured concrete cellar on its perimeter. Underneath the 4″ concrete floor is a 10″ layer of crushed stone.

Framing for the outer shell was done with 2 X 6's, set 24 inches on center, and the gaps were filled with 6″-thick fiberglass insulation. The inner shell was framed with 2 X 4's, 16 inches on center, insulated with 3-1/2″-thick fiberglass. Roof insulation consists of 6 inches of fiberglass, and the inside surfaces of both shells have 6-mil-thick polyethylene vapor barriers. All walls and ceilings are covered with fire-resistant drywall, and the interior floors are made of wood.

To minimize heat loss, the only openings on the north side are the double-pane kitchen window and the entrance door from the air-lock vestibule. On the east and west walls there is a total of four small windows, each double-glazed and fitted with movable insulation. The south wall (the entryway for the home's principle heat source, sunlight) is about 60% glass on the first floor and 40% on the second . . . all the glazing is double-pane and fitted with draw drapes.

The vertical portion (first floor) of the greenhouse's facade is double-glazed (totaling 175 square feet), while the angled second-story section is fitted with 513 square feet of 1/4″-thick plexiglass.

The combination of cellar windows, awning vents, and the large louvered attic vents at each end of the roof peak keeps air moving through the greenhouse during the summer, and heavy-duty roller shades housed under the angled portion of the greenhouse control solar gain. Furthermore, all of the vents have insulated shutters, which can be closed to prevent heat loss in cold weather.

The living area on the two floors within the inner shell totals 1,600 square feet, and the greenhouse glazing—vertical and angled—adds up to 688 square feet . . . or 43% of the floor area. That's a considerably higher window percentage than is found in most envelope houses. In fact, it just could be too high, requiring more venting and shading than should be necessary in the summer, and perhaps losing as much heat from those last few percentage points as is gained in the winter.

Two solar water heaters have been installed inside the upper glazing of the greenhouse, along with an insulated storage tank set at a higher level in the attic to permit thermosiphoning. The preheated water is piped to the electric water heater in the cellar and greatly reduces utility costs.

Design calculations indicated that in order to maintain a living area temperature of 65°F on a cloudy day in the frigid months of December and January, the Reeves would need 7.500 kilowatts (KW) of electric heat per hour . . . or 120 KWH in a 16-hour waking period. To be on the safe side, they installed heaters with a total capacity of 12.720 KW and also planned to put a woodstove in the living room as a backup heat source in case of a power failure. In northwestern Connecticut where the winters can be (and usually are) long and chilling, they felt it best to have a safety margin.

The Reeves estimate that the cost of building a double-shell home added at least 25% to their total construction fees, when compared with the expense of erecting a superinsulated, conventionally heated house with the same amount of living space. Paying back that premium from fuel savings will take 20–25 years—an excessive length of time, of course—but the Reeves were willing to accept this for the sake of comfort and convenience.

HOW THE HOUSE PERFORMED

Of course, in order to truly rate the performance of a building in terms of thermal efficiency, one has to do more than add up the utility bills at the end of the winter. The Reeves' solution was to install a thermistor-type thermometer with 12 remote sensors located indoors, outdoors, and throughout the air space between the two shells. By standing in one location, punching buttons, and reading a dial, Bob could find out, at any time, what the temperature was at any of those 12 locations. This information was taken down at more or less regular intervals throughout each day and entered in a log. By this method, the house's internal temperatures could be compared to outside conditions and a performance profile established.

(Before going more deeply into the performance analysis, two terms should be defined. *Cloudy days* are days with no direct sunshine . . . that is, daylight hours of overcast, heavy cloud cover, rain, or snow. *Sunny days* are days with at least four hours of direct sunshine. Days fitting neither of these definitions are not included in the calculations.)

During the first winter in the new home, there were no cloudy days which were as cold as −10°F, and only two cloudy days below 0°F. The average dawn temperature on the ten coldest cloudy days was a frigid 4.1°F, and the maximum amount of electricity required to maintain an indoor temperature of 65°F during the 16 waking hours on any of those days was 49.344 KWH.

It should be noted that most of the coldest cloudy days were interspersed with sunny days, so the structure retained more heat than it would have during a prolonged cloudy period. But after three or four *consecutive* cloudy days (with dawn temperatures ranging from 10° to 20°F), the house had lost much of its warmth, and more heat was required . . . as much as 58.800 KWH for the 16 waking hours. A look at figures 1 and 2 will reveal that outside temperatures on the ten sunny days were actually quite a bit colder than those on the ten

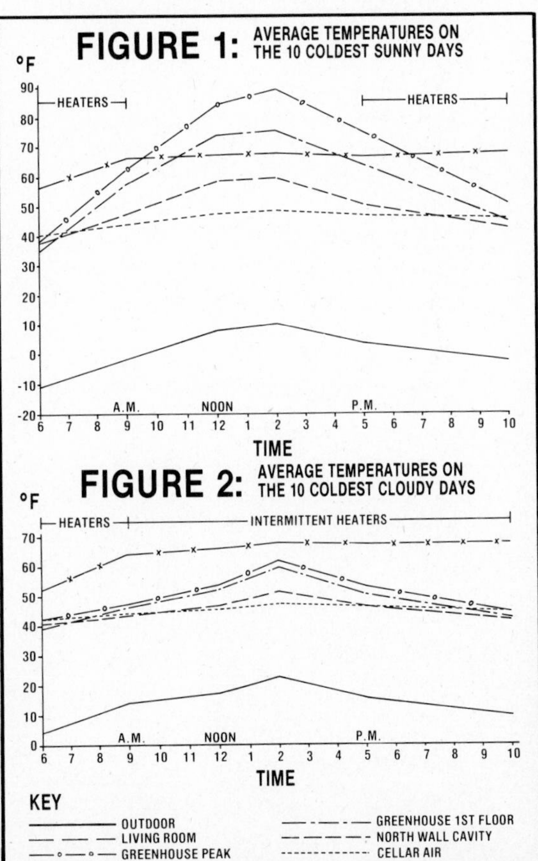

Cellar windows, awning vents, and large louvered attic vents at each end of the roof peak keep air moving through the greenhouse during the summer.

Cavities in the walls were packed with fiberglass insulation.

With only a few alterations, the home's solar heating contribution could be boosted to 90% or better.

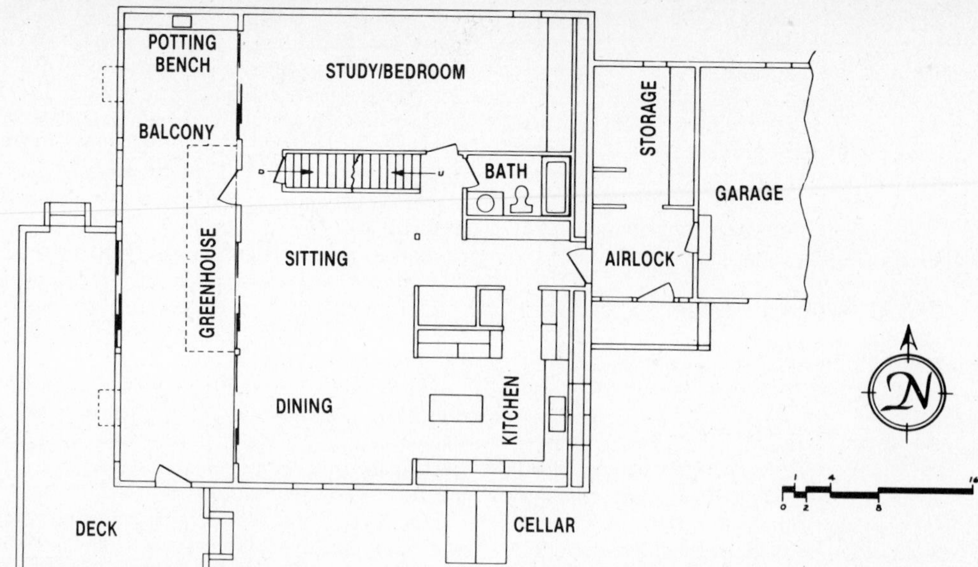

cloudy days, but that temperatures within the envelope were much higher, thanks to solar collection.

The ten coldest sunny days had dawn temperatures averaging -11.4°F, and the maximum amount of electric heating for 16 hours on any one of those days was 40.405 KWH. On the coldest day of all—when the outside temperature was -18°F at dawn, rose to -4°F at 2:00 p.m., and then dropped to -15°F at 6:00 p.m.—the total supplemental heat required only 31.152 KWH of electricity: 16.608 KWH in the early morning to bring the indoor temperature up from 55° to 65°F, and 14.544 KWH in the evening to hold that reading until bedtime. In between, the eight hours of sunshine kept the living area at 66° to 68°F without power . . . which means that at 2:00 p.m. there was an approximate temperature differential of 72°F between indoor and outdoor environments *without any kind of auxiliary heating*! Performance more than fulfilled the family's expectations: electric heat usage for the entire season totaled just under 3,000 KWH (the equivalent of the heat delivered by one cord of white ash firewood or 115 gallons of fuel oil).

SECOND THOUGHTS

After carefully monitoring the performance of their double-shell house, the Reeves reached several conclusions about how its efficiency could be improved.

One change they would make would be to omit the crushed stone under the cellar floor, and instead pour the concrete directly onto the earth, using drains to forestall flooding. They believe that the 10-inch layer of stone with its captive air spaces acts as insulation, reducing the warming effect of the earth on the concrete. As things stand, the cellar is very dry but cold. At one point the surface temperature dropped to 37°F, while the earth's temperature at that depth below grade remained at 50°F.

As far as improvements in the envelope design itself go, Bob recommends using double glazing instead of single glazing on the upper part of the greenhouse, and installing the roof insulation and vapor barrier more carefully, which he believes would result in the need for considerably less glass . . . say the equivalent of 25%-30% of the home's floor area, instead of the existing 43%. In addition, mounting the glass lower in the front wall to provide more shaded travel space above the glazing would allow the rising air to gain greater momentum before reaching the roof peak. Furthermore, to reduce air-flow turbulence at the entry to the roof passage, he recommends running collar beams faced with plasterboard across the top of the attic, thereby decreasing the angle of direction change that the circulating air makes at the roof peak.

Double glazing the upper section of the greenhouse would have two other benefits, as well. First, it would eliminate much of the frost that forms on the upper glazing surfaces on extremely cold nights (and which melts and drips when warmed by the morning sun). Perhaps more important, double glazing the entire greenhouse would reduce nighttime heat loss, allowing a wider variety of plants to be grown than is possible now. Of course, one option would be to mount insulating shades, but the expense and mechanical problems of operating them at a 57-degree angle argue against that solution.

Finally, the inner-shell vapor barrier has proved to be unnecessary since those walls never become cold enough for condensation to occur . . . another tribute to the efficacy of the double-shell concept.

There are always small improvements which can be made on any design, but—with only the alterations outlined here—the home's solar heating contribution might be boosted to 90% or better.

The collectors and tank for the home's solar water heating system can be seen through the open framework of the greenhouse roof. Sunlight entering the solarium through the front and roof windows falls on flowers and furniture, making the "front room" a great place for basking, even on the coldest days.

PERFORMANCE MONITORING: SOME CONCLUSIONS

Intensive monitoring of the Reeves' home over a full heating season generated some interesting information.

If the inner shell, insulated as it now stands (with 3-1/2 inches of fiberglass in the walls and 6 inches in the roof), were detached from the outer shell and monitored as a complete, freestanding house, its *heat loss* during the past winter would have totaled 93,787,200 British Thermal Units (BTU). Over the same period, the inner south-facing glass wall could be expected to *capture* 34,431,600 BTU, leaving a net loss of 59,355,600 BTU to be made up by conventional heating. If that system were electric, it would require 17,500 KWH of power to maintain a temperature of 65°F during the sixteen waking hours. The supplemental heat used during the past season—3,000 KWH —is only 17% of that figure.

If the inner shell stood by itself but were super-insulated with 6 inches of fiberglass in all the walls and 12 inches in the roof, its electric heat requirement (after allowing for gain for the south-facing glass) could be estimated at 13,750 KWH. The 3,000 KWH actually consumed by the home was only 22% of that figure.

WINTER'S TALE

Of the several interesting conclusions to be drawn from the monitoring log, perhaps the most provocative was that the colder the outdoor temperature, the better the double-shell system worked. During the most frigid part of the winter (from mid-December to early February), the average outdoor reading at dawn was 7.3°F. By 2:00 p.m., when the outdoor temperature had usually peaked, the average heat gain at the bottom of the thermal loop (in the cellar) was 5.8°F. On the ten warmest days during the period, however—with the average outdoor temperature at 26.2°F—the average gain in cellar air temperature was only 4.9°F. Now contrast those figures with the ones for the ten *coldest* days (when the average dawn reading was -11.4°F) which showed an average temperature gain in the cellar of 8°F! (See Fig. 3.)

This paradox reflects the improved performance of the convective loop caused by increased heat loss from the north-facing roof and wall. As more heat is lost from the building envelope, the air becomes heavier . . . sinking faster and increasing the flow rate in the loop. To gain heat, you have to lose some, but the net result is positive.

And it works remarkably well in terms of living area comfort. The lowest interior temperature at dawn during the winter was 55°F . . . without the use of supplemental heat during the sleeping hours. Within one to three hours, electric heaters could raise that reading to 65°F. On cloudy days, intermittent auxiliary heating was needed to maintain that temperature, while on sunny days no extra heat was required until evening.

Another fact discovered during the monitoring was that the envelope appeared to work more efficiently on cloudy days than on sunny ones. At dawn, the temperatures throughout the loop were relatively uniform . . . within a range of 5°–6°F, at most. By 2:00 p.m., the highest temperature was always at the greenhouse peak, and all other readings were at fairly consistent ratios to that of the peak (see Figs. 1, 2, and 4).

At 2:00 p.m. on the ten coldest sunny days, the greenhouse at shoulder level on the first floor had reached an average of 78% of the peak gain (measured at the top of the greenhouse and considered as 100%). Midway down the north wall (within the envelope), the temperature averaged 42% of the peak level . . . while it had dropped to an average of 16% in the cellar.

At the same hour on the ten coldest cloudy days, however, the first floor greenhouse location had reached an average of 99% of peak gain, while the north wall figure stood at 53% and the cellar at 26%. There was less heat overall, of course, but a higher proportion of the available BTU was being drawn around to the bottom of the loop on cloudy days than on sunny ones.

Actually, the fact that *any* heat was gained on cloudy days was, in itself, a pleasant surprise. And there has been no day—including those of heavy rains and snow storms—when the greenhouse didn't gather some heat. The lowest such gain (measured at the greenhouse peak) was 6°F, and on the same day, the cellar picked up 3°F. (Because the basement walls and floor were colder than the air, it follows that the gain was attributable to circulation within the thermal loop.)

Though more heat is gained on sunny days than on cloudy ones, it's at diminished ratio, and it's difficult to know whether the drop in efficiency is caused by stagnation at the peak, turbulence, or a greater rate of heat loss resulting from the larger temperature differential between the indoors and outdoors.

HEAT STORAGE

Contrary to the widely held belief that the cellar of an envelope house serves as a heat sink, this one seems to hold very little warmth. While air temperatures in the cellar often rose 10°F (or more) during the day, the surface of the concrete walls never gained more than 3°F, and the floor slab no more than 2°F. Air passing through the cellar at night (in reverse flow) picked up only enough heat to keep the greenhouse peak 2°–3°F warmer than its first level. Instead, significant storage occurred in the structure of the house itself . . . especially in the 6-1/2 tons of plasterboard on the walls, ceilings, and airway surfaces. On cloudy days immediately following a sunny one, walls and ceilings lost their warmth slowly, becoming chilly only the third successive cloudy day.

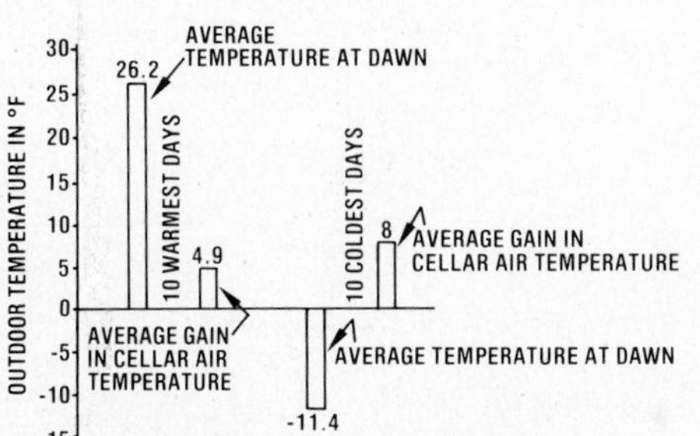

FIGURE 3: DAWM TEMPERATURES AND CELLAR GAINS

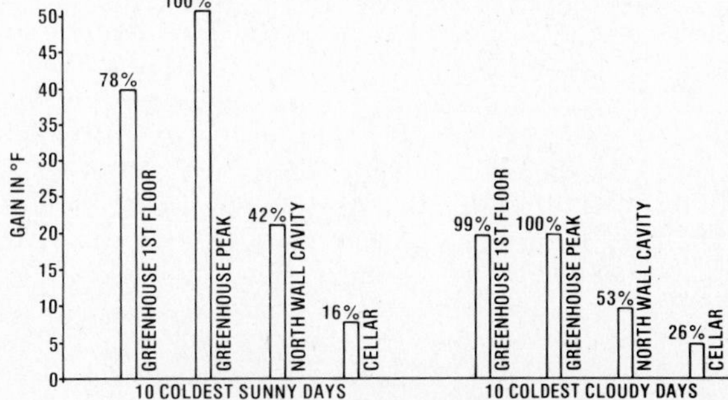

FIGURE 4: HEAT GAIN IN °F IN VARIOUS PARTS OF THE ENVELOPE

The colder the outdoor temperature, the better the system worked.

Intensive monitoring of outside weather conditions and of temperatures in the dwelling's air loop, rock storage and living spaces enabled Robert Reeves not only to draw comparisons between the efficiency of his home and a similar conventional structure but also to closely examine the house's thermal behavior.

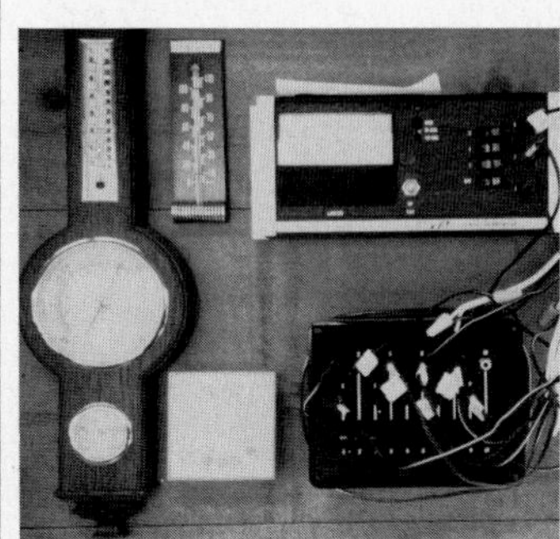

GOING SOLAR IN THE SIERRAS

To meet the challenge of both heating and cooling their home in a climate that can experience 50°F daily temperature variations, Otis and Jane faced their home slightly away from true south and took full advantage of the terrain and the location of existing trees. Sun-facing glazing and the greenhouse admit solar energy during the winter, and the solar collector on the roof provides hot domestic water. Latticework and eaves shade the windows in summer, and clerestory windows help with ventilation for their dwelling in the Sierra Nevada foothills.

PHOTOS BY OTIS WOLLAN

Otis Wollan and his wife Jane Mulder wanted to be out of the city and into a solar-heated house of their own, and they wanted to do so *quickly*. They were dead set upon becoming energy self-sufficient . . . though they didn't want to end up living in a building that looked like a wooden version of Skylab. The couple believed—despite the skeptics' claims—that two average people could design and build their own solar-heated house, and they set out to prove that they were right.

Well, a mere seven months after breaking ground, Otis and Jane moved into their new home which may appear to be—in many respects—a rather conservative blend of well-known passive solar techniques. But the proof of the pudding is that the house—built entirely by the owners' own hands (except for digging the excavation)—can be kept warm all winter with one cord of wood . . . and it was constructed at a price that won't keep the couple in debt the rest of their lives.

SOLAR ORIENTATION

The climate of the Sierra Nevada foothills isn't known for extremely bitter winters. At the 1,700-foot level—where the house is located—there are normally only a few days of subzero temperatures and a couple of feet of snow each year. It's actually the winter "monsoons" —when cold rain often falls for as many as three weeks on end—which pose the most significant solar-heating problem.

But, the real solar-home-design challenge (in that climate, at least) is to provide for both heating *and* cooling. Temperatures over 110°F and a 50°F difference between the nightly low and daily high aren't uncommon.

In order to be sure that the home could perform the dual functions of heating and cooling, the couple had to adapt "accepted" solar principles to their own location and climate. Instead of facing the major window area due south, for instance, they angled the "sunny side" five degrees to the east. This stance helps the structure even out the wide range of daily temperatures by capturing badly needed early morning rays and rejecting some of the less desirable afternoon ones.

Also, existing trees to the east and west protect the dwelling from the summer sun's intensity, as detailed in the sun path diagram. During the warm months, the sun rises and sets a little north of due east and west. The California live oak to the east shields the house before 9:30 a.m., and the grove of oaks to the west provides shade after 4:30 p.m. (after all, trees are about the most efficient passive solar energy components available). And in the winter—when ol' Sol rises further to the south—neither stand of timber casts its shadow on the walls of the house.

LET THE SUN SHINE IN

As you can see in the photos, the southern exposure of the solar bungalow has plenty of windows. In fact, the greenhouse—which was added several months after the rest of the house was finished—brought the total glass area on the south wall up to 416 square feet. The conservatory functions both as a solar collector and as an air lock to prevent heat loss from the main house. During the daytime the heat collected by the solarium can be vented—as needed—into the living room by opening the inner door and windows. Then, come evening, the doors are closed and warmth for the room is drawn from the battery of black 55-gallon drums full of water which line the walls.

The hothouse has been one of the most successful features of this owner-built solar home. The temperature in the glazed structure will often, at dawn, be in the "safe for plants" 50°F range . . . even when the mercury outside has plunged to well below freezing. In fact, because they were without the greenhouse during their first winter in the house, the couple has a pretty good idea just what the addition did for heat-collection. The first year's cold spell ate up 2-1/2 cords of wood and $28 worth of propane. But

NORTH
SUN PATH DIAGRAM
40° NORTH LATITUDE
SHADE
SHADE
WESTERN HORIZON
EASTERN HORIZON
SUMMER SOLSTICE
WINTER SOLSTICE
SOUTH

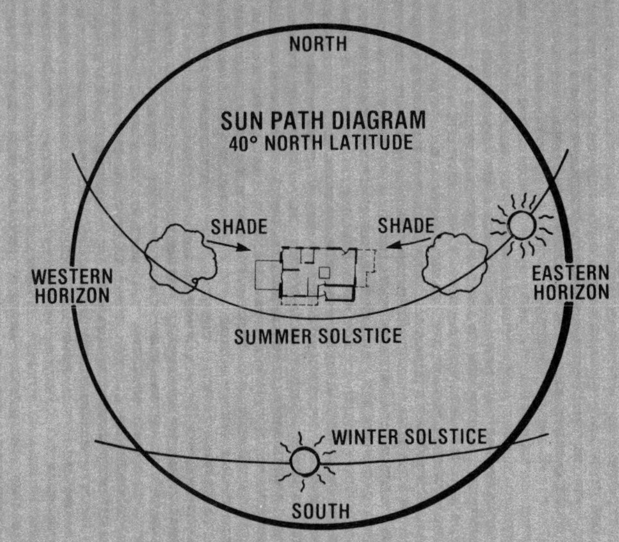

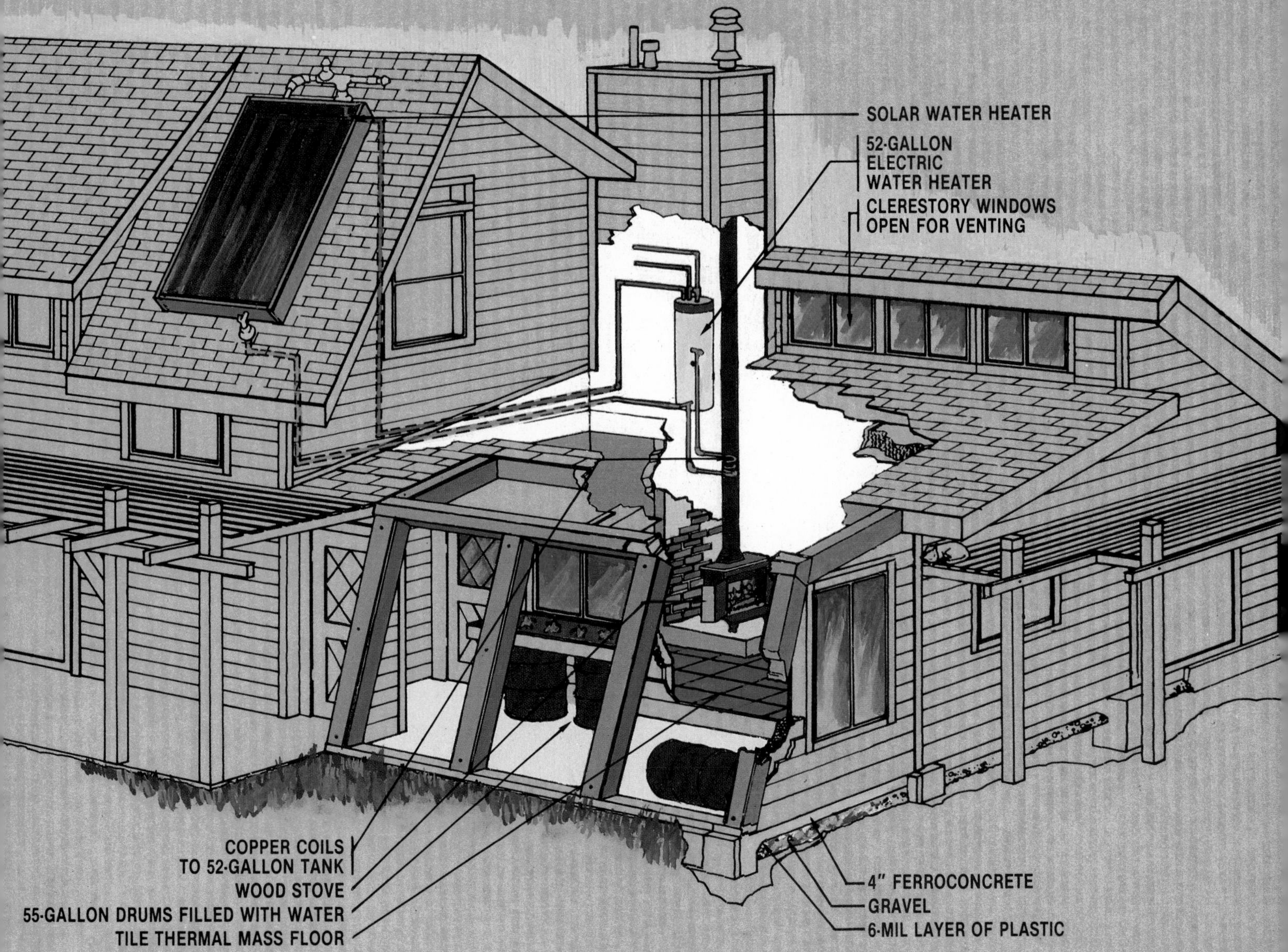

SOLAR WATER HEATER
52-GALLON ELECTRIC WATER HEATER
CLERESTORY WINDOWS OPEN FOR VENTING
COPPER COILS TO 52-GALLON TANK
WOOD STOVE
55-GALLON DRUMS FILLED WITH WATER
TILE THERMAL MASS FLOOR
4" FERROCONCRETE
GRAVEL
6-MIL LAYER OF PLASTIC

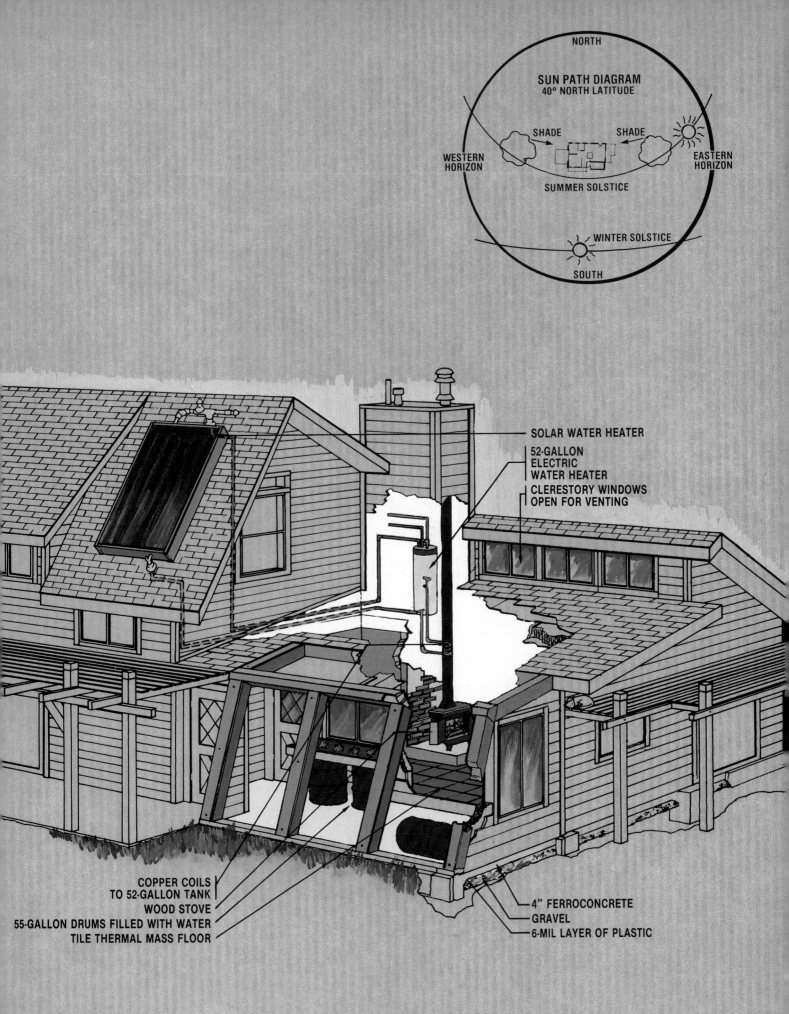

Winter's low-angled sunbeams warm over two-thirds of the home's floor area by direct radiation.

with the greenhouse grabbing additional warmth from the sun, only one cord of wood and *no* propane were used the following winter. (Otis did turn on the heater once . . . to see if it still worked!)

Not surprisingly, the temperature variation in the greenhouse is a little rough on some house plants. But vegetables thrive there all through the winter, and regularly provide a fresh green bonus at the dinner table.

During the summer, however, few plants could survive the intense heat in the solarium. After discovering that not even an extensive ventilation system was able to keep the hothouse *cool* enough, Jane and Otis devised a system for turning the greenhouse—when the dog days hit—into a covered porch. As you can see in the "Glazing Detail" diagram, the glass on the walls is removable and a shade can be attached to the roof . . . and the former "hotbox" becomes a pleasant place to relax on a sultry evening.

CATCHING SOME RAYS

Winter's low-angled sunbeams pass through the southern glass and warm over two-thirds of the home's floor area by direct radiation. Brown floor tiles—which are set atop a four-inch layer of concrete, a 6-mil piece of plastic, and a gravel base—*absorb* that heat and hold it for release during the night. To help prevent heat loss through the perimeter of the slab, all the edges of the concrete thermal mass were insulated with two inches of polystyrene and metal flashing. In addition, a Franklin-style stove is housed in an adobe fireplace which, by way of its earthen material, lends its famed heat-retaining abilities to the "house warming" cause.

The use of the floor as a thermal mass has been effective for the home in *this* climate, but the couple hesitates to recommend such an approach universally. The heat gained through direct sunlight beating on the brown tile surface has had much less tendency to migrate to shaded areas than they had expected. People in areas with less sunshine, or lower ground temperatures, might find a tile floor uncomfortably cool during extended periods of inclement weather.

GETTING INTO HOT WATER

Solar systems can have a number of small problems and *still* work fairly well. Most of the couple's difficulties arose from the way they applied "open loop" water warming.

They were doggedly opposed to "closed loop" systems . . . not only because of their complexity and expense, but also because such setups demand that a toxic antifreeze compound be kept circulating next to the potable water supply. No matter what clever safeguards could be added to such a system, the couple didn't want one.

So they constructed their own open loop solar H_2O heater (shown in the accompanying drawing) which is based on a standard 52-gallon electric hot water tank with a 30-amp wall switch added to override the built-in thermostat and to allow them to activate the electric heater when *they* want it on. The tank is connected to a 40-square-foot collector mounted on the south-facing roof. They built the 5′ X 8′ collector with a 2 X 6 redwood frame, two inches of fiberglass insulation, a metal sheet, and five passes of copper water pipe covered with sheet-metal "tents".

Otis and Jane learned later that their design was a little bit off base. In the first place, they should have stuffed more water-carrying tubes into their collector by putting the pipes four to five inches apart rather than the 12-inch spacing they chose. Furthermore, the two inches of fiberglass insulation cannot sufficiently preserve the heat gained by the system. But, on the plus side, the decision to fasten the tubes to the metal plate with clamps rather than by soldering *did* prove to be a wise one. Judging by all the temperature-caused stressing and buckling that goes on between the pipe and plates, solder joints would almost certainly have broken.

From the collector, water is drawn—down into the 52-gallon tank—by a 1/20-HP Grundfos stainless steel pump. Two temperature sensors—one located at the base of the collector and the other at the inlet to the tank—monitor the temperatures and report the findings to a differential thermostat which operates flow control valves in response to the temperature variation. Water is pumped when the collector becomes hotter than the tank.

Unfortunately, the couple also failed to do their homework thoroughly when it came to preventing a nighttime freeze-up in their hot water system. They originally opted for an inexpensive thermal-recirculation setup—which works by keeping water flowing through the collector all night—rather than a costly automatic draindown design.

As it turns out, thermal recirculation works fine where freezes are very rare, but in the Sierras—where ice frequently forms during *numerous* consecutive evenings—the draindown method would have been much more efficient. A good deal of heated water was wasted by pumping it back through the tubing at night to save the collector from disaster . . . so now they drain the system manually.

Despite such errors, the solar water heater actually does produce an adequate supply of warm water. On a sunny day it supplies about 30 gallons of scalding liquid. Still, Otis and Jane *do* believe that if their inital design had been better thought out, they could be getting as much as 60 gallons of "free" hot water each day.

HOME IS WHERE THE HEARTH IS

Fortunately, the couple seldom has to depend on their electrical water heater for backup, since the wood stove can substitute for the sun. Twenty-five feet of 1/2″ soft copper tubing is coiled around the stove's chimney and then tapped into the 52-gallon tank.

The combination of wood and solar water heating has kept winter electric bills low, despite the use of enough "juice" to run a very busy electric dryer (for scads of diapers), a 1,000-watt bathroom heater, and their well's 1-1/2 horsepower pump. During the summer—when Otis and Jane employ a *solar* dryer (the clothesline)—their bills drop off to about half the amount of the winter ones . . . even though they often have to irrigate heavily using electric pumps.

Most of the solar collectors are part of the building itself and take the place of regular, non-solar components. And insulation doesn't cost money . . . it saves it.

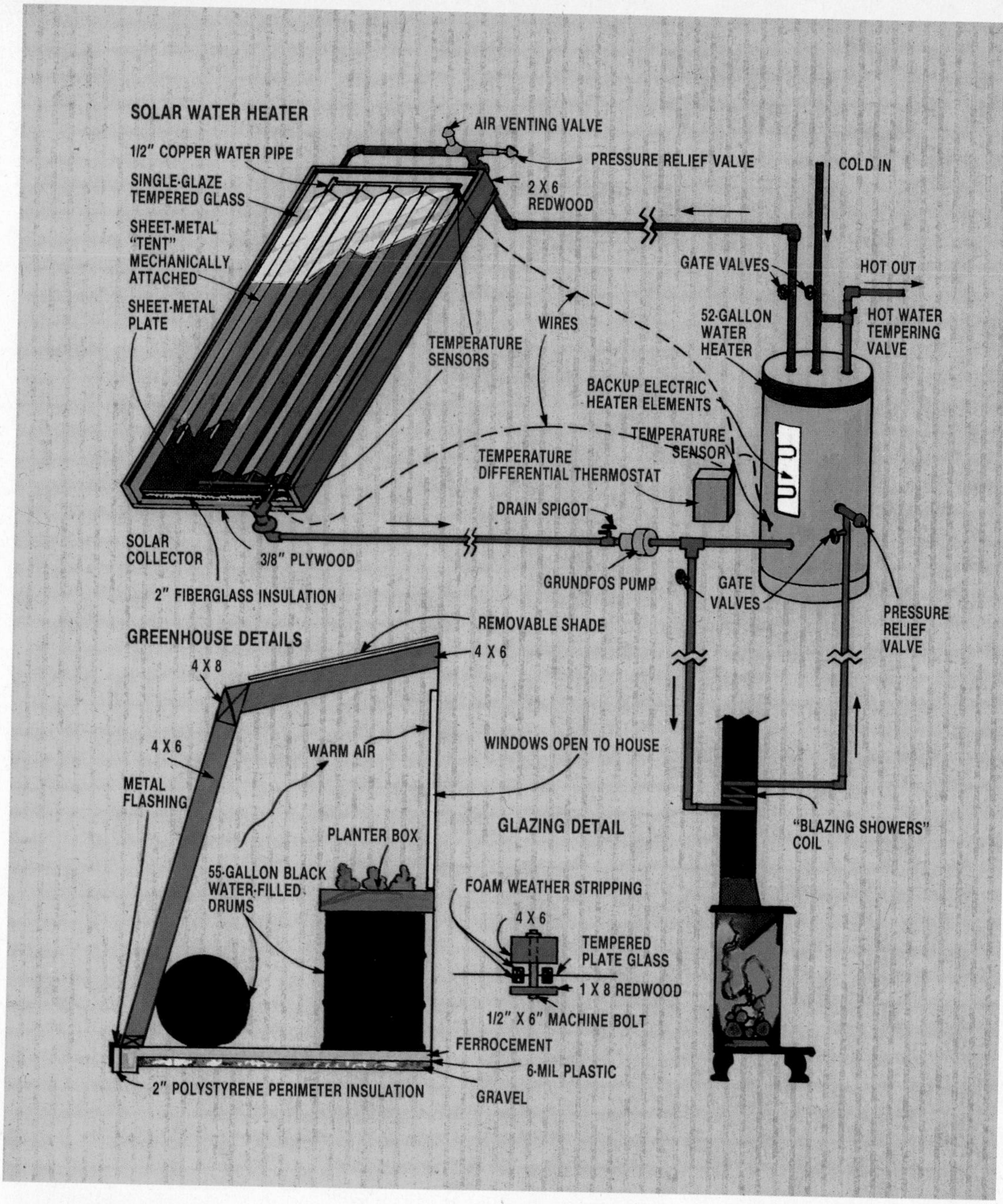

BARGAIN BTU'S

It's very difficult to determine—in constructing a passively heated house—which costs are specifically solar expenses. Most of the home's sun "collectors" are part of the building and have taken the place of standard (nonsolar) components. Furthermore, many of the energy-saving features were no more expensive than their "ordinary" counterparts would have been. For example, the floor tiles cost about the same as other quality coverings, since the couple scouted around a little and purchased them from the factory—as production overrun "firsts"—instead of paying retail prices. Some "extra" dollars *were* spent on R-19 wall and ceiling insulation, double weatherstripping on all doors, and thermopane glass. But—even though the benefits of such heavy insulation may have finally become accepted by most Americans—it should be emphasized that insulation doesn't *cost* money . . . it *saves* it. Few other items in today's housing market offer such a rapid return on an investment.

An extra $200 was spent to have the excavation dug where the sun would do the most good, rather than where the job could have been most expediently done. Add to *that* specifically solar cost the several hundred dollars in materials and controls they put into their water heater, and you'll be pretty close to the end of the couple's "goin' solar" expenses.

Of course, the greenhouse isn't what many people would consider to be a standard portion of a home (at least not yet), and an argument could be made for incorporating its cost into the sun-heating bill. But the solarium does much more than merely collect sunlight. The glass house also subs as a delightful foyer, a garden, a humidifier, and a playroom for frolicking children.

Otis and Jane put in some back-breaking construction work through summer and fall, but they wouldn't have had it any other way. Solar energy isn't the wave of the future for this couple . . . because it's warming their living room right now!

PASSIVE SOLAR IN ONTARIO

The Peter Fluker residence, located 90 miles north of Toronto in the province of Ontario, Canada, represents a successful balance between comfortable, attractive living space and energy efficiency. With 65% of the building's heating requirements satisfied by the sun (in a climate that experiences 8,500 heating degree-days annually), it can't be considered completely solar self-sufficient, but few naturally warmed homes are . . . and the expense is offset by the aesthetic qualities of the open, outdoorlike atmosphere of the structure.

In planning his family home, Fluker—a designer by profession—felt that it should take into account the concept that people and their residences are part of, rather than isolated from, their environment.

To accomplish this, Peter spent a good deal of time studying the terrain and coordinating the building's design in order to let the land do its share in making his home a functional success.

The several-acre tract is well isolated from the road by a generous accumulation of deciduous trees growing on a gentle south-facing slope. This foliage provides shading in the summer season, yet is developed enough to allow a breeze to reach the structure beneath its umbrella of leaves.

The house itself rests at the peak of the slope and is heavily bermed to the north . . . and to further the effect of this berming, Peter shaped his home's cedar-shingled roof to direct winds away from the dwelling's south-facing skylight area. The house was designed as a modified pentagon . . . both to encourage air flow around it and to maximize its southern exposure.

PHOTOS BY MICHAEL MAYNARD AND GILDA RAYBURN

The modified pentagonal floor plan maximizes the home's southern exposure and creates an interior that harmonizes with the natural outdoor setting.

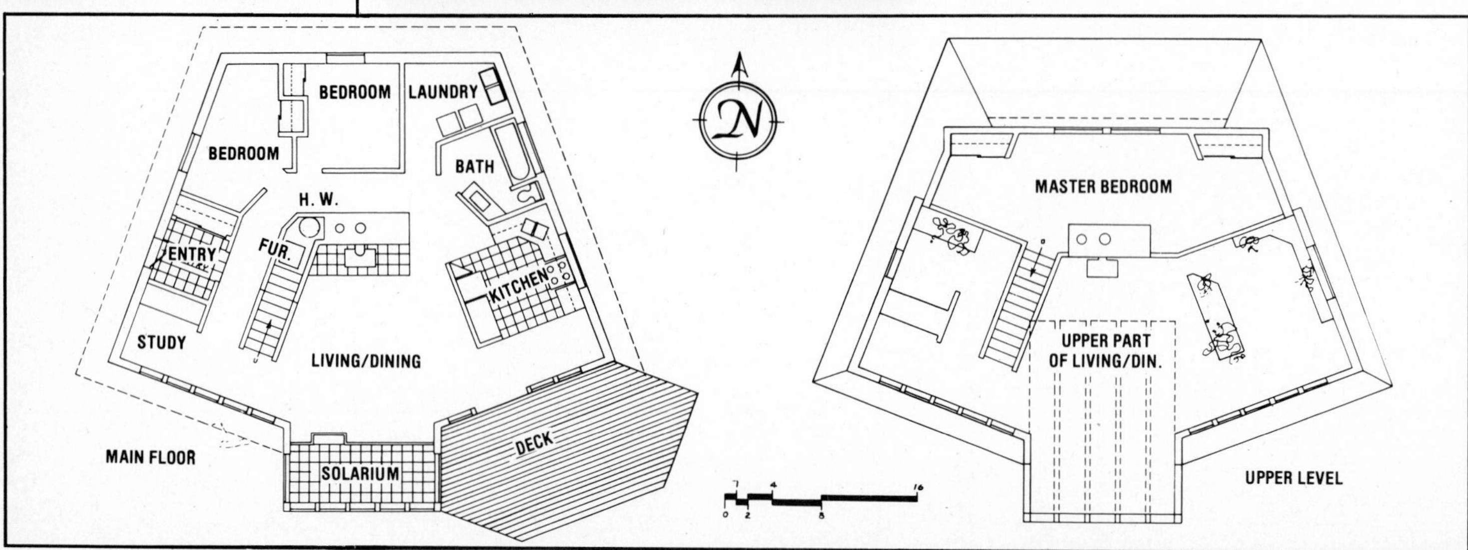

DESIGNED TO FUNCTION . . . BEAUTIFULLY

Fluker's design is fairly straightforward: It's a direct-gain, passive solar structure with a total of 1,750 square feet of living area. More than half the main floor is directly exposed to the sun—either through the 186 square feet of south-southeast- and south-southwest-facing thermopane glass, or the 360 square feet of skylight collector surface—and the master bedroom on the upper level gathers its light, across a 3-1/2-foot parapet, both indirectly from white-painted ceilings and walls and immediately through the roof portion of the skylight. (The triple glazing on the west, east, and north faces is minimized to a total of 70 square feet and is responsible for less than 9% of the building's total heat loss.)

In order to provide for heat collection and storage—yet still work within the concept that the structure itself should be a storage medium—the designer incorporated several systems into his home's construction.

First, the entire slab was poured over an insulated (R-16) bed and an air-handling system. The surface of this concrete foundation was fitted out with dark, heat-absorbing slate in the solarium, hearth, and kitchen areas, but—because it affords a softer, warmer feeling—carpeting covers most of the remaining living space.

Then, to take maximum advantage of direct solar gain (and to provide a structural and aesthetic focus), a concrete block column veneered with slabs of charcoal-gray slate stretches from floor to ceiling at the center of the house.

Absorbing solar heat isn't its single thermal function, though. The pillar also serves as a chimney for the Fisher woodstove and incorporates a central duct that's connected to the air-handling network buried in the slab. By using the low-speed fan of the backup electric furnace duct constantly for air circulation throughout the heating season, Fluker was able to create a flow loop that draws stagnant air from the peak of the building—where it collects naturally—into a vent at the top of the central column, and on through its core duct and those passageways of the system beneath the floor.

In this manner, both the backup and solar heating systems are integrated: Any convective warmth from either the woodstove or the furnace must travel through the recirculation storage mass, and the Fisher's radiant heat is also absorbed directly by the masonry from the outside. Also, the warm-air distribution network reduces temperature differences at the high and low levels of the house. And—since the floor is heated from beneath—the effects of any loss of direct solar gain that result from the use of carpeting are diminished.

Finally, to insure that the entire structural package would be sufficiently insulated from the elements, Peter protected the walls and roof to a factor of R-32.

The Fluker residence was also designed to stave off the effects of summer's heat . . . and this was accomplished, for the most part, as naturally as possible. The floor in the greenhouse area is vented to the exterior at ground level, and—by way of the normal high- and low-pressure situation created by prevailing wind flow over the structure—cool air from the forest bed is drawn into the house at that point and pulled upward to pass out through a row of functional clerestory windows high in the master bedroom's north wall.

Although the massive skylight is protected from insolation by the summer foliage, this shading is not as pronounced during periods of seasonal transition . . . so to subdue the sun's rays through the spring and fall months, the designer is currently installing a motorized shutter system on the ceiling beams. This, of course, will not only prevent unwanted sunlight from entering the house, but it will also noticeably improve the structure's ability to retain warmth when the skylight is "closed off" at night.

AN ECONOMIC SUCCESS

Since completing his residence, Peter Fluker has spent a good deal of time analyzing the structure's strengths and weaknesses. In all, considering the harshness of the Canadian climate, he feels that his objective—the creation of a minimum-energy-consuming, attractive living space that would allow him and others interested in passive solar housing to understand the concept—has been successfully met.

Heat-absorbing slate plays an important part in solar heat retention in the Canadian designer's house.

While the glazed-in living area seems part of the snowy outdoors, the bright sunlight keeps the area warm, making it a snug place to be during the chilly Canadian winter.

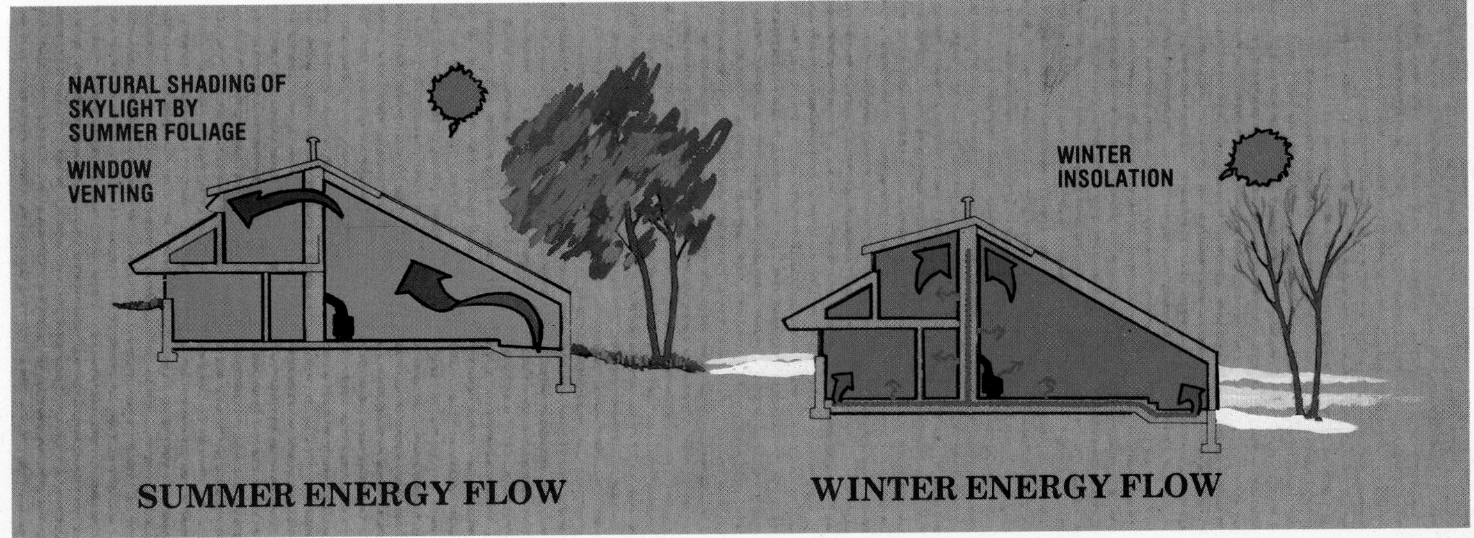

ADOBE ABODE CUTS COSTS

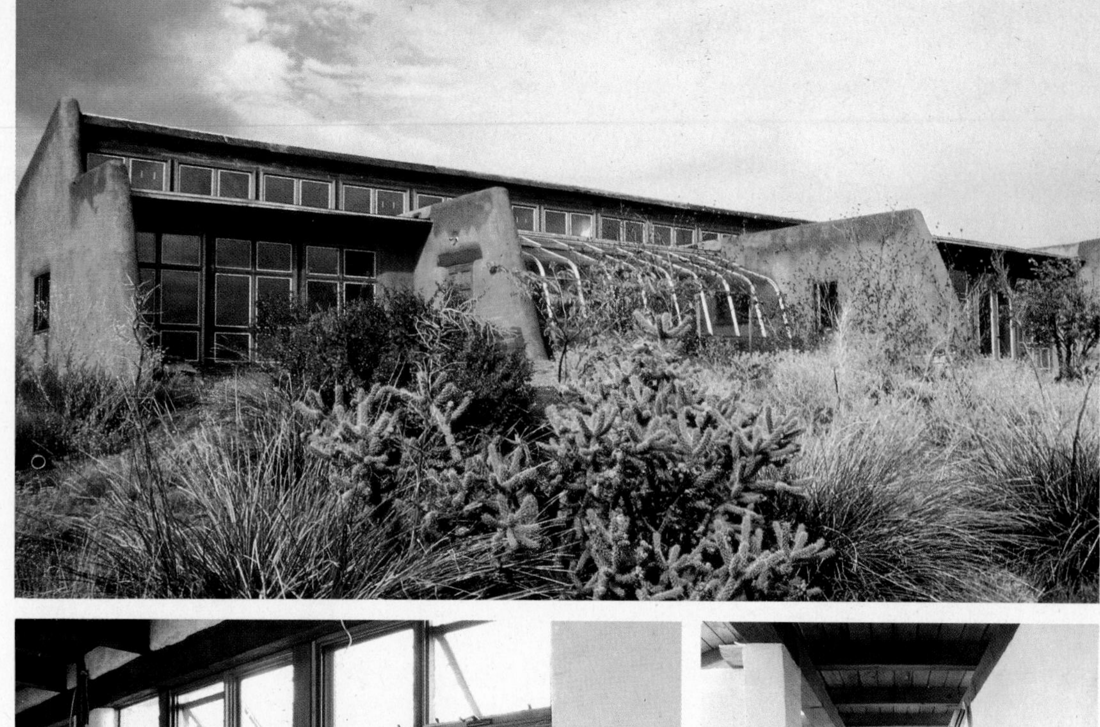

Vertical glazing in the ground floor and the clerestory on the adobe's south side totals 500 square feet and runs nearly the length of the building. These windows admit low angle winter sunlight, helping the greenhouse heat the domicile, but in summer the rays striking the glass from higher in the sky are reflected. Brick floors and interior walls—which are open at the top for air circulation whenever possible and are shaped into arches and curves—store thermal energy for nighttime use. Because of concern about water usage, a composting toilet serves as part of the building's "plumbing".

To many people, adobe dwellings are the ultimate expression of resource-conscious architecture. Built of bricks formed from the right blend of local mud and straw, such structures seem to rise smoothly from the soil.

Adobe offers that kind of satisfaction and several things more. That the adobe walls can be rounded, curved, and arched to form smooth transitions is an aesthetic plus. And, of course, no fancier of the Southwest (and its American Indian/Spanish heritage) can ignore the thousands of years of tradition that are wrapped up in earthen construction.

But adobe offers some pragmatic advantages, as well. From a thermal standpoint, for example, the material provides a great amount of mass for heat storage (though it is somewhat less dense than concrete). Thus the interior partitions and exterior walls (when insulated on the outside) become performing parts of the passive solar design. Also, for anyone with the right combination of ingenuity, energy, and persistence, adobe has proved to be a very inexpensive material from which to build a home.

Designed by California architect David Wright and incorporating state of the art solar engineering features, the 3,000-square-foot residence featured here was built by Dave del Junco, who—with others—set nearly 8,000 4" X 10" X 14" adobe blocks to produce a beautiful and delightful home at about a third the cost per square foot of a conventional structure.

ORIENT EXPRESSLY

The locale for this home—set at 6,000 feet above sea level in the rolling southwest New Mexico highlands—seems precisely tailored for high-percentage solar heating. The 80% possibility of sunshine is as close to a guarantee of solar gain as you'll find, and the high desert's day-to-night temperature extremes (with swings of up to 60°F in a 12-hour period) are a problem that the indigenous building material—adobe—was made to solve.

The footings were set so the building would face 15 degrees to the east of south . . . to encourage morning gain and discourage intense afternoon rays. Then wall extensions and overhangs were plotted to effectively screen summer insolation. (With highs of 100°F, keeping cool in summer can be nearly as important as staying warm during the 4,400-degree-day winter.)

To further bias the structure's performance toward winter gain, no angled glass was used. Instead, two levels of vertical glazing—totaling 500 square feet in the ground-floor south wall and the clerestory (with operable venting windows), which runs most of the length of the 100-foot-long roof—pull in low-angle rays but reflect the higher-angled sunlight of the warmer seasons.

ADD MASS

Solar heat is stored in the tremendous mass of the building materials which make up the house. Sunlight reaches all the way to the inner surface of the north wall—through the clerestory—in December, and the interior partitions (also laid up with 10"-wide adobe blocks) receive direct gain, as well. Another major thermal mass feature is the brick floor, which consists of about 13,000 masonry units set in a bed of sand (for leveling) over eight inches of earth on top of a 6-mil vapor barrier . . . all of which is insulated by 1"-thick extruded polystyrene.

INSULATE THOROUGHLY

Rigid foam was used to insulate the exterior walls and roof of the dwelling. Two-inch-thick foam boards were nailed (with metal roofing disks) to the adobe walls, and then stucco was applied, once a chicken-wire mesh had been hung. Three inches of polystyrene was also sandwiched between the wooden ceiling and the metal roof.

Of course, the great weight of adobe requires adequate support. Therefore, the building's footings are reinforced poured concrete measuring 18" wide and 10" deep . . . and the foundation rises another foot above grade (in the 10"-wall width) to prevent water from being drawn from the ground up into the adobe by capillary action.

Dave used 6" X 10" wooden bond beams (end-lapped and pinned) to tie the walls together at the top and to distribute roof load. Concrete also makes an acceptable bond beam, but in this case the builder located a large supply of Douglas fir timbers at a very reasonable price. In fact, all the bond beams, lintels (door- and window-top supports), rafters (8" X 8" timbers on 5'6" centers), and even the roof decking were prepared from material purchased at an abandoned mine site near Bisbee, Arizona. The beams—from trees grown in Washington and Oregon—had been sitting in the desert sun for 15 years and had thoroughly dried.

All of the building's wiring was installed as the walls went up, and plumbing was vastly simplified by having only three supply locations (kitchen, bathroom, and greenhouse) and a gray-water drainage field. The only toilet in the building—and, according to Dave, the only sort that *should* be used, especially with the loose New Mexico soil—is a composting unit. Hot water will eventually come from a series of finned tubes set across the upper glazing of the greenhouse.

AND ENJOY THE SAVINGS

Although it took better than a year for del Junco, family, and helpers to build this adobe house, it's the labor savings ("sweat equity") that can make an adobe home a bargain. And del Junco claims that this house is only a median example of the possible savings: "An adobe house can run $10 per square foot if you scrounge everything possible and make the rest yourself, or it can run $40 per square foot if you purchase all new materials."

In the long run, this adobe house will save its occupants far more. Through three winters, there has yet to be a single BTU of international backup heat used. The lowest interior temperature has been 58°F, and the highest has been 80°F. So for individuals with a little tolerance for cool mornings, the message is: With proper design and construction, in a cooperative (though not necessarily warm) climate, 100% passive solar heating and cooling are possible!

Built at about a third the cost per square foot of a conventional house, the solar design and thermal mass of this house also cut reliance on commercial energy.

Wall extensions and overhangs on the south face of the 100-foot-long house provide shade during the summer, helping the dwelling remain cool and livable.

SAVING RAYS FOR RAINY DAYS

Back when most of the world was still scoffing at the notion that the sun could be a viable source of home heat, a retired carpenter and construction millwright named Henry Mathew built a six-room solar house on Oregon's cool and very foggy coast. During the 16 years since Mathew built that home, his self-designed system—which consists of 725 square feet of water-type collectors and an 8,000-gallon storage tank—has furnished 75% of his Coos Bay home's heat in bad years, and 90% to 95% most of the time! (In fact, University of Oregon scientists were so impressed by his low electric bills that they undertook monitoring his system with a battery of instruments.)

AHEAD OF HIS TIME

Henry's long-time interest in solar energy was first kindled when—as a boy—he listened to his father say "someday people will store *solar* heat in the ground". Then, some 30 years later, his father (by that time, a retired lawyer living in San Diego) wrote to him: "If we could buy some of this inexpensive desert land down here and irrigate it with a solar-powered pump, we could make some money."

Even though his father backed out of the project after reading a book on the subject, Henry did some further reading and decided to build a solar home with the intention of improving upon existing designs.

Henry's intended improvements were mostly based upon his conviction that not enough attention had been paid to heat storage . . . especially in areas like Coos Bay where rainy periods—with no sunshine at all—can last up to three weeks at a time. He also believed most collectors were far too small, about a third as large as they should be. So, as he went to work designing his super-system, Henry planned that both the collectors and the storage capacity would be big enough to satisfy his needs.

HOW IT WORKS

The Mathew home's rooftop collector consists of a south-facing, 5-foot-high, 80-foot-long array, installed 7° from vertical. The frame is made of wood backed with plywood and a 1-1/2" thickness of fiberglass (for fireproofing). The heart of the unit is a corrugated sheet of aluminum coated with flat-black paint. A horizontal, galvanized iron, parallel-fed 1/2" pipe runs along each corrugation, and these are tied snugly to the aluminum sheet with wire. Three slightly overlapping glass panels (they're 1/16" X 20" X 30"), placed 1-1/2 inches away from the aluminum, are used to make up each individual panel. Near-vertical headers are positioned at the ends of the collector—one to bring water in and the other to let it out—and arranged so that no liquid can leave until the collector is entirely full.

Another collector of the same general design (it has 325 square feet of surface area) sits on the ground in back of the house, and there's a small unit on the east side that flows into Henry's electric water heater. "A pump forces water to the little collector," Mathew explains. "From there it runs to the east leg of the backyard unit, flows through it, then goes to an overhead pipe, where it connects with the collector on the roof of the house. When the sun's shining and the collectors are stagnated, the water temperature can rise to as high as 175°F."

DOUBLED EFFICIENCY

Normally, according to the University of Oregon's studies, the water temperature would

Henry Mathew believed that most solar collectors were a mere third as large as they needed to be and that too little attention was paid to heat storage. He overcame those two problems by incorporating a huge rooftop collector and an 8,000 gallon water tank into his first sun-heated home. A window wall passively warms the garage/workshop.

Mathew's solar heating system provides his home on the Oregon coast with "nice, quiet, even heat".

be raised only 5° if it were to flow straight from one end of the rooftop collector system to the other (of course, over a series of passes, the temperature gain would be much higher), but this ingenious gentleman has doubled that per-pass figure by simply gluing a single layer of aluminum foil to the roof with black plastic cement.

After the water is warmed by the collectors, it flows into a 7′ X 10′, 8,000 gallon tank, which Mathew welded together himself right on the premises. This container is buried beneath the house and is surrounded by a 6″ to 18″ insulated air space that accommodates a cold-air intake and a hot-air outlet.

During the summertime, the tank's water stays at about 100°F. Then in September and October—just when the heat begins to be needed—the temperature reaches its peak. Following that, there are usually several weeks of rain, and the water will start to cool down . . . however, the tank's large storage capacity still allows it to keep the house warm through that period until—by the middle of December—the area starts to get some sunshine again.

Whenever the thermostat shows unfavorable solar collection conditions, the pump automatically stops, and all the water returns to the tank. Then, when the rooms need heat, hot air from the space around the tank flows—by convection—out of a grill high in the living room . . . while cold air returns to the tank through an intake positioned below the fireplace.

"The system provides a nice, even, quiet heat," Mathew points out. "During the coldest months it keeps the living room at 75°F, while even the bedrooms and baths, which have no heat vents, often reach 65°."

There's also a large garage/workshop on the west end of the house, but it's *passively* heated . . . by an attached greenhouse. The home displays a passive solar component, too . . . a seven-foot overhang along the south side of the dwelling, which lets the sun stream across the front living area in the winter but shades the same rooms in the summer.

MORE NEW IDEAS

Encouraged by the success of his first solar home, Henry Mathew has built a second house. Even though it's a scant mile from his first one, it's farther inland where both summer and winter temperatures are more extreme . . . so he's overbuilt the solar heating system with three rows of rooftop collectors (backed with metal and built to withstand 350°F temperatures) and a 9,200-gallon storage tank insulated with 3-1/2″ of fiberglass all around.

Naturally, Henry has encountered new problems to solve . . . such as the troublesome refusal of the three collectors to drain back into the storage tank simultaneously. This caused air to get into the line which—in turn—could cause a loss of pump-power if it were to start operating just as a bubble hit it. He solved the problem by putting in about three feet of 6″ pipe to allow the bubbles to rise out of the system.

He also found that his new, larger storage tank, which he built in four parts, was subjected to great changes in pressure when the pump started . . . and eventually one whole section caved in. He had to weld a lot of heavy steel over the top to reinforce it.

"I can't really say that I had any other problems," says Henry with a smile. "However, I did make a lot of changes in the piping system as I went along . . . because I just seemed to keep getting new ideas."

After all, pioneers always do!

When the rooms need heat, hot air surrounding the water storage tank flows—by convection—up and through a grill high in the living room wall . . . while cold air returns to the tank through a vent below the fireplace. Two solar collection units in Mathew's yard preheat water that is then pumped to the rooftop collector, providing enough heat to warm the dwelling even during extended rainy periods which promote the area's lush vegetation.

A HOUSE WITHIN A HOUSE

The large expanse of glass on the south wall and roof of the Whittles' Blue Ridge Mountain home gives the family a commanding view of the surrounding hills and valleys, as well as serving as the "power source" for the dwelling's heating and cooling system.

Few new housing designs have drawn as much attention—or caused as much controversy—as has the double envelope. Pioneered in 1977 by Lee Porter Butler and Tom Smith in a house near Lake Tahoe, California, the building technique has gained an enthusiastic following while the *theory* behind it created a stir among solar designers.

When the Smith house was built, the dynamics of its performance were theoretical . . . and many architects and engineers involved in the use of energy-efficient building methods reserved judgement pending the availability of data on the efficiency of distribution and storage of the solar heat taken in through the home's large south-facing glass area.

Today, there are hundreds of double-shell houses across the country, which have incorporated into their designs features similar to those found in the home of Tom, Claire, and Tommy Whittle, built in the Blue Ridge Mountains of Virginia. Few experts question the fact that thermal-envelope buildings are quite efficient, though some quibbling continues over how well they work compared to *other* passive solar designs.

A REVIEW OF THE THEORY

The "collector" system for a thermal-envelope house is a heat-producing solar space, which in many climates can double as a year-round greenhouse. It's the method by which the sun space is incorporated into the structure's heating system that sets this sort of dwelling apart from other types of solar-heated houses.

As the term "double envelope" implies, such a building is actually a house within a house. The exterior shell is load-bearing and generally has a minimum of R-19 insulation. Between the outer and inner skins lies an air space (usually at least a foot wide) which extends from the east to the west end of the house under the north-facing roof and down the north wall. The inner wall is generally thinner—since the small temperature difference between the building's interior and the air space requires less insulation—and supports only the structure of the living space. The passageway between the two walls is linked to the greenhouse by a crawl space or basement, which allows air to return to the glazed solarium (which constitutes the entire south side of the house) through gaps in the sun room's floor.

The circulation of air through the envelope is entirely passive. The system takes advantage of the fact that sun-heated air rises in the greenhouse and enters the envelope at the room's peak . . . while the air between the shells—and particularly that along the north wall—loses heat and falls. The current then flows through the passageway and the subfloor area, and returns to the sun space from below.

Furthermore, as the air passes through the subfloor area, some of the heat it still holds is absorbed by the surrounding earth, rock, and masonry. These massive materials take in and store the warmth as long as they're cooler than the circulating air. During the evening, however, the storage temperature may actually exceed that of the circulating air, and the thermal mass gives up heat.

A double envelope taps its storage passively by reversing the convective loop. During the night the structure's greatest heat loss is through the expanse of glass in the sun space. That cooling causes air to fall to the floor of the greenhouse, while the (relatively) warmer air of the storage area rises and is forced *up* the north wall cavity. The continual imbal-

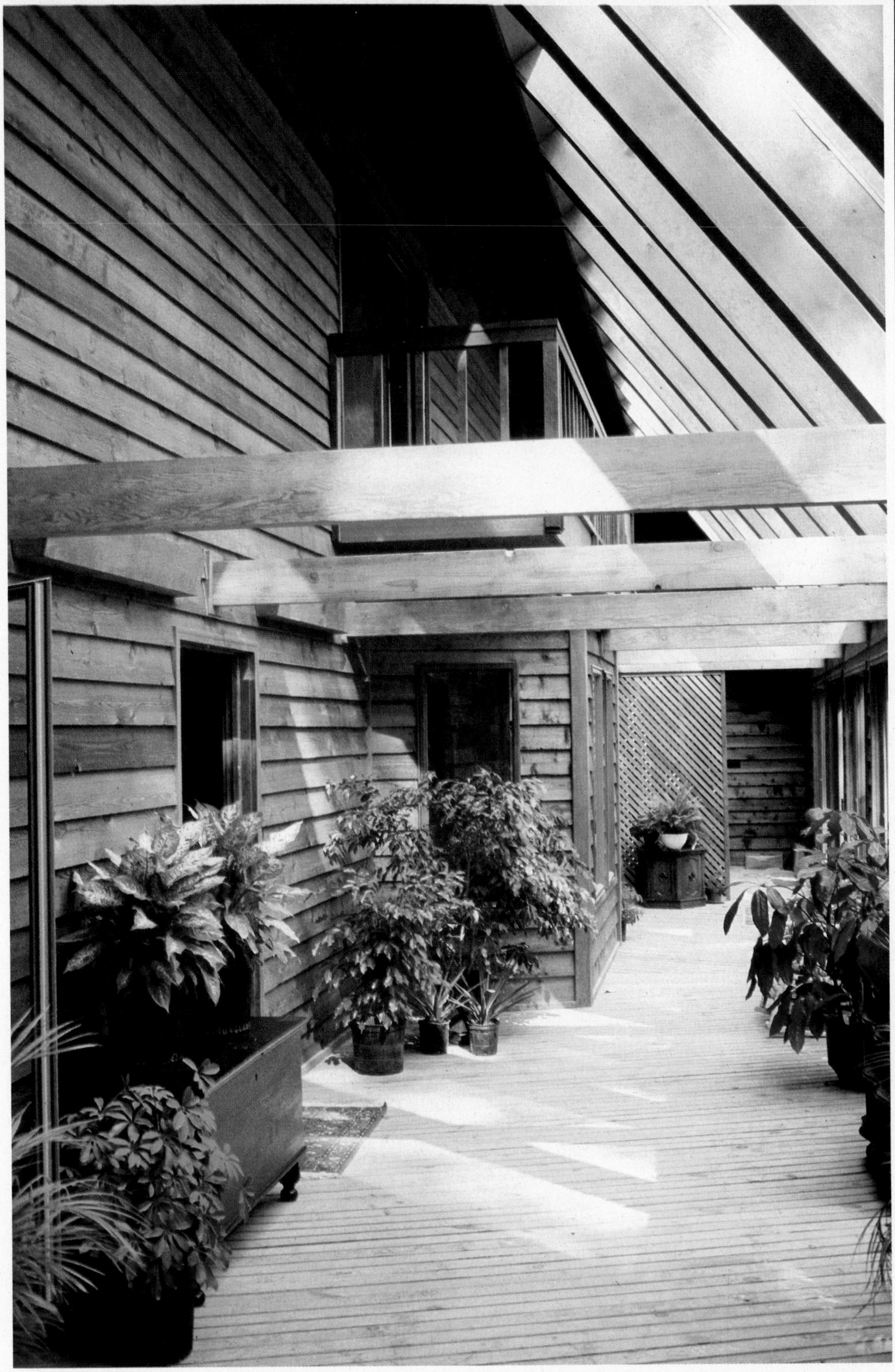

Surplus heat is stored in the crawl space for use on cloudy days.

ance in temperature keeps the loop flowing, moving warm air through the house.

In the summertime, however, the sun space is likely to gain far too much solar energy . . . despite the fact that the tilted glass is oriented to admit winter sun. To prevent overheating, vents are usually set into the roof peak of an envelope house, allowing the hot air to escape. And in some designs, "cool pipes" (air intake tubes buried in the ground) are linked to the crawl space so that earth-temperature air can be drawn in and distributed.

The energy-saving capabilities of the envelope design are numerous. For one thing, a great deal of solar heat is taken in through the greenhouse, and at least some excess warmth is stored in the crawl space for use during the night or on cloudy days. Consequently, most

Greenery growing year round in the solarium not only adds beauty to the house, but helps maintain a comfortable humidity level in the Virginia home. The main entrance is an air-lock vestibule at the west end of the greenhouse.

Constant, gentle air movement lends a "balmy feeling" to the interior.

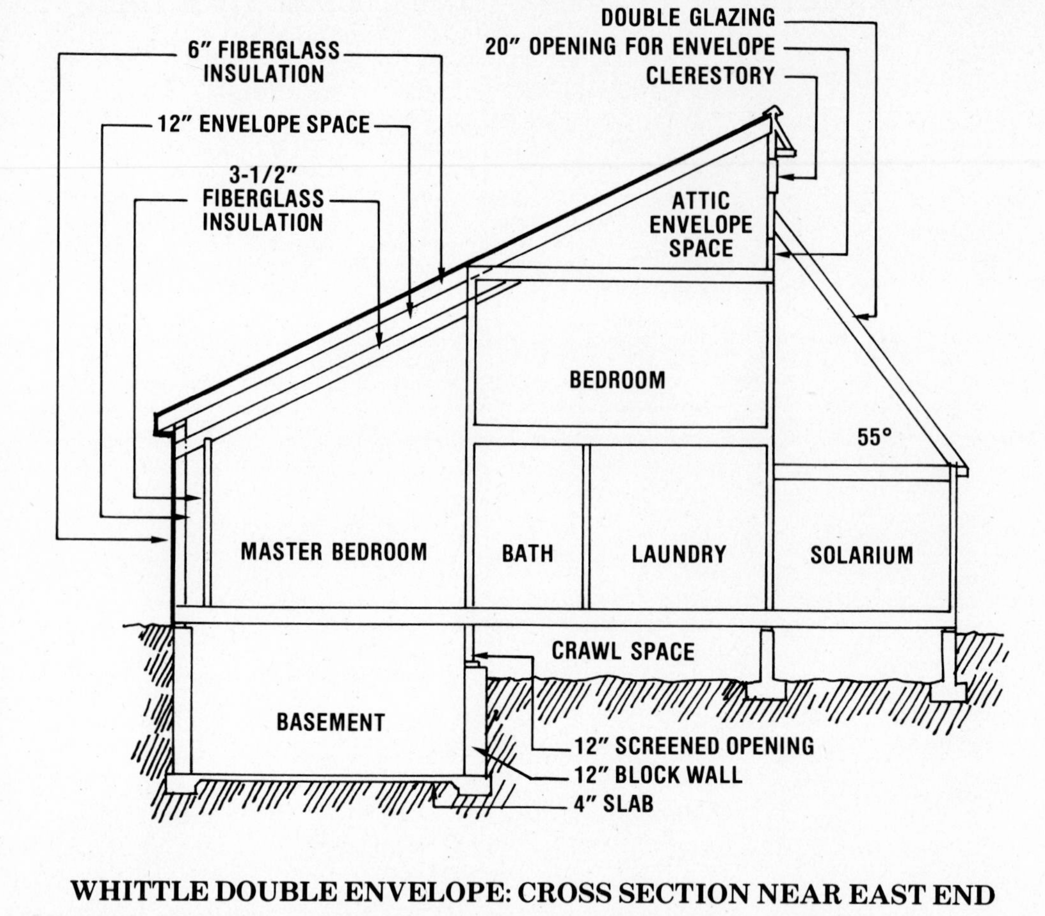

WHITTLE DOUBLE ENVELOPE: CROSS SECTION NEAR EAST END

double-envelope houses require very little backup heat. In fact, they often satisfy 80% (or more) of their thermal needs directly from the sun.

Now there's no question that a large part of the energy efficiency of such structures results from their thick insulation. The two shells and large air gap produce a total R-value that typically exceeds 30! In addition, the double walls reduce infiltration (direct air leakage) to the living space and dramatically improve the thermal resistance of any north-facing windows . . . because of the roughly 12"-wide air space. (In fact, that gap can, in effect, increase window R-value by as much as four . . . without producing the condensation that tends to be a problem in conventional double- or triple-glazed windows.)

Another thermal benefit of the envelope concept shows up in the form of comfort. Because the air circulating inside the envelope is significantly warmer than that outdoors, the difference in temperature (or Δt, in heating engineers' lingo) between the living area and the air passage is relatively small. Thus the heat loss for the inner wall is less than that of a single wall whose total R-value equals the double envelope's. As a result, the surfaces of the envelope's interior walls remain warmer than would those of equally insulated single-layer walls.

Envelope home residents also enjoy pleasantly stable humidity through the winter, since moist greenhouse atmosphere is continually circulated through the air space and can be admitted to the living quarters by cracking a door or window. (In the summer, however, excess humidity—and heat—is vented at the sun-space peak.) Furthermore, the constant but gentle and silent circulation of air prevents stagnation and lends a balmy feeling to the interior environment.

A GOOD EXAMPLE

The Whittle home—built by Alternative Builders, a regional Virginia contracting firm—experiences about 4,800 heating degree-days annually. The double-envelope design was particularly appealing to the Whittles because it combined energy efficiency with lots of glass . . . and they definitely didn't want to be shut off from the view of the lovely mountains surrounding the site.

Consequently, as they worked with Alternative Builders on the design of their home, the Whittles decided to incorporate two small windows on the north side of the structure and two more on the west end (to provide a view of the sunset). On the eastern exposure, however, there are only three tiny windows and a below-grade door (for basement access from the outside). The main entry is an air-lock vestibule located at the west end of the sun space, and there are two other exterior doors in the solarium.

The exterior wall is framed with 2 X 6's on 24-inch centers, and the cavities are filled with fiberglass insulation. All the windows in the outer shell are double-glazed, including 420 square feet of sun-space glass angled at 55° to take maximum advantage of the winter sun. An additional 160 square feet of vertical glass

The family is able to relax in quiet comfort as the house silently takes care of its own heating requirements without the aid of a noisy furnace.

is set into the front of the solarium, and a short row of crank-open windows serves as the vent at the roof's peak.

The inner shell is framed with 2 X 4's, on 16-inch centers, and is fitted with 3-1/2" fiberglass insulation. The wall is positioned so that the air space is no less than 12 inches, and—in fact—it's a great deal wider in the portion of the passage that doubles as an attic. Vapor barriers of 4-mil polyethylene line both sides of the air space . . . to keep moisture from penetrating the insulation and to prevent fiberglass shreds from getting into the circulating air. Since the temperature difference between the inner wall and the buffering zone is small, the inside-shell windows were single-glazed.

To comply with fire codes, Alternative Builders designed and built a damper—situated in the north wall—that's controlled by a fusible link. In the event of a fire, the device will close and prevent smoke from moving through the envelope.

The building's subfloor loop consists of a partial basement and a 40-inch-deep crawl space. The latter has four inches of earth lying atop a sheet of 4-mil polyethylene (for moisture protection). The earth itself is uninsulated, but the foundation and footings are lined with 1" extruded polystyrene. The backup heater for the dwelling, a large woodstove, is installed in the basement . . . so that the heat it produces can circulate in the envelope.

Air returns to the greenhouse through its floorboards, which were made by ripping 2 X 6's, then spacing them on the joists in a pattern that allows one square foot of open area for each foot of the solarium's length.

THE CONTROVERSY AND THE LATEST POOP

Much of the quibbling about double-shell houses centers on the fact that the air cavity must *lose* heat (particularly in the north wall) in order to power the convective loop. And it's true that, given the relative temperature difference between the interior and the cavity, and the cavity and the outside, most of the passageway's lost BTU *will* escape to the outdoors.

Technicians have calculated that the efficiency of the convective circulation system provided by the double envelope is far lower than that of a blower system powered by an electric motor. And there's a growing consensus among designers that the double envelope suffers a slight loss of thermal efficiency because of its air circulation system, as well. The trade-offs would be the noise of the blower and the need for electricity to run it.

Early doubts about whether or not the envelope flow pattern actually reverses at night have recently been shown to be misplaced in most cases. Though the flow rate is undoubtedly much slower at night (perhaps about two-thirds of the daytime air movement, according to a computer simulation developed by Joe Kohler and Dan Lewis of Total Environmental Action, Inc.), the double-shell dwelling's greenhouse *is* warmed at night by air circulating from the crawl space through the north wall and roof cavities.

The question of how much heat is actually stored in the crawl space is much more difficult to answer, however. The rate of thermal transfer to the earth or gravel depends on a number of factors . . . including the moisture level in the storage medium (water stores much more heat, and transfers it more quickly, than does earth), the possibility of stratification of air flow (with the warmer air collecting near the floor and cooler air sinking down against the earth), the particular type of soil involved, and the temperatures of the air and the earth. Rough estimates of storage capability suggest that only between 10 and 25% of the available BTU can be stored, but even at that relatively low rate, it's now acknowledged that the tempering effect of the earth on the envelope air does play an important role in the design's energy efficiency.

Though there's much more known today about the double-envelope concept than was the case when the Smith house was completed, it's obvious that the available data still don't answer all questions. Thermal-envelope houses are very popular among owners because they're both efficient and pleasant to live in. And when one considers that the raging controversy among experts really concerns only a few percentage points of efficiency one way or the other, the double envelope is likely to enjoy even greater popularity in the future.

Owners find double-shell homes efficient and pleasant to live in.

Clerestory windows at the roof peak allow hot air to escape during the summer, and limited window space on the ends helps reduce heat loss in winter. Custom kitchen cabinetry and an open design in that room are representative of the structure's pleasing interior.

AN ATTIC CATCHES THE SUN

As an architectural feature, the peaked roof is practically a fixture in American housing. It's a fundamental portion of the structural design of "balloon" frame construction, where its trusslike aspects distribute live loads (such as snow cover) and the dead weight of the building materials to load-bearing walls. The peaked roof also sheds precipitation, can be built to overrun the exterior walls to form shading eaves, and provides an attic that often winds up "wasted" space.

But what use is the attic itself? For one thing, it makes the installation of insulation in the ceiling easy. And in some cases, it can be accessed as storage space. In general, such places are too hot in the summer and too cold in the winter for human habitation, and in terms of energy efficiency, they make only a minor contribution as a buffer zone.

However, Helio Thermics, Inc. has developed a solar heating system that uses a building's south-facing roof and attic as a solar collector. Instead of shingling the roof, they simply double-glaze it. With some black paint on the interior surfaces of the attic and an air distribution system, they managed to create a voluminous solar heater for a minimum of construction cost.

THE SITUATION

The home Jim and Gail German built incorporating an attic collector is tucked in the high end of a narrow hollow and is well shielded from the wind by the topography and both evergreen and deciduous trees to the east, north, and west. To the south, poplars bare their limbs in winter providing a clear shot to the sun down the little valley. At the winter solstice, when the sun makes its lowest arc through the sky, the Germans' site gets direct insolation beginning about 9:30 a.m. and lasting to 3:30 p.m.

A glance at an expected-sunshine chart for eastern Tennessee where their home is located shows an annual average of about 55% . . . but that figure belies the fact that during January (the time of most severe cold) the expected percentage drops to about 40. From a solar standpoint, then, the 3,500 degree-days usually experienced in Knoxville don't tell the entire heating story.

In looking for energy-efficient heating systems for their home, Jim and Gail were fully aware of the limitations imposed by their climate. And as they developed criteria they found that four particular factors kept cropping up. To make effective use of solar gain, the first prerequisite was to have low overall heat demand. Next, excess insolation on sunny days would have to be efficiently stored for less bountiful ones. Third, at least some gain would be important even on overcast days. Last, but far from least, the system would have to be reasonably priced.

The large expanse of double glazing on the south-facing roof of the Germans' eastern Tennessee home takes the place of conventional roofing materials and allows the sun's rays to enter the attic collector. Deciduous trees partially shade the house in the summer but then allow the sun a clear shot during the winter.

The Germans found that a marriage of heavy insulation and a Helio Thermics air system promised to meet their needs best. They contacted the local dealer for the Greenville, South Carolina firm's products and arranged to meet to develop plans. At about the same time, the couple applied to the U.S. Department of Housing and Urban Development (HUD) for a grant to purchase and monitor the solar heating equipment.

THE BUILDING

Construction of the 1,270-square-foot residence began—with the Germans pitching in—by pouring the footers and laying the block foundation so that about three feet of north wall could be bermed above the floor level. Then the entire concrete perimeter was insulated with 3″-thick extruded polystyrene.

Before the floor joists could be added, the rock storage bed had to be built. The approximately 400-square-foot, 15-inch-deep space contains some 27 tons of washed and graded 1-1/2″ to 2″ limestone rock sitting on two inches of polystyrene insulation. The hot and cold plenums were formed by stacking 8″ concrete blocks, and the sides of the box were insulated with 3″-thick polystyrene. And to prevent loss into the house through the floor, the top of the storage bed was insulated by 6″ fiberglass fitted between all of the floor joists.

The exterior walls of the building were framed with 2 X 6's on 24-inch centers. The spaces between the studs were filled with fiberglass insulation, and all the wood joints were thoroughly caulked to prevent air leakage. One-inch-thick polystyrene went on the outside of the stud wall, and then finally, the building's exterior was covered with lapped cedar boards.

On the inside of the frame walls, a 6-mil polyethylene air/vapor barrier was carefully installed and lapped to prevent infiltration, and the jambs of all the double-insulated windows were blown full of insulating foam. The outside walls and ceilings of the living area were finished in 5/8″ drywall (for maximum thermal mass), and the interior partitions were covered with 1/2″ drywall. For a final measure of thermal protection, the two exterior doors are insulated steel.

UP UNDER THE ROOF

It's above the living area where the Germans' home really starts to get interesting. The ceiling joists were interspersed with 6-inch batts, and then another 12 inches of fiberglass was blown in on top of that. Directly above this insulative layer a floor was framed up to form the collector base. Access to the above-ceiling area is by a ladder in the garage (to prevent living space infiltration), and an

It's above the living area that the Germans' home really starts to get interesting.

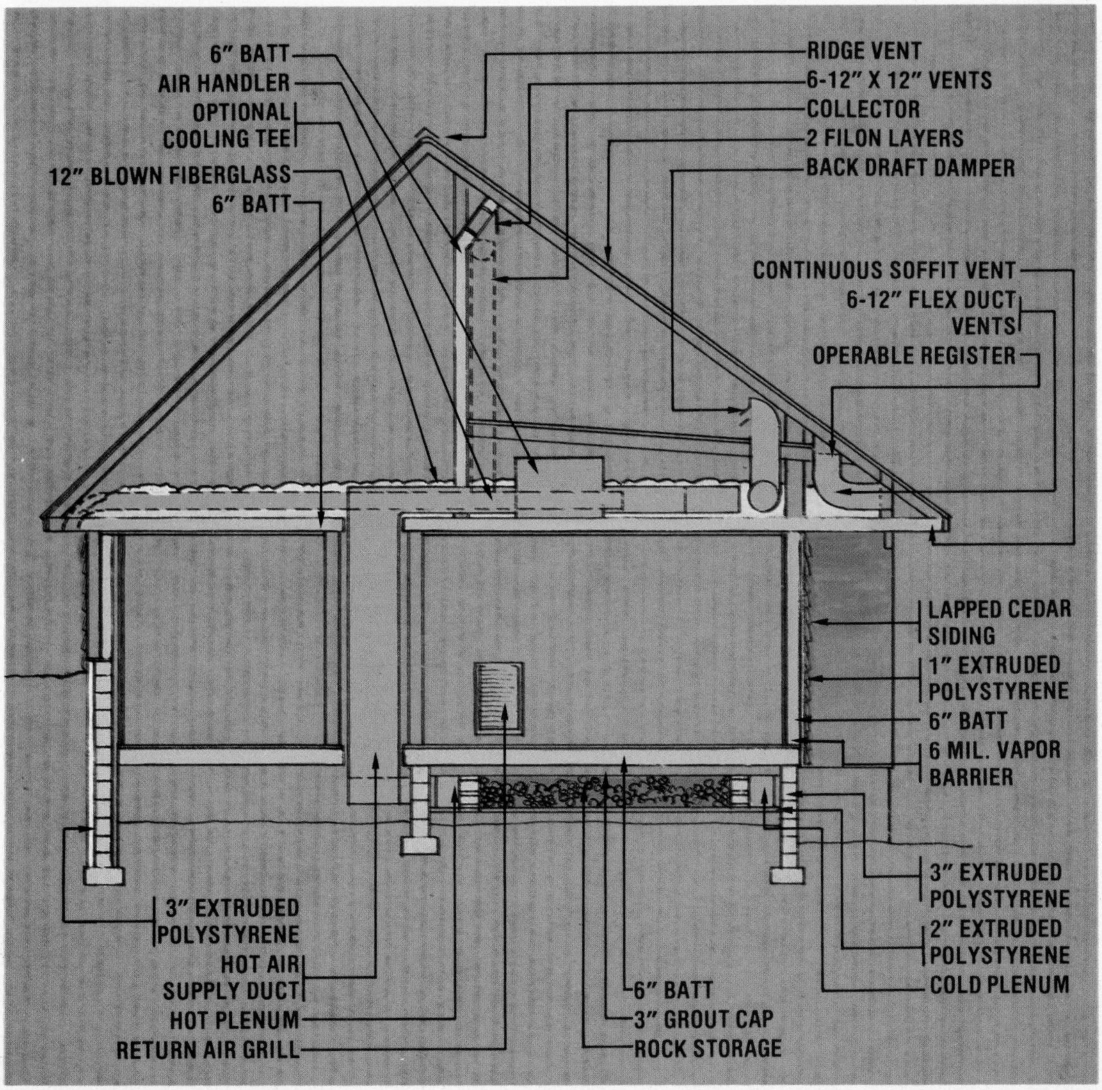

Since he had an electronics background, Jim elected to install the air handler himeslf.

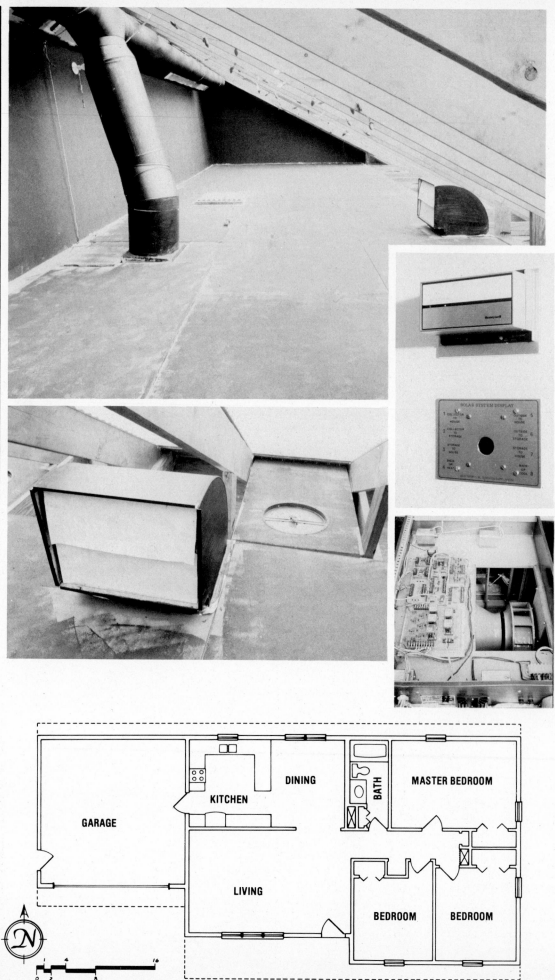

Air heated in the collector is ducted to the living area or to storage through a duct at the high point of the enclosed attic area, and cooler air is returned to the heating chamber through a duct near the edge of the house. Over the eave, a vent can be opened in the summer to help cool the house. Controlled by a wall-mounted panel, the system features a microcomputer, which decides which of the air handler's modes of operation is needed at any given time.

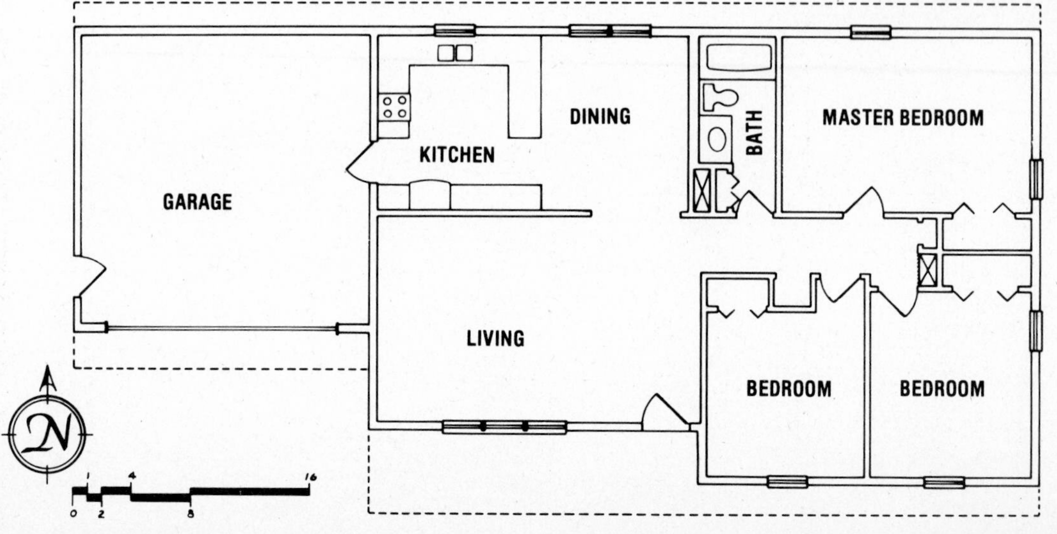

insulated steel door separates the ventilated north portion of the attic from the collector. This portal is framed into an insulated 2 X 6 stud wall that rises to a point about one foot to the south of the fully vented roof peak.

The sheathing for the collector space is currently particle board, but the HUD researchers want Jim to add a special Celotex Corporation collector material—consisting of foil-faced polyisocyanurate foam with a Typar coating—atop the inexpensive sheathing. The government team's primary concern apparently is with the use of wooden materials that might outgas in what could be become a very warm area.

Assuming that the system functions properly, however, the attic temperatures should seldom exceed about 115°F. The collector is electronically controlled to begin delivering heat to the rock storage area whenever the attic temperature reaches a differential of 15°F, and the blower doesn't shut off until that gap has been narrowed to 3°F. Collected heat can also be delivered directly to the living area below any time the attic temperature exceeds the reading on the thermostat in the hallway on the first floor.

The heart of these goings-on is the Helio Thermics air handler. This blower-equipped box has eight potential modes of operation—when equipped with the optional cooling "T"—all monitored by sensors located in the collector, rock storage, and living areas. By way of a quartet of solenoid-operated valves, the 1,500-CFM industrial continuous-duty fan can [1] supply collector heat to the house, [2] supply collector heat to storage, [3] supply storage heat to the house, [4] switch on and deliver backup warmth from strip heaters in the ductwork, [5] draw north-side outdoor air in and deliver cool air to the living area, [6] pump that cool air to storage, [7] deliver the stored cool air to the house, or [8] pump backup cooling—from an air conditioner element—into the house. (The Germans' home is not equipped with the cooling options.)

Since Jim has an electronics background, he installed the air handler himself . . . with advice from the local dealer. And though most Helio Thermics-equipped homes have their air handlers on the first floor, Jim and Gail were unwilling to give up floor space in their economically planned dwelling. So the device was put in the attic and, to prevent vibration, hung with chains from the framing that supports the collector floor.

Air is drawn into the control center through a 12"-diameter duct which runs the length of the collector's high point. After being pulled into the distribution box, the solar-heated air may be pumped down to the crawl space for storage or delivered through ceiling registers to the rooms. Air returns to the collector from the rock storage *or* from a register at the end of the bedroom wing's hallway by way of a round duct set in the front center of the collector floor.

As you can see in the photos, glazing actually replaces the conventional roofing materials in this attic solar heating system. Thus the avoided costs of sheathing, tar paper, and shingles can be deducted from the required capital outlay for the system. The 640 square feet of glazing consists of four-foot-wide corrugated fiberglass panels of a length appropriate to the particular collector (16 feet at the German house). Ripple board is nailed to the white painted rafters (which *must* be accurately spaced on 24-inch centers), and the first layer of glazing is set horizontally and caulked. The second layer of fiberglass panels is Du Pont Tedlar-coated for ultraviolet light protection and is nailed through—with the units overlapped—to every third ripple board peak. (If the rafters are not evenly spaced, then the four-foot-wide panels will have no firm base for mounting.)

Of course, the idea of having a solar collector so large that it provides plenty of headroom for a six-foot person is a bit of a novelty. And like so many other people who've taken the plunge into solar energy, Gail and Jim do enjoy having the only glazed roof on the block.

But its contribution to home heating is not the large collector's only virtue. The solar room makes an excellent area for drying fruits and herbs and has often doubled as a daytime sauna. What's more, laundry dries quickly inside the "solar dryer" during summer when the collector is vented. (Using the collector for this purpose during its functional months might add too much moisture to the air.) Jim and Gail are also installing an accessory which will heat their domestic water.

HOW WARM?

The solar heating system has provided all the heat for the home, except for an extended spell of cloudy, cool weather. During the heavy months of winter, strip heaters have drawn about 2,300 kilowatt-hours (KWH) of power from the TVA lines . . . or an average of about 800 KWH per month. On the partially cloudy or overcast days, the active system does function, albeit intermittently, but the Germans have found that their attention to proper placement of south-facing windows has paid off in providing significant *passive* solar heating. There hasn't been a single day since the couple moved in that the building hasn't gained some heat passively, and on sunny days all the collector's heat can go to storage while direct gain takes care of immediate thermal demand.

HOW COOL?

In the Knoxville area in July or August, the mercury can push into the high 90's and low 100's, while the humidity teeters around saturation. Consequently, any solar design for the region should have behind it some serious thought about keeping the heat out.

In the German's home, carefully planned overhangs provide shading from the spring equinox to the fall. During the hot months, manually operated vents are opened at the front of the collector (they connect to screened soffit openings) and at several points along the top of the attic partition to allow heat to escape through the roof-ridge vent.

By keeping their well-insulated abode sealed up during the day and then opening windows once it cools off at night, Jim and Gail can consistently undercut the daily high by 15°F without any air conditioning.

The air handler can be equipped for eight different modes of operation, each designed to match the needs of the house to outside conditions.

A front porch with steps leading to the drive at the front of the house beckons visitors and provides a seat with a view.

A COOL FLORIDA HOUSE

Nestled among deciduous trees and bermed with earth, the house sports a bright, pleasant interior in the living and dining area. Attic hatches in the bedroom admit light and allow heat to either exit or enter the home's interior.

In north Florida's subtropical panhandle region—where summertime humidity can average a clammy 82%, and temperatures in the 90's aren't noteworthy enough to comment on—cooling a dwelling is usually of greater concern than is warming it. On the other hand, though, heating requirements can't be ignored altogether, since the region is subject to nearly 1,600 heating degree-days during its cold season.

The folks at Tallahassee's Mad Dog Design and Construction Company felt that, by taking advantage of several "tried and true" building techniques and coupling them with modern thermal conditioning methods, they could come up with a house that would be comfortable throughout the year ... but which would require little or no utility-supplied power for heating or cooling.

A WELL-PLANNED DESIGN

Essentially, the Florida builders used several passive methods—backed up by two active systems—to insure a pleasant interior climate during the hot summer months. First and foremost, the earth-sheltered structure relies on natural ventilation, combined with heat-gain prevention, to maintain a comfortable internal environment. Borrowing from traditional local designs, the Sunshine Staters utilized high ceilings, continuous attic-linked soffit vents, and strategically placed windows to encourage the flow of air throughout the house.

For example, the south-facing solarium/greenhouse area incorporates ceiling-mounted outlets that can be opened, in case of overheating, to allow warm air to duct into the attic and out the soffit vents. Similarly, in the house itself—which is separated from the solarium by a quartet of sliding glass doors—unwanted warmth can be vented around four movable 8′ X 8′ insulated ceiling shutters. These horizontally hinged overhead "flaps" are mounted in light wells which are framed into the front of the attic and faced with acrylic glazing. When the electrically operated sky shutters are three-quarters open, pockets are formed, which accumulate warm air and direct it upward ... while permitting plenty of indirect light to brighten the rooms below.

Other heat-controlling elements in the unique design include [1] roof overhangs above the skylights, [2] solar screening over the greenhouse windows during the warmer months, [3] insulated draperies on the sliding glass doors, and [4] ceiling insulation with an R-value of 28. Additionally, the builders have taken advantage of deciduous trees to help shade the structure in the summer months.

Another factor that contributes to the energy efficiency of the Tallahassee residence is the dwelling's earth sheltering itself. Calculations made prior to construction had indicated that a large portion of the necessary tempering could be accomplished by using the soil as a massive heat sink, since about two-thirds of the building's wall area—as well as its entire floor—were slated to be below ground level. However, data gathered later showed that earth temperatures low enough for cooling purposes could be found only at a depth greater than five feet ... so, to compensate for the fact that the earth-bermed structure was not *wholly* engulfed in soil, the Mad Dog designers merely insulated its surrounding earthen ramparts with a 2-inch-thick Styrofoam beadboard skirt that extends outward eight feet from the home's concrete walls.

This protective "collar"—after being covered with waterproof sheeting *and* 12 inches of backfill—serves to minimize the effect of the sun and ambient air on the soil below (creating stable and comfortable temperatures at a depth of only four feet, even during the hottest months). It also provides an effective watershed that directs surface flow away from, rather than along, the sides of the building.

And the innovative designers also took the opportunity to bury a Givoni air tube (named after its developer, Dr. Baruch Givoni) and a temperature sensor deep within the berm ... allowing the home's residents to force cool evening air through the system to offset the effects of any heat gained during the day.

Many of the same features that prevent heat accumulation in the summer can act to retain warmth in the winter. Because the sun is low and the deciduous trees have shed their leaves by then, the house receives ample insolation through the unshielded solarium glazing and the fully opened ceiling shutters ... which can be closed at night to hold the day-gathered warmth. Furthermore, the contact between the earth berm and the massive structure provides a 45-day "thermal lag", which, in effect, permits the earth-stored temperature extremes of the late summer to be

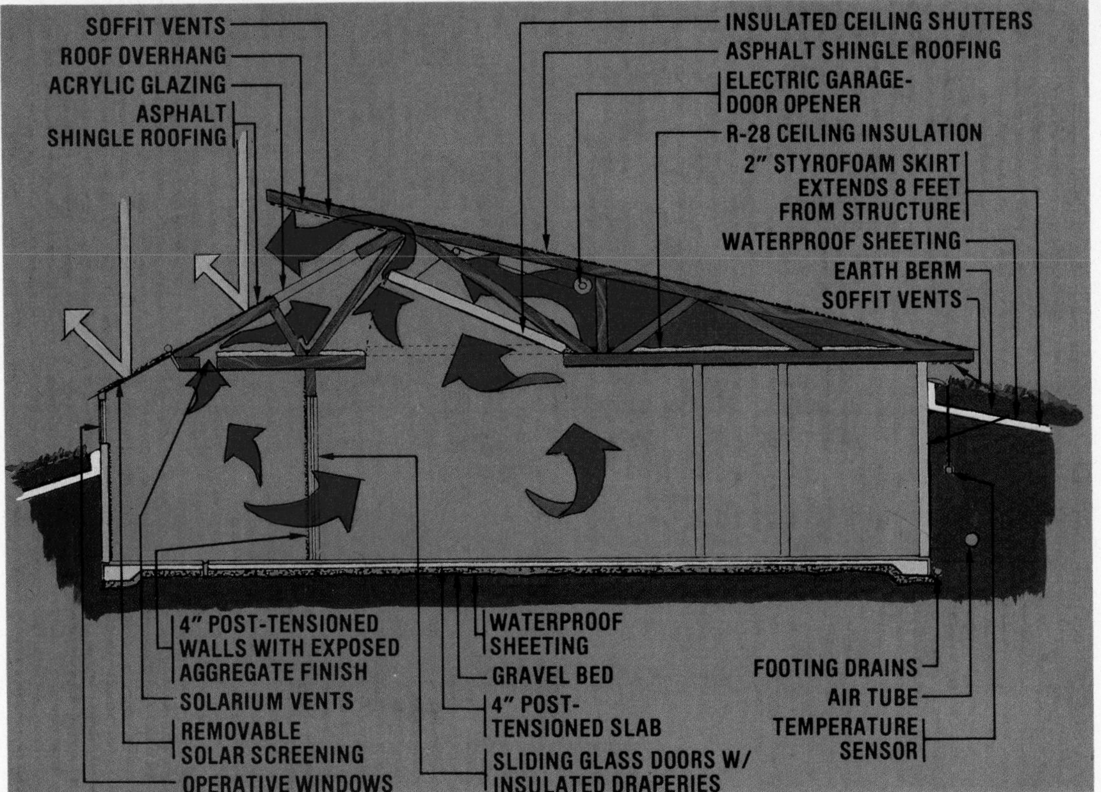

The owner found after living in the house for a year that its heating and cooling systems work even better than expected.

dissipated over a period that extends about a month and a half into the cool season, thus helping with the heating load.

ENGINEERING CUTS COSTS

Normally, an earth-sheltered structure will start its "life" as an assembly of filled concrete block walls resting upon a reinforced monolithic slab . . . or, alternatively, 8- to 12-inch poured bulkheads, on footings, surrounding a "floating" foundation. However, because the soil found at the building site has low permeability and is potentially unstable, the designers decided to utilize *post-tensioned* components, which would stand the effect of lateral loads or twisting resulting from shifting earth much better than would conventional methods of construction.

Post-tensioning, a comparatively new technique in the home-building industry, is in many ways ideal for use in earth-sheltered construction. Most important, it imparts additional compressive and tensile strength to any member upon which it's used. Unlike regular reinforced concrete construction (in which the steel rebar can begin to resist a load only after the concrete itself has *failed*), a post-tensioned component incorporates a network of interwoven cables—encased in lubricated plastic sleeves and cast in the middle of the slab on three-foot centers—which are pulled to a tension of about 30,000 pounds after the pour sets, and locked in place by means of engineered wedges mounted in stressing anchors. This fantastic force puts the concrete under constant compression and increases its strength *without* the need for excessive mass.

Equally significant, post-tensioning can be accomplished right at the building site, using little special equipment. This do-it-yourself factor, in turn, allows for some creativity on the part of the builders . . . as evidenced in the Tallahassee home by the exposed aggregate finish on the solarium's interior walls: They were poured in forms lined with a one-inch layer of river rock, then removed with the stone facade intact.

Finally, the use of the "pulling after pouring" technique can help cut materials costs. Recent studies of post-tensioned structures and "typical" earth-sheltered buildings show that only about half as much steel, and perhaps 40% as much concrete, will be required when a house is tensioned rather than conventionally poured . . . *and* the resulting shell is less likely to crack. So, although waterproofing is still necessary with any post-tensioned wall, the use of exotic (and costly) materials can be eliminated.

Because the north Florida dwelling was primarily designed to provide passive cooling rather than heating, the people at Mad Dog chose not to insulate the concrete mass. Instead, they merely poured their floor slab over a bed of gravel and waterproofing, installed footing drains, then tilted up the previously poured-and-tensioned wall panels and positioned them in perimeter slots that had been cast into the foundation.

And, rather than covering the building's top with a layer of earth (which would have upped the materials expense), the designers merely installed oversized roof trusses, and built a conventional—but well-insulated—asphalt-shingled "lid" . . . accepting what they feel are only minor thermal losses as a result. After living in it for nearly a full year, the owner stated that the home works even better than she expected . . . thanks largely to the fact that she thoroughly understands how it functions, and willingly takes an active part in matching its capabilities to the fluctuations of the weather.

Taking advantage of a woodsy setting *and* good planning, this Florida house provides comfortable living year round by incorporating several design features. Energy savings—for a knowledgeable owner—are considerable.

SUN AND EARTH COMBINE IN ADOBE

With a large greenhouse connecting the two wings of the house and collecting the sun's energy, and massive earthen walls storing the heat, solar rays provide a full 80% of the home's heating needs. Impressive attention to detail as seen in the spiral staircase makes the dwelling especially attractive.

Douglas and Sara Balcomb spend their winter evenings barefoot, in an 80% solar-heated adobe masterpiece. The Santa Fe, New Mexico area, where their home is located, is nestled against the treeline in the cool, dry foothills of the Sangre de Cristo Mountains . . . just about one of the best places in this country to make use of solar energy. However, though it is blessed with abundant sunshine, the capital of the "Land of Enchantment" also has a *real* need for heating.

Although most people think of New Mexico as warm desert country, Santa Fe—which is perched just at the 7,000-foot line—is actually slightly *cooler* (on an average) than Denver, Colorado! While Santa Feans seldom have to suffer through more than a few consecutive days of subfreezing daytime highs, the mercury *does* plummet below zero on some winter evenings, and the town's average annual snowfall is more than three feet.

In fact, in heating energy terminology, Santa Fe has almost 6,000 heating degree-days. For comparison, Denver averages about 5,700 heating degree-days, and New York nets approximately 5,250. And—just as an extreme example—Edmonton, Alberta, Canada rings in at almost 11,700 degree-days.

It's not too surprising, then, that the hillsides above the quaint old historical New Mexican community (it was established around 1610) are dotted with adobe homes equipped with a wide range of solar heating equipment. And one of the most attractive (and successful) examples of this combination of new-age technology and age-old earthen home construction methods belongs to Douglas and Sara.

The Balcomb home is known as Unit One, because it was the original dwelling in a planned environmental community called First Village. Architect William Lumpkins—with solar engineers/designers/builders Susan and Wayne Nichols—chose to blend a selection of solar techniques . . . rather than invest capital and energy in one system.

The resulting hybrid solar design consists of a greenhouse, a thermal-mass wall, and two rock heat-storage beds equipped with fans. This solar collecting system is not only fully integrated into the building's design (and thus made attractive) . . . it really *works*. In the high-energy-demand New Mexico highlands environment, Unit One is 80% solar heated to a minimum temperature of 65°F. So, with 4/5 of the "warm-up" duties handled by ol' Sol, the Balcombs' backup electric heaters consume an average of only 850 kilowatt-hours per year. (Many folks would be overjoyed to use that little in one *month*!)

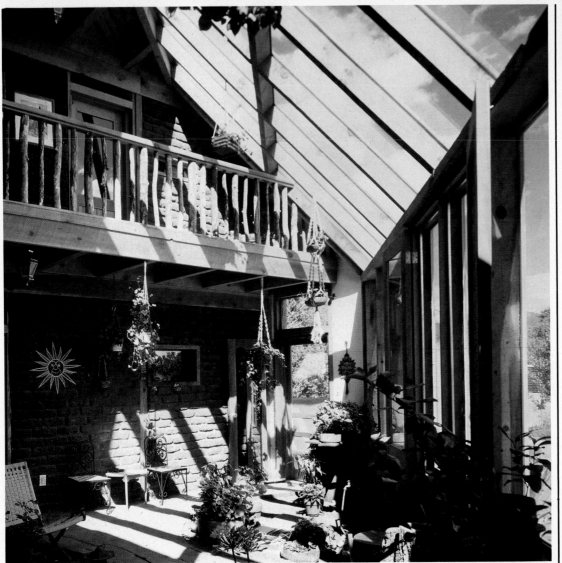

The adobe home provides a "natural warmth" making "standard discomforts" associated with winter things of the past.

THE GREENHOUSE EFFECT

More than 80% of Unit One's solar-collected warmth enters passively through the 409 square feet of double-paned thermal glass which forms the greenhouse. The L-shaped home is entirely faced—along its southern exposure—by this solarium. Two-thirds of the solarium's 24 standard patio-sized 32″ X 76″ glass panels are angled at 60° to throw sunlight on an adobe wall which separates the greenhouse from the living area. The other eight double-glazed panes stand vertically—at ground level—and the center two can be opened to provide ventilation.

The earthen wall—which tapers from a 14″ thickness at its base to 10″ at its peak some 20 feet above the floor level—is the primary storage and transfer system for Unit One's solar heating. By noon on a chilly winter day, the surface temperature of the wall will climb to as high as 110°F. Then slowly—over the course of the next ten hours—that heat works its way through the earth-brick barrier. By 10 p.m. the inside of the wall reaches about 80°F . . . and keeps the living area warm through the remainder of the night. By morning, however, most of the heat has dissipated . . . leaving the adobe ready to temper the living area through the day (when—even in the winter—the home's interior would otherwise warm rapidly). This slow transfer of the heat of the sun is an example of what solar engineers call indirect gain.

But there is a direct-gain element in the passive system, too. The air in the greenhouse is—of course—also sun-heated . . . and this warm, moist (*and* oxygenated by the plants) air can be introduced into the upstairs and downstairs by simply opening doors into those areas. Thus the Balcomb home is not only solar heated, but also has its own air filtration and humidification system. As Sara says, "It's a natural warmth. Many of the standard discomforts usually associated with winter are now things of the past: including cold feet, static electricity, dry skin, and morning sore throat. . . ."

STORING THE EXCESS

The majority of Unit One's solar-heating methods are totally passive, requiring no controls, no fuel, and no maintenance. But had the home's planners stopped at that point, much of the incoming energy would have been wasted. The fact is that—even on winter days —the greenhouse frequently draws in *more* energy than can be transmitted through the wall . . . and that's where Unit One's active solar system comes into play. Rather than just

The bulk of the heat is collected in the glazed solarium where plants can be cultivated year round, adding humidity and oxygen to the air in the adobe. Walls outside the structure itself carry the theme of the dwelling into the landscaping.

The massive adobe walls both serve as nighttime heaters for the dwelling and act as insulators against heat loss.

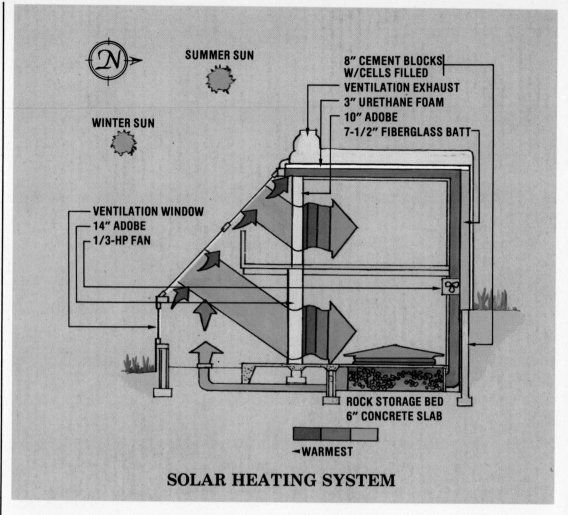

SUMMER SUN

WINTER SUN

8" CEMENT BLOCKS W/CELLS FILLED
VENTILATION EXHAUST
3" URETHANE FOAM
10" ADOBE
7-1/2" FIBERGLASS BATT

VENTILATION WINDOW
14" ADOBE
1/3-HP FAN

ROCK STORAGE BED
6" CONCRETE SLAB

◄WARMEST

SOLAR HEATING SYSTEM

vent this excess heat to the outside, the modern adobe's designers added a storage system.

Beneath the building's living room, dining room, and kitchen lie two rock storage beds—one 2′ X 10′ X 19′, and the other 2′ X 10′ X 15′—containing a total of 50 tons of 3″- to 5″-diameter cobblestones. These heat storage bins are connected, by ducts, to the greenhouse. Whenever the solarium's air temperature rises more than five degrees *above* that of the stones, air is forced down from the top of the greenhouse and into the rock beds . . . by two fans located in the backs of the bedroom closets. Thus the Balcombs can enjoy 70°F floors—with the heat being transmitted by convection through the 6″ slab—as well as 80°F walls.

Unit One's primordial "batteries" also provide the dwelling with a heat-storage capacity which can see the Balcombs through extended spells of inclement weather. And—while the home's two- to three-day storage capability doesn't match the staying power of a more expensive, totally active collector setup—Dr. Balcomb points out that a passive system *is* (in one way, at least) more efficient: Even on the snowiest Santa Fe day, Unit One's solar features are still absorbing *some* energy . . . because dispersed sunlight is better than none at all. But the *active* collector unit that provides the Balcombs' domestic hot water supply requires more *intense* light to operate. (For example, there have been a number of days since Unit One s completion when there was a passive solar home-heat gain, while the water heater didn't receive enough sunlight to operate at all.)

Adobe construction allows features such as this corner fireplace to be incorporated gracefully into the walls of the structure without breaks for using different materials.

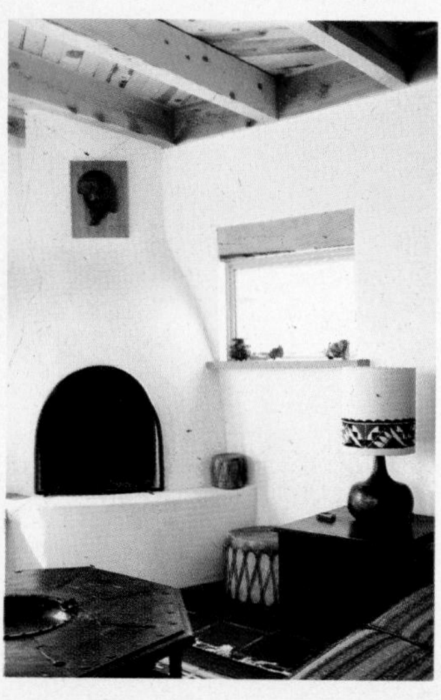

HANG ON TO WHAT YOU'VE GOT . . .

It's impossible to build and maintain an energy-efficient house without proper insulation, and the Balcomb home is no exception to this rule. The thermal mass wall—which serves as the dwelling's nighttime heater—is also (in effect) an insulator. The wall's heat transfer function prevents any significant heat loss since the outer surface losses are turned into inner surface gains. The building's east and west walls, however—which are also constructed of adobe—are more directly insulative. Though their mass *does* tend to delay inside temperature changes—just as does the greenhouse wall—they *don't* transfer any significant amount of solar heat to the home's interior.

The north-facing wall is buried below ground level to a depth of four and a half feet. This subterranean portion is built of 8″ concrete blocks (with the cells filled for extra insulation) and is sealed with plastic roofing cement and 2″ of rigid polystyrene. Above ground level, the northern wall consists of a stucco-covered frame of 2 X 8 studs on 16″ centers . . . and is insulated by a 1-1/2″ layer of fiberglass batt, a vapor space, and then six more inches of fiberglass batt. Three inches of urethane foam in the roof complete Unit One's insulation package.

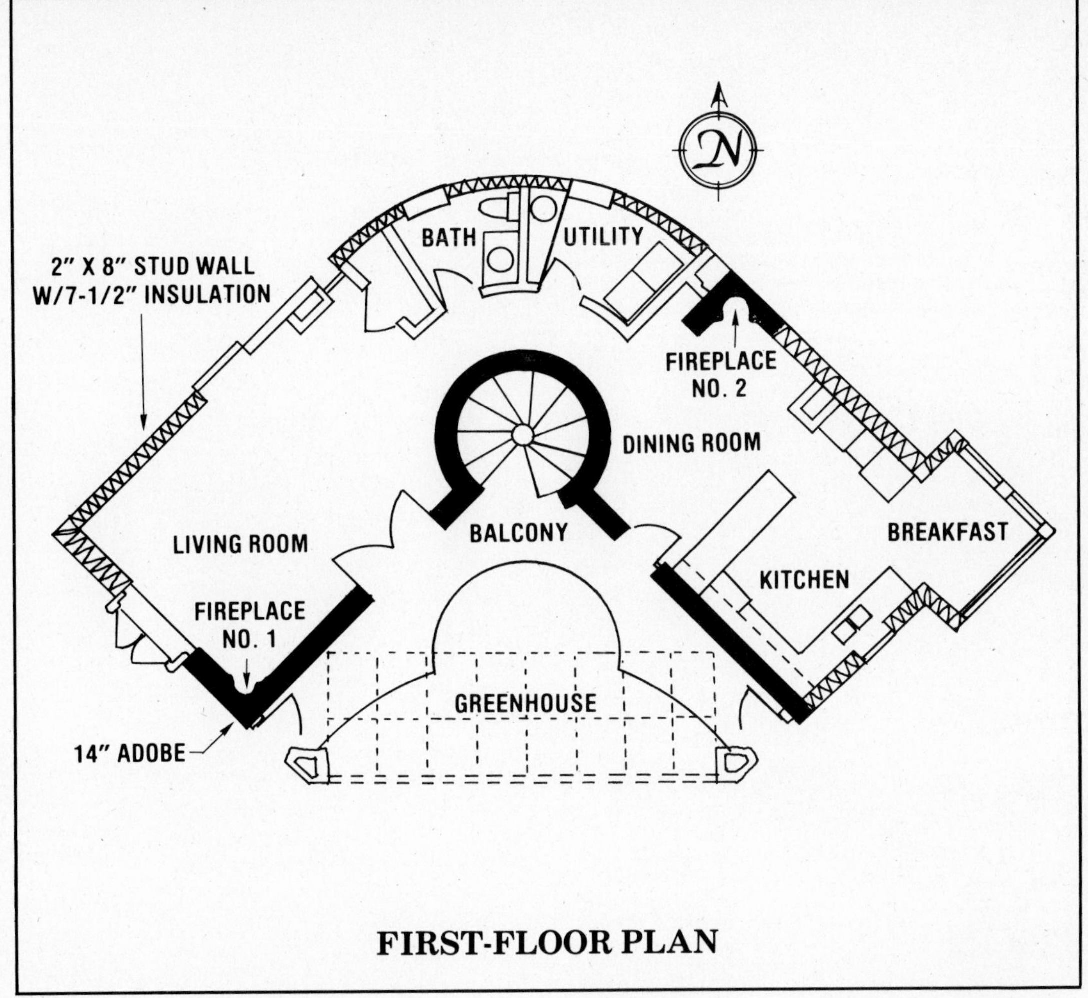

FIRST-FLOOR PLAN

Temperature fluctuations are minimal in the living area, with only a few degrees separating the daily highs and lows inside the dwelling.

AND GET AMAZING THERMAL STABILITY

There is a popular misconception that life in a passively heated solar home involves some compromises . . . such as donning or shedding clothing when the weather changes and lighting fires for extra warmth.

Sara Balcomb, however, has a bone to pick with such "myths": "I believed all that *myself*, until I lived through a winter in my passive home." And Dr. Balcomb's careful records of year-round temperatures in Unit One certainly show that the supposed necessity for compromise *is* a misconception . . . at least in this particular solar abode.

The dwelling's thermal mass wall and insulation—combined with its 20% active storage capability—conspire to keep Unit One's inside temperature incredibly stable. During a typical December, for instance, the Balcombs' living area's temperatures vary by a grand total of 4°, from 67°F to 71°F.

Sara says that it takes about two days for the house to react to a change in weather, and that there is never more than a 5° swing in any 24-hour period. The actual recorded extremes for the house are a low of 65°F in February (limited by the electric baseboard units which are thermostatically controlled at 65°F) and a high of 76° on a 97°F summer afternoon. And, as Sara points out, "A variance of 21° is hard to achieve even with conventional air conditioning . . . but we did it simply by natural means."

Temperatures do fluctuate in the greenhouse, naturally . . . on many days by as much as 35°F. This rise and fall is merely evidence of solar heating at work. Still, the coldest temperature the Balcomb's plants have ever had to tolerate was 45°F (on a -17°F winter night), while the hottest summertime high was 98°F.

And, of course, the solar techniques that heat Unit One also function to keep the Balcombs cool in the summer. When the sun is at its higher "warm season" angle, a roof overhang and the balcony shade the adobe wall from any direct sunlight. The mass of the wall then serves as a stabilizer . . . and thoroughly negates the radical temperature extremes of the desert day and night.

The storage system can also be used—by reversing its thermostatic control—to cool the rock beds at night and transfer the chill during the following day. To prevent overheating of the greenhouse during hot spells, the builders positioned vents at the base of the vertical windows and at the top of the staircase. Natural convection currents can thus introduce cool air through the lower vents and usher heat out the upper ones.

Study the photos of the dwelling for a moment. To an adobe fancier—and the lure of an earthen home "growing" out of the land is very real to many folks—the Balcomb house, more than just being an energy-efficient structure, falls somewhere between shelter and art.

Freeflowing lines and curves characterize adobe architecture, creating a blend of the practical and the aesthetic.

SYSTEMS JOIN IN A HYBRID

The appearance of the hybrid is contemporary and hardly unconventional. Windows not facing south are limited in size and number and are joined to plenums.

Aspects of superinsulation and double-shell housing designs were combined to form the "Hybrid Geotempered Envelope" system.

Understandably enough, when an energy-efficient house design proves itself practical, the concept tends to catch on. The popularity of the double-envelope principle serves as a good example, as does the recent interest in superinsulated structures.

But taking "good" one step further and incorporating the best features of several proven systems compatibly into one design can result in a still more flexible package than any one of the original layouts . . . and that's probably the simplest way to describe what the folks at Natural Energy Design—a Middletown, Rhode Island architectural and consulting firm—did when they worked up what they refer to as their "Hybrid Geotempered Envelope" system.

THE HOME HAS A PAST

The hybrid concept has its roots in one of the original Lee Porter Butler–designed Ekose'a homes which was built for Robert Mastin, who now happens to head up Natural Energy Design. Mastin, who helped construct his dwelling and was professionally interested in confirming its theory of operation, spent months tinkering with the system trying to establish its flow patterns, ascertain the significance of its abundant south-facing glazing, determine the extent to which solar heat was stored in the structure's mass, and improve its summertime venting.

However, in the midst of his seat-of-the-pants experimentation, Brookhaven National Laboratory, under the sponsorship of the U.S. Department of Energy, was preparing a series of case studies of innovative energy-efficient residences . . . and chose the Mastin house as the subject of a scientific evaluation of double-envelope thermal performance.

Instrumentation (nine thermistors for temperature measurement, three hygrometers for logging relative humidity, and two recording pyranometers for calculating insolation on horizontal surfaces) was installed to monitor the passive system and provide data which would allow Brookhaven researchers to estimate the home's auxiliary wintertime heating requirements, analyze the contribution of each individual feature, and suggest modifications that might improve its performance.

In short, between his observations and Brookhaven Lab's documentation, Bob Mastin was able to determine exactly where his own home's strengths and weaknesses existed. Subsequently, he set about to design a completely *new* structure that, he hoped, would take advantage of the attributes common to double-envelope designs while borrowing the best feature—cost-effective energy conservation—from superinsulated structures . . . at the same time eliminating one of the less desirable characteristics sometimes found in that type of dwelling, namely light-restricting, limited window area.

TWO FOREBEARS

A brief look at both superinsulated and double-envelope designs should help to explain

The solarium provides a bright, pleasant atmosphere and also helps heat the house, while the rock-faced hearth and chimney house a fireplace for visual and physical warmth and an interior duct that is part of the envelope's convective loop.

Conservation through heavy insulation is the secret, and the double envelope part of the design provides air circulation.

what Mastin's goal was to be in crossbreeding the two types of structures. It's generally accepted that the typical superinsulated home is probably the most efficient residential house design around, when compared to other designs on the basis of initial cost and energy use per square foot of floor space.

And conservation is the secret: Superinsulated homes are so well protected from heat loss and infiltration that thermal energy requirements are a mere fraction of those typical of a conventional dwelling . . . so much so that internal heat sources such as kitchen appliances, lights, and body warmth can supply up to one-half of the home's heat.

Unfortunately, this "silver lining" has a cloud around it: In order to guarantee maximum R-value and minimum wind leakage, the windows—nothing but trouble spots so far as heat loss is concerned—are often reduced in size and number, sometimes at the expense of aesthetics. (The general rule seems to be to limit the south-facing glass to 8%, and all other glazing to 4%, of the floor area . . . which is about half the percentage of glazing found in conventional American houses.)

Enter the double-envelope house. This kind of structure has several advantages in its own right.

First, because the envelope home has insulated outer *and* inner walls separated by a foot-wide air space, it effectively provides a tempered buffer belt around the entire living space (including the interior glass.) The air in this "belt" is warmer than that on the outside, so conductive heat loss—especially from glazing—is reduced.

Also, the envelope design deals with wind infiltration (ambient air being forced into a structure on its windward side and interior air being pushed from it at the leeward) in a very straightforward manner. Any intruding breezes simply find their way through the loop and then exit the envelope out the low-pressure side.

Finally, the double-shell design incorporates a full-width, south-facing solarium . . . a feature which not only helps to circulate air in the convective loop, but also allows plenty of light to enter the living area through an inner set of sliding glass panels.

A COMPATIBLE PACKAGE

How, then, does the Hybrid Geotempered Envelope that Mastin designed combine the features of both of these popular house designs? To begin with, its east, west, and north sides utilize double 2 X 4 superinsulated wall construction and are filled with 12 inches of fiberglass batting.

The structure's south face—like that of a double-envelope home—features a solarium that's separated from the living area by glass doors, but which is part of an envelope air loop connected through vents in its ceiling and floor. The loop itself, rather than passing along the roof and north wall as in a typical envelope design, takes a short cut by way of a duct built into the central masonry chimney, which returns air to the basement with the help of a thermostatically controlled fan located at the peak of the solarium.

Finally, the windows in the three "solid" walls borrow from both the superinsulated and the double-envelope camps: There's one in both the inner *and* the outer 2 X 4 "skins" (placed, of course, so they're opposite each other), but the gap between each pair of casements is bridged with wooden slats spaced 1/4" or so apart . . . and solid planking—fastened at the sides of each window set and extending from the top of the upstairs frames, along the first-floor jambs, and down into the basement—creates an earth-coupled, tempered-air vertical plenum between the glazing units.

According to the home's designer, the hybrid's benefits are at least fourfold: [1] Its centrally located chimney stores both solar and wood-derived warmth while providing the means for interior air circulation. [2] The window plenums not only furnish the desirable tempered air gap between the light-admitting exposed and inner panes, but also allow a tem-

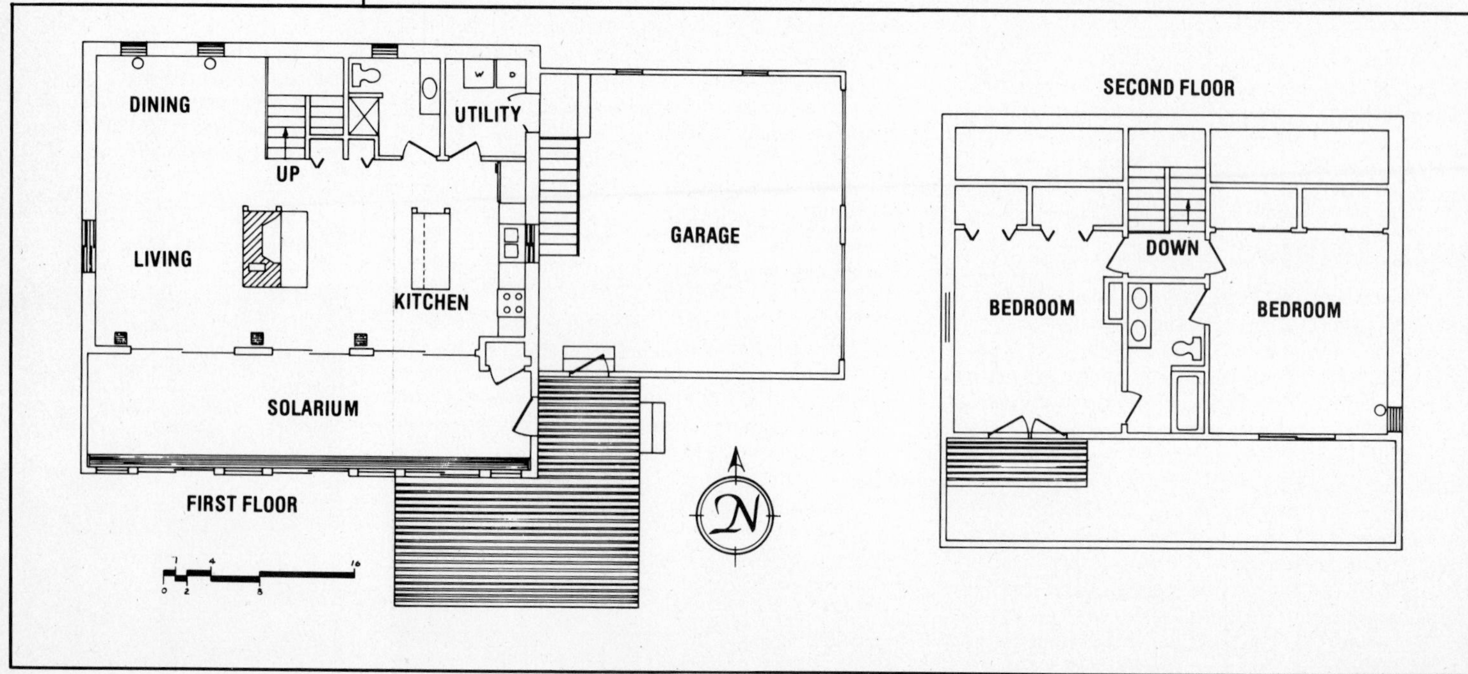

perature-moderating, ground-coupling effect . . . which simply means that the basement can give up its low-grade heat to the shafts if their temperature should fall below that of the earth. Also, since all the window ducts terminate in the basement "plenum" beneath the house, any air leakage from outside is routed around the living space. [3] Sufficient ventilation—an important consideration in nearly airtight superinsulated homes—is available to the hybrid house through natural infiltration if the solarium's inner doors are opened to allow the envelope's tempered air to circulate to the interior. [4] The interbred structure can function well on both overcast and sunny days, since its superinsulated shell allows near-maximum thermal protection, while its sunspace lets natural light enter the dwelling, generating both usable and storable warmth, on bright days.

In addition to these positive factors, there are several others worth mentioning. Bristol, Connecticut contractor Joe Riccio—who built the Hybrid Geotempered Envelope home featured here—pointed out that, because its construction is essentially conventional, its cost compares favorably with that of other custom-built homes in the neighborhood . . . and the HGE design eliminates the fire code problems often associated with structures that fit strictly into the double-envelope category.

. . . THAT SEEMS TO WORK!

With regard to aesthetics and performance, the home's owners—Ed and Terry Gianzinetti—couldn't be more pleased with their "baby" . . . which, by the way, is the first of its kind. The system now maintains interior temperatures in the mid to upper 60's . . . even when thermometer readings outside have been as low as 24°F. And, coupled with an occasional fire in the hearth, it has been more than adequate to keep the 2,000-square-foot living area comfortable.

Obviously, it may be a bit premature to claim the hybrid as the "home of the future", but—judging from its initial performance—it might just be the answer that a lot of folks are looking for.

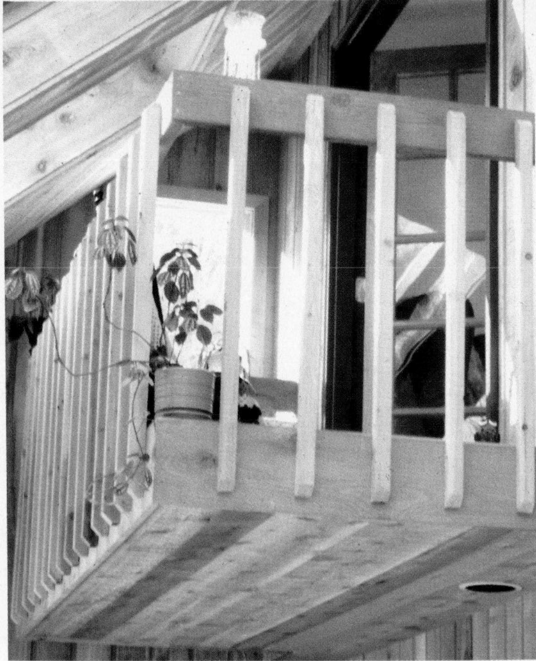

The hybrid might just be the answer a lot of folks are looking for in energy-efficient housing.

A balcony extends from the main bedroom into the sunspace under the large windows mounted on the south-facing roof and is reached through double doors, which admit heat and light to the sleeping quarters. Double casement windows create an air gap to help preserve warmth.

PASSIVE SOLAR BUT NOT SPARTAN

Careful planning from site selection to finishing the interior paid off in Randall Lankford's North Carolina home, built mainly with scrap materials and a lot of care. The large porch allows those living in the home to savor the pleasant outdoors of the mountainous region.

Back in 1976, Randall Lankford decided to erect a house on a parcel of land nestled in the mountains of North Carolina where he'd spent his childhood. Since he had a limited amount of cash available, but enough carpentry experience, ideas, and willing acquaintances to compensate—he felt—for his lack of capital, the determined Tarheel embarked on a building project that wound up involving a lot of swapping and the help of two good friends: designer Jeff Warren and artist Stan Caton (the latter individual contributed a good deal to the aesthetics of the completed structure).

PLANNING PAYS

Randall's initial task was to find a suitable construction site, and—after walking his property and listing the positive and negative aspects of several potential spots—he finally settled on a location that offered accessibility, available water and power, and good solar orientation. Once this chore was out of the way, he bartered with a neighbor, who, as it turned out, was more than willing to trade his expertise with a bulldozer for the largest of the trees that had to be removed (the *remaining* felled timber would later heat the Lankford residence for two full years).

That swap, however, was just the *first* of a long series of informal transactions that decreased the Carolinian's dependence on hard cash. Shortly thereafter, in lieu of hiring a crew to do the foundation work, Randall merely hosted a barbecue party at which only one rule prevailed: If you don't work, you don't eat! Needless to say, before the day was over the job was complete . . . and as far as we know, there wasn't a single complaint to be heard from the well-fed construction workers.

But Randall's most successful piece of "horse trading" took place when he began scouting about for framing materials . . . and discovered that new lumber was just too expensive for his limited budget to handle. "So, we took on a job dismantling a few old warehouses for their roof timbers and blocks, then went on to strip some houses in an area where a new section of highway was coming through." The lumber taken from those to-be-demolished buildings didn't cost Randall a cent, and all he needed were a few basic tools, a dry storage area, and a '48 Ford pickup!

Other exchanges helped to further reduce the cost of the structure, including (once the house was dried in) a swap of carpentry for temporary room and board, and a trade of landscaping services for some of the hardy and plentiful vegetation native to the Lankford homestead's mountain terrain.

A COMMONSENSE PASSIVE DESIGN

The 2,800-square-foot structure (2,200 square feet of it is heated) *purposely* wasn't designed to be a "typical" house. For one thing, Randall planned—from the outset—to provide his subsistence heat with wood or coal, and to back that up with whatever solar gain he could realize during the day, so the three-level dwelling had to allow for the unencumbered passage of convected air. To accomplish this, the owner-builder included a raised ceiling directly above his ground-floor great room, and positioned a den and fireplace on an exposed half-story that spans the area between the open space and the building's north wall. Above that, a two-tiered, balconied third level encompasses two bedrooms, a second hearth, a bath, and a sauna . . . and is sur-

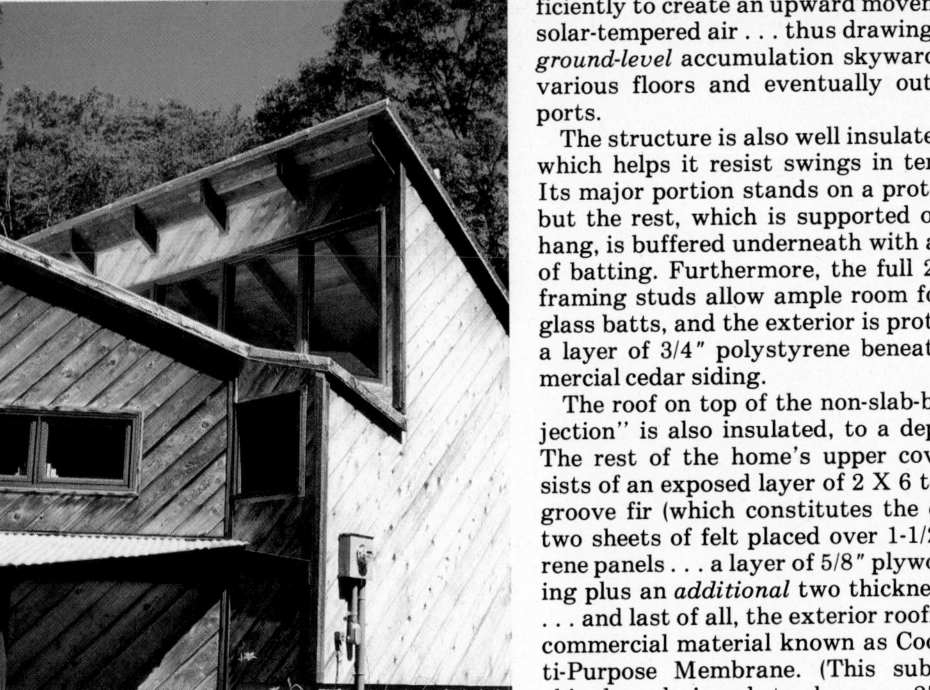

rounded by several triangular air galleries which encourage a balanced flow of warmed air from the rooms below, while providing access for both natural and artificial light. (The latter is supplied by inconspicuous fixtures made from stovepipe elbows!)

A centrally located woodburning stove furnishes a good deal of the home's heat, and 255 square feet of south-facing glazing—some of it in the form of a window wall—delivers enough solar warmth to raise the interior temperature nearly 20°F, even on particularly cold days. To improve the dwelling's heat reception/retention capabilities still further, Randall laid sections of dark gray slate (salvaged from a school demolition project) into his insulated concrete slab, installed the chimney that serves his two fireplaces 12 inches away from the nearest wall (and filled the cavity behind it with insulation) to prevent heat loss, and glassed in a greenhouse, which—with its 275-square-foot face—is designed to be a reliable and welcome source of heat during the winter. (Randall notes that sizable sections of super-thick glazing can sometimes be had—at bargain-basement prices—from local shopping centers or malls where, for insurance purposes or aesthetic reasons, perfectly good plate-glass storefronts and display kiosks are often routinely replaced when a new tenant moves in!)

Of course, the same design features that allow even distribution of wintertime heat likewise provide a source of summer cooling . . . creating, in effect, a thermal chimney. By leaving the uppermost operational windows in his house open from April through early fall, Randall can be sure that whatever sun enters through the overhang-shaded, south-facing glass wall will warm the interior air shafts sufficiently to create an upward movement of the solar-tempered air . . . thus drawing the cooler *ground-level* accumulation skyward, past the various floors and eventually out the open ports.

The structure is also well insulated, a factor which helps it resist swings in temperature. Its major portion stands on a protected slab, but the rest, which is supported on an overhang, is buffered underneath with a solid foot of batting. Furthermore, the full 2 X 6 wall-framing studs allow ample room for 6" fiberglass batts, and the exterior is protected with a layer of 3/4" polystyrene beneath its commercial cedar siding.

The roof on top of the non-slab-based "projection" is also insulated, to a depth of 12". The rest of the home's upper covering consists of an exposed layer of 2 X 6 tongue-and-groove fir (which constitutes the ceiling) . . . two sheets of felt placed over 1-1/2" polystyrene panels . . . a layer of 5/8" plywood sheathing plus an *additional* two thicknesses of felt . . . and last of all, the exterior roofing itself: a commercial material known as Cooper's Multi-Purpose Membrane. (This substitute-for-shingles—designed to have a 25-year lifespan—is made of quilted aluminum sheets, with asphalt inner layers, bonded together with plastic. It's applied to the roof with mastic, and features edges that seal to wood or to each other when heated . . . producing vulcanized seams that are designed to be impervious to water.)

One of the most *noticeable* features of the home, however, is the oak flooring, which was salvaged from houses Randall's small crew helped tear down. "We just numbered and named the back of the boards according to whatever rooms they came out of, and reinstalled them where they fit best. If we hadn't taken the trouble to mark them, we would have wasted time later, since flooring from high-traffic areas—such as kitchens—is always more worn than is that from less used rooms . . . which means that, had we jumbled it together, we'd have had to do a lot of sanding to even things up," the builder says.

HE'S READY TO DO IT AGAIN

After living in his house for several seasons, and having had a chance to reflect on the benefits and difficulties posed by the owner-built approach to home proprietorship, Randall still believes that it's a good way to avoid some of the hassles that occur when buying a home in a more conventional manner. "Except for the fact that I'm single, and thus not burdened with family responsibility, I faced the same problems most folks do and had to make some serious decisions—such as whether to procure a bank loan and take a leave of absence from my job—before embarking on my project. I also relied heavily on some good friends and my relatives, and it *still* took longer than I expected to bring the house to completion. On the other hand, my home's been appraised at about two and a half times what I've put into it—in cash—and I have the satisfaction of having done it the way I wanted to, because I shared every aspect of the job with a designer who was just as interested in the result as I was," he says.

Built with materials salvaged from dismantled buildings and with the labor of the owner, his friends, and relatives, Randall's residence has been appraised at about two and a half times the amount of money he invested in the dwelling.

Clerestory windows, found in many solar designs, are part of the home's cooling system. Opened in the warm months, they allow warm air to escape and cool air to be drawn into the structure. The multiangled roof is covered with a weather-resistant, layered membrane designed to have a 25-year life.

A SOLAR SYSTEM THAT THINKS FOR ITSELF

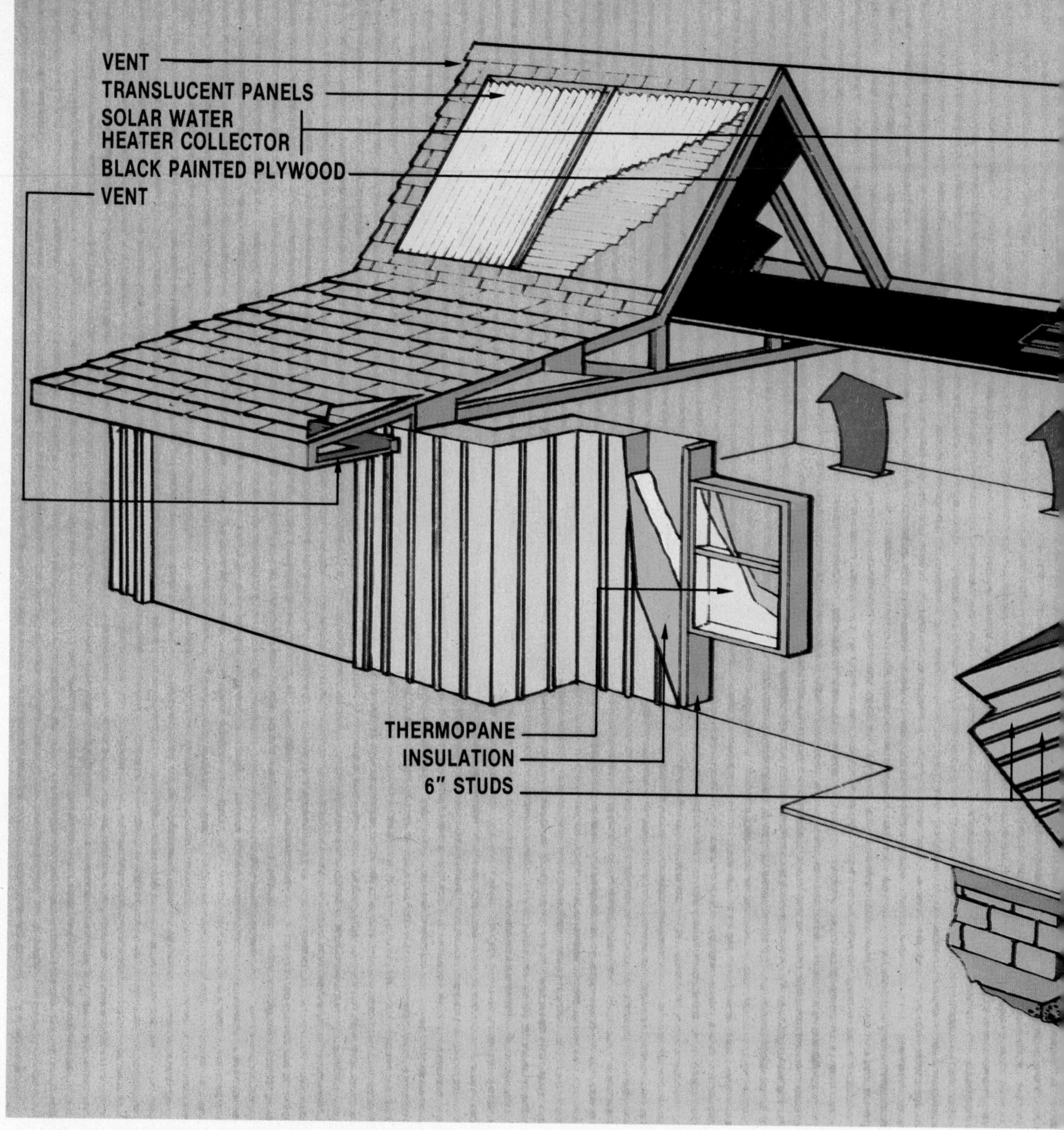

Until a few years ago, anyone who wanted to live in a solar-heated and -cooled house found the construction of that dwelling to be pretty much a do-it-yourself affair. A group in Greenville, South Carolina by the name of Helio Thermics, Inc., changed all that, by designing, building, and making readily available [1] a "standard" solar-heated and -cooled dwelling that [2] was competitively priced and [3] was among the first such structures to qualify for both FHA and VA mortgage insurance.

Helio Thermics began with little more than three brothers . . . Randy, Mike, and Larry Granger, who—in their back yard, so to speak—studied some U.S. Department of Agriculture research data (which are freely available to anyone) and then designed, built, and refined an exceptionally clever solar-heating and -cooling system.

FIRST THINGS FIRST

The Granger brothers "began at the beginning" by concentrating on the more prosaic (although, in some ways, more important) aspects of their system, such as framing the exterior walls with 2 X 6's, which accommodate twice the amount of insulation recommended for the area. The ceiling was also double-insulated, and all the windows were double-glazed.

The initial added cost of these features was more than offset by the brothers' economical approach to the collector, usually one of the most expensive components of a solar home. Their idea was to use the attic as a "hot air solar absorber". The south-facing slope of the attic roof was set at 50° to the horizon. (The optimum angle for the placement of a solar collector is generally considered to be latitude plus 15°, and Greenville is located approximately 35° north of the equator.) Translucent, reinforced, Tedlar-coated, corrugated fiberglass sheeting was then attached—with weatherproof screws—directly to the rafters on the south side, in place of standard roofing material. To add rigidity and to increase the insulating value of the panels, the first layer was laid horizontally and the top layer was run vertically (to better shed rain, snow, and other moisture). The half-inch-thick plywood floor and opposite wall of the attic's interior were then painted flat black so the collection chamber would absorb the incoming rays of the sun more efficiently.

This was all done, quite obviously, to make

A microcomputer monitors the temperature of the dwelling and decides which of eight operational modes to select.

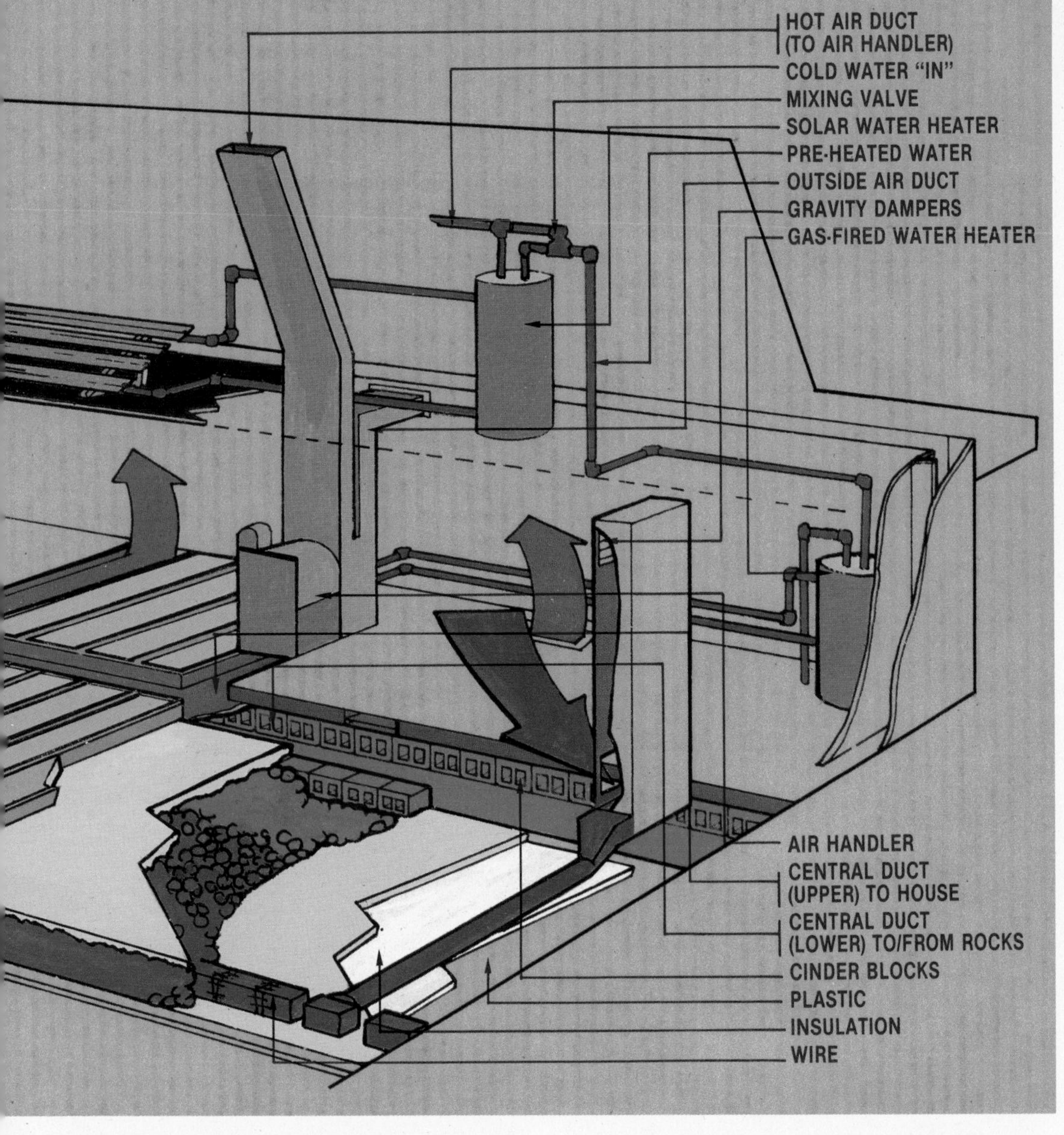

The "storage to house" mode of heat transfer for the prototype solar home can be seen in this cutaway view of the dwelling. Warm air from the rock storage area at the lower right of the diagram is drawn by the "air handler" through edge-laid cinder blocks into the lower level of the central duct. From there the heated air travels through the air handler's blower and enters the upper level of the central duct and then into ductwork leading through floor registers into the living area of the house. Cool air enters the system's return duct at the right of the drawing and returns to the rock storage area where it gains warmth before reentering the cycle.

the attic/collector a better heat trap during the winter. But what kept that double layer of translucent plastic and those absorber panels of black plywood from turning the attic into an unbearably hot solar oven during the months of July and August?

By opening a series of vents along the ridge of the attic's roof and immediately under its eaves, the Grangers found they could create a surprisingly effective natural "air conditioner" for that part of the house. In other words, the more the air in the loft was heated, the faster it rose out the ridge vents and the more it drew cool air in through the openings under the eaves.

THE DELIVERY AND STORAGE SYSTEM

Of course, if Randy and Mike and Larry had stopped right there, they wouldn't have had much of a solar-tempered house on their hands. Taken just this far and no farther, the design could provide no way to store the attic/collector's excess heat or cold (during any given period) for use at a later time.

So the boys tucked 1,100 cubic feet (60 tons) of washed, egg-sized rock under the building. And they connected this "heat sink" to the attic with a network of ducts, dampers, and louvers so that a blower (the Grangers called it an "air handler") could draw air—either hot or cold—from the attic. And that air could be used to heat or cool either the building's main floor or the crushed stone in the storage pit underneath. And—if stored—the captured warmth (or "coolth") could always be extracted from the storage area on demand and blown into the house's living space by the 1,600-cubic-foot-per-minute fan (driven by a half-horse electric motor) that was the heart of the building's air handler.

THE LITTLE "BLACK BOX"

All very well and good. It's easy to see how the Helio Thermics house captured hot air in its attic on a sunny winter day (or cold air on a cool August night) and then blew that air into either the structure's living quarters or its rock storage area for use at a later time. But it's also easy to see that the mere adjusting of vents and louvers and dampers could soon turn into a full-time job for someone.

So the Grangers built a full-time "someone"—an electric control unit—right into their

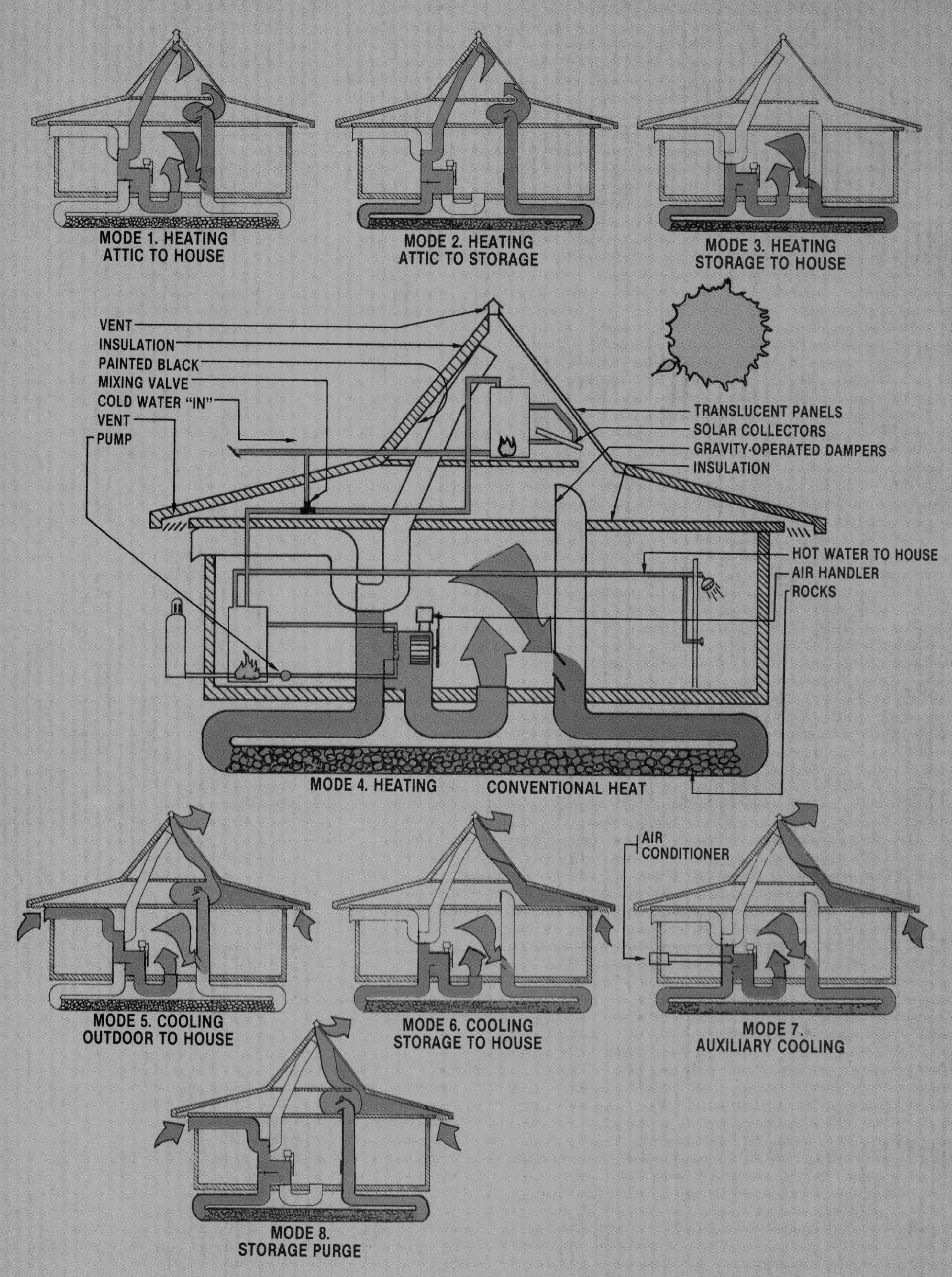

MODE 1. HEATING
ATTIC TO HOUSE
MODE 2. HEATING
ATTIC TO STORAGE
MODE 3. HEATING
STORAGE TO HOUSE
VENT
INSULATION
PAINTED BLACK
MIXING VALVE
COLD WATER "IN"
VENT
PUMP
TRANSLUCENT PANELS
SOLAR COLLECTORS
GRAVITY-OPERATED DAMPERS
INSULATION
HOT WATER TO HOUSE
AIR HANDLER
ROCKS
MODE 4. HEATING
CONVENTIONAL HEAT
AIR
CONDITIONER
MODE 5. COOLING
OUTDOOR TO HOUSE
MODE 6. COOLING
STORAGE TO HOUSE
MODE 7.
AUXILIARY COOLING
MODE 8.
STORAGE PURGE

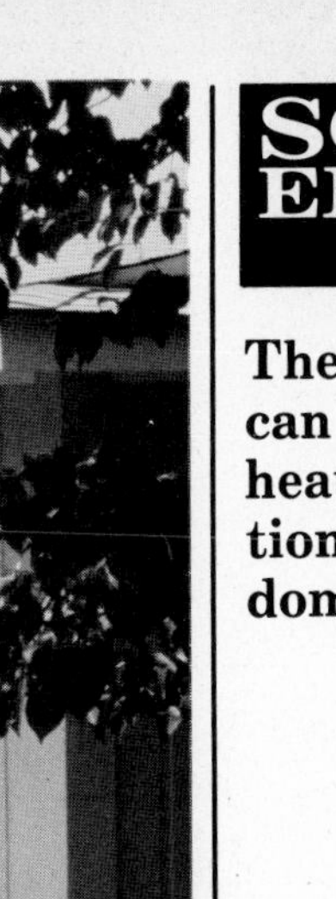

The sun's warmth can also be tapped to heat a large proportion of the residents' domestic hot water.

house to continuously take care of this chore. The "solid state black box" was of the same size and complexity as a small TV set and, just like most modern color TV's, had removable circuit boards for easy service and repair.

The control unit (actually a microcomputer) constantly monitored the temperature in five locations: [1] the building's collector/attic, [2] the structure's living area, [3] the central portion of the rock storage pit, [4] the outer edge of the storage area, and [5] the atmosphere surrounding the house. With this continually updated information always in "mind", it then decided which heating or cooling source and what mode of operation (there are eight modes) would most economically keep the building's living space at the temperature set on the black box's console dial.

As it deemed necessary, the control unit would [1] heat the house with BTU drawn down from the attic and [2] stash those therms away in the storage pit below. Then again, it could decide to [3] pull some of that collected warmth back up out of crushed stone and distribute it to the structure's living area. Or it could even [4] tap into a very small supplemental source of heat to augment the solar collection and storage system during unusually long periods of overcast weather.

The control unit was also built to [5] cool the building with outside air or [6] cache some of that coolness in the storage bin. And it could [7] make the decision to draw collected cold air from the storage area under the house and blow it into the living space, or even [8] distribute the output of a regular air conditioner.

THE BACKUP HEATING SYSTEM

The Grangers are quick to admit that—just like most solar-heated structures—their Helio Thermics house could be temporarily "put out of business" by three or more consecutive midwinter days of heavy cloud cover. Unlike a great number of other sun-warmed buildings, though, theirs was so well insulated that it could be supplementally heated with nothing but an ordinary 50-gallon, quick recovery, gas-fired domestic water heater!

Hot (140°F) water pumped through a heat exchanger, something like an automobile radiator, in the air handler was used to warm the air passing over the exchanger's coils. This heated air was then distributed throughout the house. Interestingly enough, the water returning from the exchanger was still hot enough (130°F) to pipe right into the dwelling's plumbing for washing, bathing, and other household uses.

The expense of heating with hot water was easily recovered *on a regular basis* directly from their building's attic/collector. Black-painted copper tubing was laid out on the attic's floor with one end of the bed connected to the bottom and the other end to the top of an electric water heater's tank (the unit's heating element was removed). This very simple solar-powered heater could warm water to a simmering 170°F, and it supplied the Helio Thermics prototype with a large part of all the hot water its residents needed.

THE BACKUP COOLING SYSTEM

Even though it was never actually necessary to supplementally cool the Helio Thermics house during its first summer, the Grangers did do a limited number of experiments with the idea just to see how it would work.

"You can bolt a big air conditioner right into the building's ducting and use it to 'overpower' any uncomfortable heat in the house on a really hot day if you want to," said Mike. "We think it's a lot smarter and less costly, though, to use a much smaller conditioner and just run it on the few nights when the outside air temperature doesn't drop enough to cool the rocks in the structure's storage bin. On such nights, the small conditioner can be used to cool the storage pit . . . and the rocks can be used to cool the house on the following day."

. . . AND THE LIVIN' IS EASY!

In spite of the apparent complexity of the air handling system, neither a degree in thermodynamics nor tolerating idiosyncrasies only an inventor would live with were needed to live in a Helio Thermics house. On the contrary, the dwelling boasted all the modern comforts that most Americans have come to expect . . . or at least to want.

The various heating and cooling cycles of the attic/collector system are demonstrated in these drawings. In the first four modes of operation, the vents in the eaves and at the roof peak are closed to retain heat during cool weather. For warm-weather cycles, illustrated in modes 5 through 8, the same vents are opened, allowing a convective current to help draw hot air out of and cool air into the living area. While the heating and cooling system in this house is agreeably unconventional in design, the outward appearance of the dwelling can hardly be considered unusual.

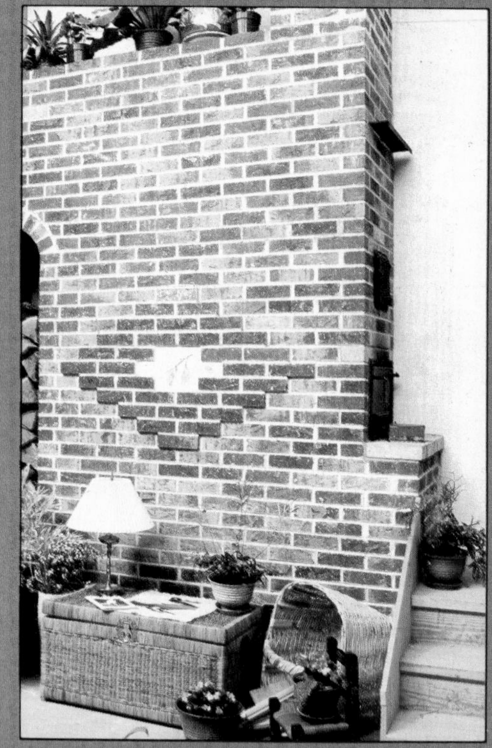
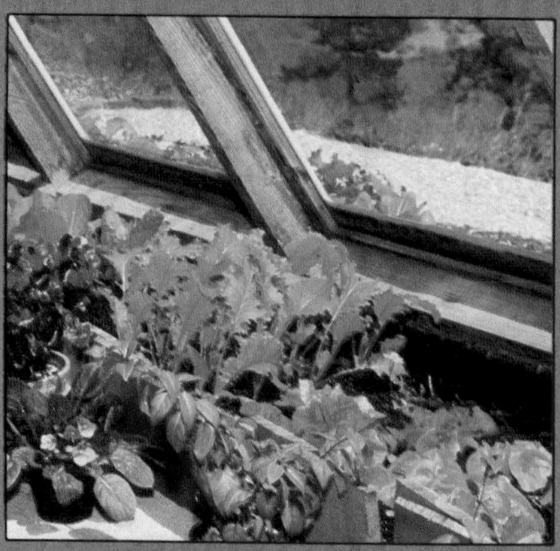
 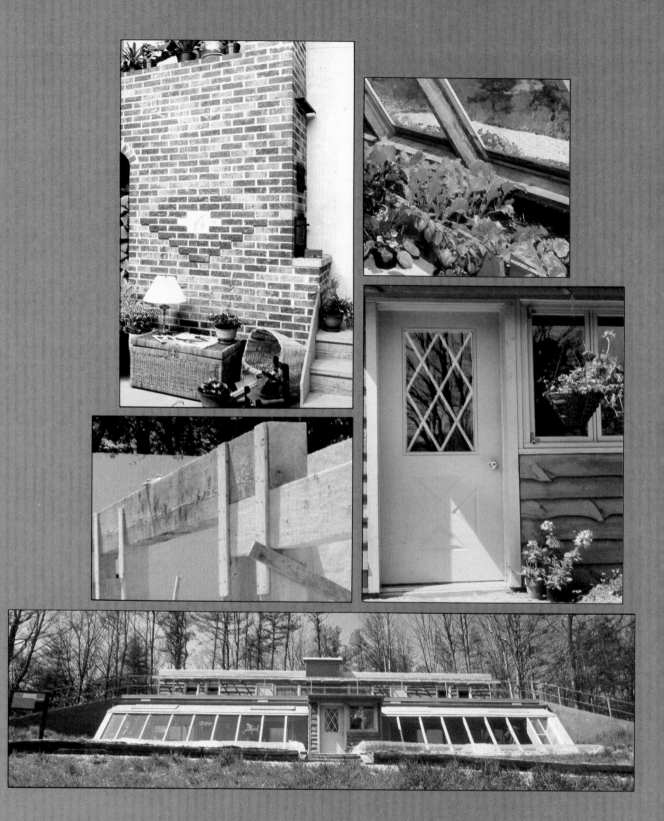
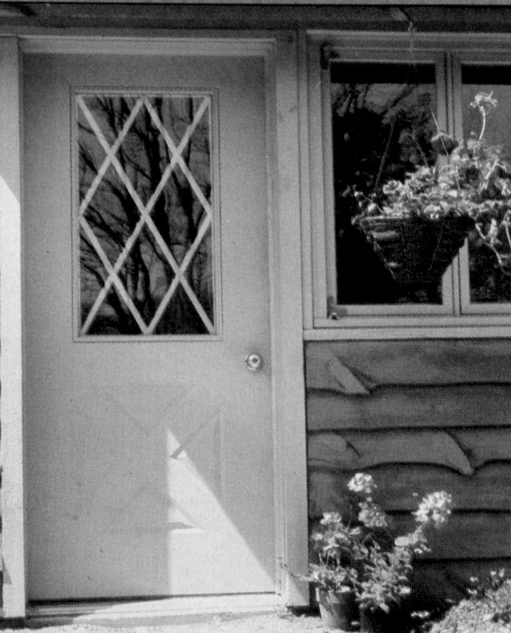
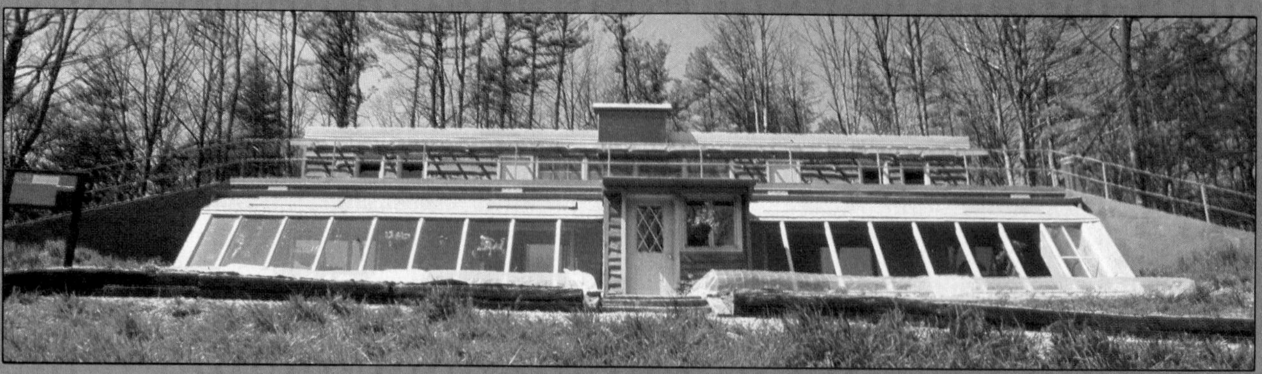

ALTERNATIVES COMBINE IN A TEST HOUSE

With groundbreaking in April 1981 on a south-facing slope in the western North Carolina mountains, construction was begun on My MOTHER's House, designed to incorporate and test many of the energy-saving building techniques being used today by people concerned with reducing their dependence on nonrenewable energy sources.

Fabricating this structure at THE MOTHER EARTH NEWS® Eco-Village was a learning process for the research and construction teams, who gained a great deal of knowledge and expertise as they worked . . . often in consultation with a number of alternative-building specialists.

Though much care and attention were given to planning the earth-sheltered, solar-heated, energy-efficient house, the design process continued throughout construction as adaptations were made to accommodate new ideas or to make the best possible use of the available materials . . . as you will see in this step-by-step account of the building process and in the analysis of the materials and methods used in My MOTHER's House.

Steps were taken to tailor the house to its particular climate.

BASIC DESIGN METHODS FOR WALLS

In April 1981, construction began at THE MOTHER EARTH NEWS Eco-Village on a test house incorporating innovative, energy-saving technology.

Western North Carolina's topography and climate lend themselves quite well to the earth-sheltering approach. The area is blessed with an abundance of rolling hills—which provide plenty of sites where a home can be backed into a slope without the need for any particularly difficult excavation—and soils that have little expansive (prone to slippage) clay.

The region experiences approximately 4,000 heating degree-days annually and can encounter seasonal extremes of 10° and 95°F. A glance over a local monthly temperature profile chart indicates that some home heat may be required from September through May, and that cooling would often be pleasant in July and August. Even during the hottest and coldest times of the year the temperature will change significantly from day to night.

Consequently, when the construction specialists at THE MOTHER EARTH NEWS, Inc. planned to build a solar-heated house at the magazine's Eco-Village, it was decided that the inclusion of a large amount of thermal mass—along with the added "flywheel" effect of earth berming—would essentially eliminate the need for *conventional* heating and cooling. A few additional steps were also taken to tailor the house to its particular climate.

The structure was erected on an existing 6"-thick, 25' X 60' concrete pad oriented just 5° to the east of due south. The chosen site has other excellent qualifications for passive solar heating. The open eastern exposure allows the living area to begin warming soon after sunrise. To the west, however, dense deciduous trees provide late afternoon shade during the warmer months.

The excavation into the hillside left the rear of the cut 13-1/2 feet below grade. Since that depth is too great for a "to grade" fill on a single-story earth shelter (such a design would have to support an incredibly thick and heavy layer of earth), the designers decided to build the back retaining wall to 14 feet and opt for a split-level dwelling. The *front* half of the house would then have only one story with a sod-covered roof . . . and the shed roof on the back section of the dwelling, which protrudes above grade, would be heavily insulated.

While the floor of much of the rear half of the house is raised 63 inches above that of the front, the center section maintains the same level as the front of the building with a cathedral ceiling to provide illumination *and* to serve as a thermal chimney for summer cooling. Below the raised floors of the two bedrooms, provisions were made to enclose rock heat-storage bins—which would be fed by ductwork from the peak of the cathedral ceiling—and a holding tank for solar-heated domestic water.

The incorporation of an above-grade second story into the design provides several other benefits as well. The rear bedrooms receive direct sun for both lighting and heating, and the upstairs veiw across the valley is delightful.

The walls for the earth-sheltered portion of the house reach their finished height, and the outline for the greenhouse in front of the building and the root cellar at the east end are all that indicate where those parts of the structure will be. Blocks needed to fit special locations were cut on a masonry saw.

In addition, the operable windows and the exit to the veranda created by the flat sod-covered roof satisfy most regions' building code requirements for egress from sleeping areas.

With those basic concepts in mind, the design committee began to add detail to the roughed-out plans. A root cellar—with access from the kitchen—was situated outside the main walls . . . requiring a minor addition to the slab. The sunspace/greenhouse along the front would be completely glassed, and a rammed-earth floor (treated with linseed oil) in that area would be a good addition to the thermal mass provided by the 12"-thick wall separating the living area from the solarium. Further, for back-up heat, it was decided that a high-efficiency Russian fireplace would be installed.

The remainder of the floor plan was left relatively open since the structure was not intended to be a residence but—at least in part—to serve as a meeting place for large seminar groups.

Finally, the innumerable small (but *vital*) considerations that complete a house—from a graywater handling system to electrical outlets to washer-dryer placement—were mulled over, and construction was ready to begin.

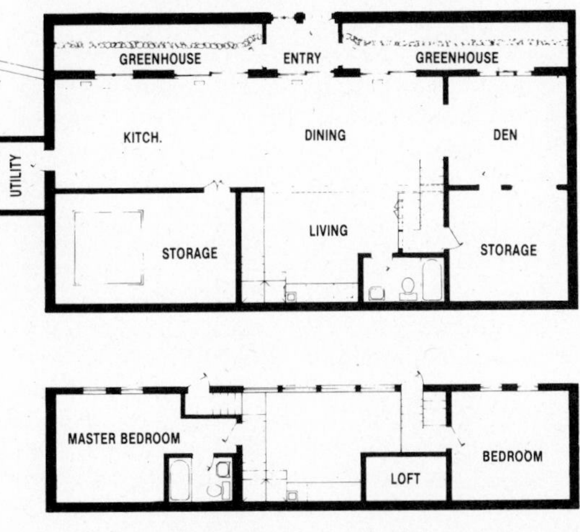

Innumerable small considerations were mulled over, and construction was ready to begin.

THE WALLS GO UP

To counter the combined forces of hydrostatic (ground water) pressure and earth berming, the Eco-Village team opted for a three-way network of redundant wall-reinforcement techniques. The necessary strength was achieved by fitting the courses and cells of 12" retaining-wall block with rebar, filling the cavities with concrete, and then covering the three block walls—inside and out—with a 1/8"-thick layer of Surewall surface-bonding cement. An expansion joint was positioned midway in the rear wall to prevent cracking . . . and for waterproofing protection, a drainage pipe and gravel seepage field were planned to conduct water away from the uphill side of the building.

Before wall construction could begin, 3/4" holes had to be bored into the slab, and 36" lengths of 7/8" (No. 7) rebar pounded into the openings. Then a single course of block was laid over the reinforcing rod . . . with mortar beneath to level out the undulations in the concrete pad. From that point on, the wall was dry-stacked (with *no* mortar between the tiers), and a section of 5/8" rebar was laid horizontally in each groove in the block.

Now laying a wall without mortar *does* allow the work to go quite a bit more quickly than would be possible when mortaring each piece, but the method turned out to have a *disadvantage* as well. Because common block is often uneven by as much as 1/4 inch, irregularities

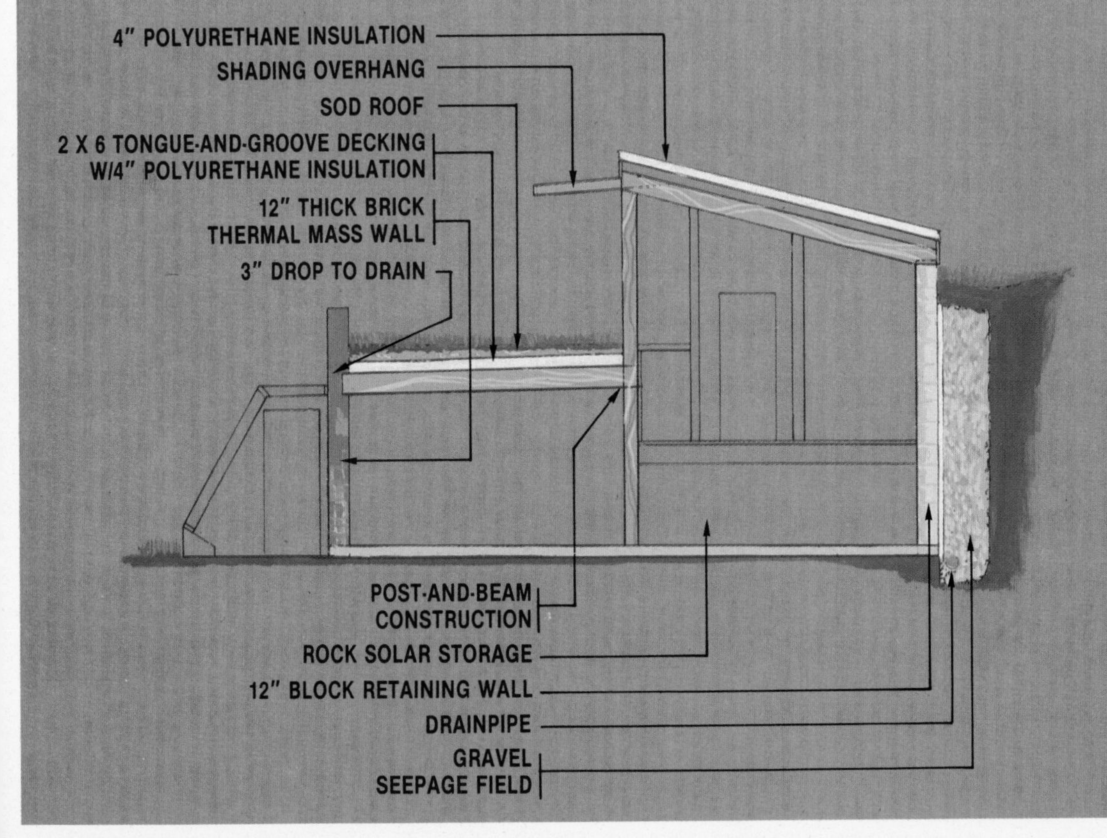

As each course of blocks was laid, a length of reinforcing bar was placed in V-grooves in the tops of the blocks.

Locally fired, high-magnesium brick was used to build the thermal mass wall at the front of the living area.

tend to develop as the courses pile up . . . and each layer seems to magnify the problems of the one beneath it. ("Trued" block can be acquired in many areas, but it's fairly expensive.) By the time the eight-foot level was reached, there were noticeable bows (or "hogs") in the walls, despite attempts to level each course.

Hence, it was necessary at that height to pour a beam all along the walls to even out the irregularities. Before doing so, though, two lengths of 5/8" rebar were dropped into each cell, the forms were built for the root cellar entrance . . . and then the cavities, beam, lintel, and door frame were poured at the same time.

As the last few of the 22 courses required to reach 14 feet were being finished, a representative from Bonsal—the company that makes Surewall surface-bonding compound—arrived with some wedges specifically designed to level dry-stacked block. Those plastic implements—the use of which is detailed in the accompanying photos—considerably speeded up the process of trueing the wall. Then the remaining cavities were poured and reinforced down to the level of the beam/lintels. Next came the surface coating of Surewall. The material is similar in many ways to stucco, except that it has fiberglass threads to add tremendous strength to dry-stacked wall. (Bonsal claims that its product is superior to mortared block walls in withstanding bending, shear, *and* impact stresses.) One 50-pound bag of Surewall—which must be mixed with 1-1/2 gallons of water—will cover approximately 40 square feet (when spread to a 1/8" thickness). Furthermore, it's available in white, gray, and six pastel colors . . . and thus can serve as a finish coat.

It's difficult to reach a firm conclusion about the economics of using Surewall. The materials cost does exceed that of a simple mortared masonry wall, but—according to Bonsal—labor time can be reduced by as much as 30% when the product is used.

People who decide to build a similar house should at least consider opting for continuous-pour concrete, however, because the team's calculations indicate that filling the cells and lintels for the 12" block walls used up enough concrete—about 70 cubic yards—to pour an identical length of 8"-thick wall, which would be the structural equivalent of the block bulkheads. Furthermore, the required forming plywood can be used later in the construction process for roof decking or flooring.

A THERMAL MASS WALL

The clay content of western North Carolina soil, while tricky to work with for drainage, helps to support a thriving brick industry. Consequently, it was decided to build the mass wall at the front of the living area from locally fired, custom-ordered, high-magnesium brick. (The magnesium darkens the material and improves its thermal properties.)

The wall was laid up three bricks (12") thick to provide a thermal lag time of between six and eight hours. Of course, the partition was tied into the slab with rebar at the bottom . . . and alternating corner blocks left in the side retaining walls allowed for the keying of the brick to the rest of the structure.

Since the brick bulkhead needed to be terminated at a height of 7-1/2 feet to allow space to fit the beams for the sod roof, the use of poured concrete lintels was impractical. Instead, two sections of 1/4" X 6" angle iron were welded together to bridge each of the window and door openings, and brick was laid directly on top of the metal. At the same time, allowances were made at the top of the wall for ducts to trans-

Block-leveling wedges were used in between the upper courses of block, making it easier to keep the tops of the tiers even. A fiberglass-laden surface bonding cement was applied to the faces of the dry-stacked walls.

port greenhouse-heated air to the roof peak where it could be picked up and delivered to the rock storage.

ABOVE-GRADE BERMING

In order to supplement the structure's thermal mass, wing walls were designed to angle out from the front of the building and hold backfill while allowing for some above-grade earth berming. The wing walls were built the same way as the main retaining walls with an inch of polystyrene foam insulation separating them thermally from the rest of the structure.

ROOF SUPPORT FRAMEWORK, SHEATHING, INSULATION

While *designing* the earth-bermed solar shelter, several different means of supporting the sod-covered roof on the front half of the house were considered . . . including precast, prestressed, and cast-in-place concrete, trusses, and even steel beams. But after hashing out the advantages of the various approaches, the designers chose a wood post-and-beam arrangement . . . both because it could be economically built from local materials with basic hand tools *and* since the huge timbers required would be attractive additions to the interior.

The ten vertical members (or posts, which are lined up to bear the weight of the beam) are 8 X 8 hemlock pine, acquired from a local lumber mill. The original plans specified 6 X 8's, but the sawyer had only 8 X 8's on hand, so rather than wait to have the smaller timbers cut, it was decided to widen the central wall thickness from 6" to 8" to accommodate the larger members. Each post was secured to the slab with a 10"-long piece of 1/2" rebar that was pounded into holes in both the concrete *and* the wood, and the posts at each end of the building were also tied to exterior walls with 3/4" bolts.

Of the remaining eight uprights, a total of four were positioned at 6-foot intervals from each end of the building, and the remaining four were arranged to provide additional support for the central spanning beam, while also making room for a stairway.

Since an 8 X 16 kiln-dried Douglas fir timber would span the middle of the living area, with 6 X 12 hemlock beams as the shorter end-members of the same span, the posts had to be longer beneath the big beam in order to raise it far enough to provide adequate ceiling height. (The 6 X 12's would become part of an internal partition, so their clearance wasn't important.) The builders allowed for this necessary jog by using longer posts and by setting the 8 X 16 atop the ends of the 6 X 12's. For added security, the beams were notched to a depth of 1-1/2" so that each post could be keyed into the horizontal timbers. In addition, all the posts and beams were joined with 1/4" steel plates and 1/2" bolts, nuts, and washers.

The rafters for the front half of the house consist of 4 X 12 sections of hemlock, spaced 36" on center. These 12'10" and 13'6" crosspieces span from the central beam (where the long ones were set on the 6 X 12's, and the shorter

The huge timbers needed to support the earth-covered roof are attractive additions to the decor.

The heavy beams were notched to fit their support posts. The horizontal timbers support the load of the earth-covered section of roof and the eight-inch-thick second-story front wall. The center timber rests on top of the ones coming from the ends of the house, giving more headroom in the passageway. The rafters under the sod roof span the gap between the center beam and the thermal mass front wall.

Everyone working on the project was enthusiastic about the simplicity and economy of post-and-beam construction.

timbers were butted against the central 8 X 16 and suspended from 2″ angle iron hangers) to one brick width short of the outer edge of the thermal mass wall. Then more brick was laid around and against the ends of the timbers.

The stout framework is built to withstand the 147 pounds per square foot of pressure exerted by the framing, roofing, sod, moisture, etc., but it also offers the beauty and warmth that many feel can be provided only by wood. Everyone who worked with the big timbers became quite enthusiastic about the simplicity and economy of post-and-beam construction.

ROOFING

An interesting product—one that's been around for many years but seems now to be enjoying a real growth in popularity—was put to use atop the building. It's Homasote: a 2-1/2″-thick, tongue-and-groove roof sheathing that can be combined with the same manufacturer's 4″ polyurethane insulation, called Thermasote, to yield an R-30 roof that's only 6-1/2″ thick.

Furthermore, beyond Homasote's fine *insulative* value, the sheathing has a couple of other important advantages. First, the 2′ X 8′ sheets can be laid very quickly . . . and the material not only has a water-resistant outer coating, but a white vinyl interior that functions as a finished ceiling.

Unfortunately, however, it was estimated that Homasote couldn't quite provide the strength needed to span the 36″ gaps between the rafters of the *sod-covered* portion of the house's roof. So the full 6-1/2″ marriage of sheathing and insulation was used on the *rear* roof of the house only . . . and sturdier 2 X 6 tongue-and-groove pine decking with Thermasote was used to insulate the earth-loaded front roof.

Once the 2 X 6 decking was laid down (a process that was made more time-consuming by the need to trim the rafters with an adze to keep the boards level), the roofing went on quite rapidly. It took a four-man crew just two days to apply the Thermasote to the to-be-sodded area, and both Homasote and Thermasote to the 2 X 10 rafters (spaced on 24″ centers) on the second story. Of course, *lifting* the roughly 80-pound panels did prove to be a bit of a task, but the speed with which the panels could be nailed down compensated for the extra effort.

What's more, the cost of the Homasote Company's products turned out to be quite competitive with that of a comparable conventional roof . . . and when one totals the potential costs of the customary framing for insulation, applying decking, and finishing the interior ceiling, the recycled paper products begin to look very economical.

CAPPING THE BRICK WALL

With the roofing in place on the front of the house, a parapet bordering the sod roof area was built atop the 12″-thick thermal mass wall. First, to form an insulating barrier between the two sections, bricks were laid along the outside row of the three-brick-thick wall and between the rafters (which rested on the thermal wall) along the inside row of bricks. The 4″ hollow between these two rows of bricks was filled with vermiculite, as were the voids of a tier of 12″ concrete blocks laid on top of that brick. Also, to further minimize heat loss from the mass wall, the mortar used in the insulated section consisted of eight shovels each of sand and vermiculite, to one bag of mortar mix. Finally, the remainder of the parapet wall was built solid with bricks laid in a three-wide configuration as in the mass wall itself, below.

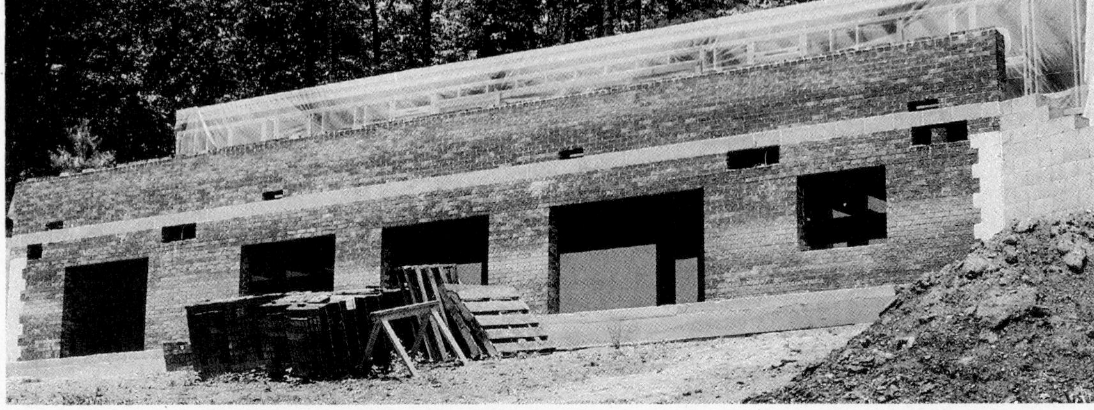

Roof sheathing for the rear section of the building provides both insulation and a finished ceiling, and it was easy to install. A continuous vapor barrier was installed to seal the second-floor wall, and the high-magnesium brick wall at the front of the lower floor's living area stores heat.

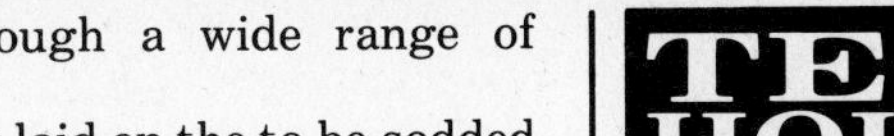

WATER-PROOFING AND ROOFING

The earth berming on three sides and the partial sod roof called for by the split-level design of My MOTHER's House presented the builders with two separate waterproofing challenges. The vertical bermed walls needed both to shed surface water and to resist hydrostatic pressure (including drainage from the hillside behind the building). The sod roof, on the other hand, while not subject to any great hydrostatic pressure, needed to be impervious to standing water left by rainfall on the nearly horizontal surface.

Consequently, two different kinds of waterproofing were used and, although either of the substances selected could conceivably have been used in both applications, each material's unique qualities made it particularly suitable to the separate task for which it was chosen.

RUBBER ON THE ROOF

Specialized elastomeric membranes have been used in conventional built-up roofing applications for quite some time, and several rubber manufacturers have elected to market the products for earth-shelter waterproofing applications . . . primarily in response to the burgeoning demand caused by new enthusiasm for the "underground" homes. On the recommendation of a manufacturer's representative, 0.060" EPDM material was chosen. It is resistant to degradation from ultraviolet light and remains flexible through a wide range of temperatures.

The rubber mat was laid on the to-be-sodded surface *and* sealed in a little more than one morning's time. The membrane was rolled out atop 1/2" particle-board sheathing, with protective patches of the rubber added at each junction of the 4' X 8' partical board panels to prevent the possibility of a corner's lifting and puncturing the EPDM. Two different adhesives are used when working with Carlisle's elastomeric membrane. One cement bonds the EPDM to itself (for use in situations where two sheets of the mat must be joined to span a wide roof), and the second glue sticks the rubber to other materials.

The EPDM waterproofing was not much more difficult to lay down than a living room carpet. The cut-to-length rolls can be relatively heavy . . . but once the burden is positioned, laying the mat is easy.

After it's spread in place, the membrane had to be squared up, smoothed, and thoroughly sealed—with rubber cement—along all of its edges. Next, the sheet was lapped up both the parapet and the second story wall of the building and cemented along both sides. Flashing was then applied to insure that a minimun of water would get to the seal. (The edge-securing process is particularly important, since a leak along the perimeter could allow water to migrate beneath the rubber and appear at some other point inside the house. Tracking down such a problem can be quite difficult.)

MUD ON THE WALLS

Though elastomeric membranes *can* be used on walls, the procedure required in such cases is considerably more difficult than is that used when working on a horizontal surface. The

The waterproofing membrane was not much more difficult to lay down than living room carpeting.

An elastomeric membrane provides waterproofing for the earth-covered roof. The material was rolled out on the sheathing, and its edges were sealed with rubber cement. Sheathing was placed over the membrane for insulation and protection and was then covered with rock, which helps provide drainage for the roof.

Bentonite clays tend to absorb a small amount of water and become impervious to further penetration by the liquid.

weight of the material makes rolling it up or down a wall a struggle, and the difficulty is increased by the need to prevent the rubber from being stretched (since it will eventually return to its original size). In addition, the sheets must be attached to the vertical surface as they're put up.

Of the several different materials considered for waterproofing the bermed walls, a trowel-on bentonite clay produced by Effective Building Products, Inc. was selected. As described by the Bentonize system patent holder, Dr. Bryan "Mac" McGroarty, bentonite is a clay mineral which was created—geologists speculate—as the result of a series of violent volcanic explosions that took place in the Aleutian Islands about 150,000,000 years ago. It is thought that winds carried the ash from the eruptions in a southeasterly direction, and that the material was eventually deposited in a highly alkaline sea which then existed in the Black Hills region of South Dakota and Wyoming.

Bentonite is valuable, in today's marketplace, primarily because of its remarkable reaction to water. An electrical charge, which is an inherent property of the platelike structure of sodium montmorillonite (the particular form of bentonite used to make Bentonize), is partially discharged to surround water . . . which causes the plates to separate slightly, producing a gelling of the material. Therefore, bentonite clays tend to *absorb* a small amount of water—which could cause the mineral to expand to as much as 22 times its normal size if it were unconfined—and then become nearly impervious to *further* penetration by the liquid.

The expansive clay is also quite stable. It can be wetted and dried an indefinite number of times (after all, who knows how many such cycles the material has gone through in the last 150 million years?) . . . is unaffected by sunlight . . . and can be frozen, heated to over 400°F, or even exposed to ionizing radiation without losing its useful properties.

The challenge that faced Dr. McGroarty—when he began to work with bentonite—was to develop agents that, when added to the mineral, would both help it stick to walls *and* keep it stable (that is, unexpanded without drying) for packaging and application. As a result of his research, Bentonize includes a patented mixture of organic resins (from soybeans, for example) and alcohol, which keeps it workable. The product is entirely nontoxic and requires a minimum of energy to produce.

The gray mud—which can also be purchased in a spray-on form—was scooped from five-gallon buckets and applied like stucco (with a hawk and trowel) to a depth of about 3/16″ (*small* imperfections can be overlooked, since the bentonite will expand to fill minor gaps). One bucket of Bentonize will cover about 60 square feet of wall, and will remain workable for approximately two hours after application.

Under Dr. McGroarty's supervision, the waterproofing was applied to the bermed walls of the house in less than a day. The clay had to be covered quickly with a protective layer of polyethylene before a thunderstorm blew in. (If Bentonize were exposed to water *before* the backfilling was done, the material would expand and slough off the wall.)

The following morning expanded polystyrene insulation was stuck to the "mud blanket" using dabs of fresh Bentonize as glue (the boards could have been applied directly to the waterproofing if backfilling could have been done immediately). Though the insulative panels *do* add to the thermal efficiency of the house, their

Bentonize was troweled onto the underground part of the walls, and polyethylene was added to protect the sealing compound. Sheets of insulation were stuck to the outside of the plastic, using gobs of the patented bentonite clay compound for adhesive.

primary function is to protect the Bentonize from being damaged by rocks in the fill earth. Still, *two* inches of polystyrene were applied instead of the standard inch in coating the upper six feet of the waterproofing . . . in order to reduce the loss of heat to the cool (in the winter) top layers of dirt.

The Bentonize clay was easy to apply, and the material's flexibility should allow it to seal any small cracks that may form in the block wall. Unlike many asphaltic preparations, its life span promises to be effectively unlimited. Furthermore, it may be that no other firm selling waterproofing materials actually *encourages* individual builders to do the work themselves.

HEAT EXCHANGE SYSTEM, BACKFILLING

With winter almost upon My MOTHER's House, the crew was hard at work getting the unfurnished structure ready to weather the coming storms. And beyond the innumerable seasonal details to be taken care of—which included installing insulation, sealing, shingling, and flashing, to name a few—one component had to be finished that really wouldn't be needed until the next summer. The pipes for the natural cooling system needed to be buried before the backfilling and grading were completed for the all-important feature of earth berming.

THE EARTH AS HEAT EXCHANGER

Since soil is far less willing to conduct heat than is air, the temperature of the earth below the frost line remains comparatively constant throughout the year. At 25 feet down there's essentially no change in the ground temperature . . . though at shallower depths the tempering effect is weaker. In general, however, the earth six feet or more below the surface will stay fairly close to the average *annual* air temperature for the area.

And, of course, that stability of ground temperature is the key to the energy efficiency of earth-sheltered homes. The soil surrounding such structures is likely to remain in the 50°F to low 60°F range so the buildings lose less warmth in the winter and gain less heat in the summer than they would if their walls were exposed to outside air, which in most areas drops well below 50°F.

However, earth sheltering doesn't eliminate the need to exchange a home's interior air at least once every two hours. (Such a change is required to maintain adequate oxygen in a house and to prevent the accumulation of carbon dioxide and toxins emitted by gas appliances, woodstoves, and the building materials themselves.) In a very well-insulated dwelling, the task of heating or cooling this "new" air to room temperature can account for a substantial portion of that building's thermal energy requirements.

In order to limit the difference between the temperature within a house and that of the exchange air that must be introduced, a few pioneers have been experimenting with arrangements of buried "breathing" tubes by means of which the natural heat sink of the ground tends to warm or cool the indrawn air

Earth sheltering doesn't eliminate the need to change a home's interior air at least once every two hours.

Drainage pipes from the base of the foundation share trenches with plastic irrigation pipes through which earth-tempered air can be drawn into the dwelling. The intake ends of the cool tubes are capped with screens and shields.

Little technical information is currently available on the use of passive ground-source heating and cooling systems.

almost to its own temperature. For the most part, such systems have been used to provide cooling, so they've been nicknamed "cool tubes". In truth, however—since, in cold weather, they bring in outside air that's already warmed above ambient temperature and doesn't require as much energy to be brought up to indoor comfort levels—they can contribute to efficient home heating, too.

Because the use of passive ground-source heating or cooling systems is so new, little technical information is currently available. So the crew's design decisions were based on a few rudimentary principles gathered mostly from folks who'd already tried similar setups. For example, the thermal conductivity of metal pipe isn't substantially better than that of the plastic variety . . . therefore, less expensive, durable irrigation-type PVC was chosen. Originally, the 12″ size was going to be used (though any diameter between 8″ and 18″ would have been acceptable), but eventually 15″ pipe was picked . . . simply because it was readily available.

To take advantage of the most stable ground temperatures possible, the pipes were buried as deep as was practical . . . a full ten feet. At the same time perforated plastic drain lines were run around the building's foundation with their outlets laid in the same trench as the cool tubes. The slope of the hillside made the task of draining all the pipes an easy one. Water that condenses in the tubes (the situation arises in summer, when the relative humidity of the warm air is increased to saturation by the cooling effect of the earth) runs downhill to drains located at the air entrances.

The available data suggest that cool tubes are effective for only about 60 feet in one run: After that distance, the temperature difference between ground and air—in a tube where air is flowing at an adequate rate—becomes too small for thorough heat transfer. Consequently, two 60′ lengths of the 15″ tubes were used . . . with one entering at the front of each end of the structure. A ducting channel in the slab then runs the length of the mass wall, to allow the cool (or warm) air to be distributed evenly. This trench also serves as the runway for the 2″ PVC kitchen sink drain.

Though blowers could be used to pull air through the tubes, convection does the job in My MOTHER's House. A row of vents built into the peak of the roof encourages air to flow up the pipes, through the house, and out the openings. Information from other folks who've tried it indicates that the natural flow of this "thermal chimney" should be more than enough to change the air in the house several times an hour if desired. During the winter, only a small amount of venting will be used, since the very frequent air changes that are so conducive to summertime comfort aren't needed when the chill is on.

Once all the pipe was laid in place and glued, and the trenches filled in, one group built and installed intake screens/covers for the tubes, while the rest of the team finished off the plumbing exits and began backfilling against the dwelling's walls.

The task of pouring the fill into the excavation had to be handled very slowly and carefully, to prevent the earth from dislodging the polystyrene insulation. Fill dirt was added to a level of about 1-1/2 feet below the edge of the roof on the back of the building. At that stage, a 6′-wide sheet of 4-mil polyethylene was laid along the entire length of the building, to prevent water draining off the roof from running directly down along the wall. The plastic was

Gravel covers the drainpipes that run along the base of the back wall. Fill dirt was added to a level a foot and a half below the back roof line and then covered with a sheet of polyethylene projecting six feet from the building. This was then topped with more earth.

secured beneath the shingles and flashing, and then the remainder of the fill was moved into place. No attempt was made to compact the earth as the filling progressed since doing so might have damaged or shifted the insulation.

Finally, before the first heavy frost, the roof was sodded, and some rye grass was started on the berms.

HYBRID SOLAR COLLECTION AND STORAGE SYSTEM

Though the earth-sheltered home relies primarily on passive solar gain, a passive/active heat distribution and storage system was also installed to allow visitors to examine this alternative. And the setup—though not strictly necessary for keeping the house warm—proved to be quite impressive.

NEAT AND ON THE ROCKS

Because of the extensive use of glazing on the south side of the house, two areas can—on sunny days—become warmer than is necessary: The sun-heated air tends to gather both in the greenhouse and at the peak of the second-story roof. Of course, the presence of 90°F-plus temperatures at those two locations doesn't pose a comfort problem for the structure's occupants (and it would be easy enough to vent the excess heat, anyway), but why let all that warmth go to waste?

Consequently, it was decided to set up a ducting system that could capture heat from both spots and either direct it to the floor area immediately or store it for future use. The accompanying flow pattern diagram should give you a good idea of how the air paths connect the different parts of the building.

During collection, warmth is pulled actively (by a 1/3-horsepower blower) from the greenhouse and from a triangular passageway that runs along the peak of the second-story ceiling. The air is routed through ductwork (it's made from fiberglass board) to an enclosed, rock-filled storage area located beneath the east-end bedroom floor. The box was built from plywood (with a supporting framework) and insulated with polystyrene board, then the bottom of the container was lined with 8" X 16" concrete blocks . . . placed on their sides and spaced about an inch apart. The crew handpicked a little over ten tons of approximately 3"-diameter washed river rock to fill the storage bed to a level about 6" below the top.

To give the rock bed the capability of handling both storage and heating, openings were cut at the top and bottom of the east and west ends, and plenums were built from fiberglass ductboard to encase each of the two pairs of openings. Each chamber has a valve inside which will join either its top or its bottom rock bed opening to the connecting ductwork.

With the system in its storage mode, air from the greenhouse is drawn through a passage that connects to the roof-peak duct where it joins

Why let all that warmth go to waste?

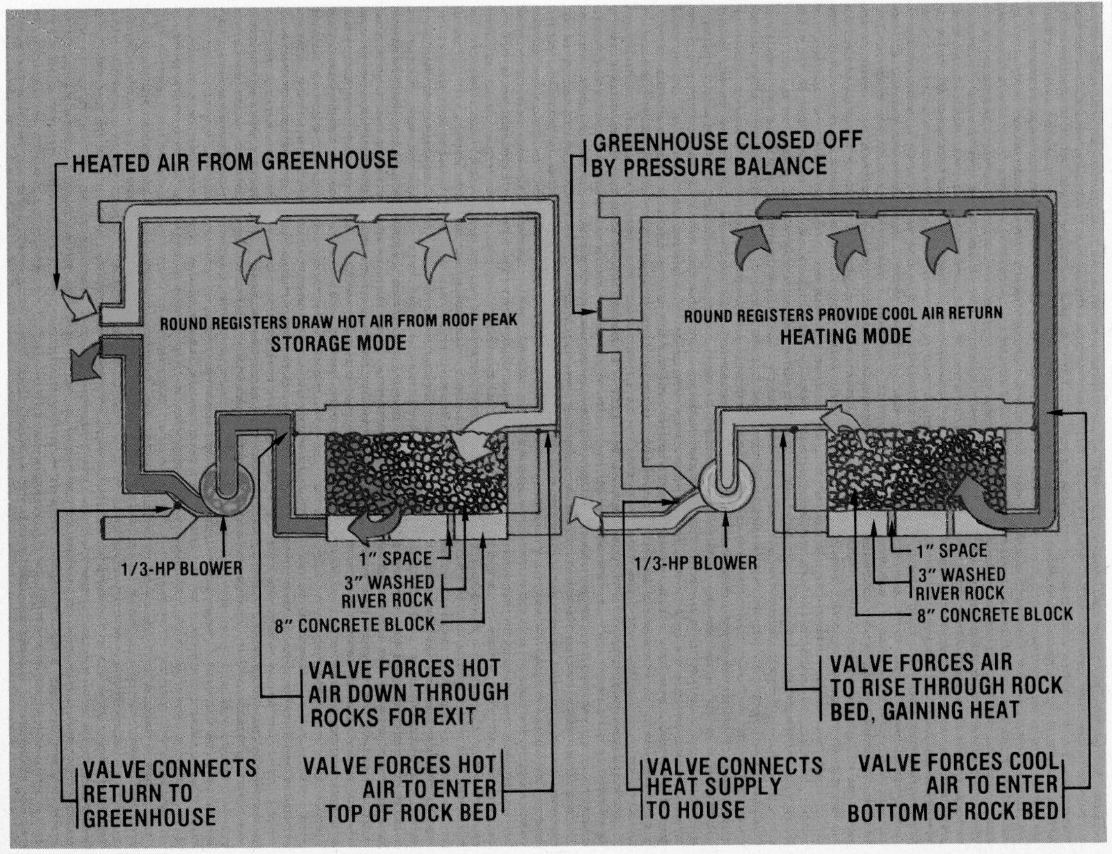

A few passive links were made between the greenhouse and the living area.

more solar-heated air that's pulled in through round registers set into the bottom of the nearly roof-length chamber. From there the combined masses of warm air drop down to the east end of the rock bed, and the valve in that plenum directs the warmth into the top of the storage. As it passes among the rocks, the heat is left in the cooler material, and the air exits by slipping between the blocks . . . through the cores . . . and then out of the box. The cycle is completed when air reaches the blower and is pushed through the return duct to the greenhouse to be heated again.

When the heat from the rock bed is needed in the home, the valve on the east end of the storage area forces air to enter the bottom of the box, while that on the west end makes it exit at the top. Meanwhile, yet another valve closes off the greenhouse return, thereby directing the warmth gathered from the rocks into the living area. Of course, the air that's entering the rock bed—in either the heating or the storage mode—comes from the roof-peak duct and helps to prevent warmth from stratifying near the ceiling. At the same time, the passage connecting the greenhouse to the roof-peak duct is still open . . . but, because the return air duct to the greenhouse is closed, pressure balance prevents the occurrence of any significant flow through that passageway. (Naturally, the various doors and windows in the greenhouse must be well sealed.) If you're familiar with conventional forced air systems, you've probably noticed that this arrangement seems to work backwards. That is, instead of drawing cool air through a short duct, heating it, and then pressurizing a ductwork labyrinth with a blower, air is sucked through the majority of the building's passage.

It was the team's intention to make the controls for the system as stone simple (if you'll excuse the expression) as possible, and they've managed to arrange for the whole setup to rely upon one manually operated control. Of course, there are several "air handlers" on the market that will do everything this arrangement does (and more) without the homeowner's lifting a finger . . . at some expense, however.

THE PASSIVE LINK

Hooking up the hybrid collection system involved making a few passive links from the greenhouse to the living area. These include a pair of ducts running from the west end of the greenhouse back to the west bedroom. One of the passages ends next to an intake for the roof-peak duct, while the other merely spills air directly into the room. Controlling the former register and the one in the roof-peak duct itself allows air to be drawn from the greenhouse for storage or central heating, or just to flow into the room naturally.

A pair of floor-level vents were set against the front wall of the guest bedroom/den to create a passive thermosiphoning link between the greenhouse and the living area. The system allows the heat to rise to the greenhouse roof . . . flow up the pair of ducts into the upstairs west bedroom . . . spill down the stairs into the living room . . . and return through floor level vents in the bedroom/den to the greenhouse.

It's a little too soon to be sure exactly how much solar boost the house will get from the system discussed here. Early calculations indicate that the rock bed should be able to store about 3,500 BTU for each 1°F that its temperature rises above that of the home's interior. Thus a 20°F increase in that storage area could provide a very useful amount of backup heat to this low-loss building.

On the other hand, if a home were to depend to any significant extent upon rock storage for its heat, the bed would obviously have to be quite a bit larger than is this display unit (30-ton setups aren't at all uncommon). Still, the success or failure of the system won't be determined until it is established how well the rock storage will actually warm the house.

Washed, handpicked river rocks provide thermal mass for the dwelling's active heating and cooling system, which can be switched from the heating to the storage mode and back with a single lever.

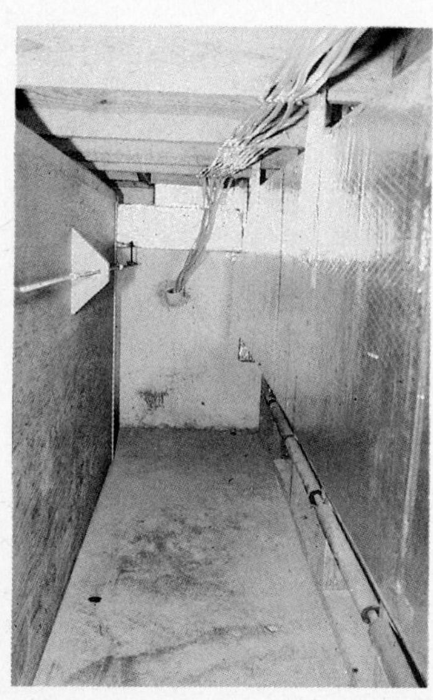

SOLAR WATER HEATER, SOLAR CHIMNEY

Of the many different systems used to heat water with the sun, only one kind of collector can claim a performance history of more than a century. The basic tank-in-a-box water-warmers first appeared in the 1870's with the introduction of the Climax Solar-Water Heater and have enjoyed varying levels of popularity since that time. Such devices go by a number of names—batch heater, breadbox, and integral passive solar water heater are a few of the popular terms—and there actually are some variations in their designs as well. However, these collectors all have one thing in common: real down-to-earth simplicity.

A typically configured batch heater consists of little more than a black-painted tank in a glazed, insulated box. The internal vessel serves as both absorber and storage container (thereby eliminating any need for the tubes, fins, and other paraphernalia common to flat-plate collectors), and water is moved through the system by either gravity or line pressure.

Today, most batch heaters feature reflective surfaces—on the inside of the box, surrounding the water container—which bounce sunlight back onto the tank for maximum efficiency.

BRINGING IT ALL BACK HOME

Practical problems got in the way when it came to designing a collector for the house. First of all, the plan was to mount the unit in one of the east-end windows of the earth shelter's greenhouse. The tempered glass could serve as the outer glazing, and the moderate environment inside the sunspace would keep the collector in service throughout the below-freezing winter months. Although the sections of greenhouse glass are 84" high, they are only 33" wide ... so the design was seriously restricted from the beginning.

Then, a search for off-the-shelf tanks introduced yet another problem. Because of the glazing width, a vessel larger than 12" in diameter could not be used without greatly compromising the device's reflective capability . . . but the only available 12" tank, a glass-lined unit used as a ballast in hydronic heating systems, was only 60" long. That meant, in effect, a sacrifice of almost 24" of available glazing height.

REFLECTIONS

The first part of the project involved creating an involuted reflecting surface. This curve can be formed by wrapping a string around the cylinder in question, tying a pencil to the end, and tracing the line formed as the string—held taut—is unwrapped. Because the curve's radius increases, and does so at a rate determined by the diameter of the cylinder, light rays that strike the involute tend to bounce in toward the cylinder. Two curves—one for each side of the tank—are needed.

As attractive as the involute shape is, though, it's no easy matter to form one from common materials. So, after a couple of unsuccessful attempts, a shortcut version of the

The basic tank-in-a-box waterwarmers first appeared in the 1870's.

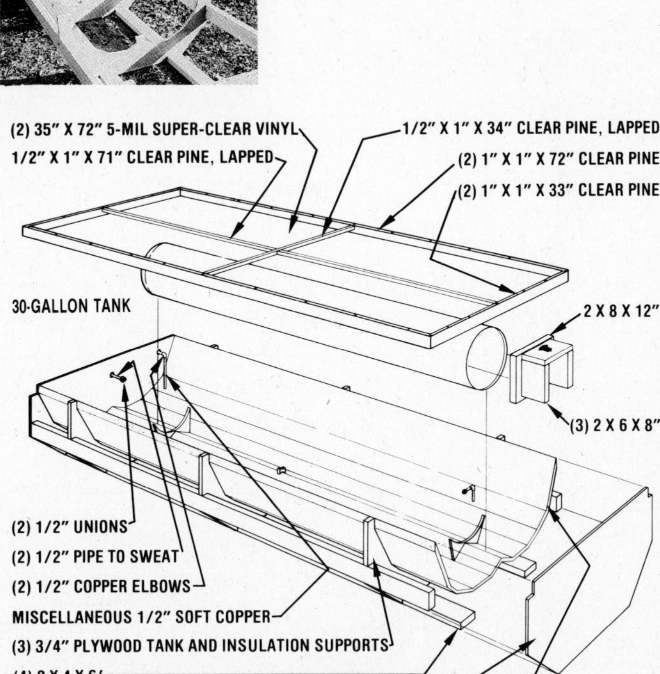

The tank of the solar water heater is surrounded by reflective insulating material mounted in a frame constructed of plywood and 2 X 4 stringers.

The involute curves of the reflector bounce light rays back in against the cylinder.

The water heater, with its own plastic covering, is mounted inside the easternmost window in the greenhouse.

curve was used. It involved using a series of flat surfaces to approximate cords of the involute.

In order to get the series of faces to reach the sides of the box, the cord arrangement was modified. The first surface was described by drawing a line out from the cusp (the point on the circle where the involutes begin) 3 inches to intersect a tangent to the circle at a right angle (this can best be accomplished with a carpenter's square). Then the line was extended another inch.

The next surface was formed by the same technique, proceeding from the end of the now 4″ first line (again, the new line must be perpendicular to a tangent at its 3-inch point). Two more 4″ segments were determined in a similar fashion, and the final 10-3/8″ reflector was also positioned by setting it perpendicular to a tangent intersecting it 3 inches from its starting point. The accompanying scale drawing can be used to prepare a template for cutting the reflector parts.

GETTING FRAMED

The frame for the batch heater consists of five plywood ribs tied together with 6-foot 2 X 4's. The three center sections, which carry most of the weight, are formed from 3/4″ plywood . . . while the two end pieces are cut from 5/8″ sheets. As you can see from the drawing, the ribs include extensions, which serve as support for the tank . . . and the lowest of the 3/4″ braces—also shored up with a frame of 2 X 6's—extends down to connect to the mounting system beneath the box.

Reflectors were cut from a single sheet of 3/4″ X 4′ X 8′ foil-faced polyisocyanurate foam insulation (marketed under the brand names Thermax and R-Max). Each of the two 4″-sections that start at the cusp must have one edge angled about 30° to fit up beneath the tank. The 10-3/8″ outer segments should also be trimmed off separately, but you can save some time in forming the three center reflectors for each side—and maintain the integrity of the inner sheet of foil—by slicing from the back to (but not through) the foil along lines 4″ in from each side of two 12″-wide sheets.

Because the tank didn't extend the full length of the 6-foot box, additional angled pieces of insulation were used to bounce light back onto the tank from the open end areas. (Depending on the dimensions of your unit, this step may not be necessary.) All the reflective sections were taped together with adhesive-backed aluminum duct wrap. At this point, the hot and cold lines were run out through the insulation (installing unions at the tank so that the vessel can be removed easily), and the holes were sealed up.

For glazing, 5-mil vinyl was mounted on a frame of 1″ pine by glueing and stapling panels of the plastic to the wood.

THE SUN AS EXHAUST FAN

The natural air conditioning arrangement in this earth-sheltered structure depends on cool air (chilled as it flows through 15″-diameter plastic pipes buried roughly 10 feet deep in the ground) being drawn into the house as heated air exits the building through a roof-peak vent and through a solar chimney.

The dwelling's thermal tower is connected to the roof-peak vent in the center of the second story and is fabricated from sheet metal, insulation, and fiberglass-reinforced glazing. The 48″-high, 72″-long box has one 10″-wide passage through which house air moves (it has just about twice the cross-sectional area of the cool tubes, to avoid impeding flow), and a sealed

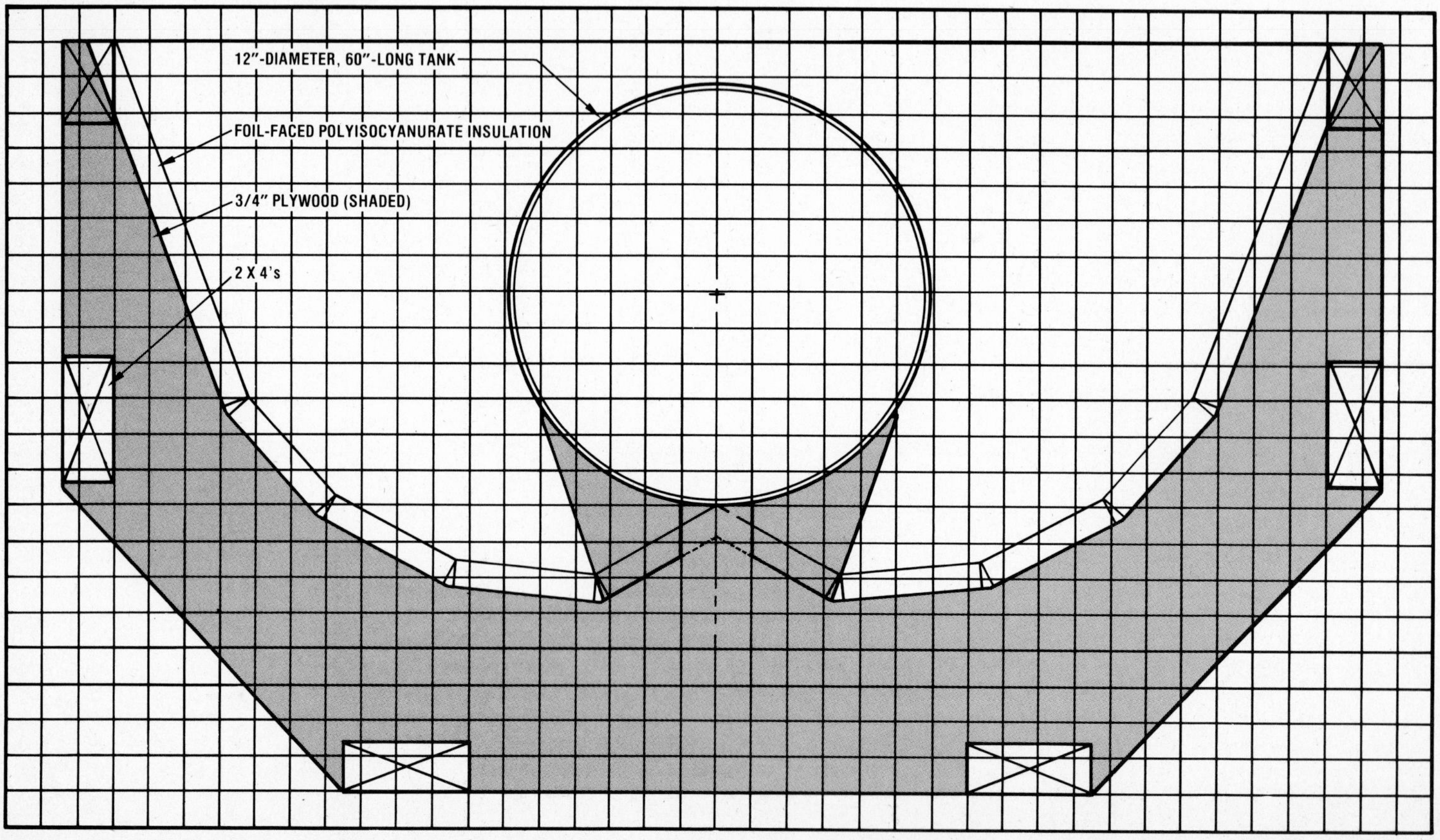

12″-DIAMETER, 60″-LONG TANK
FOIL-FACED POLYISOCYANURATE INSULATION
3/4″ PLYWOOD (SHADED)
2 X 4's

1-1/2″-deep solar collection chamber, the back of which is black-painted sheet metal. As this dark surface is heated by the sun, the air behind it is also warmed and rises, spilling from the top of the solar chimney and pulling more house air into the chamber. A ridge cap prevents rain from falling into the tower, and a hinged flap shuts off flow on demand.

RUSSIAN FIREPLACE

Auxiliary wood heat—largely because of its relatively low cost—is probably the most popular form of backup for energy-efficient buildings. Nowadays, most people choose steel- or iron-bodied stoves, since such heaters are widely recognized to be far more efficient than are conventional fireplaces. However, more and more individuals are discovering the attributes of the so-called *Russian* fireplace, which is even more efficient.

In Europe, massive masonry "stoves" have long been in general use. Historically, of course, the open hearth dates back to the Dark Ages, but even the comparatively advanced (by *today's* standards) Russian fireplace predates Ben Franklin's famous heater. At one time, the *grubka* (as it's called) was commonplace in rural Russian homes, and the concept actually arrived on our shores when a White Russian community formed in Richmond, Maine sometime around the turn of the century.

A massive masonry fireplace is quite different in concept from a modern "airtight" woodstove. The common metal heaters provide warmth over extended periods by working under predominantly *starved* combustion-air conditions. The Russian heater, on the other hand, has an unrestricted air supply and burns its charge of fuel rapidly. The high-temperature flue gases that are generated in the long, narrow firebox are then forced to wind their way through a series of baffles built into the brickwork above the firebox. In the process, a very large percentage of the heat is given up to the masonry. In a typical Russian fireplace, a load of fuel will be all but out after only three hours, but the warmth that's been absorbed by the bricks will continue to radiate for another *seven to nine hours*!

Obviously enough, it would be difficult to load up a 7,500-pound mass of bricks and move it into a laboratory for testing. Consequently, it isn't often easy to compare performance figures for Russian fireplaces with those for conventional heaters. The work that has been done, however, suggests that the very best masonry heaters may have efficiency ratings approaching 90% . . . exceeding even the best metal-bodied stoves.

But the list of the advantages of Russian fireplaces doesn't stop with improved efficiency (which, incidentally, could result in a saving of a third or more of the wood needed to warm the same area with a conventional woodstove). Masonry stove owners also encounter very little creosote accumulation, because of the high-temperature, efficient combustion typical of such units. Of course, a low-smoke fire does minimal damage to our atmosphere, as well, since free-breathing combustion yields less carbon monoxide and particulate matter than does the choked variety.

The warmth absorbed by the brick will continue to radiate for another seven to nine hours!

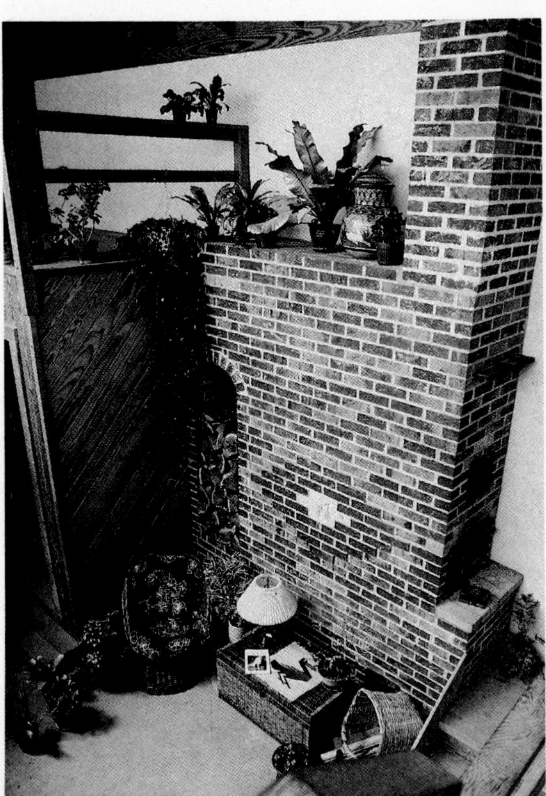

Backup heat for the building is provided by a Russian fireplace, which, because of its mass, keeps exuding warmth long after its fire has died. A firebrick-lined combustion chamber is surrounded by the red brick outside of the efficient heater.

The fireplace should be centrally located, and its hottest end should project into the living area where family members spend much of their time.

There are, however, a few restraints to consider before (and *while*) planning a massive masonry heater. The several-ton devices are obviously a bit more complicated to install than metal heaters, and they require a stout foundation to support their weight. In fact, Russian fireplaces are best used in new construction, where they can be planned into a building for proper orientation. The warmest part of such a stove's surface (where temperatures can reach more than 150°F) is the end farthest from the loading door. In turn, the fueling end is the coolest, while the two long sides tend to be about equal in warmth.

Consequently, the fireplace should be centrally located, and its hottest end should project into an area where family members spend much of their time. In some cases, it proves advantageous to position the loading end in another, less used, room. And it's even possible to extend the top of the heater through the floor into a second story. (Be aware, though, that the brick surfaces of Russian fireplaces do require adequate clearance from combustible objects.)

A quick glance at the accompanying photos will reveal that some of these orientation principles have been violated in building the grubka at My MOTHER's House. Because of the need to accommodate as many as 100 people at a time—during demonstrations—in the mainroom, it wasn't possible to place the heater where it would have been located had the house been planned as a residence.

After reviewing several interesting plan packages, the decision was made to use drawings by Basilio Lepuschenko . . . because of the designer's fine reputation *and* because of the simplicity of the brickwork, which is well within the abilities of many *non*masons.

The Lepuschenko masonry stove can have either three or five baffle passages which are oriented vertically above the firebox. The exhaust gases pass from the outlet end of the firebox and then travel through this masonry heat exchanger back to the loading end of the fireplace where they rise through a conventional 8" X 8" chimney.

Because of the proposed location of the firebox loading and chimney cleanout doors—which would be reached from the first landing of the staircase—and the fact that the brickwork could also provide *solar* heat storage if it were high enough along the wall, an extra-thick base was built for the fireplace. A passage was left below the firebox in the center of the rising courses of exterior brick so that ashes could be dumped down to a collection area below, and—at floor level—an 8"-square cleanout door permits ash removal.

The baffle section of the fireplace is some 13 courses high, and the passages are capped with the two halves of a split 17" X 17" flue tile. The brickwork in this area had to be carefully planned, but laying the courses wasn't difficult. Approximately 1,600 bricks were used for the fireplace and chimney, though Mr. Lepuschenko estimates that 1,000 should be sufficient for a shorter model, built with its firebox only a few courses above floor level. Naturally, the masons made a few alterations of their own to the design as they went . . . including the addition of a wood storage arch (which you'll see at the left of the main part of the fireplace) and the convenient shelf that extends before the loading door. You may also notice a little bit of fancy bricklaying on the front, into which a handmade tile (produced by one of the artisans at the Eco-Village craft shop) is set.

Hot air from the firebox travels through a baffle chamber covered with tile halves before exiting through the chimney located at the same end as the masonry heater's firebox, cleanout doors, and damper.

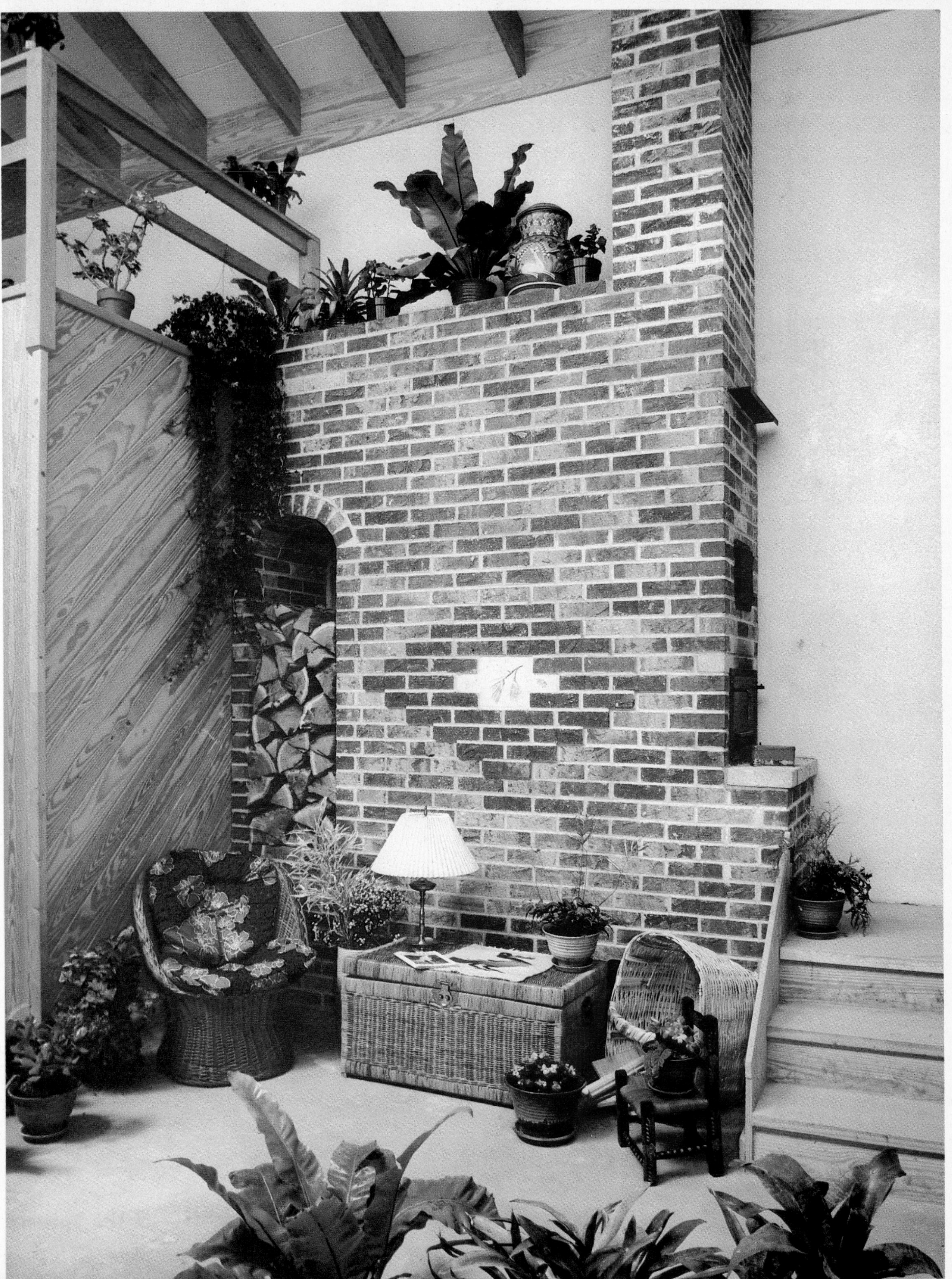

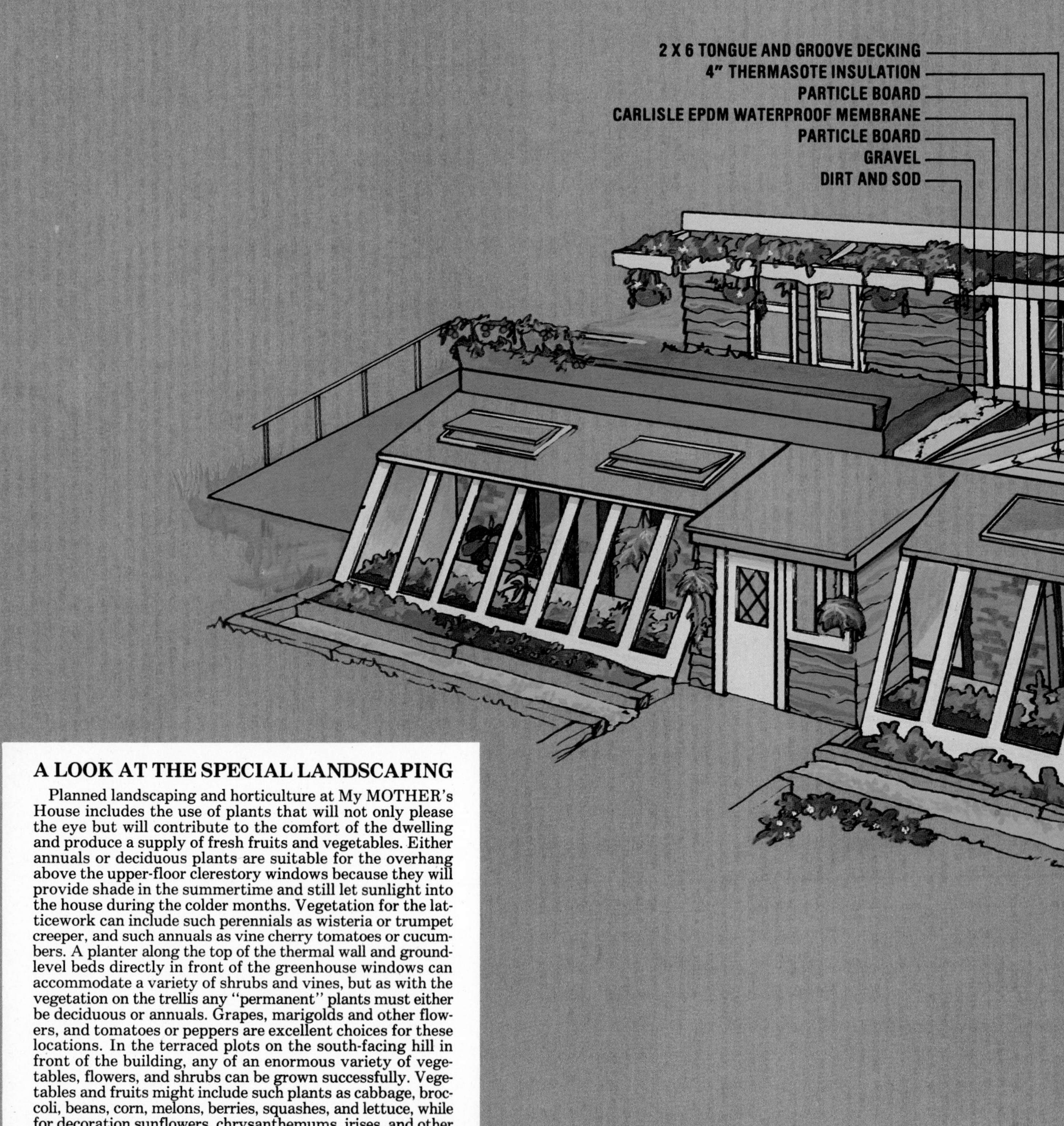

A LOOK AT THE SPECIAL LANDSCAPING

Planned landscaping and horticulture at My MOTHER's House includes the use of plants that will not only please the eye but will contribute to the comfort of the dwelling and produce a supply of fresh fruits and vegetables. Either annuals or deciduous plants are suitable for the overhang above the upper-floor clerestory windows because they will provide shade in the summertime and still let sunlight into the house during the colder months. Vegetation for the latticework can include such perennials as wisteria or trumpet creeper, and such annuals as vine cherry tomatoes or cucumbers. A planter along the top of the thermal wall and ground-level beds directly in front of the greenhouse windows can accommodate a variety of shrubs and vines, but as with the vegetation on the trellis any "permanent" plants must either be deciduous or annuals. Grapes, marigolds and other flowers, and tomatoes or peppers are excellent choices for these locations. In the terraced plots on the south-facing hill in front of the building, any of an enormous variety of vegetables, flowers, and shrubs can be grown successfully. Vegetables and fruits might include such plants as cabbage, broccoli, beans, corn, melons, berries, squashes, and lettuce, while for decoration sunflowers, chrysanthemums, irises, and other ornamentals might grace the landscape. Azaleas and rhododendrons provide some shade for the shorter plants. Almost everything growing around the structure received an early start in the greenhouse.

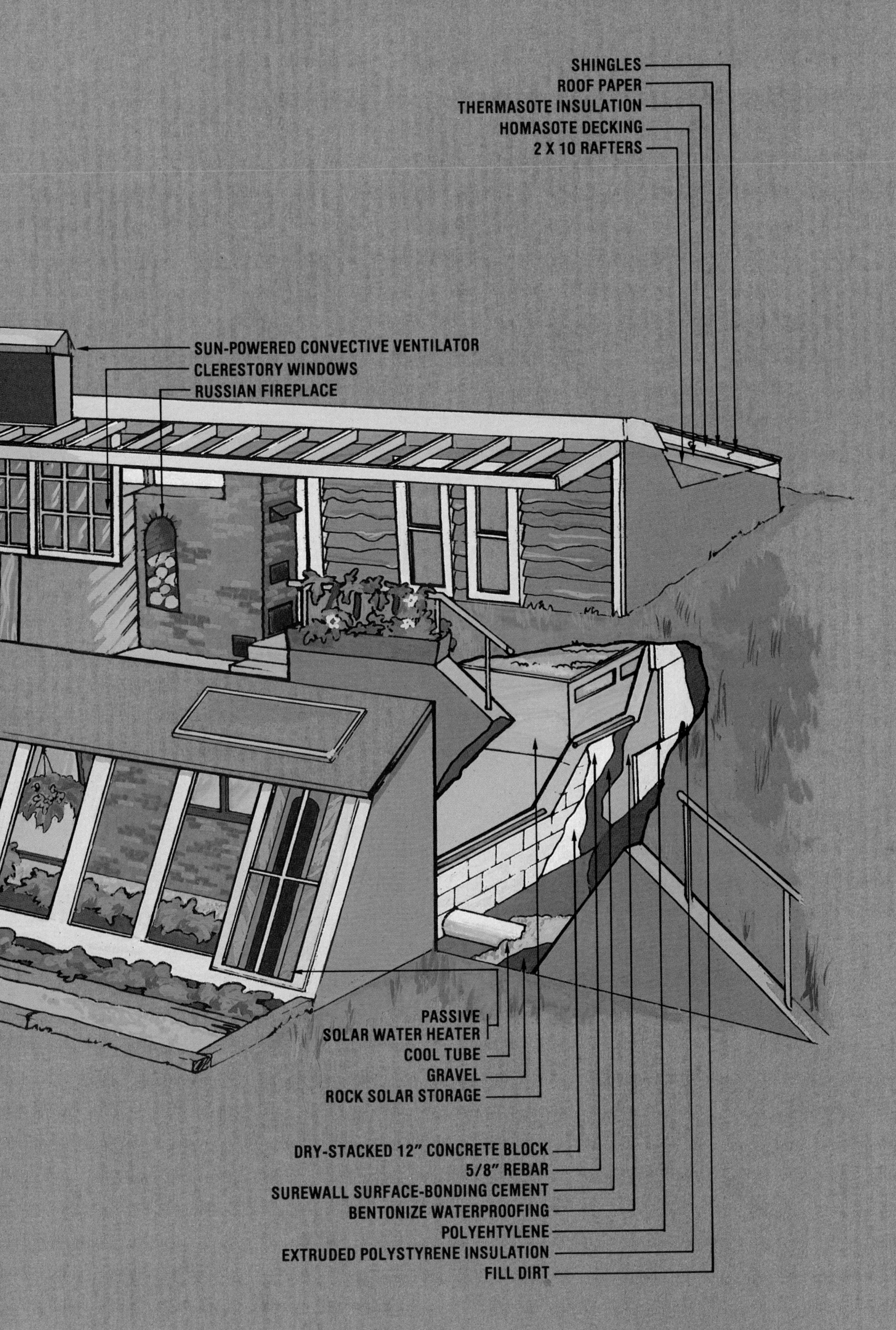
SHINGLES
ROOF PAPER
THERMASOTE INSULATION
HOMASOTE DECKING
2 X 10 RAFTERS
SUN-POWERED CONVECTIVE VENTILATOR
CLERESTORY WINDOWS
RUSSIAN FIREPLACE
PASSIVE
SOLAR WATER HEATER
COOL TUBE
GRAVEL
ROCK SOLAR STORAGE
DRY-STACKED 12" CONCRETE BLOCK
5/8" REBAR
SUREWALL SURFACE-BONDING CEMENT
BENTONIZE WATERPROOFING
POLYEHTYLENE
EXTRUDED POLYSTYRENE INSULATION
FILL DIRT

The building could have been built for considerably less money, but bear in mind that changes involve compromises.

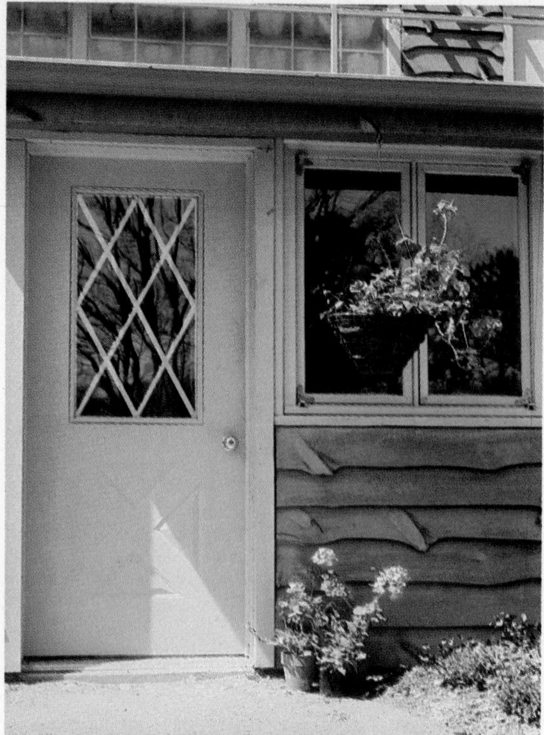

Passing through the front door of My MOTHER's House, one enters the greenhouse.

A CRITICAL LOOK AT MY MOTHER'S HOUSE

With My MOTHER's House pretty much finished, some of the people involved in designing and constructing the earth shelter got together to analyze the project. Here are some of the topics that were raised at that meeting, as well as a breakdown of a few of the costs involved in building that structure.

THE COSTS

The records show that a total of $48,855 was billed to the underground house project, and this amount included materials, contracted labor (such as painting, excavation, and the application of one waterproofing system), and tool rental. Items that have not been installed are cabinetry, finished floors, closets, bathroom fixtures, light fixtures, and appliances. It is estimated that it would take another $10,000 to $15,000 to complete the building as a residence.

Furthermore, by applying common ratios of materials-to-labor for construction, it follows that between $115,000 and $125,000 would have to be spent to have such a house built by a contractor . . . with no owner help whatsoever. The average person who decides to put up his or her own home, however, would likely find the price falling somewhere between the out-of-pocket expense and these figures. Consequently, the cost per square foot for a structure built to the exact (and purposely impractical) specifications of My MOTHER's House would amount to between $40 and $85.

Of course, the building *could* have been constructed for considerably less money. Bear in mind, however, that changes would involve compromises . . . *you'll* have to decide just what represents real economy to you.

THE WALLS

My MOTHER's House has very strong walls, built from dry-stacked, 12″ retaining-wall blocks that are surface-bonded and have their cores filled with concrete and rebar. Some preliminary calculations suggest that an 8″-thick poured and reinforced concrete wall might have been substantial enough. (Please remember that each building site requires specific stress computations based on the soil type and hydrology, and that an 8″-thick wall might not be strong enough for your shelter.) It cost $4,380 to build the back and side retaining walls for the house . . . but building forms from 3/4″ plywood and pouring an 8″-thick wall would have cost about $2,750. What's more, the plywood could have been reused for subflooring and/or roof sheathing.

On the other hand, the Surewall surface-bonding cement used on the block walls produced an interior surface that did not seem to require a further finish, which saved the cost of paint or other coating. In addition, the surface-bonding cement also helped in waterproofing the exterior wall. Finally, the 12″-thick wall provides half again as much thermal mass as would an 8″-thick one.

THE SLAB

A house such as this could be built *without* pouring a slab . . . as long as the footings are adequate to support the weight of the structure and to resist tilting at the rear wall. By going that route, 35 yards of concrete (at $42 per yard) and $100 worth of wire mesh reinforcement could have been saved. An alternative flooring would have been rammed earth with quarry tile, or something similar, atop it. The total thermal mass available for heat storage would have been comparable, though the labor involved in preparing the rammed earth would have been considerably greater.

ROOF DECKING

It was decided to experiment with a roofing system made by the Homasote Company. Including the sheathing material for the above-grade roof and the 3-1/2″-thick polyurethane insulation for both roof sections, it cost $5,300 to "top off" the building. Broken down on a cost-per-square-foot basis, that amounts to $2.50 for sheathing and insulation on the rear section and $1.75 for the sod roof insulation alone. The shingled area could instead have been sheathed with 1/2″ plywood and insulated to an equivalent value with rigid board for about $1.75 per square foot, and the sod roof could have been thermally protected for $1.50 per square foot.

There are two important trade-offs to be considered, however. First, the Homasote products are very easy to apply and thus can save a considerable amount of labor. This might be important for someone who's trying to build his or her own home and hold a job at the same time. Second, the Homasote roof decking has a finished material on its inner surface. It can be laid on top of the rafters, and no Sheetrock or other drywall is needed to produce an attractive ceiling.

ACTIVE SOLAR SYSTEM

As many different materials and techniques as possible were tried during the building (a procedure that certainly added to the cost), and the active solar system was included largely for demonstration purposes. It tied up $1,125 in materials for the rock storage bed and ducts and required a great deal of labor as well. The system performs nicely, but the fireplace actually provides more than enough backup heat for the passive solar elements in the building.

COOL TUBES

Although it seemed important to experiment with various ground-source heat exchangers to cool the residence, they were by no means inexpensive. All the 15″ pipe, backhoe work, and miscellaneous ducting and registers cost $3,600 . . . which would buy a pretty big air conditioner. Of course, the cool tubes cost nothing to run, but no one knows for *certain* at this time how they compare in performance with a conventional system.

WINDOWS

Though some people might question the investment in top-of-the-line Andersen insulated windows and doors, the roughly $5,000 shelled out for them should prove to have been a bargain as the years pass.

BACK WALL INSULATION

There's been an ongoing debate among staff members about whether the 1″-polystyrene insulation that extends from the footings up the back and side walls to six feet below grade (it's 2″ thick above that) is really necessary. The thermal merits are certainly open to discussion, but everyone does agree that the insulation eliminated the possibility of condensation on the interior of the walls . . . which might otherwise have been caused by a large temperature differential. In any event, the $350 cost of the material doesn't amount to a great expense.

EPDM WATERPROOFING

There doesn't seem to be anyone who worked on the house project who isn't wholeheartedly enthusiastic about the Effective Building Products bentonite clay used to waterproof the back and side walls. People who've checked the books have raised a question or two about the rubber membrane on the sod roof, however. The installed cost of the material (with a day's help from a local roofing company) ran $1,925 . . . or $2.14 per square foot. The Bentonize, on the other hand, cost 75¢ per square foot and the labor of four men for a day.

THE SOD ROOF

The final area in which some savings might have been made as a result of design modifications is the sod roof on the front half of the house. Now it's generally agreed that there's no great thermal advantage to putting 8″ of earth on the roof of the building, and—in fact—the front roof was just as heavily insulated as the rear one anyway! The main advantages of the earthen covering, then, are aesthetic, so if you're willing to forgo the blending roof line, etc., there are some savings available. Specifically, it cost about $1.25 more per square foot, or a total of $1,125, to have a sod roof rather than to make the two roofs match.

The main advantages of the sod roof are aesthetic.

The earth-covered roof, with a railing at the front, was seeded with grass and can also be used as a veranda.

In winter months the greenhouse footing casts a shadow over some of the areas.

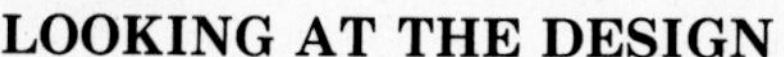

Wooden stairs beginning at either side of the Russian fireplace lead to the bedrooms. Plants and other decorative items around the fireplace give the house a touch of home.

LOOKING AT THE DESIGN

It was recognized early that the building couldn't be laid out as a residence . . . since lectures would be delivered there to groups of up to 100 people. The large open area that appears in the center of the floor plan is now occupied by 50 chairs, and when the downstairs bathroom is completed, it will have to be equipped with a ten-foot-long ramp to accommodate folks in wheelchairs. An alternative floor plan, one that might be more suitable for residential use, has been developed and is available.

The floor plan used imposed other limitations on the practicality of the house, too. For example, placing the upstairs floors 54 inches above the slab meant that the space below those floors couldn't be included in the calculated living area. Five hundred square feet of space was thereby lost and the cost per square foot was driven up by almost a third. Of course, that area beneath the floors *is* put to use . . . for the rock box where solar heat is stored and for general storage. But it does decrease usable living space.

THE GREENHOUSE

From its very inception the house project was at a disadvantage because of the need to work within the limitations of an already existing slab. For the most part, the 25′ X 60′ pad worked well for the house itself, but the greenhouse design was admittedly compromised by the foundation layout. The sunspace would be more convenient if it were at least two feet wider. As it is, the gardening area is limited and shoulder room is confined. Worse yet, the design of the footing casts shadows over some of the growing bed in the winter months.

One approach that has been suggested by workers involved in the project would be to extend the 4″ X 12″ beams that support the sod roof beyond the front wall so they could be used for the greenhouse roof as well. In that case, it might be desirable to mount the greenhouse glazing vertically . . . to limit summer heat gain and to widen the area inside the space.

THE RUSSIAN FIREPLACE

When the first report on the masonry backup heater for the earth shelter was written, there had been little chance to test the woodburner. After a winter's use, there was a problem.

After the first few powerful burns in the Russian fireplace, stress cracks developed on one side and over the loading door. Though no smoke has leaked into the room, and the heater has continued to perform very well indeed, the cracks *could* become a serious concern . . . if they widen. The big question, however, is why the unit cracked in the first place.

According to Albie Barden, who operates the Maine Wood Heat Company (which builds masonry heaters and sells plans and products related to them), there are several problems with the fireplace that could have produced the cracks. First, a portland cement was used rather than a clay mortar. The latter is far more flexible and is better able to stand the stress exerted during differential heating of the masonry materials. Second, the vertical first flue of the heater undergoes the most stress because flames lick up into it. Barden believes that some measures should have been taken to

As it now stands, the growing area of the greenhouse is limited, and shoulder space is confined.

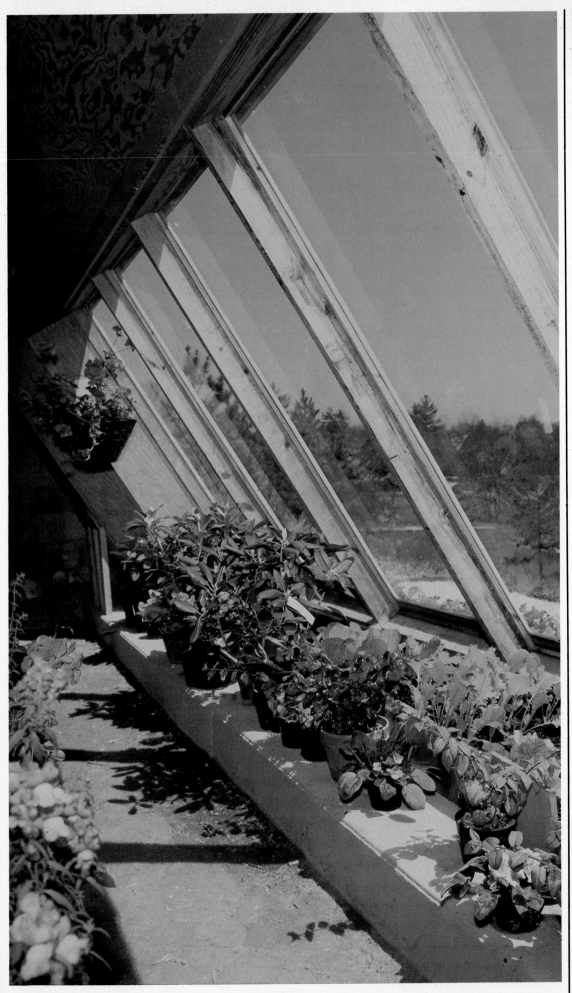

In addition to providing a year-round environment for plants, the solar greenhouse on the south face of the structure collects warmth that is then distributed by both active and passive means.

The construction and design process was fascinating and instructive to those involved in the project.

compensate for that . . . such as building double brick layers with air gaps, installing mineral wool insulation behind the firebrick, and/or increasing the passage's size. Since the side crack runs right along the first passage, overheating at that point would certainly seem to be the problem.

On the brighter side, the Russian fireplace performs beyond expectations. It fires very easily and radiates a strong, even heat for many hours after the fire has died away. There's been almost no creosote accumulation (actually, the material that does build up is more in the nature of soot), and the heater doesn't seem to consume much wood!

HARD-WON WISDOM

Some of the costs incurred could have been reduced by better planning and/or ordering. For example, 15,900 costly high-manganese exterior bricks were purchased when only 13,000 were used. That's an excess expenditure of about $350 . . . though the leftover material has been used on other projects. (The best theory of why the order was so far off is that the estimator failed to allow for the doors and windows in the front wall.)

Then about 3,000 of the bricks were wasted when the decision was made to shorten the knee wall at the front of the sod roof. The materials were ruined in knocking the wall down, and there was further expense in retopping the shorter wall and adding a safety railing.

Another approach that was taken that didn't cost much money, but can't be recommended in the long run, was the type of glazing used in the center section of the second-story windows. A double layer of fiberglass-reinforced plastic was installed on handmade frames. Unfortunately, repeated attempts to keep the plastic from buckling and to remove condensation have been unsuccessful. Fiberglass was chosen because it's inexpensive and translucent (which cuts down glare inside the house), but it might have been wiser to install translucent glass instead.

One structural aspect of the building has proved to be unsatisfactory, as well. The headers above the sliding glass doors in the brick wall are made from sections of angle iron welded back to back. For the standard-width doors, the 1/4" X 2" metal has been adequate . . . but over one exceptionally wide door, the angle iron has sagged somewhat as a result of the weight of the wall and roof above. This span is approximately eight feet, and it obviously would be advisable to use heavier material to form the header for this entrance.

In this house, the fact that the beams running lengthwise in the building aren't tied together (the section in the west stairwell was cut away to provide headroom) isn't a great concern . . . since the walls are plenty strong enough to stand up on their own. If the walls were slightly less substantial, however, the additional support of a continuous lengthwise beam might be desirable.

There was also a bit of concern that the main brick wall and the brick chimney would become thermal "wicks" and conduct heat to the outside. Consequently, a thermal break was formed in the front wall at the ceiling level by using block, filling the cores with vermiculite, and "doctoring" the mortar with insulation, as well. No simple solutions presented themselves for the chimney but—fortunately—the area there isn't too great. Still, both of these exposures undoubtedly do result in some heat loss, and it might have been better to design them so they wouldn't penetrate the building's shell.

Finally, though most of the interior of the house gets adequate daylight, natural illumination falls a bit short in the kitchen area. In retrospect, it's clear that the wall at the east end of the greenhouse should have a window in it.

The construction and design process of My MOTHER's House has been fascinating and instructive to those who were involved in the project. In the preceding paragraphs the attempt was made to lay bare their mistakes . . . for *your* benefit.

A detailed information package for My MOTHER's House is available for $15—plus $1 shipping and handling—from MOTHER's Plans, P.O. Box A, East Flat Rock, North Carolina 29826. It includes a 20-page booklet of building techniques and designs, drawings, and two different floor plans.

Clerestory double-glazed windows were installed in the wall above the sod roof and can be opened during warm weather to provide ventilation through the house. Steel plates tie the large framing timbers together and support the large roof beams.

SUPERINSULATED SOLAR HOUSES

In the cold northern regions—where the winter daylight hours are few—reliance on the sun alone for heating buildings is impractical, so reducing heat loss becomes far more important than the collection of solar energy in the design of energy-efficient dwellings. Superinsulated homes, dwellings that require less than 15% as much space heating as do conventional houses in the same area, have been developed in both Canada and the northern United States, and the results of the techniques applied by the energy-conscious designers have been measured and evaluated for several years now.

But superinsulation means a great deal more than merely jamming an abundance of insulative material into walls, floors, ceilings, cracks, and crevices. Heavy insulation, careful consideration of the size and placement of multi-glazed windows, attention to sealing the structure against the infiltration of cold air, and the inclusion of a mechanism to circulate fresh air are the basic design elements needed to create a superinsulated house.

CUTTING ENERGY USE IN CANADA

Dwellings in the Saskatoon Energy Showcase were not unconventional in appearance, and the use of superinsulation may prove a boon to people who live where solar energy is less than abundant.

Noteworthy indeed is a house that can endure between 10,000 and 11,000 heating degree-days per year while functioning well on wintertime heating bills of only a few dollars per month. But such is the record of not one, but 14, energy-efficient homes comprising the Saskatoon (Saskatchewan, Canada) Energy Showcase project. The secret of their success lies in superinsulated construction, the technology that Canadian builders have obviously found to give a lot of energy performance for the dollar.

The characteristics of a superinsulated house, according to William Shurcliff (who has written extensively and cogently on the subject), are [1] the dwelling is located in a cold (4,000 degree-days or more) climate, [2] it receives only a small amount of solar energy, and [3] it is so well insulated and airtight that it needs less than 15% as much space heating as that required by a conventional, comparably sized house built before 1974.

BUT FIRST, A LITTLE HISTORY

The construction techniques and approaches used by the builders participating in the Saskatoon superinsulated housing program resulted from research on the project's predecessor . . . the Saskatchewan Conservation House, which was the first Canadian low-energy dwelling.

This house—built in 1977 near Regina, Saskatchewan, under the aegis of the provincial government—was intended to use 10 to 15% of the energy required by a conventional home. It had large amounts of insulation, including an insulated foundation, double- and triple-glazed windows (some of which were equipped with mechanical shutters), and passive and active solar features. The project resulted in an airtight dwelling that required only 4.8 to 19 million BTU/year for heating. (By comparison, a typical house in the same area uses between 95 and 142 million BTU annually.)

From this model, researchers made two generalizations: It *is* possible to build an extremely low-energy house in a severe climate . . . and it is *not* cost-effective to employ an active solar heating system in far northern areas.

ON TO THE ENERGY SHOWCASE

It was time, then, to make a large-scale test of the knowledge gained from the Saskatchewan Conservation House . . . so an ambitious building program—slated to take place along one block in a Saskatoon development—was devised. In essence, the Energy Showcase would demonstrate whether superinsulation technology could feasibly be employed by established builders, and whether it could provide affordable, comfortable homes for moderate-income families.

The project started in 1980 as a cooperative venture of the governments of Canada and Saskatchewan, the Saskatoon branch of the Housing and Urban Development Association of Canada (which coordinated the participating builders), and the city of Saskatoon. Construction companies were invited to submit plans for low-energy houses for which there were two stipulations: The homes had to

The key is to build an airtight building where cold air can't seep in and heat can't leak out.

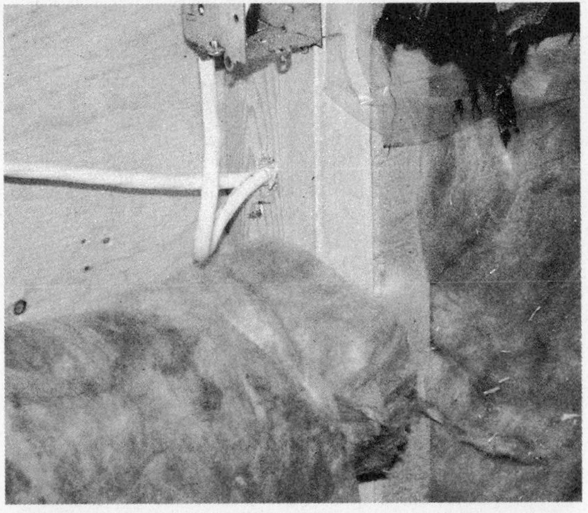

Heavy insulation and airtight vapor barriers characterize the Energy Showcase houses. Heat exchangers provide ventilation in the buildings, whose wall thickness is given away by the foot-wide windowsills.

have less than 2,150 square feet of heated space, and the plans couldn't differ significantly from the builders' conventional designs. Aside from these criteria, the contractors were given free rein in arranging the living area, employing heating technologies, and testing energy-saving features. Fourteen plans—to be built by 13 different companies—were chosen.

All of the homes were built on speculation . . . however, each builder received a grant that averaged about 7% of the home's total cost to compensate for the extra expenses incurred in designing and equipping a superinsulated house.

At the time they were built, the houses, which are now all privately owned, ranged in price from $65,000 to $120,000 (in 1980 Canadian dollars), with the average residence costing about $85,000. The average cost-per-square-foot came to between $40 and $45 Canadian, which was considered reasonable for a moderate-income family seeking low-energy housing in Saskatoon.

WHAT MAKES THEM WORK?

The term *superinsulation* means more than just a house crammed with fiberglass batts. The Energy Showcase homes do have more insulation than is customary, but unless that additional insulation is used in conjunction with certain building techniques, it won't insure a low-energy house.

The key—as Canadian researchers learned from the Saskatchewan Conservation House—is to build an airtight dwelling where cold external air can't seep in, and heat (from solar gain or intrinsic sources) can't leak out. In order to minimize air leakage/heat loss, the following methods must be used in combination:

- *Additional insulation.* In the Saskatoon program, these areas received extra insulation: the walls (to between R-30 and R-60) . . . the roof (up to R-60) . . . and the basement walls (from R-20 to R-30). Research now indicates that basement floors also should be insulated up to R-15 for concrete and up to R-30 for a floor above a crawl space.
- *A continuous air/vapor barrier.* This is a sheet of 6-mil polyethylene that literally shrouds the home's shell. The wrap is carefully overlapped at all breaks, and is joined with acoustical sealant (a pliable, single-component, butyl rubber).
- *An air-to-air heat exchanger.* All of the Energy Showcase homes are equipped with these simple blower-augmented machines, which are vital in airtight houses to induce air changes, remove odors and indoor pollutants, and prevent excess humidity. The devices also reclaim heat from exhausted air.
- *Attention to glazing.* The Energy Showcase homes typically have a window area equaling 5 to 10% of the total heated floor space, a proportion similar to that of other houses in Saskatoon. (This is not necessarily applicable in less severe climates where a home may have a window area equaling up to 20% of the floor space.) The designers tried to locate the majority of the windows toward the south to utilize solar gain, and they employed triple and/or quadruple glazing.

Typical superinsulated wall construction combines the heavy use of insulative materials with a thorough sealing of the building.

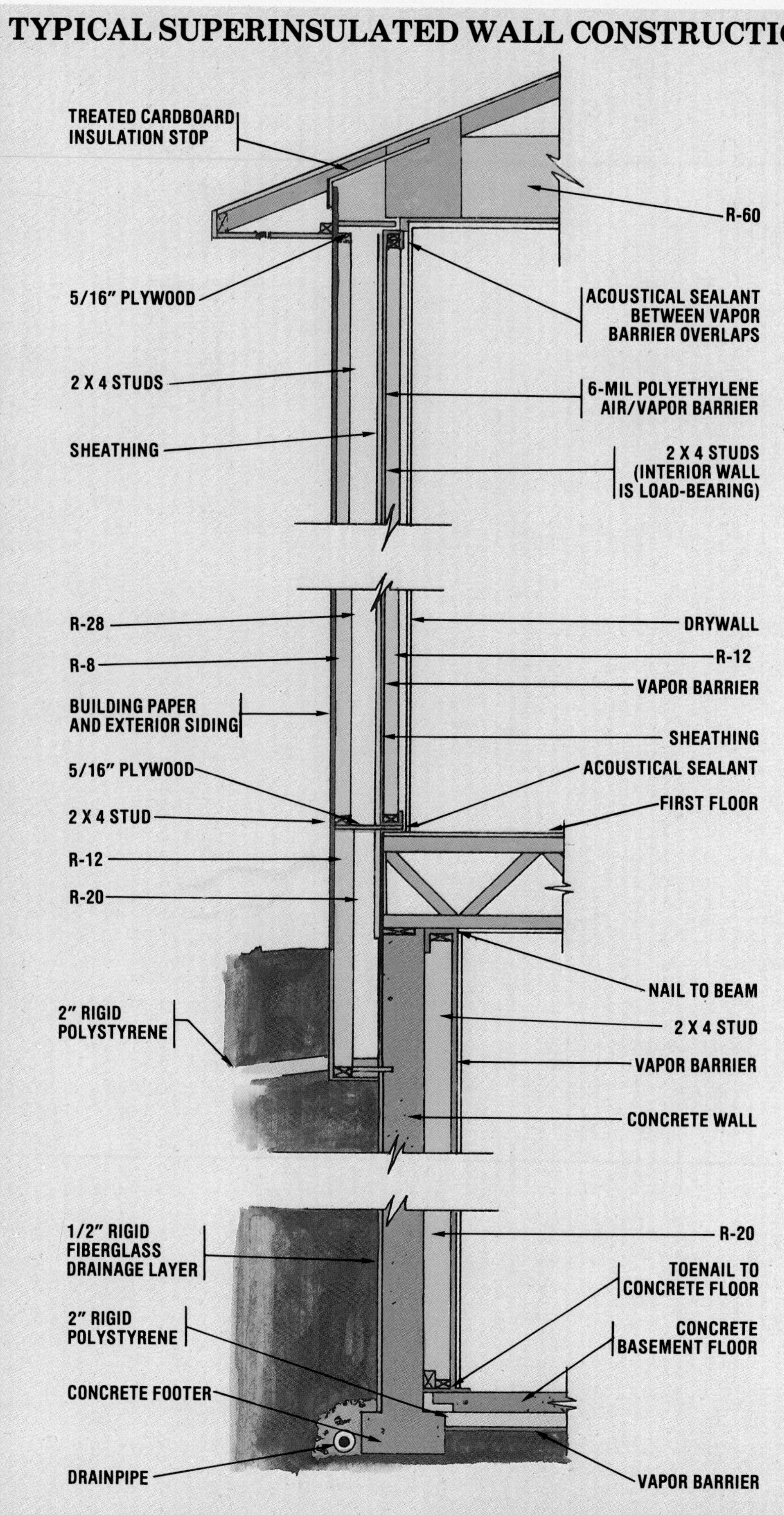

Because of their airtight design, the mass of the building materials, and the care exercised in siting, superinsulated houses require very little backup heat.

If all of these measures are taken (and if the quality of craftsmanship is high), the result is a dwelling of acceptable size that can be heated for only a few dollars a month in fuel.

The Energy Showcase homes also incorporate other energy-efficient features such as pairs of insulated, steel-encased exterior doors hung in the same jamb, airtight furnace rooms (the sealed compartments limit the infiltration of cold air used in furnace combustion), stack dampers, prewarming tanks (these receptacles, which are plumbed into the water heater, hold the cold incoming Saskatoon city water until it warms to room temperature), and air-lock entries. Some of the designers exhibited considerable ingenuity in reclaiming lost heat . . . in one home, the warm exhaust from the clothes dryer, along with that from the over-the-range hood, is filtered and then routed back into the residence.

Furthermore, some of the dwellings have passive solar features such as additional thermal mass, Trombe walls, mechanical shutters, and greenhouses. But the more heavily "solar" designs have not yet proved more efficient than the more conventional homes.

THE DOUBLE WALL

Most of the Energy Showcase builders elected to use double-wall construction for the exterior shell to achieve the high R-values they sought. In a nutshell, a double wall consists of the interior finish (drywall) . . . the interior framing (most often 2 X 4's, on 16" centers, since this wall is load-bearing) . . . a layer of insulation representing about one-third of the total sandwiched between the studs . . . the continuous air/vapor barrier . . . sheathing which lends rigidity to the vapor barrier, keeps it from bellying, prevents the insulation from shifting, and provides "racking" strength to the structure (5/16" plywood is frequently used for this layer) . . . one-third more of the insulation . . . a 2 X 4 exterior stud wall with the remaining one-third of the insulation placed between the studs . . . and the building paper and siding. Some builders preferred to construct the double wall as a unit, gusseting it top and bottom with plywood before lifting it into place.

The accompanying diagram—which depicts a cutaway of a typical double wall from roof to foundation—should make the foregoing explanation clearer . . . but there are a few construction details that may not be readily apparent in the drawing.

Builders of superinsulated homes go to great lengths to seal the vapor barrier at all possible points of air leakage. Many contractors purchase the polyethylene in 10'-wide rolls, a convenient size for wrapping eight-foot walls because it allows a workable overlap to join with the ceiling and the basement wall vapor barriers. Breaks in the wall wrap are joined by overlapping the polyethylene by two or three inches, running a generous bead of acoustical sealant between the two layers, and stapling the seam to a rigid backing.

The air/vapor barrier is applied directly to the ceiling, and this polyethylene is sealed to the top of the wall wrap (the drywall is installed after the ceiling wrap is secure). Recessed ceiling lights and interior entrances to the attic are avoided in order to insure the integrity of the vapor barrier. R-60 insulation is added above the ceiling through an exterior attic hatch.

Likewise, the vapor barrier lining the basement walls is carefully sealed to the bottom of the first floor's wrap . . . and the basement floors and walls are insulated. In some cases, Saskatoon builders used extruded polystyrene to insulate the foundation. (Since a superinsulated house does require an insulated, vapor-barrier-wrapped basement, there is a growing enthusiasm among Canadian builders for wood-framed basements. They've found that such basements are easier to insulate, less expensive to construct, and somewhat drier than those of concrete.)

One of the advantages of the double wall is that it permits most of the electrical, plumbing, and ducting work to be performed within the interior stud wall, so that the vapor barrier remains intact. When the wrap must be broken, though, workers try to seal the slits with polyethylene patches and acoustical sealant to avoid infiltration. (Some electricians use *polypans*—20-mil-thick plastic pans—that are placed behind the metal electrical boxes to minimize air leakage. The pliable containers can be sealed tightly with acoustical sealant and staples.)

Door and window jambs are framed in plywood and receive individual polyethylene wraps, which are secured to the walls to minimize air leakage.

Once the builders are certain that the exterior shell of the house has an air-tight vapor barrier, interior partitions are erected.

HEATING NEEDS

Because of their airtight design, the mass of the building materials used, and the care exercised in siting, superinsulated houses require very little backup heat (this is the main reason that the active solar heating systems have not proved cost-effective in such designs). Most of the Energy Showcase homes are equipped with gas furnaces, but the homeowners have found that even the smallest of these commercially built units—rated at around 50,000 BTU/hour—are too large.

In a home designed and owned by Al Treppel, a scaled-down version of the boiler/radiator/forced-air system used in high-rise office buildings heats the dwelling. Treppel fitted his domestic water heater with a radiator coil over which air can be circulated. When auxiliary heat is needed, a thermostat allows hot water to move into the coil and warm the air, which is blown through the ductwork of the house. Treppel's gas bills—for hot water *and* heat—average between $12 and $15 a month.

Arnie and Charlene Wudrick own a more conventionally heated home, where a 55,000-BTU/hour gas furnace heats more than 2,000 square feet. (One researcher has estimated that the Wudricks' ranch-style home actually needs a unit capable of delivering only 25,000 BTU/hour.) The Wudrick's gas bill for a ten-month heating season totaled about $80.

Despite their different heating methods, the Treppel and Wudrick residences produce energy performance figures comparable to the other houses in the Energy Showcase. During one

While miserly wintertime fuel consumption was of prime importance, designers were also concerned with comfortable warm-weather performance.

Special measures were taken around windows to minimize heat loss and infiltration. The houses in the Showcase were carefully monitored to measure their energy efficiency.

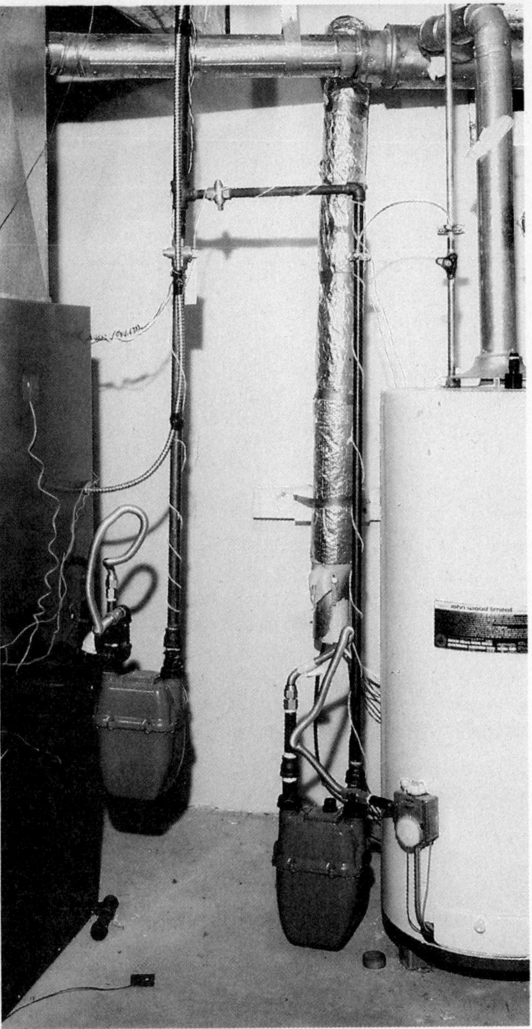

monitored ten-month period, the heating bills for the Saskatoon abodes ranged from $59 to $143 . . . or from $6 to $15 a month. In slightly different terms, the Energy Showcase homes required between 30.8 and 74.7 million BTU for one winter's space heating, or about 75% less fuel than houses that were previously considered to be energy-efficient. The design goal for the project was 17,500 BTU per square foot per year (BTU/sq. ft./yr.), and the Showcase homes ranged in their requirements from 13,000 BTU/sq. ft./yr. to 38,000 BTU/sq. ft./yr.

While miserly wintertime fuel consumption was of prime importance, designers were also concerned with comfortable warm-weather performance, since Saskatoon's daily maximum temperature average is above 70°F. Thus far, there have been no serious problems with overheating, and contractors believe they can correct the few hot spots that have cropped up with additional shading overhangs or the installation of shutters to limit solar gain.

IRREFUTABLE PROOF

The home's energy consumption figures were derived through extensive monitoring of all the houses during a period of 13 months by the Energy Research Group of the Department of Mechanical Engineering of the University of Saskatoon. Every 15 minutes, a computer recorded information on electricity and gas consumption, the temperature inside each house, and external weather conditions. Furthermore, Canada's National Research Council monitored one home that was left vacant for a year, conducting tests with simple electric space heaters and infiltration studies using tracer gas.

The Energy Showcase homes have also been pressure-tested for airtightness. Based on pressure-test results, the Treppel home, one of the better performers in the group, had an air leakage rate of only about 0.02 air changes per hour (with an air-to-air heat exchanger in operation, the structure's air change rate is about 0.25 air changes per hour). Conventional, poorly sealed houses have uncontrolled air change rates of between about 0.3 and approximately 1 per hour.

Additional tests have indicated that although the houses are airtight, there are no apparent health problems . . . probably because of the use of air-to-air heat exchangers.

LOWER FUEL BILLS AND HEIGHTENED EXPECTATIONS

All in all, the Energy Showcase project has had its effect, in a remarkably short period of time, on construction in the Saskatoon area. Since its opening month, when 45,000 persons toured the homes as part of a "superinsulation open house", hundreds of homes incorporating the technology have been built in the area . . . some with the assistance of interest-free loans extended by the province, and many by individuals and private construction companies. Essentially, the program has established new standards of construction for a cold-weather climate.

While it's likely that superinsulation's biggest selling point is demonstrably lower heating costs, there are several other factors furthering the technology's popularity. First, this is a flexible building method that can accommodate many different housing designs (the Showcase, for example, featured split levels, ranch-style homes, and bungalows).

Second, a superinsulated home is not as dependent on optimum solar siting as are typical active or passive sun-heated dwellings, and thus the construction method may prove to be a boon for folks forced to cope with less-than-favorable exposures.

Third, superinsulation is an unobtrusive technique. The foot-wide windowsills—which resemble bay windows from the interior—are about the only visible indications of the dwellings' unique wall construction and are viewed by buyers as an interesting feature.

The Energy Showcase has proved—among other things—that extremely energy-efficient houses can be built by established contractors and enjoyed by the average family.

Tests indicate that although the houses are airtight, there are no significant health problems.

Furnace rooms in the buildings—which rely little on solar energy gain—are airtight.

READY-TO-MOVE HOUSING

One of the most fascinating aspects of the burgeoning interest in superinsulated housing in Saskatoon has been its effect on established contractors. As the benefits of this particular energy-efficient technology have been demonstrated, building professionals have expanded their repertoire of construction techniques to accommodate the desires of fuel-conscious home buyers.

Perhaps the first to recognize and respond to this shift in consumer demands was D & D Construction, Ltd., a company based in Saskatoon, Saskatchewan. Back in late 1980, brothers Marcel and George Denis—owners of the firm—became sold on superinsulation and decided to concentrate on building low-energy homes.

However, the Denis brothers added a new twist to the enterprise: They switched the focus of their construction company from framed-on-site residences to "ready to move" (or RTM) housing. And so the first transportable superinsulated house was born.

The contractors offer 17 different models, ranging in size from 950 square feet to 1,600 square feet. Each home features double-wall construction, with the inside wall consisting of 2 X 4 studs 16 inches on center, R-12 friction-fit insulation, a 6-mil polyethylene continuous air/vapor barrier, 3/8" plywood sheeting, and a 4" insulation-filled space (with an R-value of 12) between the walls. The outside wall is framed in 2 X 4's on 16-inch centers and has R-12 friction-fit insulation, caulking in every joint to eliminate air leaks, and 3/8" plywood on the exterior, over which the customer's choice of siding is applied. These double exterior walls have a total insulation value of at least R-36, and the ceiling is insulated to a value of R-60.

Other energy-efficient details in the D & D homes are triple-glazed windows (with half-inch air spaces between the panes), insulated steel entry and storm doors, and air-to-air heat exchangers (currently, the company is installing vänEE models with an airflow rate of 200 cubic feet per minute), which are ducted out of each bathroom, the laundry room, and the kitchen.

As with the Saskatoon Energy Showcase homes, the D & D houses give little indication from the interior or exterior that they're energy-efficient. The deep windowsills—framed with solid mahogany jamb extensions—give about the only clue to the foot-thick walls. (Joe Meehan, sales representative for the firm, notes that the windowsills can actually be a selling point: "Most folks see the wide window ledge and say, 'What a nice place to put plants.' ") However, the superinsulation features become apparent when the homeowner starts receiving his or her fuel bills: The dwellings require about 75% less fuel to heat than residences of a comparable size without the energy-efficient construction.

The superinsulated RTM's are finding a ready market in the Saskatoon area, particularly among the region's farming community (one reason for this success might be that rural residents are the most vulnerable to power failures). The prices in late 1980 for the ready-to-live-in homes ranged from about $33,000 to a little less than $53,000 (in Canadian dollars) depending on the floor space. Meehan estimates that—in addition to the cost of a lot—approximately $12,000 is necessary to complete the house . . . for building the foundation and basement (most RTM's are fitted over wood-framed basements, insulated to a minimum of R-20), for connection of services, and for miscellaneous expenses.

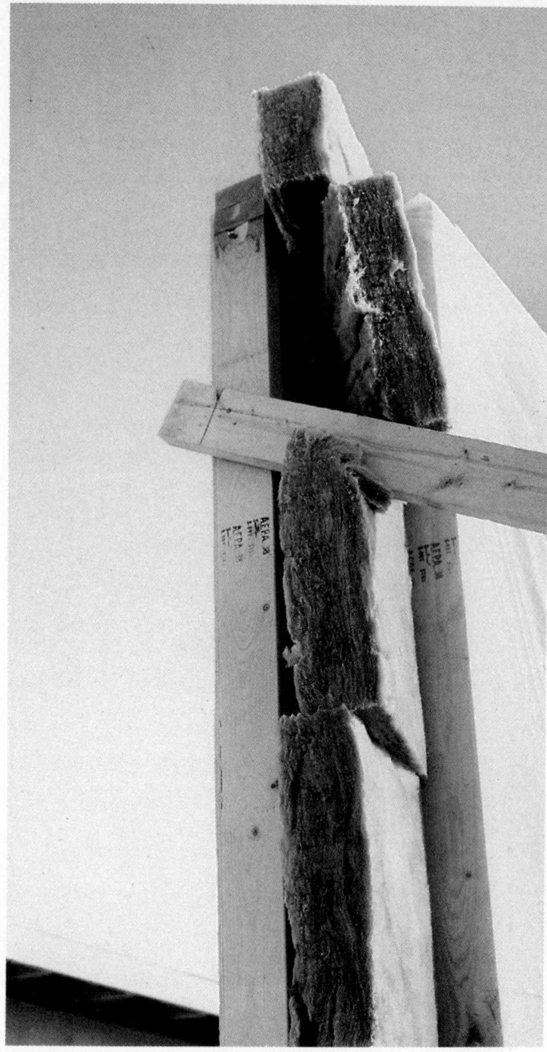

Double walls for these heavily insulated modular homes are constructed as individual units and raised into position.

Still, D & D homes are attractively priced, considering that the homeowner is getting a superinsluated house for less than the cost of a conventional RTM.

It's amazing that D & D has put superinsulation "on the road", especially given the conditions under which the houses are built. D & D's construction lot is located 15 miles east of Saskatoon on the tree-sparse Canadian prairie, and the only time the crew stops building is during the summer when the dust storms become too fierce. The accompanying photos were made in February when the temperature was a bone-numbing -25°F, and the workers kept briskly at their work, pausing only occasionally to warm their hands by space heaters.

The finished homes are 30 to 32 feet wide and may range up to 56 feet long. (The province of Saskatchewan, unlike many areas in the U.S., allows an object 32' X 56' to be moved along its highways.) While the company operates primarily within a 100-mile radius of Saskatoon, it has delivered homes to other parts of the province of Saskatchewan.

These superinsulated dwellings require about 75% less fuel to heat than comparably sized conventional dwellings.

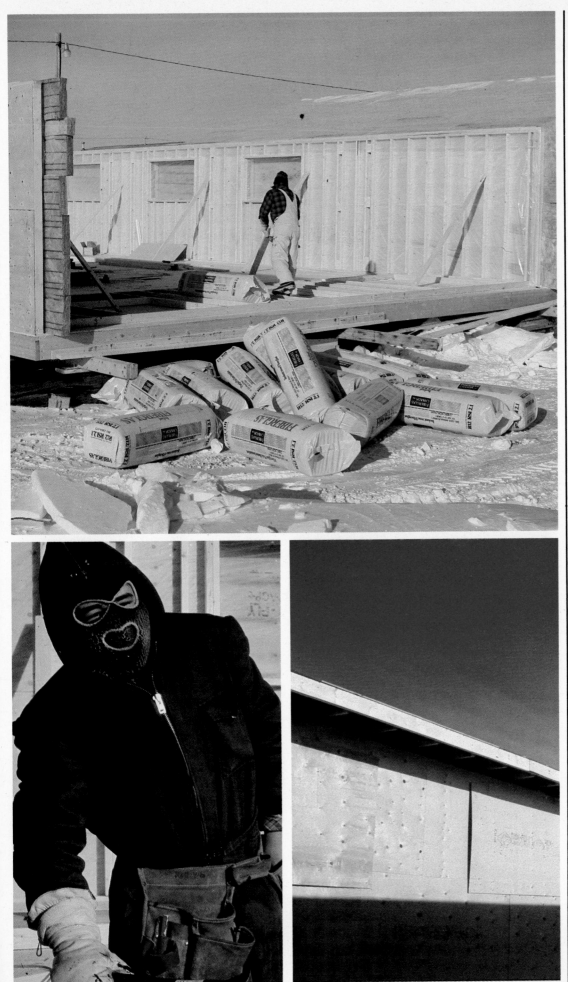

The intact vapor barrier can be seen lining the inside of the shell's walls. Workers must insulate themselves, as well as the dwellings they construct, against the cold.

INSULATE AGAINST THE NORTH'S CHILL

Though it's true that the Canadian province of Saskatchewan experiences winter temperatures more severe than those felt in the continental United States, the northern regions of the U.S. are still capable of sending a relentless chill all the way through even the warmest natured among us.

Take, for example, the state of Minnesota: The Minneapolis area (where −30°F is not unheard of) endures about 8,460 heating degree-days annually . . . only three-quarters of the total in the city of Saskatoon, yet nearly twice that of New York, and more than *five times* the norm in Houston.

Hence, it should come as no surprise that Gopher Staters have been studying superinsulation techniques closely for several years now . . . and have applied their knowledge to the construction of houses that are about as energy-efficient as those being built lately in Canada.

SEVERAL YEARS IN THE MAKING

One person familiar with the particulars of superinsulation is custom builder Dick Hand of Anoka, Minnesota.

His early examples were (by conventional standards) merely over-insulated homes built with 2 X 6 stud walls and deep ceilings to accept the additional "stuffing". But, after studying residential conservation techniques being used in Canada and Alaska, Dick strove to improve the R-value of his products even further . . . while paying more attention to important features like moisture control, air infiltration, glazing, *and* cost-effectiveness.

In an effort to document the energy efficiency of the Hand Construction, Inc. model home featured here (already carefully estimated by the Mid American Solar Energy Complex using detailed manual calculations and computer simulations), Dick arranged with the United Power Association to install microcomputer instrumentation throughout the structure. The study indicated that if a family of four were living in the house, they would consume only 2,401 kilowatt-hours of electricity for auxiliary heating from November through March.

PHOTOS BY DICK HAND AND THE MOTHER EARTH NEWS STAFF

A GOOD EXAMPLE OF THE GENRE

Though the definition of "superinsulation" varies from Massachusetts to Manitoba, the result-per-dollar-spent is the real bottom line . . . and this latest generation of "Hand-built" homes has earned a reputation in the field as being possibly the most energy-efficient in the lower 48 states.

Since 1974, the Minnesota builder has been utilizing essentially the same 2,088-square-foot, split-entry suburban design shown here, though his earlier structures used conventional framing and insulation. (Even prior to 1975, he opted for insulation specs 20% higher than those called for currently in that state's building code!)

So, by using the same floor plan and "beefing up" the structure where necessary to accommodate additional insulation, vapor barriers, and an air exchange system, Dick was able to accurately compare the energy and cost differentials between a super- and a normally insulated house of the same design.

ATTENTION TO DETAIL AND PLAIN COMMON SENSE

Obviously, the Hand house contrasts with other structures since it performs so well. But its differences lie in two areas: [1] The superinsulation features—after being carefully evaluated with regard to product performance and cost—were planned into the design rather than added on where they would fit. [2] The Minnesotan took the time to anticipate trouble spots and correct them to avoid throwing his building crews a "curve ball" on the job. This prudent premeditation saved time and tempers, and the consideration paid the workers shows up in the quality of the finished product.

On the surface, the house doesn't appear unlike the hundreds of other model homes across the country, but of course the differences lie behind the drywall and beneath the slab.

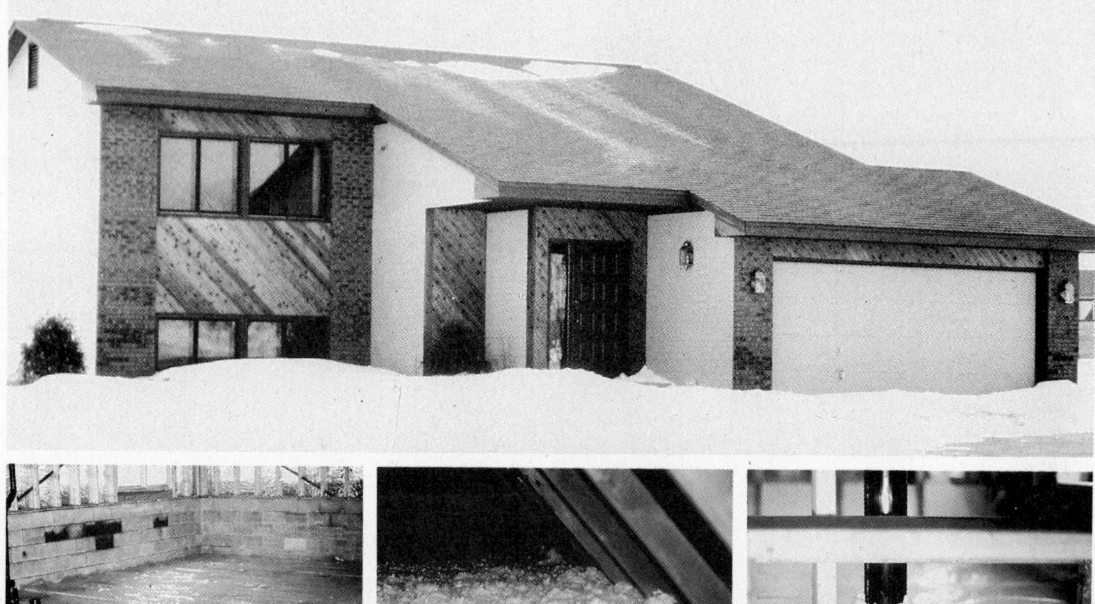

Seen in early March with snow piled all around, Dick Hand's split-entry model home required a minimum of energy to stay warm inside. Two inches of rigid insulation and a vapor barrier protected the slab, while cellulose attic fill prevented heat loss from above. Sealant foam was used to prevent infiltration.

Starting at the bottom, an 8" X 20" footing, topped with five layers of concrete block, forms the perimeter of the structure. The exterior surface of this below-grade wall is then waterproofed and insulated with 2 inches of polystyrene foam board. In much the same manner, the slab itself is isolated from the earth by 2 inches of rigid insulation under a 6-mil polyethylene vapor barrier.

The structure's upper walls are composed of two sections: the outer, load-bearing framework, which consists of 2 X 4's on 16" centers and, several inches inward, an inner skeleton of 2 X 4's that are 24 inches apart. Since the lower-level walls must support a greater load, 2 X 6's are used instead of 2 X 4's.

Beneath the siding on the exterior walls, Hand used 1" foil-faced rigid foam insulation (polyisocyanurate), then filled the hollow between the two stud walls with two layers of 6" unfaced fiberglass batts. A continuous 6-mil polyethylene vapor barrier surrounds the interior wall, and 5/8" industrial-grade interior drywall helps to hold that skin tightly in place. (In addition to the pains taken in insulating and wrapping the walls, all service entrances, gaps, and other potential leak areas are sealed with either 3M 480 tape or Polycel Two, an insulating sealant foam manufactured by Coplanar Corporation of Oakland, California.)

Naturally, the roof system had to be especially thought out to [1] accommodate extra insulation, [2] carry it to the walls, and [3] support its weight and that of the structure . . . so pre-engineered "energy" trusses were used. These hold nearly two feet of fiberglass batting, though some Hand houses have been built with 16 inches of cellulose fill in the attic instead. Air chutes as well as soffit and ridge vents allow the attic to "breathe".

The span joists which form the floor between the home's two levels aren't insulated within the interior, but they're set back on their 2 X 6 supports along the north and south walls, and a combination of rigid insulation at their exterior faces and batting at their interior ends guarantees thermal protection at that point.

The results are impressive: The slab has an R-10 insulation value, the below-grade wall about R-33 (since the concrete block makes up some of that bulwark, less insulation was used), the walls above grade R-46, and the roof between R-60 and R-70, depending upon the method of insulation used.

The windows were installed according to superinsulation Hoyle (maximize south-facing glass to gain winter heat, minimize glazing to the west to keep out summer heat, and try to keep the north-facing window area to 4% of the heated floor area), and the windows on the home's south face are triple-glazed to afford thermal protection while allowing insolation.

The north and west glazing, though, consists of two facing double-thick window units (one in each wall) . . . which not only insulate more efficiently than one triple-glazed casement but cost less and provide a buffer against outdoor noise.

SHORT PAYBACK AND LONG ENJOYMENT

Because the Hand house does not need a furnace (it requires less than four kilowatts of electric heat . . . about one-fourth that delivered by the smallest of oil burners), some expense could be spared . . . but a portion of that savings was used to install the air-to-air heat exchanger, since the structure is so tight it allows minimal infiltration. Likewise, the house *could* feature a fireplace, but the hearth's annual output of nine million BTU (per cord) would practically overheat the structure!

In terms of performance, the house sounds plenty good as it is. The builder, however, chose to go the whole nine yards by using insulated metal doors, a double entry, and an off-peak hot water system to save additional energy. While the house is more expensive to build than a conventional structure, the entire superinsulated package will give the homeowner an easy ride after only a 3.3-year payback period for the additional building cost.

The output of a fireplace would practically overheat the superinsulated structure.

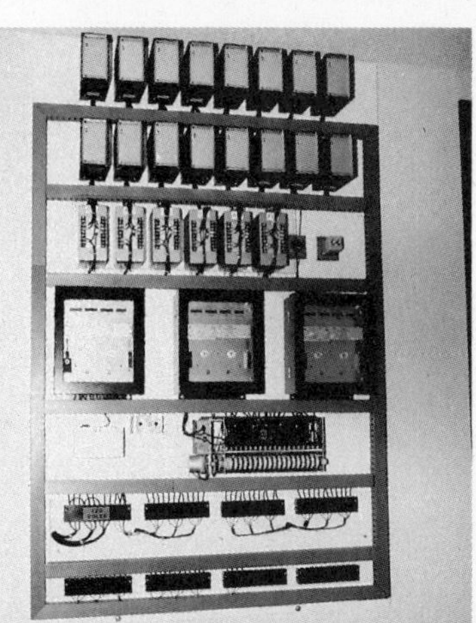

Microcomputers were used to monitor the house, which was entered through an air lock fitted with insulated metal doors. Twin windows buffer against cold and outside noise. Sealing around wires prevents air leaks, as does the critical vapor barrier that covers the extra insulation in the double walls.

THE LURE OF LOG HOUSING

In the New World, blessed as it was with an abundance of timber, it was logical that the earliest structures built by the European settlers would be log cabins. And those early colonists probably learned quickly that when the gaps between the great horizontal logs were properly chinked to keep out the wind, wooden walls did a fairly good job of keeping in the heat produced by a fireplace or a fire pit. (Timber serves as an effective insulative material because of its cellular structure: Each cell acts as its own tiny dead-air space.)

Today, people living in restored log cabins often find that the dwellings are easily kept snugly warm in the winter and refreshingly cool in the summer. But owning a log house doesn't necessarily involve finding a 150-year old structure to restore. An inexpensive cabin can be built from scratch by anyone with timbered land or access to enough large trees . . . and log houses can also be purchased in kit form. Furthermore, short firewood-length logs can be laid up with mortar to create walls by the stackwood method.

MASONRY AND WOOD COMBINE

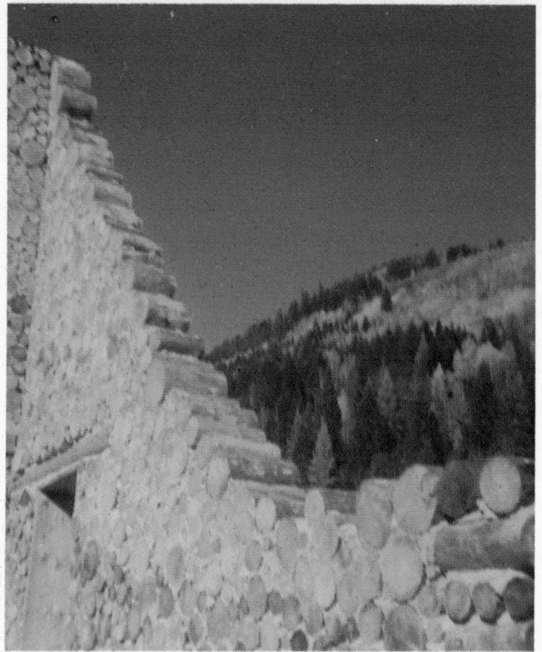

The domed roof over the cordwood walls gives a living room large enough to accommodate a homebuilt airplane. The walls are easily built without special tools and can be joined at the corners much like concrete blocks.

PHOTOS BY JENNY PRINGLE

Who'd ever think of trying to build a 2,500 square foot house for $10,000 . . . especially in the Canadian province of New Brunswick, where winter temperatures of -40°F are pretty common?

Well, a desperate man would, as was Jack Henstridge, when—in rapid succession—he was laid off his job, saw his house burn down, and listened to his VW's engine swallow a valve, turning its engine block into Swiss cheese.

NOW FOR THE GOOD NEWS

The Henstridge family had two resources to help them design and build a replacement for the home they'd lost. They received a settlement of $8,000 from their fire insurance claim (thanks to Jack's wife, Helen, who had remembered to pay the premium a month before the "big blaze"), and they had lots of free time.

Of course, whether they could buy food out of the $8,000 and still have enough cash left to finance the construction of something more substantial than a fancy two-seater outhouse was the big question . . . particularly in light of the fact that any new dwelling would have to stand up to the accumulations of snow that are typical of Oromocto, New Brunswick, winters.

Jack wondered if *anybody had ever built a low-cost house in that climate?* And then he answered his own question: "*Sure they did! The early settlers built log cabins!*" That inspiration gave Jack Henstridge his solution: He'd build a log home.

So he went to work to learn all he could about log construction by researching materials and methods and visiting restored log buildings. He took notes, made sketches, and—at the same time—began to cut the trees that he intended to use for his new home.

Jack noticed that many of the old log cabins he visited had long since lost their roofs. He also saw that some of the sill logs that touched the earth had begun to rot. So he resolved to build a strong roof over his log house by using a gambrel design *and* to keep the logs from touching the ground at any point by using a concrete slab foundation.

SHIP WITH WINGS

Jack's ambition was to create a modern dwelling while utilizing extremely old methods of construction. And he wanted the home to tell a story as well . . . to serve as a sort of live-aboard sculpture. Because of his lifelong fascination with sailing and aviation, his design resembles a ship with wings. The central living area has the floor plan of an ocean-going vessel . . . pointed in front—like the bow of a ship—while the rear features an observatory in the form of half a geodesic dome. To each side of the family's living space are winglike extensions containing the bedrooms, baths, kitchen, study and utility area. The "ship" section has a soaring gambrel roof, and each of the wings is covered with a sod roof.

THE LONG AND SHORT OF IT

The trees were felled one spring, and the 50- to 60-foot-long timbers were trimmed, peeled and racked by the following summer. In September of that year, however, Jack hit a big snag: The Canadian Army (on whose land the logs were stored) refused entry to the forest on the only day Jack had a truck large enough to do the hauling. To be sure of getting the logs out before winter set in, Jack had to cut the logs into shorter lengths so they could be trucked out later with a smaller vehicle, thus forcing him to abandon his plans for conventional log-cabin-type construction, and thanks to the Canadian Army, he conceived the idea to build a "stackwood wall" house..

True to its name, the stackwood method involves nothing more than laying up with mortar firewood-sized sections of logs perpendicular to the length of the wall. While any reasonable length of log will do, Jack opted for sections that were 9" long for the exterior walls, and 6" long for the interior partitions. His mortar consisted of a 20:5:3 mix of sand, hydrated lime, and portland cement.

The stackwood (alias firewood, cordwood, pilewood) wall is actually older than the regular notched log structure with which most people are familiar . . . even though many people think it's something new!

And it's a wonder more people haven't rediscovered this unusual building technique, since it offers significant advantages over ordinary log construction . . . such as:

[1] Building ease: Anybody who can handle a chain saw to cut an almost straight line can make his or her own building blocks. If he or she can stack the wood as the accompanying photos show, the construction of the wall is a snap!

[2] Low cost: Windfalls, "waste" cuts, and bowed or twisted timber—in short, almost *any* kind of dry wood—can be used to build a stackwood wall. The very best trees to harvest are those that have been killed—but not burned to ashes—by fire. They're already dry and virtually shrink-proof.

As for mortar, the Henstridges used only $1,000 worth of lime and cement in their house. Not bad, considering the home is 80 feet long!

[3] Soundproof design: The walls are so thick that the home's interior is unusually quiet . . . regardless of what's going on outside!

[4] Fire resistance: The mortar in the stackwood wall tends to absorb combustion heat . . . making it all but impossible for fire to spread. (Anyone who's had a house burn down, as Jack did, can really appreciate this feature!)

[5] No chinking: The mortar is largely self-healing. If a crack develops, lime leaches into the break and calcifies.

[6] No finishing: There's no need to paint or cover the surfaces inside or out. (And, when hanging things on the walls, one needs no stud-finder to know where to drive the nail!)

[7] Blends with nature: The finished appearance is aesthetically pleasing (as much—certainly—as is a stone wall, which it resembles from a distance) and blends easily into a natural background. (From 1,000 feet in the air, you would never see the Henstridge home unless you knew where to look for it as you flew over the area!)

It's rather difficult to build square corners using this method of construction, and the Henstridges elected not to try. They like the comfortable "feel" they get inside the house with its rounded corners. And, Jack points out that such curves lessen wind resistance and make the house warmer and more snug. (See the accompanying photographs for a stacking method that *does* produce square corners.)

The main drawback to stackwood wall construction may be the poor insulating properties of the large quantity of lime mortar required. Jack solved this problem by inserting hunks of polystyrene insulation between the mortar at the outer and inner wall faces. He had no trouble locating all the foam he could use in the town dump. (If you can't find enough of this material for free, wads of newspaper or chunks of foam rubber could be substituted. Furthermore, it might work almost as well to simply leave pockets of air in the walls.)

HOW DOES IT "LIVE"?

The Henstridges have lived in their "ship with wings" long enough to believe that they could hardly have chosen a home design that was more comfortable, attractive, and, certainly, *economical to build*.

Jack *does* feel, though, that if he'd had the time to wait, he would have let his logs dry for three summers instead of just one, because he found he needed to add a small amount of chinking to keep the home tight as the wood completed its final shrinking.

True to its name, the stackwood method involves nothing more than laying up firewood-sized sections of logs with mortar.

The split "firewood" can be laid to form interesting patterns.

LOG HOMES OF TODAY

The air of frontier authenticity evident in this log house can be seen in its dovetail joints and chinked walls.

When European settlers first came to the North American continent, their dwellings were, naturally, constructed of whatever materials were readily available ... in most cases, timber cut right from the forests and hewed to the desired dimensions. Of course, most of those early log cabins were primitive affairs, but they provided excellent shelter with a minimum of upkeep.

Through the years, building styles and materials have changed ... to the point where steel, concrete, and even glass are now used to construct dwellings that often don't resemble residences at all. However, the high price of goods and the rising cost of labor are rapidly turning these "modern" dream houses into nightmares ... and paving the way for a new period of log home popularity.

THEY'RE NOT JUST "CABINS" ANYMORE

To most folks, the idea of a log building conjures up visions of Daniel Boone and a drafty, ramshackle timber hut. In reality, though, twentieth century technology has improved on that concept ... and today's log dwellings not only are well-constructed, weathertight units, but also can be designed and furnished to rival even the most *palatial* of conventional houses.

Furthermore, contemporary log homes offer many advantages that more conventional structures (because of their design) simply cannot equal. For the most part, log buildings are sturdy, durable units that [1] require little, if any, attention after construction and final weatherproofing, [2] need a minimum of insulation—or none at all—to achieve sufficient thermal protection from the elements, and [3] can be built for a lower cost than can the "typical" home ... especially if the owner is willing to devote his or her share of time and labor to the project.

SCRATCH-BUILT ... OR FACTORY KITS?

Even though there are excellent factory-made log home kits available, many farmsteaders (and even suburban landowners) attempt to build their own timber dwellings from the ground up. And, although their intentions are good, these do-it-yourselfers are apt to run into three major obstacles right from the start:

[1] Even the homesteader who's fortunate enough to live on wooded acreage may not have *enough* raw material to complete a fair-sized dwelling. It takes at least ten dozen straight, disease-free logs (some over 30 feet in length) to build a large cabin. Furthermore, some tree species simply cannot be used in log home construction. (The most acceptable varieties are cedar, Douglas fir, yellow pine, poplar, and spruce.)

[2] To insure that the timbers to be used in a structure won't shrink with the passage of time (and subsequently throw the finished home "off level"), the logs must be stripped of bark and allowed to dry out thoroughly before construction. Not many novice homebuilders have the time, space, facilities, or patience to carry out this whole lengthy "aging" process successfully.

[3] A high degree of skill and a substantial amount of knowledge are required to successfully notch and fit the logs ... and to install windows, doors, floors, etc. in this type of construction.

Few would deny that a log home offers unparalleled natural beauty and charm.

So unless you're an "old pro" at building log houses, it's best to leave the preparatory work to the experts. After all, some log home firms have been in business for several decades, and during that time numerous technological advances have been made in the field.

In addition, such companies are equipped to select and prepare construction-grade logs, already have the facilities for curing green timber, and will go to great lengths to accommodate their customers . . . especially if there are any technical problems encountered during the actual building process. In fact, some manufacturers even go so far as to assemble the structures at their own location *prior* to shipping (to be sure all the components fit properly), then dismantle them and send the package on its way!

SOLID AS THE TREE IT'S BUILT FROM

The sheer sturdiness of a log home—when compared to the flimsiness of many stud-framed houses—is enough to boggle the mind. Whereas a conventional structure needs all four exterior walls *plus* some load-bearing interior partitions to support it, a log dwelling should be able to stand by itself—if need be—with one entire side removed!

This "Rock of Gibraltar" ruggedness is primarily due to the fact that—in most cases—each log in every exterior wall is a solid, one-piece section of timber, connected to its mates with sturdy joints at the corners of the house. The method of uniting these logs varies among manufacturers, of course, but generally the individual logs are "locked" together in some fashion . . . using either notches, "bolts" (these are actually long sections of threaded rod fastened into a concrete slab foundation), or standard dovetail or mortise-and-tenon wood joints.

By taking advantage of such solid connections, manufacturers can almost guarantee that a house is nearly as strong as the timbers themselves . . . and reports from around the country—including a U.S. government regional earthquake damage study—indicate that log structures are capable of withstanding an amazing amount of stress with only superficial damage.

BEAUTY ISN'T ONLY SKIN DEEP

Few would deny that a log home offers unparalleled natural beauty and charm . . . but many folks fail to realize how many practical advantages are inherent in these rustic-looking dwellings.

For one thing, the timbers themselves are efficient insulators. Although some manufacturers offer an optional "insulation package" with their houses, the fact is that—in a well-constructed log home (free from drafts, leaks, or cracks)—additional in-the-wall material is often not needed. Eight inches (or more!) of wood provide a lot of thermal protection.

As a further "plus", log dwellings can't be beat for durability . . . and their long-lasting qualities aren't limited to exterior surfaces. The inside of a house is also subject to the "hard knocks" of life (especially if the resident family includes children), and the ruggedness of a "pioneer" home is often a most welcome feature.

THE PATH OF LEAST RESISTANCE

By and large, factory kits are a practical shortcut for folks who want a log residence.

Considerably larger than average, this "cabin" features hand-peeled logs laid so no conventional chinking is needed. Virtually all manufacturers offer homes in a variety of floor sizes and with several floor plans.

Most of the aspects of construction can at least partially involve the owner/builder.

But don't let the manufacturer's list prices fool you . . . the kit price will by no means reflect the cost of the completed house. In fact, the companies themselves will be the first to admit that the finished log building can require two to four times the amount of money needed to purchase the basic kit. This discrepancy exists because the "prefabricated" kit prices don't include assembly expenses *or* the cost of installing plumbing, heating, electrical wiring, septic systems, and so forth. However, most of these jobs—especially the actual construction—can at least partially involve the owner/builder. In fact, that's the beauty of the whole kit concept: If the buyer is willing to donate his or her own time and effort, he or she can reduce the total cost of the log home by 40% or more!

Better yet, many manufacturers actually *encourage* owner participation . . . by offering detailed instructions with the kit and by promoting an "open door" policy regarding questions that may arise during construction.

The prospective buyer should know, too, that each log home manufacturer sells a different package. Some firms supply roofs and

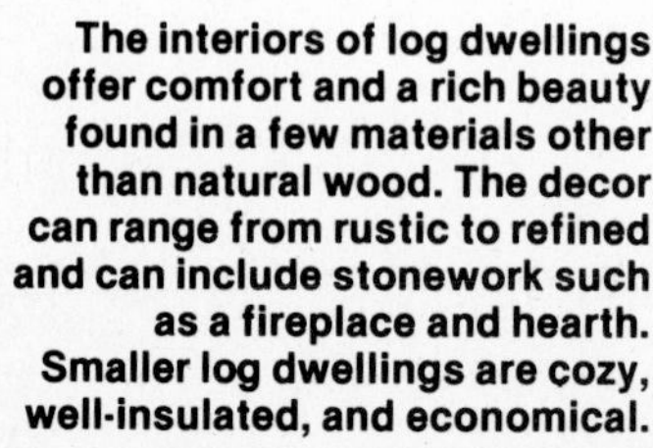

The interiors of log dwellings offer comfort and a rich beauty found in a few materials other than natural wood. The decor can range from rustic to refined and can include stonework such as a fireplace and hearth. Smaller log dwellings are cozy, well-insulated, and economical.

floor joists, others do not. Many offer options on these items . . . as well as a variety of structural and design features which can considerably alter the appearance of the original kits. So it would be worthwhile to look and ask questions before actually buying: It just might prevent a great deal of trouble later.

Financing and insurability are two other factors to consider when shopping for a log home. Fortunately, because of stringent codes within the industry—and the "success" of many log houses that have already been built —most financial institutions and insurance companies recognize the fact that timber structures are "good risks".

A contemporary log house kit might just be the happy medium—between buying a conventional home and constructing a dwelling from scratch—that many folks are looking for. In any event, it would be hard to find a type of residence that's more attractive than a "modern" timber structure . . . and there's no doubt that these substantial buildings provide far more quality—at comparable costs—than the "crackerbox" types of surburban homes that are all too common today.

Timber structures are "good risks".

LOG HOME MANUFACTURERS DIRECTORY

The following is a list of log home dealers and manufacturers active in the United States today. Although this directory is *not* all-inclusive, it represents a fair cross section of the industry. We've also included access information to the *Log Home Guide for Builders and Buyers*, a quarterly Canadian publication which should help the prospective buyer make an educated decision regarding the purchase of a log home.

AIR-LOCK LOG COMPANY
Box 2506
Las Vegas, New Mexico 87701
(505) 425-8888

ARKANSAS LOG HOMES, INC.
(Real Log Homes)
P.O. Box 959
Mena, Arkansas 71953
(501) 394-5824

BEAVER LOG HOMES
P.O. Box 1966
Grand Island, Nebraska 68802
(308) 381-0421

BELLAIRE LOG HOMES
Box 398
Bellaire, Michigan 49615
(616) 533-8633

BOYNE FALLS LOG HOMES, INC.
Boyne Falls, Michigan 49713
(616) 549-2421

BOYNE FALLS LOG HOMES
1554 Highway 93 North
Hamilton, Montana 59840
(406) 961-4421

CAROLINA LOG BUILDINGS, INC.
(Real Log Homes)
P.O. Box 368
Fletcher, North Carolina 28732
(704) 684-9867

CEDAR MARK HOME CORPORATION
2281 116th Avenue Northeast
Bellevue, Washington 98004
(206) 454-3966

DEEP SOUTH LOG HOMES
P.O. Box 286
Lookout Mountain, Tennessee 37350
(615) 821-1619

EUREKA LOG HOMES, INC.
Commercial Avenue
Industrial Park
Berryville, Arkansas 72616
(501) 423-3396

GREEN MOUNTAIN CABINS, INC.
Box 190
Chester, Vermont 05143
(802) 875-2163

GREEN RIVER TRADING COMPANY
P.O. Box 130
Boston Corners Road
Millerton, New York 12546
(518) 789-3311

HERITAGE LOG HOMES, INC.
P.O. Box 610
Gatlinburg, Tennessee 37738
(615) 436-9331

JUSTUS COMPANY, INC.
Box 98300
Tacoma, Washington 98499
(206) 582-3404

LINCOLN LOGS LTD.
Main Street
Box 135
Chestertown, New York 12817
(518) 494-2427

LODGE LOGS BY MacGREGOR
3200 Gowen Road
Boise, Idaho 83705
(208) 336-2450

LOK-N-LOGS, INC.
Route 80
RD 2, Box 212
Sherburne, New York 13460
(607) 674-4447

LUMBER ENTERPRISES, INC.
(Model Log)
75777 Gallatin Road
Bozeman, Montana 59715
(406) 763-4411

MAINE CEDAR LOG HOMES
Main Street
South Windham, Maine 04082
(207) 892-8561

NEW ENGLAND LOG HOMES, INC.
P.O. Box 5056
Hamden, Connecticut 06518
(203) 562-9981

NORTHEASTERN LOG HOMES, INC.
P.O. Box 46
Kenduskeag, Maine 04450
(207) 884-7000

NORTHEASTERN LOG HOMES, INC.
P.O. Box 126
Groton, Vermont 05046
(802) 584-3200

NORTHEASTERN LOG HOMES, INC.
P.O. Box 7966
Louisville, Kentucky 40207
(502) 228-0127

NORTHERN PRODUCTS LOG HOMES, INC.
Bomark Road
Bangor, Maine 04401
(207) 945-6413

PAN ABODE CEDAR HOMES
4350 Lake Washington Boulevard, North
Renton, Washington 98056
(206) 255-8260

PIONEER LOG HOMES
P.O. Box 267
Newport, New Hampshire 03773
(603) 863-1050

PROCTOR PIPER LOG HOMES, INC.
Peaceful Valley Road
Proctorsville, Vermont 05153
(802) 226-7224

R & L LOG BUILDING, INC.
P.O. Box 237
Mount Upton, New York 13809
(607) 764-8118

REAL LOG HOMES, INC.
(Real Log Homes)
P.O. Box 8509
Missoula, Montana 59807
(406) 721-1600

REAL LOG HOMES
National Information Center
P.O. Box 202
Hartland, Vermont 05048
Toll Free: (800) 451-4485

RUSTIC OF LINDBERGH LAKE
Condon, Montana 59826
(406) 754-2222

SIERRA LOG HOMES, INC.
(Real Log Homes)
P.O. Box 2083
Carson City, Nevada 89702
(702) 246-0590

SMOKEY MOUNTAIN LOG CABINS
P.O. Box 549
Maggie Valley, North Carolina 28751
(704) 926-0886

SUPERIOR LOG HOMES, INC
5253 Corey Road
Williamston, Michigan 48895
(517) 468-3344

TIMBER LOG HOMES, INC.
P.O. Box 300
Austin Drive
Marlborough, Connecticut 06447
(203) 295-9529

TRADITIONAL LOG HOMES, INC.
(Real Log Homes)
P.O. Box 250
State Road, North Carolina 28676
(919) 366-2596

VERMONT LOG BUILDINGS, INC.
(Real Log Homes)
R.R.1, Box 69
Hartland, Vermont 05048
(802) 436-2121

WARD CABIN COMPANY
Box 72
Houlton, Maine 04730
(207) 532-6531

WILDERNESS LOG HOMES
Route 2
Plymouth, Wisconsin 53073
(414) 893-8416

YELLOWSTONE LOG HOMES
Route 4, Box 2
Rigby, Idaho 83442
(208) 745-8110

THE LOG HOME GUIDE FOR BUILDERS AND BUYERS
Muir Publishing Company Ltd.
1 Pacific Avenue
Gardenvale, Quebec, Canada H9X 1B0
(514) 457-2045

$100 LOG CABIN

Built in two summers in Oregon's isolated Coast Range, the cabin was built using traditional hand tools and stands miles from any road or powerline. Functional handcrafted furniture graces the 10′ X 13′ interior of the structure.

PHOTOS BY BILL SULLIVAN

Living in a cozy little cabin nestled in the woods is part and parcel of the classic Thoreau-inspired lifestyle most folks dream of now and then. But the romantic vision of log-home life is shattered—for many people—by the sheer *cost* of such structures, which can be as high as that of equivalent conventional homes.

That doesn't have to be the case, however. Bill Sullivan and his wife, for example, kept down the cash outlay for their "Walden" in Oregon's coastal mountains by gathering most of the materials from the land where their house was to stand and then building the cabin themselves, using only handtools. As a result, their small home cost them only about $100 to construct . . . and the project was so simple that they believe *anyone* with access to a few basic implements and a good supply of timber could do the same thing.

FIRST STEPS

One of the ways in which the Sullivans kept the expenses down was to choose an uncomplicated design for their cabin. After researching several log house styles, they chose to build a home patterned after the Norwegian *stabbur*, which is a storehouse built on a raised foundation of pillars or stilts. A traditional *stabbur* also features extra-wide eaves, which repel rain and snow . . . small windows and a low door, which help reduce heat loss . . . and an upstairs loft, which serves to nearly *double* the available floor space.

The *size* of the cabin was limited more by the couple's stamina than by the design. They didn't want to have to deal with logs any longer than 16 feet (if they could avoid it), so the home measures 10′ X 13′ inside. Creative planning and the careful placement of doors could allow a much larger house to be built, but the Sullivans encourage first-time builders to start with an easily managed project.

With plans drawn up, the couple chose a cleared and level site with nearby water . . . pitched a couple of large tents for temporary shelter . . . and brought in enough food to sustain themselves during a summer of hard work. They also had the assistance of Bill's father—a volunteer for the duration of his vacation—whose first job was to build an outhouse. Bill himself began by marking the borders of the cabin's foundation with stakes and string. Next, he dug six holes, three on each side, to a depth of 2-1/2 feet, right at the wall line of the cabin . . . and hauled in 20 wheelbarrowfuls of large, flat rocks gathered on the property. Using four bags of mortar mix, he laid a sturdy cement-and-stone pier in each of the holes,

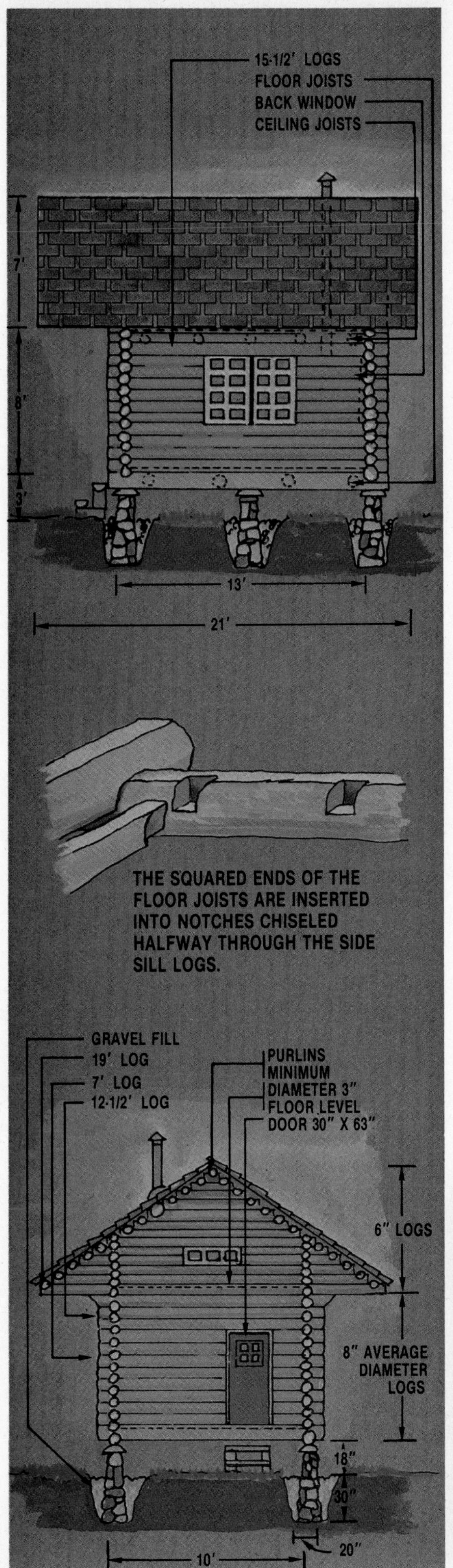

extending the supports to a level approximately 18 inches above ground. After the extra spaces in the openings were packed with gravel, the "stilts" were topped with large plates of sheet metal to keep termites and small rodents out of the cabin.

LOG FORAGING

Next on the agenda was the exciting—and often backbreaking—task of finding, cutting, and hauling in the logs that would soon become the walls of the home. (The trees were selected from a dense second-growth forest which needed thinning.) Most of the conifers earmarked for the dwelling measured seven to nine inches in diameter . . . and thus were too small to have commercial value. Working together, the couple felled each tree—using a five-foot crosscut saw—and removed the limbs. Then, with an axe or a hardwood barking spud (a two-foot-long stick with a wedge-shaped tip) they stripped the bark off each log. They found it was better to peel the logs immediately, because if the bark was left on the trunk for more than a few days, it adhered tenaciously, and had to be laboriously whittled away with a drawknife.

After the trunks were de-barked, they were cut into lengths and hauled out of the woods with the help of an old set of iron wheels pulled with ropes. (Fortunately, all the towing was downhill . . . otherwise, the couple would have needed a draft animal or a tractor to handle the chore.)

Collecting the sill logs (those that form the bottom layer on each wall of the cabin) required a special trip, since they had to be the largest of all. The builders chose trees that were at least 12 inches in diameter, so that the smaller logs *already* cut would have adequate support when used to form the upper portions of the walls. With the sill logs at the building site, Bill hewed a flat side on each piece, using an adze (a tool that looks like a sideways axe and is swung between the legs) . . . and checked the flatness of his cuts with a straight piece of standard lumber. Then the two side sills were lowered into place atop the stone pillar already constructed. Finally, he carved saddle notches into the undersides of the end sills and fitted them over the side timbers.

A FINE FLOOR

Once the sill logs were positioned, the couple decided to install the cabin's floor before com-

Trees were selected from a dense growth of forest that needed thinning.

The Norwegian "stabbur" design features a raised foundation, small windows, a low door, and wide eaves that repel rain and snow.

The couple found that raising the walls can be one of the least arduous parts of the cabin construction process.

Not far from the cabin's entrance is the woodshed, which protects the Sullivans' supply of heat. Both the house and the outbuilding are tucked into the side of a wooded hill.

pleting its walls. Bill first hewed flat four eight-inch-diameter joist logs, squared their ends with an axe, and notched them into slots chiseled halfway through the side sill logs at equal intervals along the length of the wall. (Of course, if you use dimension lumber for your floor joists, a flatter floor could be built more rapidly . . . but such boards lack the character of—*and* are more expensive than—logs.) He set the joists into notches carved *inside* the wall line, so they would be in less danger of rotting and would allow the first wall log to fit in place more easily.

Then, for the sake of simplicity, the floor was planked with 2 X 8 lumber salvaged from a demolished farmhouse. Though that underfooting served well for several seasons, the couple later completed the floor with a tar paper layer and handsome planks of 1 X 10 fir, laid at right angles to the recycled lumber (that is, *parallel* to the crosswise joists).

RAISING THE WALLS

After the cabin had a sturdy foundation and flooring, its builders tackled the job of notching and piling logs to form the walls. Now, many folks would likely pale at the very thought of lifting heavy timbers into place . . . but, surprisingly, the couple found that raising the walls can be one of the *least* arduous parts of the whole cabin construction process. First, they had to arrange the logs—by size—in the sequence in which they'd be used, keeping in mind that the large and small ends would alternate. They then cut notches near the ends of each length so each "saddle" would fit over its "neighbors". (It's a darn good idea, at this point, to label the logs somehow so you'll remember in what order to pile them on the wall.) Bill used one-side saddle notches, since the fancier dovetail and Lincoln-log notches—which are carved out on the top *and* bottom of each log—tend to collect rainwater in the upper half . . . and can even rot out in extremely wet areas (such as his location in western Oregon).

To make a saddle notch, he simply set a log on top of the timbers it would eventually rest upon and marked a semicircle, halfway through it, that *exactly* matched the dimensions of the supporting logs. Then he rolled the top log over and cleanly chopped out the notched area as marked. (If the pole didn't fit just right when he rolled it back into place, he'd continue trimming until it *did.*)

With the logs all carefully tagged and notched, the Sullivans devised a ramp—by leaning several poles against the top of the wall—and placed each timber in turn at the bottom of that incline parallel to the wall. Then a rope was tied to each end of the top of the wall, looped under the log on the ground, and brought back up to the top. Using this simple

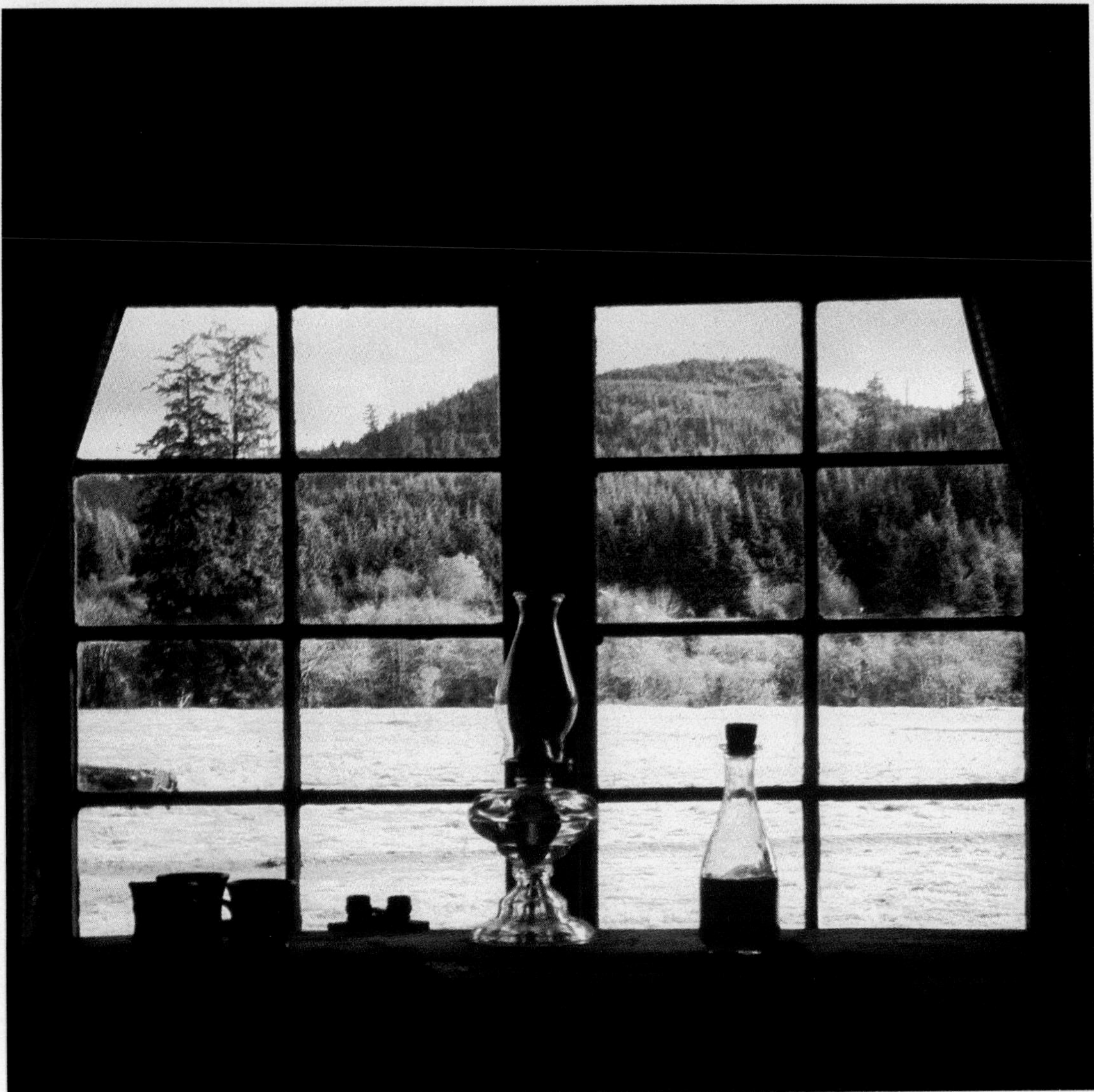

After the cracks had been chinked with cement, the cabin became comfortable and weathertight.

arrangement, the two people—pulling in tandem from the opposite side of the wall—could easily raise a heavy log and lever it into place on top.

THE SECOND STORY

When the walls had reached the proper height, the builders constructed the floor of the upstairs loft bedroom . . . using log joists just as they had for the main floor, but leaving openings for a ladder and the stovepipe.

The gables were made up of small logs—down to four inches in diameter—held in place with 29 long, straight poles that also served as purlins, or horizontal rafters, to support the roofing itself.

The cedar shakes for the roof came from a large log found at a local beach. Rejoicing at their good luck, the couple cut the timber into 24-inch bolts, and split each of those into half-inch shakes with a mallet and a cleaving tool called a froe.

The shakes were fastened right onto the purlins with galvanized nails, starting with a double course along each eave. Every row of shakes started eight inches higher than did the one before it . . . giving the entire housetop a *triple* layer of shakes. Furthermore, only eight inches of each slab is exposed to the weather, so the roof *doesn't* leak *and* will probably last for a hundred years! In addition, the ridgepole is protected by a double row of shakes that overlap four inches toward the leeward side (the slope opposite prevailing winds). Once again, the Sullivans had to remember—as they placed the roofing—to leave a hole for the stovepipe (the opening is fitted with a commercial metal flange) . . . so the flue wouldn't have to be routed through a window.

FINISHING TOUCHES

The sides of the door and window openings were framed with dimension lumber spiked into the logs. Bill built his own door with diagonally running boards and set it on hand-hewn maple hinges . . . then rigged up an old-fashioned wooden bar latch, which is lifted by a string hanging on the outside of the portal.

Since they could hear the breeze whistling through the cracks in the walls, the couple tried the Scandinavian solution of packing the chinks with dried moss, but nesting squirrels seemed to pull it out faster than they could stuff it in! After the cracks had been chinked with cement, however, the cabin became the comfortable, weathertight dwelling they'd hoped it would be.

Aside from its being economical and practical, the log cabin allows the Sullivans to enjoy a real back-to-nature lifestyle . . . and they're delighted with the solid comfort of this home that they created using only a little money and *no* power tools.

Past the silhouetted objects on the window sill, the view of the landscape surrounding the cabin is certainly priceless.

INGENUITY AND IMAGINATION CREATE THE EXOTIC

Where, how, and of what a dwelling is built are often subject not only to restrictions imposed by limited time and resources, but also to difficulties created by local climate, topography, and even the type of soil at the site. Answers to these—and other—challenges confronting individual homebuilders are being found in a myriad of forms . . . from cliff dwellings in sheer rock faces, to barges on Louisiana bayous, to a unique residence on a Hawaiian mountainside.

The experiences related here demonstrate emphatically that the problems people face in providing themselves and their families with low-cost, self-built, and—if possible—energy-efficient places to live are far from insoluble . . . and that with ingenuity and resourcefulness a comfortable home can be built that will reward its owners well for their investment of time, energy, and money.

MODERN CLIFF DWELLING

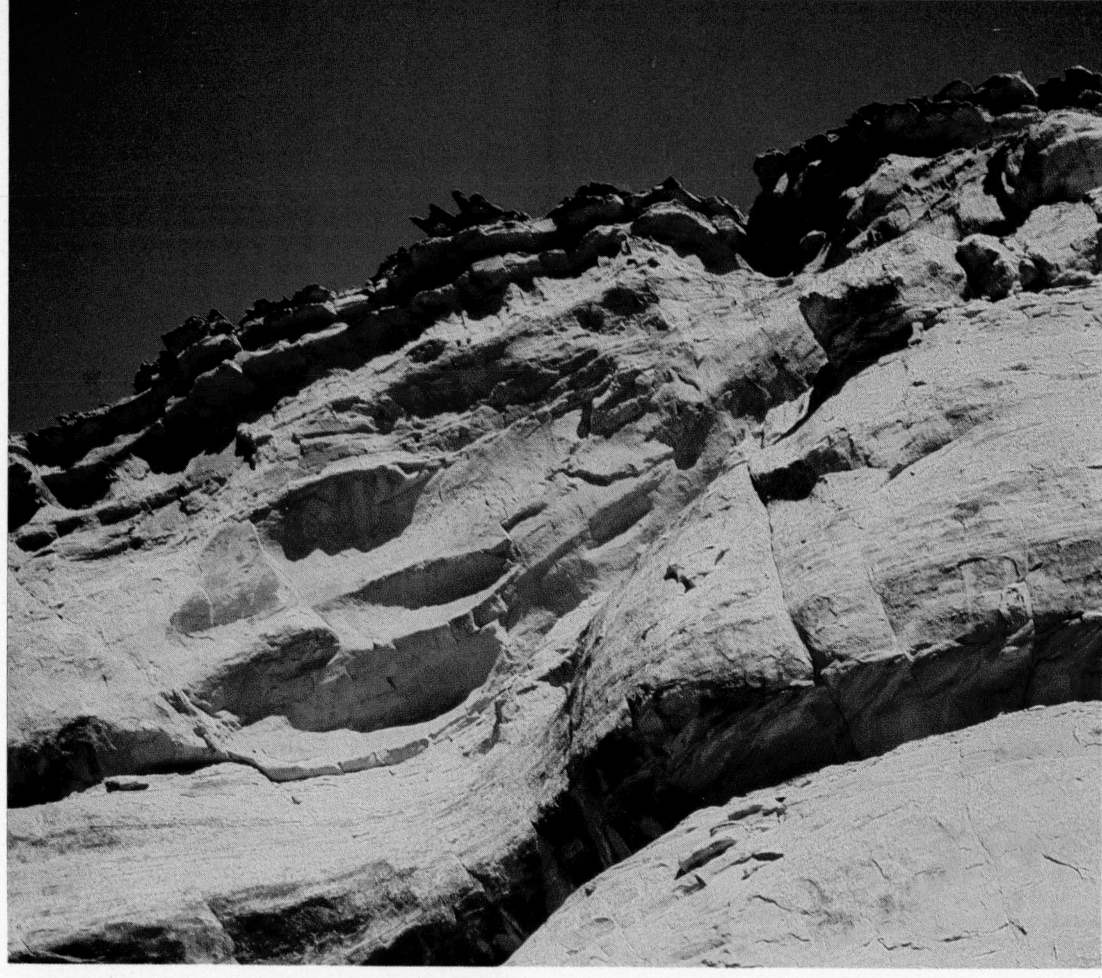

Because a cave house requires protection on one side only, the retired contractor dodged the expenses of insulation for floors, walls, and ceilings as well as those of roofing and siding.

The Anasazi (a Navaho word meaning "the old ones") built their homes in the cliffs of Mesa Verde for both practical and psychological reasons. The towering walls offered physical protection from the whims of the desert environment *and* from marauding bands of warlike nomads. But the rock itself was also a central aspect of Hopi, Zuñi—and later—Navaho spirituality . . . it was seen as the source of man's origins in the four worlds below, and as the essence of the Mother Earth herself.

An integral part of each family's abode was the *kiva*, a ceremonial chamber most often set down into the ground and entered from above. Each *kiva* had a small hole, or *sipapu*—usually in front of the fireplace—which was the pathway down to (or up from) spiritual realms. The spirits which were invited to rise through the *sipapu* were called *kachinas*.

Today, to the north of the historic cliff dwellings—near the farthest reaches of the Hopi domain—stands a twentieth century version of the ingenious Anasazi abodes. Like the pueblos (a Spanish word for "towns") of Chaco Canyon and Mesa Verde, Charles Nystrom's rock-sheltered home provides protection from the extremes of the high desert climate, and it suits his own sense of spirituality.

A PREOCCUPATION

The concept of a modern cliff dwelling was first suggested to Chuck by a friend, and it proved to be an idea that the builder just couldn't get off his mind. For five full years he researched cave and cliff houses to develop a design that would combine brightness, security, and efficiency . . . while still reflecting the Anasazi heritage. And when Chuck retired from his busy contracting practice in 1976, he set about "etching" his ideas in stone.

Nystrom hired a mining firm's demolition expert to help him make a suitable cave. They first experimented by blasting out a garage, and—after encountering no major technical problems—began dynamiting for the house. Though the detonation specialist was skilled in mine excavation, the idea of making a hole for its own sake was new to him. So Chuck urged the expert to proceed slowly and carefully . . . and nearly two months later the man-made cave was finished.

ONE WALL, NO ROOF

Once the excavation was done, the construction of the 1,920-square-foot, three-story interior actually turned out to be *less* difficult than that of a comparable "wide open spaces" building. Since a cave house requires weather protection on one side only, the retired contractor was able to avoid the effort (and expense) of placing insulation in the walls, floor, and ceiling . . . as well as that of installing waterproof roofing and siding. (However, Chuck *did* decide to insulate the floors of the second and third stories to prevent any irritating thumps and squeaks from being transmitted to the rooms below.)

Basically, the "constructed" portion of the home consists of standard 2 X 4 stud walls on 16-inch centers, with dry wall on the inside and 3/8" plywood on the outside. A two- to three-foot air space surrounds the walls—as

Charles Nystrom's latter-day cliff dwelling exhibits the earth tones of its Colorado setting.

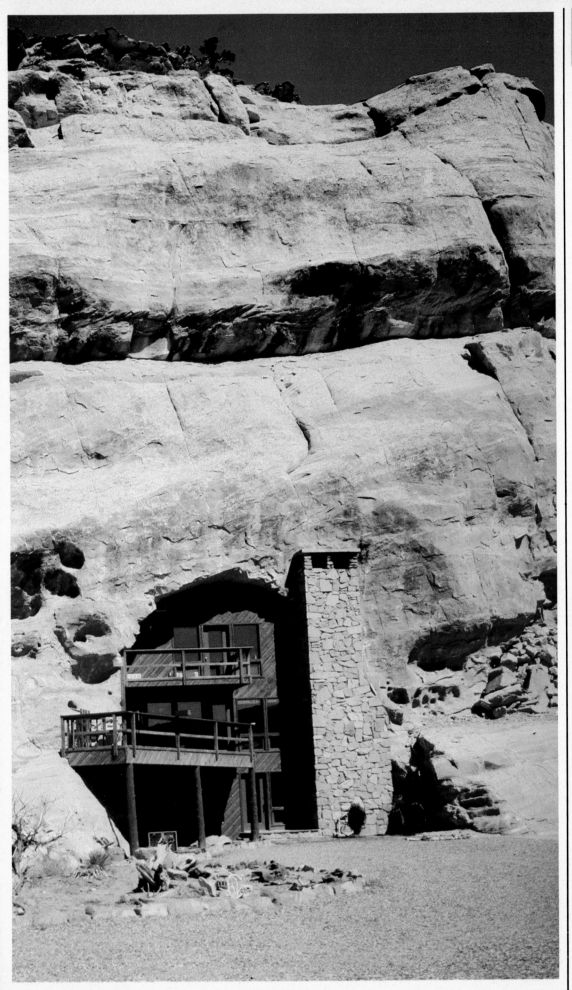

The convoluted crossbedding of the Mesozoic sandstone lends incredible texture to the interior walls of the home.

Charles Nystrom pays roughly $10 per month to heat and cool his rock-sheltered cliff house.

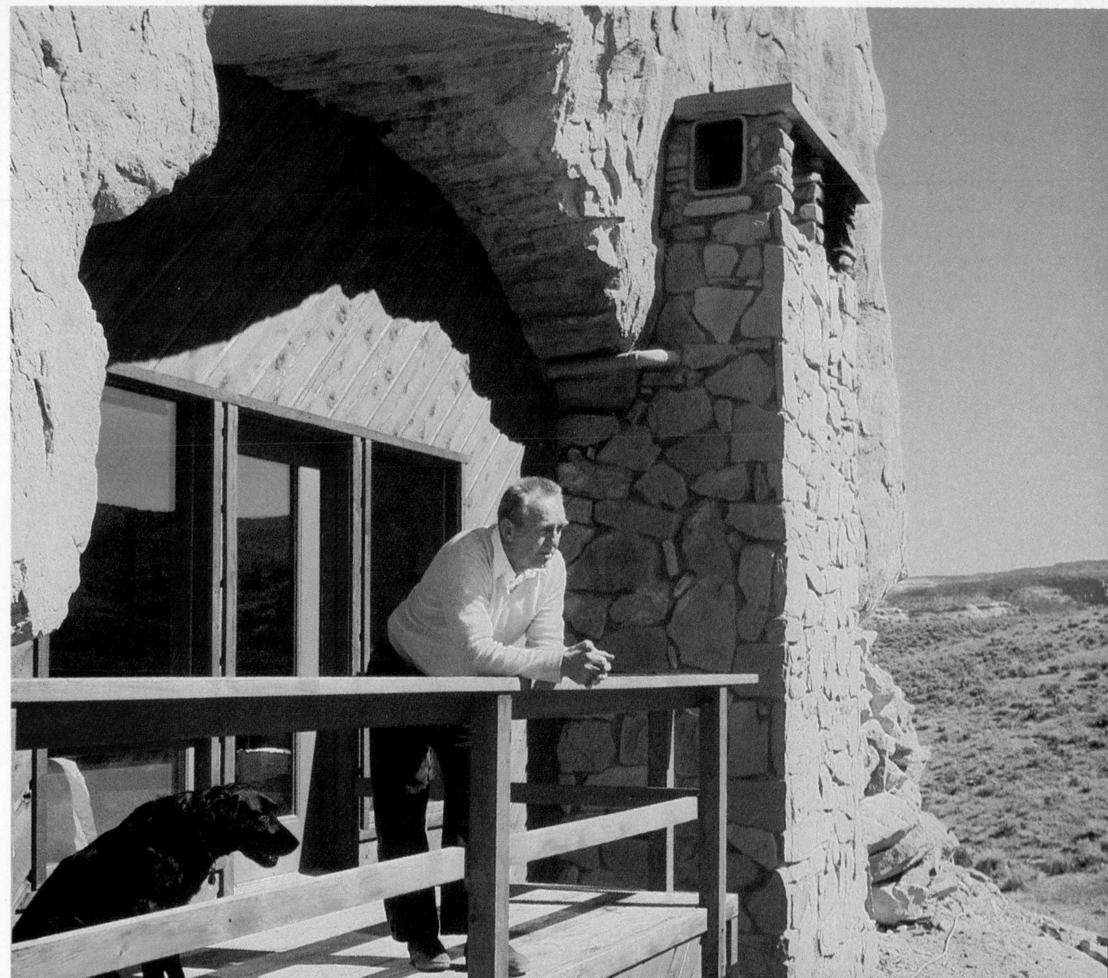

The dwelling's lowest floor serves as a den—much like a Hopi *kiva*—and has a massive stone fireplace built of rocks from the property. The carefully planned interior motif reflects a native American heritage.

well as the ceiling and floor—to provide access for the installation and service of plumbing, electrical connections, and ducting.

When construction began, Chuck didn't know whether humidity would be a problem in his cave house. However, the porosity of the surrounding sandstone, combined with the vapor barrier provided by the open space between the rock and the wall, proved to be more than sufficient to prevent difficulties.

As another benefit, the home's design allowed cabinets, closets, and even bureaus to be recessed into the air space surrounding the walls. Thus the Nystrom house tends to have a relatively uncluttered interior . . . which results in more available floor space than in a traditional home.

COMPARABLE CONSTRUCTION COST

Because a cliff dwelling offers significant savings in both materials and labor, the current cost of such a structure is about equal to that of a quality conventional home. However, Chuck hopes he can improve the economy of the concept by using recently developed hydraulic mining methods.

The actual construction of such a house is a job that almost any building contractor—or even a skilled do-it-yourselfer—can handle. Once the hole is prepared, the rest of the process is actually *less* complicated than is construction using standard building techniques.

BIG ENERGY SAVINGS

While Mr. Nystrom's cliff house cost about the same to build, per square foot, as most homes, it pays him a dividend every time he pays his power bill. Chuck's annual heating and cooling expense—in the Colorado western slope area, which has 5,500 heating degree-days—is about 1/10 that of a similar-sized tract home. (The electricity consumed serves a heat pump with resistive coils located in the distribution system for backup.)

The building's stone encasement obviously plays a large role in its energy efficiency. Only one wall touches outside air, and that bulwark is insulated with 6" fiberglass batt, as well as double-pane windows with a 1/2" air gap. The air space surrounding the other three walls, the ceiling, and the floor serves to moderate the difference between the temperature of the rock and that of the living quarters. (While the outside air temperature may jump between −30° and 110°F in a six-month period, that of the rock slowly fluctuates between 60 and 73°F!)

Another watt-saving feature is the solar gain that's made possible by the home's 200-plus square feet of southwest-facing glass. In the winter, the sun's rays reach nearly to the back wall of the house . . . while the cave's overhang and the porches protect the interior from the *summer* sun.

BRIGHT INSIDE

Many visitors are surprised, Chuck says, to find that the cliff dwelling has the light and airy feel which results from natural illumination. In fact, it's difficult to believe that the abode is actually inside a cave. By designing the structure to be relatively tall and wide, Nystrom has totally avoided the gloomy corners which can lead to that "dungeon" feeling.

He has a love affair with wood, and the house's trim and cabinetry are made predominantly of light oak, with a minimum of handles and metalwork. A motif of white pottery lamps and pots decorated with native American designs completes the uncomplicated decorating scheme.

The top floor serves as the master bedroom and as Chuck's office, while the second story is occupied by the kitchen, living room, and dining room . . . and provides the major egress. Steps—which are carved into the sandstone outcrop itself—lead up from ground level to a large overhanging porch and the front door.

A staircase at the rear of the building provides access from one floor to another, and the steps leading down from the second story take a visitor to a room of markedly different character. Slightly below ground level—and mostly shaded by the porch above—the first floor manages to be serious without being somber. In modern American terminology the room would be referred to as a den, but in a cliff dwelling it must be called the *kiva*.

Here, one of the cheerful white walls—which brighten the upper rooms—has been omitted . . . to reveal an expanse of fantastically cross-bedded sandstone braced by rough-hewn beams. The rock is actually the cave wall itself (sealed to keep down dust), and the ceiling is carefully fitted into a notch in the stone. Toward the front of the room the natural rock blends into a massive lichen-covered sandstone fireplace built by Chuck's brother Scott. And—as a small homage to his cliff dwelling forebears—Nystrom has added a four-inch-diameter hole that penetrates the hearth in front of the fire: the *sipapu*, from which the spirits come.

THE BIG PICTURE

Although the practical application of Charles Nystrom's design will be dictated by geography, appropriate cliff-bearing rock formations actually span the country—from Mexico to Canada—in a 500-mile-wide swath. Chuck feels that there are plenty of places available for dwellings like his, and he'd like to see *more* of them built.

The sandstone home seems to be a natural part of its untamed surroundings.

Steps leading to the front porch were carved out of solid rock.

TIPI IN THE FOREST

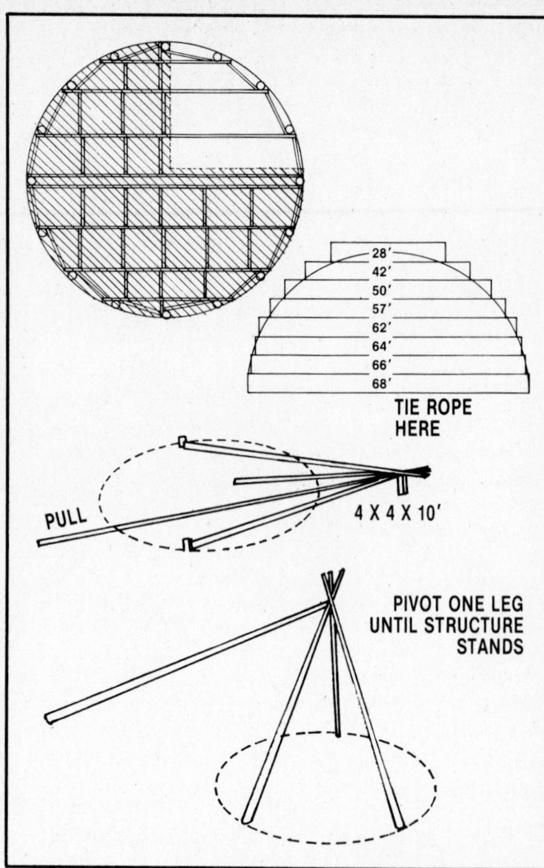

A tripod of trees forms the core of the pole framework for the triple decker, 1,000-square-foot conical home.

Michael and Judy McCoy call their dwelling Kon Tipi because—like Thor Heyerdahl's famous raft Kon Tiki—it's been an adventure both to build *and* to live in. Furthermore, the unusual home has helped them ride out the "rough waters" of economic storms.

The couple is convinced that anyone with modest building skills could duplicate their tipi. Mike *is* pretty handy with tools, and he took care of the entire job—with some help from Judy and a few neighbors—in a scant two months.

STEP ONE: THE COVER STORY

The traditional native American tipi has both an outer cover and a liner. In such a dwelling the inner wall extends from ground level to about six feet high and is secured to the insides of the poles . . . creating an air space. The McCoys chose, however, to extend the liner all the way to the top and to place both it and the cover *outside* the pole framework . . . with insulation sandwiched between the two skins.

On the average, tipis run from 18 to 20 feet in diameter. Kon Tipi, on the other hand, is a full 30 feet across, and rises 30 feet to the point where its poles meet. To provide both layers of cover for the structure, 300 yards of 54"-wide fabric were needed. After considering the advantages of various types of material, the McCoys settled on nylon-reinforced vinyl . . . since it has an outdoor life of about 20 years, is waterproof, meets California's fire-resistance standard, won't rot or mildew, and is less expensive than treated canvas.

With the material purchased, the couple cut it into strips (following the pattern shown . . . once for each of the two layers) and then, starting with the longest piece of the outer cover, glued the strips together in order of decreasing length (using Bostik 7130 adhesive). It's very important to shingle each section of fabric *over* the shorter strip that follows it so that water will run over, and not into, the seams. In all, the couple spent about 12 hours assembling the outer wall.

Quickly getting tired of the fumes produced by the glue (and deciding that needle holes, which might have admitted moisture through the outer wall, weren't a concern in the inner covering), the McCoys *sewed* the liner together. The task required another 12 hours of work with a double needle to produce two parallel seams about 1/4 inch apart. The only real problem encountered was the tendency of the fabric to pucker . . . which made it necessary to hold the material securely, both in front of and behind the needle, as it was stitched.

STEP TWO: A VAULT OF POLES

After the vinyl was assembled, folded, and stored, Judy pretty much turned Kon Tipi over to Michael . . . since she had to finish off two more months of city work before sailing into country life full time. Mike established a camp and got right to the task of selecting and cutting poles. He chose, blessed, chopped, dragged, and peeled some 16 oaks, each about 35 feet in length and 4" to 6" at the base (after peeling). Once the poles were prepared, their lower ends were treated with wood preservative.

It was short work, then, to clear and level the 30-foot circular homesite, after which Michael approached the intimidating task of actually raising the monstrous tripod that would form the core of the pole assembly. The job involved tying three trees together, at a point 30 feet from their bases, with one end of a strong 40-foot rope. Then he spread the butts of the poles apart . . . placing two together at one point on the perimeter of the prepared site, and the other (single) pole—also on the edge of the circle—roughly 25 feet away.

With that done, Michael braced the bases of the logs in place with stakes . . . temporarily propped up the joint (where the three poles met) with a 10-foot length of 2 X 4 . . . tied the free end of the rope to his truck . . . and pulled the framework high enough to allow him to grasp the base of one of the paired poles and swing it around the perimeter until the tripod stood on its own. He went on to place each log butt in its final spot by dropping a plumb line from the point at which they crossed to mark dead center of the 30-foot circle and positioning each post exactly 15 feet from the center and equidistant from the two others. It was then a relatively simple matter to add the rest of the uprights and—climbing a ladder to do so—tie their tips to the tripod's joint.

STEP THREE: FLOORS GALORE

In order to make the best use of the space that would be enclosed by Kon Tipi's fabric walls, the McCoys decided to make it a three-story home. Michael began the second floor by choosing two sturdy poles that were directly opposite each other across the circle. He then measured the distance between the uprights at a height of 6′8″ (it came to 22 feet), located a pair of 2 X 10's of that length, and nailed the planks, one to each side of the pair of poles. Parallel beams, getting progressively shorter as they approached the edges of the tipi, were added next. (These boards were used singly . . . only the initial span was doubled.)

Mike completed the framework by fastening 2 X 8 crossmembers to the joists at approximately 3-foot intervals. He planked the floor with rough-cut 1″ X 8″ oak boards . . . leaving one quarter-section without flooring *or* crossbeams, to enhance ventilation, increase the dwelling's feeling of openness, and provide access for the stovepipe and stairway.

The third floor is simply a smaller version of the second . . . and the roof—which is positioned about 18 inches below the point where the posts cross—consists of 2 X 4 rafters and plywood cut to fit snugly around the poles. There are *no* upright supports: In fact, the *only* vertical walls in the dwelling are the ones that enclose the 5′ X 8′ bathroom (two bulkheads handle that job . . . both of which were framed with 2 X 4 studs and sheathed with oak boards).

The first floor is composed of sand, covered first with heavy black plastic and then loose oak planks. A 5′ X 5′ area was left bare, except for a layer of large flat rocks, to provide a safe location for a woodstove. Of course, the ground floor *could* have been raised up on joists and even insulated, but the McCoys were pressed for both time and money . . . and they feel they can always go on to do a fancier job as their circumstances permit.

STEP FOUR: SETTING THE SAIL

After smoothing the inner wall evenly around the tipi, the McCoys stapled rows of fiberglass insulation—through the liner—to the poles, starting from the bottom. Mike spent a full day getting that job done and hauling up the outside wall, but he had to work fast . . . since an unexpected downpour would have done real damage had it hit before the waterproof outer wrap was in place.

While hanging the cover and liner on Kon Tipi, it seemed to Mike and Judy that they were unfurling the canvas on some ancient seagoing vessel. (The huge expanse of fabric *was* a real handful when the wind caught it.) They began the job by tying a strong rope to the center of the liner's straight edge . . . then they raised the fabric by means of a pulley attached to one of the poles. By standing on the roof, Michael was able to tack the liner to the framework at his feet, using lath and roofing nails.

STEP FIVE: PORTS AND PORTALS

Now, most folks don't think of windows and doors when imagining tipi life, but Michael and Judy McCoy had been able to salvage a number of panes and screens at no cost and were willing to experiment. As it turned out, cutting the openings for the viewports and entryway involved more by-guess-and-by-gosh figuring than did any other task encountered.

To build the front door/window combination, for example, Michael first selected three poles on the east side of the tipi. He then cut through the vinyl and insulation, along the line of the middle pole, starting at a point seven feet up and moving down to the ground. With that done, Mike sliced a horizontal gash, at the seven-foot mark, running from the first pole to the third. This "T" cut allowed him to fold back the vinyl and insulation.

Next, the entryway was framed in with 2 X 4's. Seven-foot uprights were fastened to the bases of the three poles, followed by horizontal—or roof-line—planks . . . which were secured to the tipi poles at the tops of the uprights. Michael claims that the job was sort of like constructing a dormer on a simple slanted roof, except that the tipi's curve made it a little more "interesting".

With the frames in place, Mike hinged the window to its upper border so that it could be pulled in and hooked to the entry ceiling on warm days. The door was set to open inward . . . the spaces below and beside the window were filled in with planks and insulation . . . the entry's 1/2″-plywood roof was topped with roofing paper, white roll roofing, and tar . . . and the vinyl flaps were stapled to the frame. The whole job turned out to be easy enough to inspire Michael to go on and build dormer windows on each floor . . . plus the 5′ X 10′ greenhouse shown in one of the accompanying photos (which provides additional light, solar heat, and—of course—a way to assure a continual harvest of vegetables).

SOME SUM:

As you'd imagine, part of the satisfaction of building Kon Tipi came from knowing that the entire home was constructed for less money than most homebuilders would have to pay for just putting in a foundation! The vinyl cover and liner represented the single largest expense but contributed to the home's durability and unique appearance. *And*, the McCoys have been more comfortable in their "home in the round" than either of them ever thought possible. Whatever future they may dream of and set sail toward in the years to come, Kon Tipi will help make "getting there" an adventure!

Kon Tipi was constructed for less money than most homebuilders pay for just putting in a foundation.

BARGE ON THE BAYOU

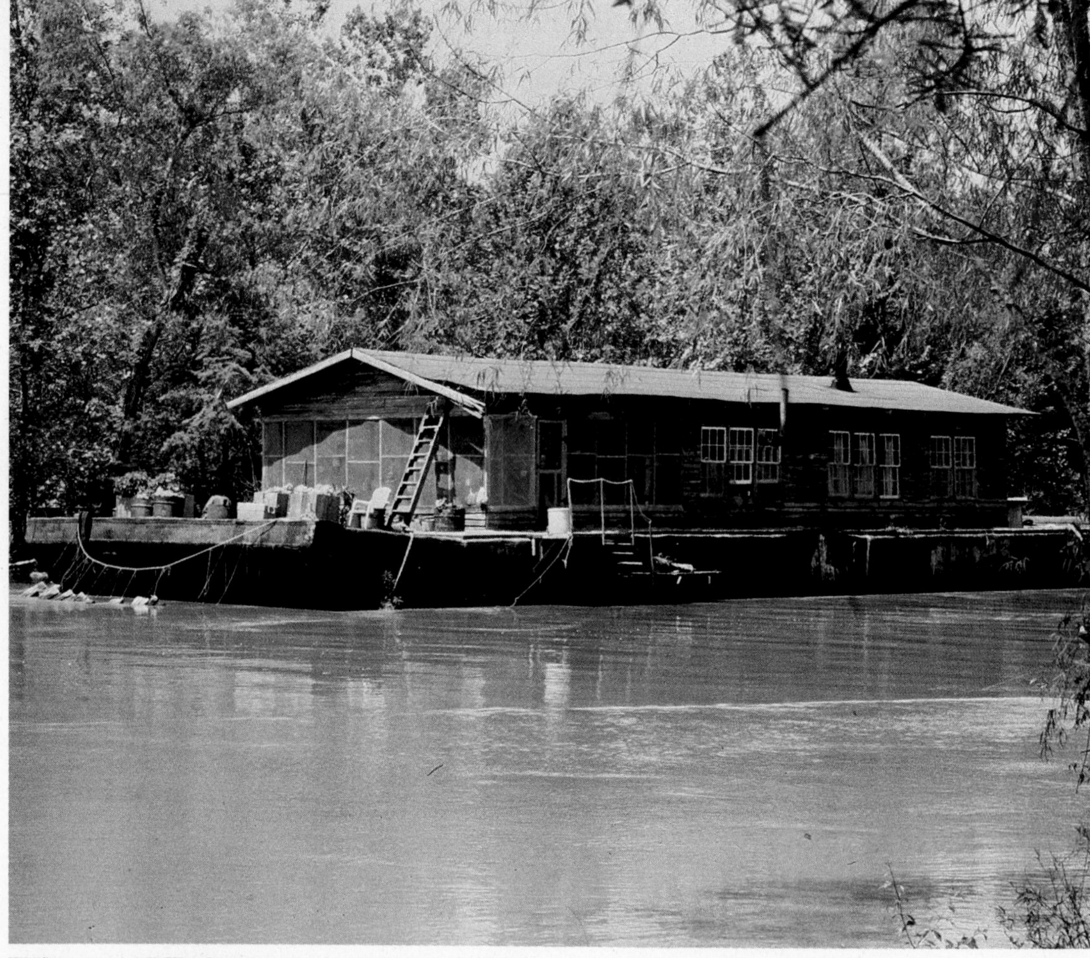

A spacious houseboat-on-a-barge is home to two cousins who willingly adapted their lifestyles to the whims of the Atchafalaya River, its bayous, and swamps . . . in return they are rewarded with plentiful fish and game and rich soil.

Raccoon feet tickety-tacked out of the back room as Gwen Carpenter and her cousin Calvin entered their ruined house through a hole where the front door used to be. The guilty flick of a retreating snake's tail seemed to say, "Pardon me . . . I didn't think you'd be coming back," as it slipped down a crack in the six-inch layer of dried gunk covering the floor. The mud had finished the demolition begun by the flood five months earlier. As depressing as her last view of their home had been—with its roof poking bravely above the brown swirl of overflow from the Atchafalaya River—it couldn't compare with the desolation Gwen now saw.

BORN ON THE BAYOU

Even as a child, Gwen's cousin Calvin dreamed of returning to the Atchafalaya Swamp where their ancestors had lived for 150 years before the area had been turned into a spillway (in 1930) for floodwaters of the Mississippi River. Following his desire to live *and* work among the silver cypress and whispering cottonwoods, the young man invested in moving his parents' vacation house out to the old family homesite in the swamp, and then—when Gwen was looking for a summer job before commencing Ph.D. work in the fall—he took her on as a fishing partner. By the time autumn rolled around, there wasn't a graduate program in the world that could have enticed her away from the wilderness home!

The two drifted through the year in a daze of enthusiasm. They painted, patched, and hung curtains in the old house. Vegetables and roses fairly *sprang* out of the black earth, encouraging the homesteaders to put in an herb garden and a small orchard. The fish and game that had attracted the first swampers were still plentiful. Gwen and Cal began to wonder how those old-timers ever could have *left* this paradise . . . until the flood of 1973 answered that question with a vengeance!

NOTHING TO LOSE

As she toured the water-wrecked home and contemplated the dreary prospect of a city apartment and the academic world, Gwen idly pried the relics of her life in the swamp from the muck with her toe: a jar of preserved pumpkin, winking in the July sun like a hot coal . . . her grandmother's ceramic soap dish, half-buried but unbroken . . . an aluminum muffin pan filled with 12 perfect mud cupcakes. Each of the buried treasures seemed to mock her yearning to stay . . . since even if the old house *could* be repaired, it might be washed away *again*.

At that point, Calvin broke into her thoughts. "Instead of fighting the water, let's try to cooperate with it. What do you think about houseboats?"

"Not much," she returned. But when Calvin described a full-sized home that could rise and fall with the water level, and that would have lots of windows, she changed her mind. So they put the word out to old friends, casual acquaintances, checkout clerks, and complete strangers that they were in the market for a barge. While that bit of information met with incredulity and guffaws, the skepticism no doubt helped to spread the news ever further. And while they were confounding friends with their daydream, they also mentioned that they were looking for a traditional Louisiana cypress *house* to recycle.

Having "placed their order", they separated . . . to earn money in whatever ways they could.

THE PRICE IS RIGHT

More than a year later, Calvin sent word that an available barge had been located in Houma, Louisiana . . . a coastal town rich in marine equipment. The 26′ X 103′ monster was made of heavy riveted steel, but at 50 years old it was considered a commercial insurance risk and put up for sale as scrap metal. And if ever there was an omen that their dreams were in the right place, it was the price . . . a low $950!

Then, immediately after the barge arrived at the building site on the Intracoastal Canal near the Bayou Sorrel Bridge, they heard that a nearby sugar plantation was selling off the houses that had been homes to generations of cane-field workers. Another $450 netted them a dwelling's worth of century-old cypress boards . . . some as long as 35 feet and others over two feet wide! The bargain also included three brick fireplaces, tongue-and-groove flooring, roofing tin, silvery aged clapboards, solid wooden doors, a massive four-poster bed, a bentwood chair, and an antique bureau!

As they pulled nails and sorted materials, they paid close attention to how the old cypress house had been framed. Just because neither of them had ever built so much as a doghouse was no reason to shrink from constructing a big home with lots of windows and a brick fireplace! Armed with crayons, paper, and a how-to building book, they drew up their plans.

The shape of the barge naturally dictated a shotgun style of architecture, rather than a four-square model . . . the Louisiana climate demanded a big screened porch and as many windows as the walls could support . . . and the pair's tastes leaned toward a home with a few large rooms rather than many small ones. The rest of the design was pretty much determined by the availability of materials. Construction started under the pessimistic eye of an old loiterer who kept mumbling, "It'll never stand." That gentleman, however, was also one of the many people who'd scoffed at the thought of even *finding* a barge in the first place, so they paid little attention to his comments.

For a while, though, it did seem that his prediction might well prove true. Each morning, they'd peer from a temporary shelter on the bank to see studs listing north or south, depending on the direction taken by the largest wake-producing towboats in the night. It became a pre-breakfast ritual to hoist the studs back to perpendicular with a rope while they braced and braced, and braced some more. Before long, Calvin tossed the carpenter's level to his bored spaniel, and from then on they just *guessed* at the constantly changing angles.

Six months from the time they started to build, the last piece of crooked molding (there's not a 90° angle in the entire house) was nailed into place. They returned the borrowed hammer, handsaw, and ladder, and had their "new" house towed to its permanent mooring in the bayou. From top to bottom, they'd spent a total of $2,500 for their floating home.

Today, after years of houseboat living (several of which brought floods), Gwen and Calvin are still learning ways to work *with* the high water. In choosing garden vegetables, for example, they give priority to late-season varieties, since a spring-swollen Mississippi could cause the fields to flood and delay the planting dates. Their chicken population is limited to the number that can be kept in a floating coop when the henhouse goes under. And since a permanent fence would rust, the chicken and garden enclosures are made up of wire-covered frame sections that can be taken down and stacked, then reassembled in minutes with a pair of pliers.

A 500-gallon rainwater cistern stays full during the wet season when the swollen bayou is too muddy for house use, but when the tank gets low (during the dry summer and fall months), the bayou provides an endless supply of clear water. And instead of regularly running propane bottles in by way of truck and boat, Calvin nestled a 150-gallon tank in its own aluminum bateau, which is easily towed in for filling twice a year.

Life on the bayou is based on the moods of the water. The high levels of spring find Gwen and Cal fishing and crawfishing, while gardening season arrives when the water falls too low for profitable catches. During the slack water of summer, Calvin takes a welding job for a few weeks, and in the dark winter months, when they spend most of their time keeping the barge's woodstove company, the cousins prepare exhibit prints and articles from photographs taken during the bayou's more spectacular seasons.

There's no fear of floods when your home is a barge that can rise and fall with the river's water levels.

DOME AND PYRAMID MERGE

In one of the oldest towns in the state of New York—Southold, Long Island—stands one of the newest kinds of houses in the world. Dubbed a "pyramoid", the building has features in common with both a geodesic dome and a pyramid, and the combination results in an amazing amalgam of aesthetics, comfort, economy, strength, and energy efficiency. The unique dwelling is the home of Don Lubov (its inventor and designer), his wife Linda (a professional photographer and craftswoman), and their two small children.

"To me, it's sculpture," says Lubov, an artist by profession, who studied architecture and engineering in order to bring his brainchild to reality, "the biggest sculpture project I've ever conceived and completed."

THE SOURCE

Don was teaching art at East Carolina University when the idea for the design—a result of "playing" with the configuration of a carbon molecule—began to take shape. At about the same time, he read about Buckminster Fuller's work with dome dwellings, and he saw a similarity between Fuller's ideas and his own concepts. Subsequently, Mr. Fuller and the World Games staff encouraged Don to keep working on his notion.

The art teacher spent the next five years on the road, traveling some 33,000 miles to investigate alternative lifestyles and house shapes. When that pilgrimage/apprenticeship was over, Don settled down to translate his ideas into concrete and lumber. Today, he and Linda (who gave the shape its name) can testify to the practical benefits that go hand in hand with the mathematical beauty of the structure's clean geometry.

COZY AND COMFORTABLE

To begin with, the 1,200-square-foot, two-story house (plus a usable basement) requires about 50% less energy to heat than a conventional dwelling of the same floor space. The design itself saves 25% . . . by literally cutting corners: The shape reduces the ratio of shell area to floor area (the "cover ratio") from the approximate 4:1 of traditional rectangular architecture to 3:1, resulting in a 25% smaller volume of inside air to heat (or cool). Another 25% is saved as a result of insulation and the integrity of doors and windows.

The house is heated, upstairs and down, by a Fisher Baby Bear woodstove. The midget heater, burning two to three cords of wood per winter, can maintain an inside temperature of 75°F, even when the thermometer outside

The pyramoid design cuts costs by literally cutting corners . . . the result is a smaller volume of inside air to heat or cool.

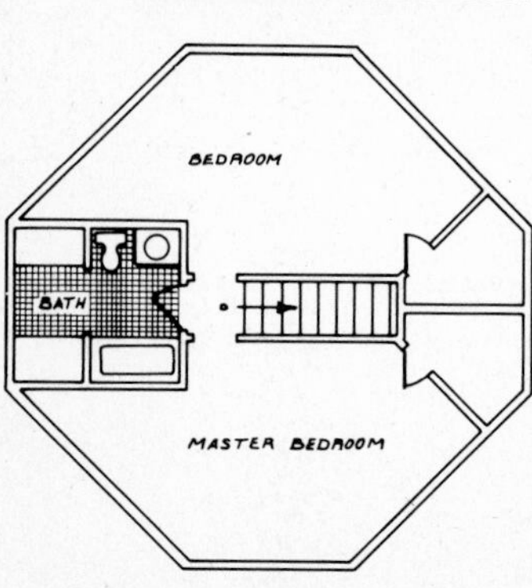

reads 0°F, and icy ocean winds claw the shore. To satisfy local building codes, each room is also equipped with an electric baseboard heater . . . so far, entirely unused!

Of course, a geodesic dome has an even better cover ratio than a pyramoid—about 2:1—but as Don discovered in his research, not everybody is really comfortable with a round house. So it's an advantage of the pyramoid that the actual floor of the main level is square: The rooms there allow for easy furniture arrangement, and they *feel* conventional. By the time a newcomer notices the unusual wall/ceiling angles, or climbs to the second floor—which, because of the level at which it intersects the sides of the house, is octagonal—he or she is far more ready to accept the occasionally "different" appearance.

Don and Linda have exercised considerable ingenuity in making use of the structure's odd corners. One in the living room, for example, perfectly houses the little woodstove . . . others serve as display space for Don's lithographs and Linda's colorful photos . . . and some disappear neatly in closets and storage space. Upstairs, in the master bedroom, a sloping wedge of upholstered wall serves as a headboard for the master bed . . . at a relaxing angle for reading or watching television.

The interior of the Lubovs' home is cheerfully light and airy, too . . . thanks not only to the skillfully created decor, but also to the big sliding glass doors (opening onto a large, pleasant deck) and windows that slope to catch the sunlight. The small proportion of glazing to insulated siding and roofing is another energy-saving feature, of course, and despite the fact that the windows appear to be tiny, the rooms are bright. Indeed, visitors frequently exclaim that the house is "much bigger inside than outside"!

PUTTING UP AND SHUTTING UP

The construction was accomplished in three months by just four men—Don, his father-in-law (Saul Millman), and two friends—only two of whom had previous house-building experience. With the labor expense thus kept at a reasonable level, the basic pyramoid was built for almost exactly *half* the cost of a comparably sized conventional house in the area.

Because Don and Linda both work at home, they decided to build their house with a usable basement to provide studio, workshop, and darkroom space. So construction began with excavation . . . then a 25′ X 25′ concrete floor and the reinforced walls were poured . . . and the entire foundation was waterproofed with tar before being backfilled on three sides.

Building the pyramoid was simplified by the fact that the exterior is composed of 12 congruent right isosceles triangles, their only difference being the wedges attached along their sides to fit the angles at which they meet. Each three-cornered frame, braced with 2 X 6 studs on 16″ centers, was constructed flat and then raised into position. Sole plates bolted to the foundation's upper edges formed bases for the four outward-sloping triangles (as shown in the photos), and eight additional triangles completed the shell.

Once locked together with bolts, the 12 panels created a structure of impressive strength. "A hurricane might roll it over, or an earthquake drop it into a hole," Don comments, "but I believe it would hold its shape."

Inside, the main floor spans the foundation and is supported by six Lally columns, set on their own footings and later concealed in the walls of the basement stairs. The upper floor rests on the downstairs partitions. (Because the exterior shell is completely self-supporting, the interior partitions can be placed according to the owner's pleasure.) The outer walls were insulated with fiberglass (to R-19) and the ceilings with both fiberglass and rigid urethane insulation board (to R-22). Then the entire interior was simply covered with plasterboard and painted.

The Velux windows Don chose are Danish-made units complete with double glazing, weatherstripping, and flashing. And they're ingeniously convertible: Since they pivot at the center, they can be opened a mere crack, swung wide, or flipped all the way around so that the outsides can be cleaned from inside the house.

The sliding doors to the deck and the front entrance, set vertically into outward-sloping walls, create their own overhangs . . . which serve both to protect them from wet weather and to shade them from the high summer sun. In addition, a custom-fitted storm/screen unit at the front door provides an air-lock entry.

Of course, ventilation is an essential—especially on days when doors and windows must be closed—to avoid moisture buildup . . . so the builders created a blower-equipped "false attic" under the roof, and installed vents in the eaves. (The system also exhausts hot air in the summertime to keep the house cool.)

FUTURE TALK

Having lived in their new home for a few years, Don and Linda know that a pyramoid *works* . . . but that's just the beginning, because the design is capable of many variations. Plastic stretched over lightweight frames could make a greenhouse or a tent . . . there are plans for a luxurious four-bedroom, three-bath version . . . and one of Don's fondest dreams is to make available a prefab kit for a 250-square-foot "cabin" pyramoid that would house two people.

In addition, pyramoids could be clustered in a number of ways: "overlapped" in double or quadruple units to achieve new shapes and an even better cover ratio, or ringed around a courtyard for use as condominiums, offices, or a motel.

What's more, the designer has suggestions for even greater energy efficiency. For example, much more could be done to improve solar gain: "Our deck faces east," Don explains, "because we wanted it to be cool on hot afternoons. But if you were to put the deck and its glass doors on the south side—and let deciduous trees provide your summer shade—you might even want to let the stove go out on sunny winter days." Also, the front deck could be glazed in, creating a greenhouse, and thermal mass for heat storage could be added in the basement.

In short, the pyramoid possesses unplumbed potential . . . it's only *started* to strut its stuff!

With labor expenses kept at a reasonable level, the basic pyramoid was built for almost half the cost of a comparably sized conventional house in the area.

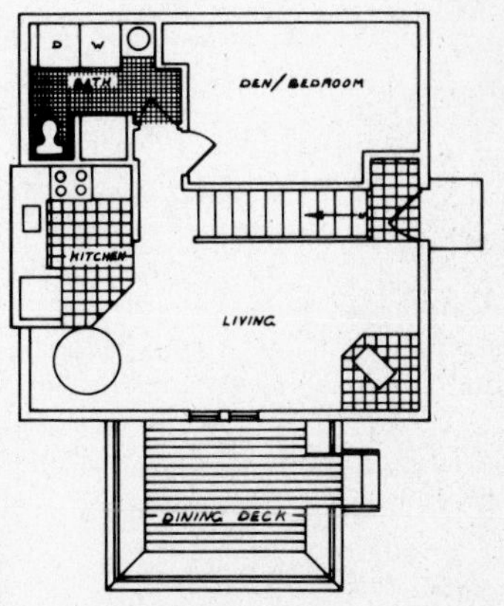

A HOME FROM A WATER TANK

Unlike most country-bound folks, who spend years planning the details of their move back to the land, George Lundburg and his family fled urban Oahu to five undeveloped acres on the "big island", Hawaii, without much more than high expectations and a solid conviction that life would get better.

It would be nice to tell the story of how they simply charged off into the country without money, skills, or clearly defined goals and successfully homesteaded a tropical paradise. Nice, yes, but that isn't exactly the way it happened. The true story is that George and his wife and daughter found themselves, within four short months after making their move, in a dismal situation.

CAMPER BLUES

Their goldfish and three dogs might not have minded being squeezed into a camper halfway up the family's hilly property on the very rainy Hamakua coast, but George, his wife Kay, and daughter Sally felt their close quarters shrinking after months of all but steady rain. At first, a set of house plans drawn by a student architect gave hope, but with the realization that they couldn't afford the wood necessary to build the structure, their dreams turned to despair. And George's initial optimism began to give way to a sense of urgency . . . as he realized that they desperately needed a sizable, economical home.

Then, on a rare sunny day while he was tending his Chinese pea patch, inspiration hit. As George hoed, he took mental inventory of his possessions . . . good acreage, a promising building site with terrific views, the camper, and an enormous, disassembled 25,000-gallon water tank that he had bought and moved to his new property. Gradually, he began to see in the tank more than a pile of rotting redwood boards stacked near the camper. Maybe, just maybe, he thought, there was enough there to build a house.

If he'd been asked about it ten minutes before, Lundburg would have replied that the mess of wood was of dubious value and had, up to the moment, been more trouble than it was worth. Funny how inspiration can give a person a fresh perspective!

Before he left Oahu, George had read an advertisement that offered three of the tanks for sale. They'd been disassembled and removed from the cliffs above Kaaawa after having served as holding tanks for that town's water supply since just after World War II. Each was formed of slats three inches thick, six inches wide, and fourteen feet high . . . about 100 pounds of redwood per slat. The steel bands that encircled the tank, holding it together, were over a half-inch thick. The floor was more than 20 feet in diameter.

When he first read the advertisement, George thought that one of the tanks might make an ideal irrigation reservoir on his future homestead. But he decided against the idea when he read the asking price: $3,000 per tank . . . well above what the Lundburg's modest budget could bear. He forgot the whole thing until he saw another ad, a month after his move, for the one tank that remained. This time the asking price included a P.S.: "or best offer." Maybe, thought George, a $1,500 offer would take it. He decided to try. Much to his surprise his bid was accepted . . . and then his troubles really began.

The entire stack of planks lay festering in a banana orchard from which it had to be transported, first by truck to a shipping dock on the coast, then by barge 200 miles to the island, after which the whole mess still had to be gotten somehow to the hillside property. Staring at the heap in the dankness of the banana forest, George could only say "*Auwe!*" That's Hawaiian for "Oh brother!"

CHAIRMAN OF THE BOARDS

It's a bit painful for George to recount the story of the days spent loading the unwieldly planks on a rented flatbed truck. Fortunately the sellers were a compassionate bunch and helped a lot. So did Lady Luck, who led him to a friend who had a banding machine he could use to package the planks. Then, on the other end of the haul, a new neighbor, Harvey, took pity on the struggling homesteader and contributed his labor plus the use of a ten-wheel logging truck and a forklift to help move the cargo off the barge and up the 2,500-foot rise to the new Lundburg domain.

A 25,000-gallon redwood water tank becomes a yurt-like home. Fertile acreage supports a vegetable plot.

After the major pieces were hauled, George spent an entire week shuttling back and forth in his aging pickup, toting precariously balanced loads of components—braces, beams, flooring, ribs, and bands—far up the inclining acreage to a spot next to the camper . . . which then served as the Lundburg's home.

Having gained a somewhat intimate acquaintance with the tank's components—one by ponderous one—George began to harbor a growing suspicion, then close to an absolute conviction, that the thing wouldn't "hold water". What he had, he became certain, was a bona fide redwood white elephant. Little wonder, then, that his spirits began to soar when he perceived new potential in that old water tank . . . and decided to convert that horrible heap into a habitable house!

A wise man knows when he needs help. So, in recognition of his own lack of skills, George hired Ambrose Pollack, a carpenter who is also a bit of an artist, to help design the home. Without the benefit of Pollack's mechanical and artistic input, George is convinced the final result might have been a gloomy shed.

THE TRANSFORMATION

The first big task was to recondition the redwood itself. Every board was cleaned and smoothed with an electric planer powered by a small gasoline-fueled generator. After George finished his work on a plank, Kay treated it with termite repellent and water seal and applied a final coat of Danish oil to the surfaces that would form the interior of the dwelling. Presto! Years of use and neglect, as well as the ravages of both wet and dry rot, were erased. There was little similarity between the seasoned lumber he hauled to the building site and the moldering mass he struggled with during the trip from Oahu.

Next, George and Kay laid a post-and-piling foundation and assembled the tank on top of it. Interestingly, the dynamics of the structure eliminated any need for conventional bracing. The inward pressure exerted by the hoops that secure the boards in their cylindrical arrangement is offset by a resisting force created by the meeting of the slats' sharply beveled edges, resulting in a sturdy stand-up enclosure similar to a yurt.

Clambering over 14-foot-high walls to get into and out of the under-construction dwelling became rather bothersome, so doorways were soon cut out. Around that time, near-disaster struck.

George was working alone, perched on a ladder at the top of the tank, when he fell to the ground and shattered a heel bone. He crawled 350 feet to the camper, applied ice, and hobbled down the hill for help. One of the few cars that use the hillside road every day stopped, and George soon received medical attention . . . but he was flat on his back for the following six weeks.

By the time George (still on crutches) returned to work on the house, he had built a scale model of the new dwelling using greeting cards. This miniature brought the family's ideas to life and helped guide them through the remaining construction on the full-sized model.

Before long, the Lundburgs were able to stand back and admire a solid, comfortable, attractive and very unusual residence they'd built themselves . . . from a run-down old water tank.

TIME FLIES

The family has since spent two years in their abode. Daughter Sally is nine, and John, the newest Lundburg, is 18 months old. The couple has made a few additions to the home, also, and plans to continue expanding it. They stay happy, snug, and dry . . . even during their island's infamous driving horizontal rainstorms (which caused leaks between the slats before George solved the problem with a thick coat of clear boat-bottom epoxy). The former water tank now keeps water *out*!

In terms of self-sufficiency, the Lundburgs have come a long way from the dismal days spent cramped in the camper. George does still find it necessary to take an occasional job to pay for food and supplies, but the family is convinced that they're on their way to a really self-reliant lifestyle. George knows they'll get there, mostly because in the process of converting that dilapidated old tank into comfortable living quarters, they underwent a remarkable transformation. They learned to do . . . and to *make* do.

The mechanical and artistic input of a hired carpenter produced a workable but imaginative design.

After planing and treatment with termite repellent, water seal, and a final coat of Danish oil, the redwood planks formed not only the exterior of the home, but the rustic interior shown here. A spiral staircase provides access to upper and lower levels.

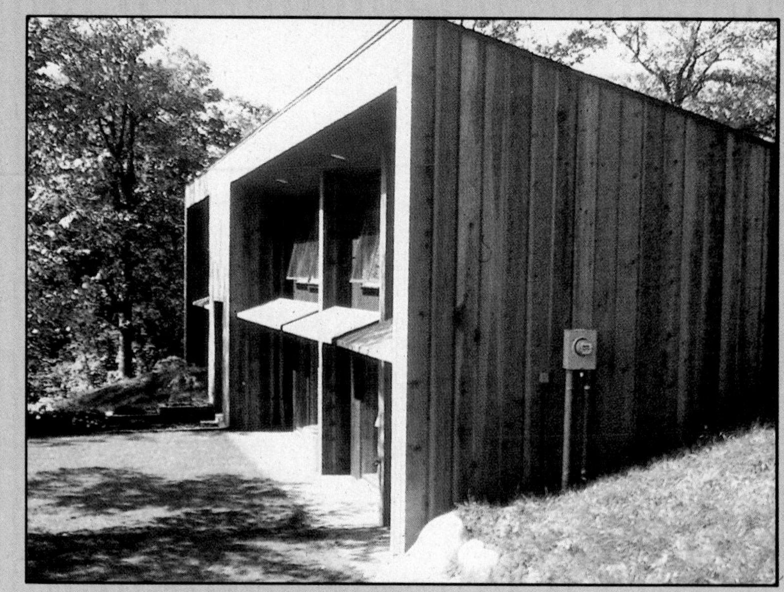
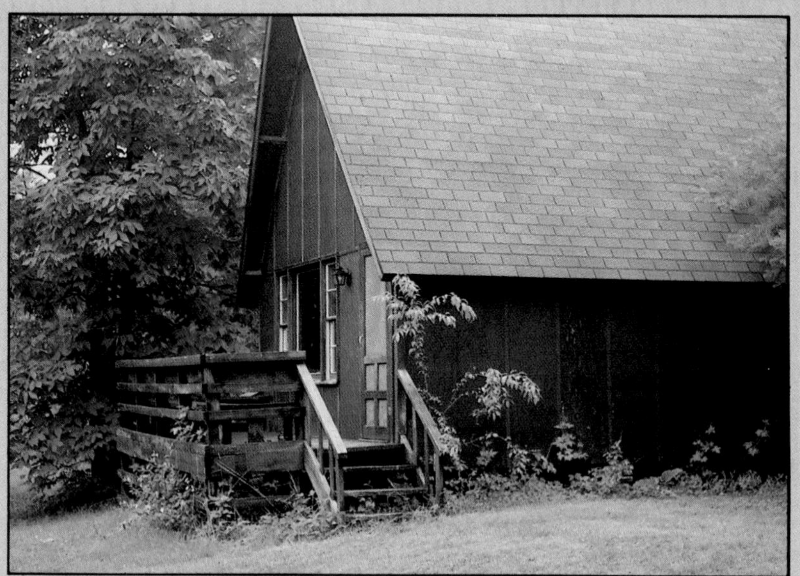
 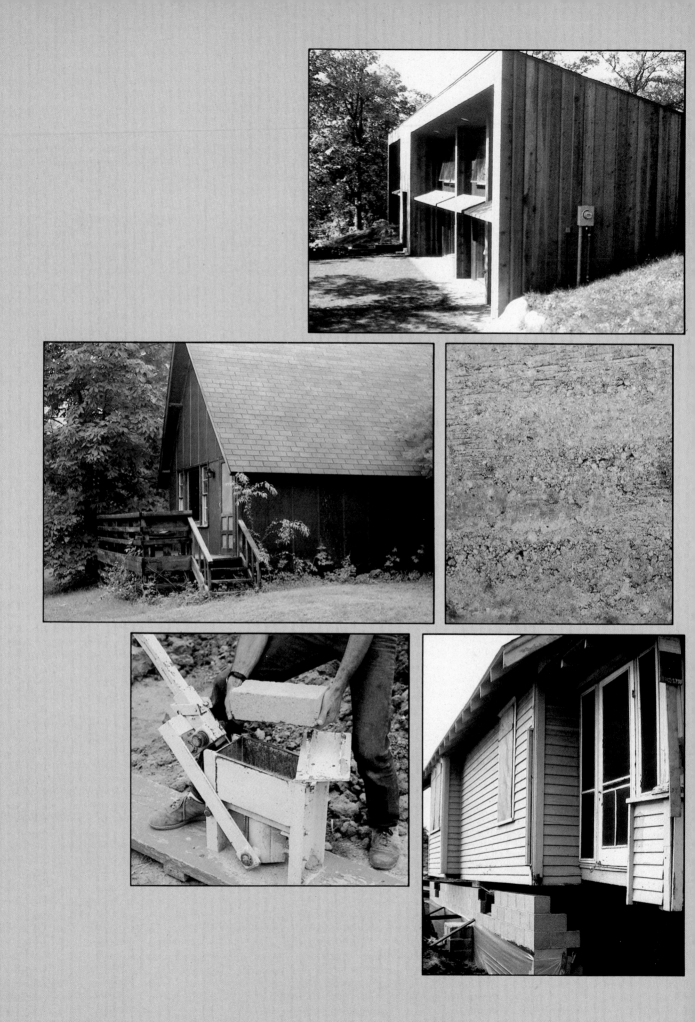
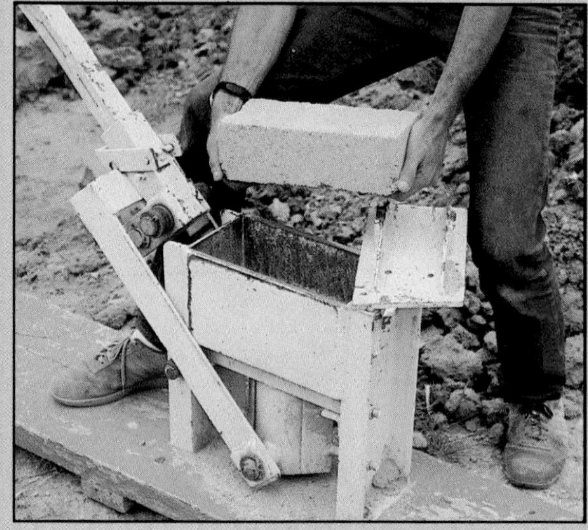
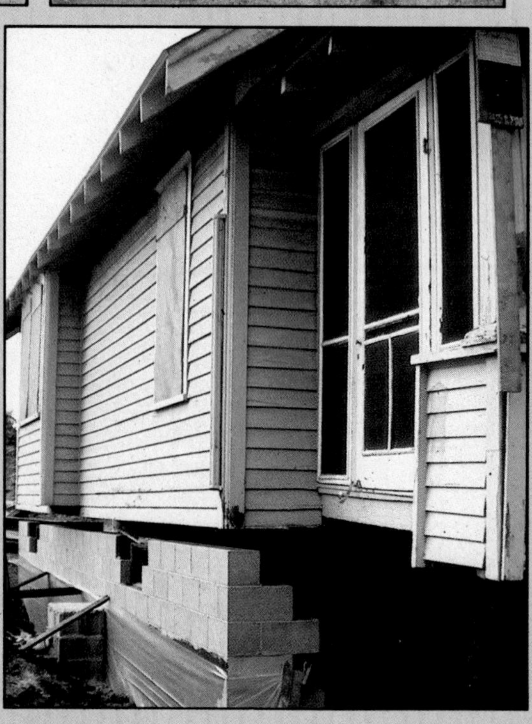

IDEAS AND TECHNIQUES

The hurdles and stumbling blocks encountered when building or buying a dwelling are many and varied, and the ways in which people meet the challenges of the different aspects of planning, constructing, or purchasing a home are just as numerous and diverse.

The material that follows deals with some of the available options and describes how a few people achieved their dreams of efficiency and economy without sacrificing their basic living requirements. For instance, an energy-efficient home doesn't need to be too far removed in design from a conventional house . . . on-site earth can be compressed to form walls at considerable savings . . . leasing property with an option to buy can reduce or eliminate a lump-sum down payment . . . and building on the foundation of a burnt-out structure can offer real moneysaving possibilities.

CUSTOM BUILT ENERGY SAVER

A BLEND OF THREE ENERGY-SAVING FEATURES

It seems natural to take advantage of as many conservation strategies as possible when planning a day-lit dwelling . . . and that's precisely what Minneapolis architect Tom Ellison did when he designed the house featured here.

Ellison's client was very specific concerning his requirements. The structure had to be bright and pleasing inside, highly energy-efficient, and yet comparable in price to other custom homes in the area . . . a tall order indeed, and one that was complicated by the fact that the building site sloped to the south at roughly a 3:1 ratio.

To achieve these objectives—and to blend the structure well into its pitched, heavily wooded setting—the designer relied upon the three basic passive conservation techniques available to him: [1] earth sheltering, [2] superinsulation, and [3] passive solar design.

THE DARK SIDE OF "GOING UNDER"

Generally—at least when dealing with a conventional, aboveground, wood-framed residence—it's less expensive to go with a two-story layout to achieve a desired amount of floor space, simply because there's less surface area to deal with.

But, as Ellison points out, when he applied that strategy to the construction of earth-sheltered houses, some interesting differences appeared which actually would have increased the overall cost of the project. "When you start going deeper into the earth, as would be the case when excavating for a dual-level building, stresses—that is, lateral earth pressures—go way up. But they don't increase arithmetically in proportion to the depth as in a straight-line relationship . . . they become greater along an upward curve. So instead of having to build an underground two-story house just twice as strong, it must be about four times as sturdy . . . and this, of course, adds expense."

Also, there are some other considerations peculiar to subterranean structures that can drive the cost of construction up. One is the use of retaining walls at the sides of the building, which are expensive if done well.

In addition, good waterproofing, regardless of the method used, comes dearly . . . a lot more so than the asphalt shingles that would be used to protect a conventional house from the elements, for example.

Finally, insulation is a factor: Extruded polystyrene, specified for below-grade installation, can be up to *five times* as costly per R-value as fiberglass batting . . . and if the roof is thinly earth-covered, and thus not contributing thermally to the structure, it must be very carefully protected with a reliable rigid insulation, at the expense of the budget.

PHOTOS BY TOM ELLISON AND JOHN FULKER

TRIMMING OFF THE FAT

First, Ellison scrapped the notion of a two-story structure and replaced it with a single-level layout planned around an elongated concrete slab.

Then he specified one story of reinforced concrete block walls with 4-1/2" rigid insulation above grade, tapering to 1-1/2" below. Rather than berm completely around these exposed faces—which would require the use of earth-retaining wing walls to the south—the Minneapolis designer chose to sacrifice a relatively small amount of surface area to the elements to save expense.

Finally, he did away with the whole concept of an earth-covered roof with its inherent cost considerations and settled upon a series of pre-engineered, clear-span wooden truss joists over a wooden subframe. Their 20" depth was able to accommodate two 9" fiberglass batts (with sheathing and gypsum board, the resulting R-60 value is equivalent to that of the roof of a superinsulated dwelling), and the exposed surface was covered with conventional shingles. By sticking with this simple shed-roof layout, Tom was able to keep materials costs down, as well as to make the later installation of a continuous vapor barrier—and its drywall covering—easier by virtue of the fact that partition walls could be put in after the main interior surfaces were finished.

Below grade, the structure was sealed with Bituthene, though bentonite would have been an equally good choice. Of course, a drainage system was used around all the footings.

And, rather than finish the south wall's upper section with block, Ellison decided to use wood stud framing filled with fiberglass batting and covered with wood sheathing over rigid insulation.

PASSIVE SOLAR IN PRACTICE

Although the use of passive solar techniques was critical to the design, too much reliance on dark-colored interior mass would have stood in the way of the owner's desire for a bright inside environment. Ellison, then, based his storage medium decisions on a commonsense rule of thumb: The low-mass wall surfaces must be white to deflect and diffuse radiation so it reaches—and is absorbed by—the exposed high-mass interior surfaces, which should be dark.

To put this formula into practice, he made use of a 16"-thick sand bed within the borders of the insulated footings. A layer of rigid polystyrene beneath the sand isolates it from the earth, and dark quarry tile, set over the concrete slab atop the granular bed, absorbs the energy and transfers it downward.

In a similar fashion, he used the east and west walls as part of an integral storage medium . . . but this time by using rock-faced exposed block masonry on these interior surfaces. These block walls are darkened with a wood stain, which offers a rich hue along with thermal absorption capabilities sufficient to offset heat loss through the windows in those areas.

Supplemental heat comes from an electric forced-air furnace and reaches the living area through supply ducts located in the sand beneath the slab. The return is mounted at the peak of the roof, and can be operated independently as an air-handling system to circulate solar- or wood-heated air.

For cooling purposes, Ellison included adjustable sunshades and operable clerestory windows. The site is heavily wooded, so keeping cool has not been a problem.

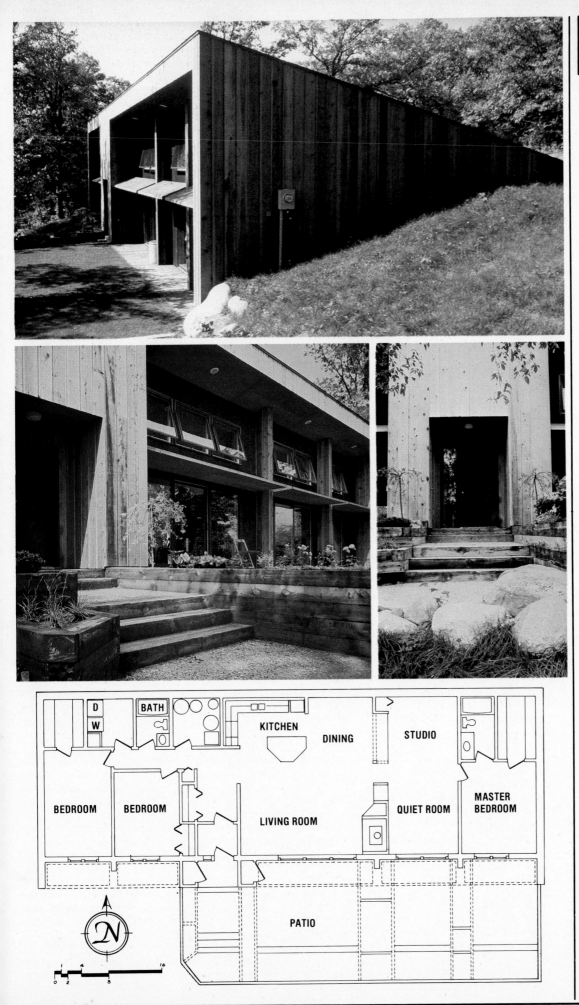

The structure had to be bright and pleasing inside, extremely energy-efficient, and yet comparable in price to other custom homes in the area.

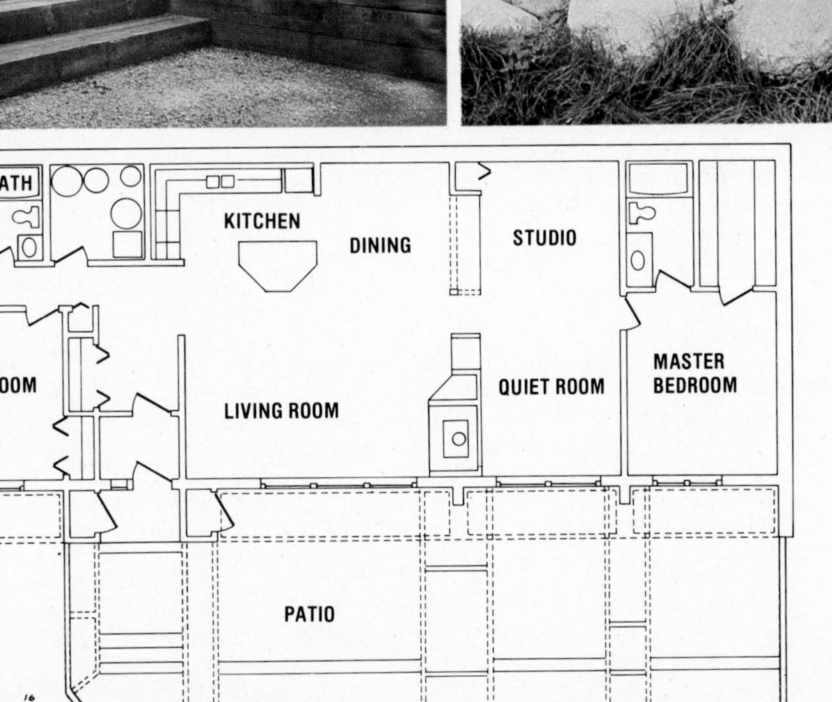

Earth berming, superinsulation, and passive solar features were combined for functional and financial success in this Minneapolis residence. The recessed, operable windows are sheltered from the wind and shaded from summer sunlight, while allowing solar energy to enter the dwelling in winter. The air-lock double entry helps prevent heat loss.

BACKUP HEAT

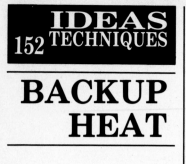

No matter what kind of energy-efficient home you might choose to build, you'll probably need some sort of backup heat during the coldest and/or cloudiest spells. And picking the appropriate system is an indispensable part of planning . . . one that might not be as simple as you would imagine it to be.

Of course, it's important to obtain auxiliary BTU as inexpensively as possible, but in today's very airtight, energy-efficient buildings, there are other concerns as well. In fact, for the class of houses known as superinsulated (as well as other types of tight buildings with heavy thermal protection), it's gradually being recognized that, for the health of the inhabitants, combustion appliances should be avoided . . . even if they have flues which vent the exhaust gases outside.

So for homes that are very tightly sealed, it would be best to consider one of the three options in electric heaters . . . including the conventional space heater, the quartz radiant heater, and the electrical heater with water storage and tempering. For slightly airier structures, the combustion appliances (including kerosene, oil, gas, coal, and wood) may still be acceptable alternatives.

SUGGESTED LIST

Anyone who's done any shopping for a heater of the types described here already knows that there can be a big difference between what is actually paid for one of the devices and the list price. Of course, discount department stores may offer several types of products at substantial savings. What's more, there's significant variation in size, quality, and price within the specific categories. These considerations make it difficult to assign exact values for cost.

But to have any fair basis for comparison, an average of suggested retail prices is the only reasonable cost from which to figure. In the accompanying chart, the cash outlay is split into three divisions (low, medium, and high), which should help to absorb some of the retail pricing variation.

$ PER BTU

The cost of delivered BTU is a subject of significant controversy. Advertising is full of claims and counterclaims as to the benefits of one kind of device versus those of another. To add further confusion to the heating cost question, the price of energy varies considerably throughout the world: There are regions, for example, where electric rates are half what they are in other areas.

As a basis for this comparison, average national energy costs in effect during March 1982 are used here. And the efficiency numbers have been established according to the following criteria.

Electric heaters are generally considered to be 100% efficient, but there is some loss in the delivered versus metered power. Therefore, we've used 95% as the figure for electrical efficiency. (Though the heaters themselves are very efficient, the production of electrical power is not particularly so, averaging only 30% plant efficiency.)

All of the combustion appliances have been calculated as having external venting systems. While chimneys are standard for wood, coal, oil, and gas heaters, many people are still allowing portable kerosene heaters to exhaust into their homes. Several different pollutant hazards are posed by this approach, and most manufacturers are already—or are on the verge of—recommending that kerosene heaters be equipped with flues. Consequently, though kerosene heaters have had efficiency ratings touted as 90% or better, venting the flue gases (and moisture) outdoors cuts that figure to little better than 80%.

Wood and coal stoves have been widely claimed to have 55% efficiency . . . a rating that should be within 5% of all the well-made conventional products. A few new solid fuel heaters are coming onto the market (the better catalytic woodstoves and some wood gasification devices, for example) that can exceed that average by as much as 25%. In addition, these more efficient stoves are generally much cleaner than the established line of appliances. Anyone considering a solid-fuel stove should look into these newer products.

Gas and fuel oil space heaters (without air distribution ductwork) have reasonably well-established heating efficiencies of from 55% to 75%. In general, you can expect a gas appliance to be a little more efficient than oil. And today, at least, both natural and bottled gas are significantly less expensive than fuel oil.

CONVENIENCE

Though the first two criteria discussed here are probably of primary importance to anyone who's looking for backup heat, the amount of effort individuals are willing to expend to keep the appliance fueled may vary greatly. Some people may not object to cutting and/or splitting logs for a woodburner . . . but from a practical point of view, to obtain the amount of heat generated by burning 150 gallons of fuel in an oil heater, the woodstove owner will move 3,000 pounds of wood at least once.

Coal burners do not require as many pounds of fuel to be carted into the home, but they do require more frequent ash cleanout than do wood heaters. In addition, it's difficult to imagine that anyone would enjoy gathering a load of coal.

EMISSIONS

Every backup heating system considered here involves some sort of combustion (and therefore pollution) . . . with the exception of nuclear and hydroelectric powers, which obviously present concerns of their own. Electric heaters *are* nonpolluting in the home, however, and the size of the *producing* facilities makes it possible to limit regional air pollution by sophisticated means (though the available technology isn't always put to use). As mentioned at the beginning of this article, electric resistance heating is the runaway favorite for airtight homes where pollutants such as carbon monoxide, nitrogen oxides, carcinogenic polycyclic organic matter, particulates, and other products of combustion can leak from an appliance and easily accumulate to dangerous levels.

In addition, electric heat does not impose any burden on the fresh air supply in a home. A woodstove, on the other hand, may use as many as 15 to 20 cubic feet of air per minute to support combustion. While this level of air consumption wouldn't be a problem in most conventional homes, a building which changes its air only once every four or five hours could have slightly reduced oxygen levels and would definitely be forced into additional air changes, along with the attendant energy losses.

The overall outdoor emissions from the stacks of these various combustion heaters are now beginning to be quantified, and it appears that wood and coal stoves emit the greatest amount of pollutants per unit of energy provided. The hazards of those compounds that spew out of chimneys aren't quite so well understood, however. For the time being, the most that can be said is that all of the different heaters produce emissions which pose a danger to plant, animal, and human health.

If this analysis seems to produce few favorites, don't despair! The fact that the heaters discussed here are meant only for backup is a sign of real progress. For the comfort of our pocketbooks and the quality of the air we breathe, we all hope that we can cut back on energy consumption. Perhaps these backup heaters should be thought of as the last vestiges of a passing era.

If this analysis seems to produce few favorites, don't despair.

BACKUP HEATER COMPARISON

ELECTRIC

TYPE	INITIAL COST	$/MILLION BTU DELIVERED	CONVENIENCE	INDOOR EMISSIONS	MISCELLANEOUS
fan-equipped resistance	low	18	excellent	insignificant	utility dependent; portable; will overheat room without thermostat
quartz radiant	low to medium	18	excellent	insignificant	utility dependent; portable; directional; may stratify air less than others
water storage resistance	medium	18	excellent	insignificant	utility dependent; limited portability; gradual heat release prevents overheating and limits stratification

COMBUSTION

TYPE	INITIAL COST	$/MILLION BTU DELIVERED	CONVENIENCE	INDOOR EMISSIONS	MISCELLANEOUS
kerosene (modern)	medium	13	moderate	significant	portable; utility independent but uses fossil fuel
kerosene (old style)	low	19	moderate	significant	portable; utility independent but uses fossil fuel
fuel oil	medium	18	excellent	significant	usually utility dependent for ignition
gas (natural)	medium	8	excellent	significant	can be utility independent but uses fossil fuel; overall low emissions
gas (propane)	medium	15	excellent	significant	can be utility independent but uses fossil fuel; overall low emissions
coal	high	9	poor	significant	utility independent; high overall emissions
wood	high	8	poor	significant	utility independent; probably highest overall emissions

FIVE DAYS TO BUILD A CABIN

Among the later additions to the cabin was the 6′-wide front porch, shaded from the hot afternoon sun by deciduous trees. The tall roof allows plenty of room for the sleeping loft, and a woodburning stove vented through the fieldstone chimney keeps out the chill of a cool mountain night.

PHOTOS BY LESTER E. HARRIS, JR.

When Lester Harris took on the job of operating a biological station in the Allegheny Mountains of Highland County, Virginia, he found himself faced with a serious problem: namely, how to house his family during the summer school sessions.

His employer, a small private college, had no funds for extra staff lodging . . . and Lester's year-round home was in the far eastern part of the state (which meant he couldn't commute to the outpost). What he needed, then, was an "overnight" cabin that the five of them—Lester, his wife, their two teenage sons, and their teenage daughter—could build quickly, easily, and inexpensively, right on the biological station grounds, and live in during the summer months.

In terms of design, such a lodge would have to be [1] weathertight, [2] sturdy enough both to withstand the gusty storms common to the area *and* to shed the loads of snow that occasionally build up there, and [3] spacious enough inside to give the six-footers in the family (Lester's sons and himself) more than just the tiny amount of stand-up room they'd find in a conventional A-frame cabin.

AN INEXPENSIVE SOLUTION

The Harrises were able to solve their housing problem quite nicely by building a 16′ X 24′ "modified A-frame" cabin . . . one that they erected in a *mere five* daylight-to-dark workdays.

DAY ONE

The Harris family spent their first day digging twelve 2′-square, 2′-deep holes for the foundation's footings, pouring six inches of concrete (made partly with gravel from a nearby stream) into each hole, and gathering stones for the piers.

DAY TWO

First thing the next morning, they began to lay up a dozen 12″-square concrete-and-stone piers to a height—above grade—of about a foot. While the mortar was still wet, they inserted a long bolt (the threaded end of which previously had been heated and bent at a right angle) head-down into each of the ten outer piers . . . then—with the aid of a borrowed level—Lester evened up all the columns.

When the concrete had begun to harden, they [1] set the 2 X 8 stringers atop the supports, [2] marked the spots at which the bolt tips met the beams, [3] drilled in the beams at these points, and—finally—[4] bolted the stringers in place atop the piers.

DAY THREE

The next task was to nail 2 X 4's along the insides of the four longest stringers . . . after which 2″ X 8″ X 7′8″ joists were notched at both ends, so they could ride on the two-by-fours, and spiked in place 16″ on center. (Note: To insure a roof overhang of at least 4″ at the building's rear, the last four pairs of joists were spaced 14″ on center.)

Atop the completed gridwork, they nailed a board subfloor and built a finished floor of 3/4″ A-C waterproof plywood (the same kind of plywood later used for siding and roofing). With such heavy flooring material, they had no need to place tar paper between the layers of wood to act as a moisture barrier.

Next, they constructed the entire rear wall of the cabin—plywood siding and all—flat on the newly constructed floor, using 3/4″ X 4-1/2″ carriage bolts (with flat and lock washers beneath the nuts) to connect the rafters and studs. Then they raised the wall as high as they could by hand, pulled it into final upright position with the aid of a rope tied to a pickup truck, and checked the structure very carefully for "plumb" (to make certain that successive rafter/stud frames would be properly aligned) before nailing it to the floor.

With the rear wall up and standing, they proceeded to [1] bolt together the first of five rafter/stud frames, [2] raise *it* upright, [3] spike the structure to the floor, and [4] connect it to the back wall with sheets of plywood siding (which eliminated the need for further bracing of any kind).

This procedure was repeated for each of the next four rafter/stud frames, using additional plywood siding to brace the structure as they went along. (Note: The sheets of plywood were applied rough side out and spiked in place, first with 16-penny common nails, then with 8-penny commons.) By overlapping the lowermost siding panels with—and nailing them to—2 X 8 stringers surrounding the building, the builders came up with a solidly constructed, well-anchored framework.

DAY FOUR

On the fourth day, the Harrises [1] built the cabin's front wall on the ground (and raised it into place with lots of sweat and push), [2] nailed ridge boards and purlins to the rafters, and [3] hammered down the plywood roofing, using a combination of 16-penny and 8-penny nails. Before the day ended, the front roof overhang (which required two sheets of plywood, each cut lengthwise at an angle) was framed and built.

DAY FIVE

On the fifth day they set the windows, hung the doors, shingled the roof, painted the entire building with redwood-colored preservative, and put in the loft floor and railing. Their cabin in the woods was up!

LATER ADDITIONS

Of course, certain additions were made later to the basic cabin, such as a 16′ X 16′ rear deck . . . a 6′-wide front porch . . . a handmade fieldstone chimney (which took the better part of a year to complete) for the woodburning stove . . . and 1-1/2″-wide lattice-strip battens on the outside wall, to cover the gaps between the sheets of plywood and improve the dwelling's outward appearance.

One nicety not required was a bathroom, thanks to the proximity of the biological station's washhouse facility (which happens also to be the source of the family's water). Likewise, since they eat all their meals in the camp dining hall, the family elected not to install kitchen equipment. But the cabin does have lots of sleeping space . . . which is all its residents really wanted in the first place!

The cabin provides lots of sleeping space, which is what the residents really wanted in the first place.

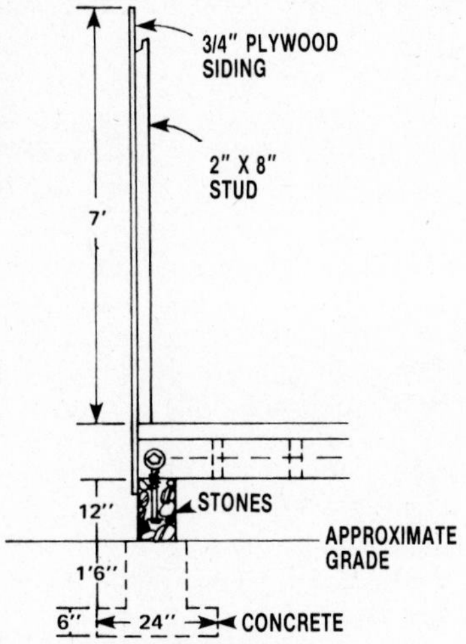

3/4″ PLYWOOD SIDING
2″ X 8″ STUD
7′
12″
STONES
APPROXIMATE GRADE
1′6″
6″ 24″ CONCRETE

FIGURE 1

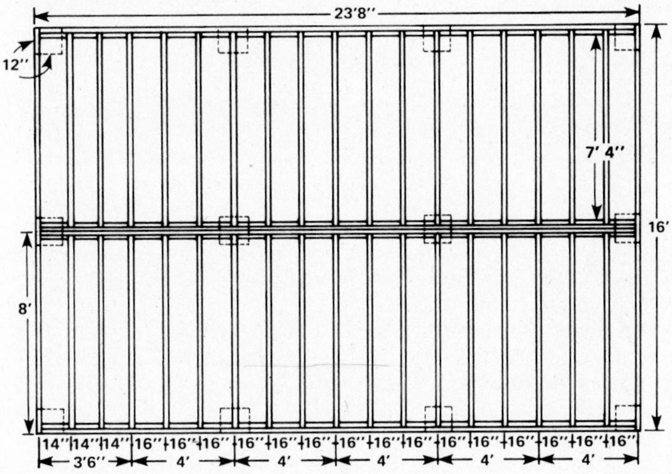

23′8″
12″
7′ 4″
16′
8′
14″ 14″ 14″ 16″ 16″ 16″ 16″ 16″ 16″ 16″ 16″ 16″ 16″ 16″ 16″ 16″ 16″
3′6″ 4′ 4′ 4′ 4′ 4′

FIGURE 2

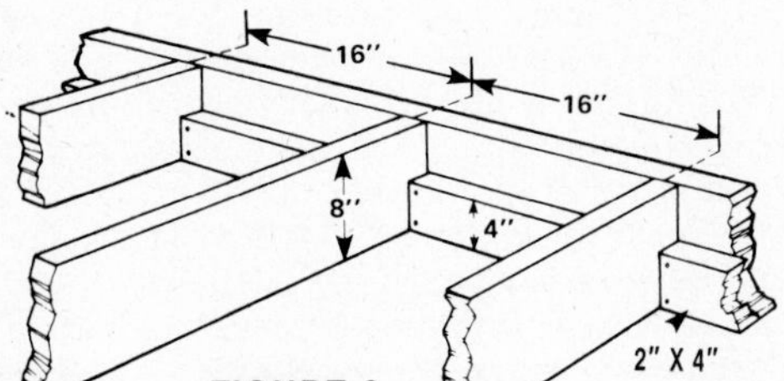

16″
16″
8″
4″
2″ X 4″

FIGURE 3

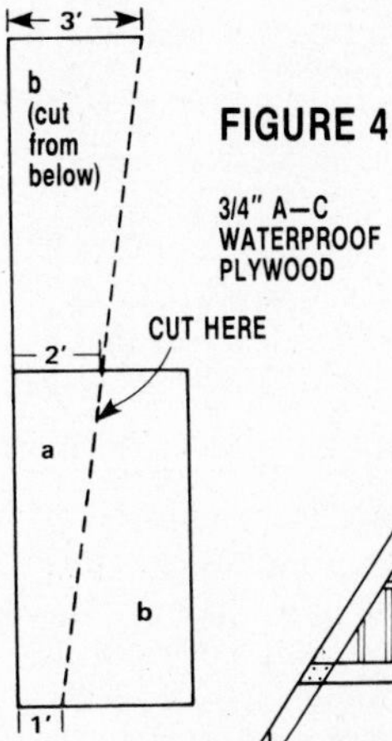

3′
b (cut from below)
2′
CUT HERE
a
b
1′

FIGURE 4

3/4″ A—C WATERPROOF PLYWOOD

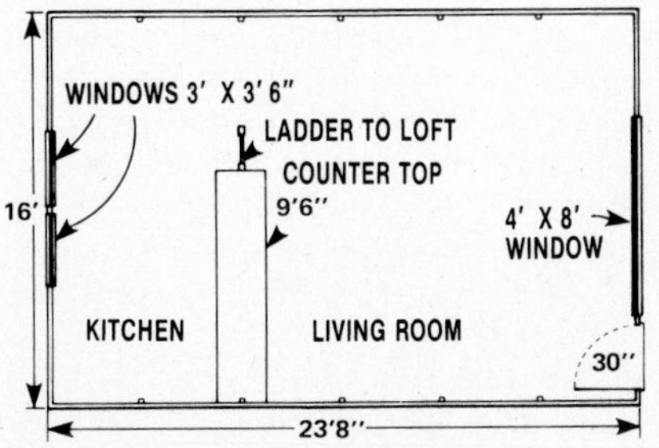

WINDOWS 3′ X 3′ 6″
LADDER TO LOFT
COUNTER TOP 9′6″
16′
4′ X 8′ WINDOW
KITCHEN
LIVING ROOM
30″
23′8″

FLOOR PLAN

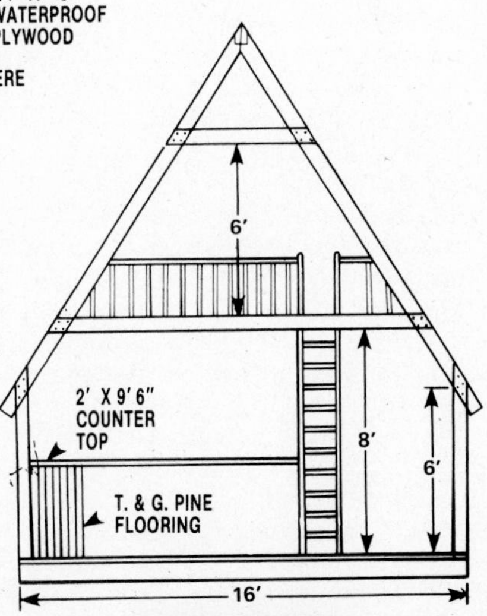

6′
2′ X 9′ 6″ COUNTER TOP
8′
6′
T. & G. PINE FLOORING
16′

CROSS-SECTION OF CABIN

LIVING IN THE EARTH

In an era which tends to celebrate the new and shun the old, rammed earth construction stands out as a paradox: After all, the millenniums-old building method may well *also* be the technology of the future.

No one knows exactly when the first rammed earth edifice was built, though historians agree that the process was employed by the Romans—during the heyday of that nation's empire—to build structures in conquered lands. In fact, the Romans spread the use of earth construction throughout Europe . . . and today, in France (where rammed earth is knows as *pisé de terre*), numerous 400-year-old rammed wall homes *still* shelter their occupants with a measure of comfort and security which no "modern" frame dwelling can offer.

Because rammed earth has such a low rate of thermal conductivity (it's actually near zero), warmth takes almost 12 hours to work its way through a 14"-thick wall. The half-day heat transfer rate makes the material a perfect substance for providing thermal mass in passive solar construction . . . since the sun's warmth will actually be reaching the interior of the house during the cold hours of the night.

In addition, the compressional strength of rammed earth can be as high as 625 PSI, which—though it's only two-thirds the value of a similar thickness of concrete—makes a rammed earth building nearly as durable as a bomb shelter.

Why—if rammed earth construction is *so* strong and *so* time-honored—hasn't this building method caught on in the United States? Well, the fact is that it did . . . once. Back in the 30's, Ralph Paddy (of South Dakota State College) conducted extensive research into earth mixtures and building forms.

Then—in 1938—the U.S. Department of Agriculture actually erected an experimental community of rammed earth buildings. The results of that test were quite positive: The USDA's final report noted that rammed earth structures—which would last indefinitely—could be built for as little as two-thirds the cost of standard frame houses. The earthen abodes were also shown to be considerably less expensive to heat and cool, and—because the homes were labor (as opposed to material) intensive—it was clear that they would allow do-it-yourselfers plenty of opportunity to save money.

We can only speculate as to why postwar America snubbed the rammed earth concept: Perhaps the modest *pisé* technique seemed too basic in the face of our newly formed technocracy. Or it may have been the construction industry—which depends so heavily on material-intensive methods for its livelihood—that helped deprive rammed earth of its rightful position in building. Furthermore, the public's then-increasing yen for miracle synthetics certainly had something to do with the lack of acceptance of so "earthy" a technique.

Fortunately, attitudes are changing. People are returning to any number of time-tested ideas and techniques that have been scorned for the last several decades . . . *including* the concept of rammed earth construction. And at the center of this "back-to-the-land-for-building-materials" movement stand David and Lydia Miller, who have been proponents of rammed earth homes for more than 40 years, and occupants of such dwellings since 1945.

The Millers initially encountered the building-with-soil process in an article from a 1937 issue of *American Home* magazine. Later—during their travels to Europe in the 30's—their interest in the new-old construction technique continued to grow as they corresponded with English and German architects who had successfully used the method.

The contemporary lines of the Millers' home hardly even hints at the fact that the rammed earth building process dates back to the heyday of the Roman Empire.

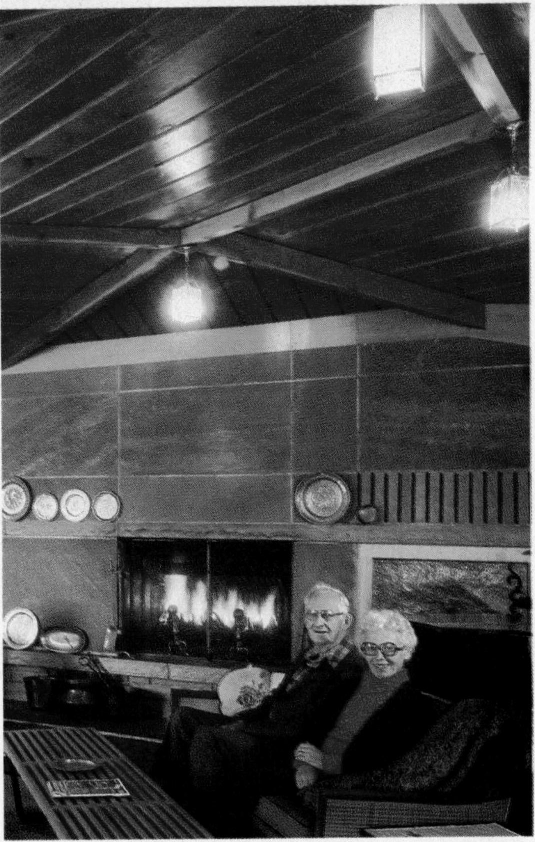

In 1940, David and Lydia met J. Palmer Boggs, an environmentally oriented architect and professor of architecture at Oklahoma State University. Together, Boggs and the Millers built their first house in 1945.

Then, in 1949, after the couple had been airlifted out of Berlin (where David had spent two years as a civilian legal analyst for General Lucius Clay), the architect teamed with the Millers again—in Greeley, Colorado—to build the rammed earth structure they live in today.

EARTH SOLAR

Since David and Lydia's present home was Boggs's second collaboration on a rammed earth dwelling, the architect made use of his previous experience to produce a design that—though more than 30 years old—could still be called advanced by today's standards.

From a distance, the Miller home—which rests atop a gentle knoll on the outskirts of town—looks similar to many of the sprawling ranch-style houses built in the late 50's. But as you turn up the tree-lined driveway, you can see several external features that set the structure apart from any run-of-the-mill residence. For example, on the east side of the building—where two perpendicular walls meet—the thickness of the bulwarks (14 inches of earth plus an inch of stucco covering) becomes apparent. In addition, there's a surprising lack of glass on the front of the house . . . to prevent heat loss from the northern exposure.

Most of the north-facing glazing is set around the front door, which is framed by a pair of beautiful sandstone columns (mined in Lyons, Colorado). However, the northside bedrooms *do* have windows to admit natural light, and a line of glazed vents runs along the roof level in the living area.

Despite the lack of glass on the street side of the house, the home's interior is kept bright by the extensive *south*-facing glazing. In addition, because the house arcs gently to match the sun's path, light tends to penetrate deeply into particular portions of the building at specific times of day.

For example, the morning sun shines into the bedrooms in the east wing and heats both the wool-carpeted floor *and* an interior 12"-thick rammed earth wall. By the afternoon, however, old Sol has slipped around and is beaming in through the living room's huge double-insulated picture windows. More of the woolen floor covering—as well as much of the inside north wall and the massive sandstone fireplace—catches these rays and stores their warmth away for future use.

On really frigid days, the Millers can produce additional warmth by circulating hot water through pipes embedded in the 4" concrete slab floor. This auxiliary heating system was initially served by a gas-fired boiler, but the Millers have recently installed additional water-heating components: placing three 4' X 8' solar collectors on the roof, and a water-heating device in the living room fireplace . . . all of which were tied into the home's original gas-fueled water heater.

Naturally, rammed earth walls do just as good a job of cooling as they do of heating. The excess warmth of a particularly hot day doesn't reach the interior of the house until nightfall . . . when the outside air has cooled. Plus, Palmer Boggs designed a few special features into the Miller home to help the walls do their cooling work. The southern side of the house is equipped with eaves to provide shade during the summer months, and louvered vents are located at the bottom and top of the wall to allow convective ventilation. However, Mrs. Miller finds that it's never necessary to open more than one of the vents, and that not even a number of successive 95°F days can raise the inside temperature above 75°F!

PROOF IN THE LIVING

There are also a number of subtle advantages to the use of massive earthen walls . . . pluses which contribute to the comfort of this venerable form of passive solar living. Besides doing a great job of insulating and storing heat, *pisé* also allows more air exchange than does any comparable material. Thus a rammed earth house breathes (and doesn't tend to become clammy as does a concrete structure).

The thick walls also provide a feeling of security which goes *beyond* their warmth and strength. And it's hard to beat a 14" layer of earth for soundproofing.

DOWN TO EARTH

Perhaps the best feature of rammed earth is that almost anyone can build with it. Most people have the necessary raw materials in their own backyard. And, if you're willing to supply the labor, a rammed earth dwelling can be far less expensive than a conventional (energy-inefficient) house of the same size.

Rammed earth homes lend themselves to construction on a community level. The spirit of such group effort harks back to house raisings during our country's earliest years.

Rammed earth walls do just as good a job of cooling as they do of heating.

This method of construction yields a solid, thermally efficient wall that is aesthetically pleasing as well.

RAMMED EARTH FROM THE GROUND UP

Though the composition of finished rammed earth walls has frequently been compared to that of sandstone, it actually more closely resembles the rock type called conglomerate. Sand *is* one of the major soil-construction components, and clay does bond the materials . . . but aggregate, with rocks up to an inch in diameter, is also included in *pisé*.

The earth in a rammed wall can usually be dug from the excavation that's made for the home's foundation. Topsoil, however, can't be included in the mixture and should be set aside for gardening uses . . . while the ground that *is* used must be composed of about 30% clay and 70% sand and small stones. Such a ratio is common in many parts of the country, but roadbed aggregate must be added to especially clay-heavy soils.

Once earth with the right composition is located (or mixed), the material must be broken up with a rototiller and sifted through appropriately meshed screens to remove any large rocks. (The Millers have stones as large as an inch in their walls, but some rammed earth builders specify using nothing larger than half-inch pebbles.) After the consistency is uniform, water is added to give the mixture the proper adhesion. The ideal raw material is just damp enough to ball up in your hand . . . but will still break apart when dropped. Such a consistency is usually reached by using about 12% H_2O, but the ratio varies, depending on the *exact* proportion of clay in the soil.

A rammed earth wall is built on a foundation that is at least as wide as is the bulwark itself (remember, the soil—in its final compressed form—will weigh about 140 pounds per cubic foot). The foundation can be composed of either poured concrete or specially prepared rammed earth that has been fortified with the addition of 10% cement.

To build the wall, the forms (which are detailed in the accompanying illustration) are clamped onto the foundation—the top of which is dampened slightly—and four to five inches of prepared earth is dumped directly atop the moistened concrete.

This dirt is then tamped with a flat-bottomed device (such as a concrete filled bucket with some sort of handle embedded in it) which provides about two pounds of weight for each inch of its diameter. To tamp properly, just lift the ram and then let it drop . . . continuing the process until the tamper no longer makes any indentation in the earth. You will find that ramming will compact the loose dirt to about 50% of its original height, so each layer will eventually take up between two and three inches of space.

To continue raising the walls, dampen the previously tamped earth, throw in more dirt, and repeat the procedure described above. Once the form is full, you will then take away the wedges, slide the boards off, remove the 1/8" steel straps, and move the form up for the next level.

The ends of the walls are truncated by sliding a vertical board inside the outermost metal straps and packing the dirt against this barrier. Then, once you've squared one wall, a corner can be formed by simply butting the next wall perpendicularly against the original one.

The Millers now believe that it's not necessary to cap a rammed earth wall with concrete, though their 30-year-old home *does* have a six-inch layer of the mix poured on top of the compressed soil. (Some rammed earth builders are still employing the concrete cap on their walls, while others compromise by mixing cement—in a 1 to 10 ratio—with the last couple of beds of earth.)

You can incorporate windows and doors into the massive walls by framing the proposed openings with 2"-thick lumber (of appropriate width) and tamping the earth around the frames. Plumbing and wiring may also be built into the *unpacked* walls . . . but both junction and switch boxes should be temporarily plugged—with a piece of lumber—to prevent them from collapsing during the ramming process.

It can take as long as several years for a rammed earth wall to dry completely (and the strength of the material increases during the curing period), but the forms can be removed as soon as you've finished tamping. Then—two days after the wall is completed—framing, nails, and other connections can be added. You'll have to act quickly, though, because within another two weeks the rammed earth will be too hard to get a nail into . . . unless you first drill the wall with a masonry bit.

After the initial 14 days have passed, it's no longer necessary to protect the rammed earth from rain . . . though moisture will still be able to penetrate the *pisé*. Therefore, exterior and interior coatings are more or less a matter of your own aesthetic preference. The Miller home has an external covering of stucco (over chicken wire) and a layer of plaster on the inside, but David and Lydia plan to leave the walls in their next house bare. They find the natural light-brown color of the rammed earth to be quite pleasing.

The limitations on size for rammed earth buildings come more from practical than from structural concerns. There *are* "soil skyscrapers" in Europe that are as tall as five stories, but building a structure over two stories high involves lifting that would be prohibitive for the do-it-yourselfer. In addition, because it's difficult to set floor joists directly into a rammed earth wall, most two story *pisé* buildings use a ledge—created by *narrowing* the wall thickness on the inside—to brace the support timbers at the second level. Thus a *three*-story building with a 12"-thick top wall would have to have a 16"-thick bottom wall to allow enough material to form joist ledges . . . and would be too thick to be heat-efficient (heat from the sun doesn't have time to reach the inside surface of walls over 16" thick).

The various steps involved in building a rammed earth wall involve evaluating the soil, sifting the dirt, building forms, fitting them with earth, and compressing it by tamping. Doorways and windows are framed, and the wall grows around them.

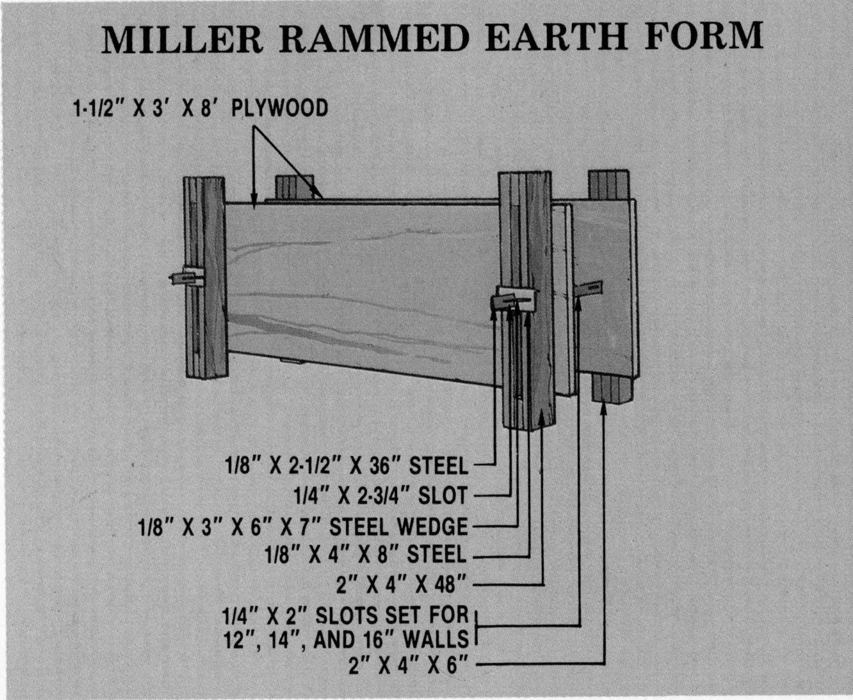
MILLER RAMMED EARTH FORM
1-1/2" X 3' X 8' PLYWOOD
1/8" X 2-1/2" X 36" STEEL
1/4" X 2-3/4" SLOT
1/8" X 3" X 6" X 7" STEEL WEDGE
1/8" X 4" X 8" STEEL
2" X 4" X 48"
1/4" X 2" SLOTS SET FOR
12", 14", AND 16" WALLS
2" X 4" X 6"

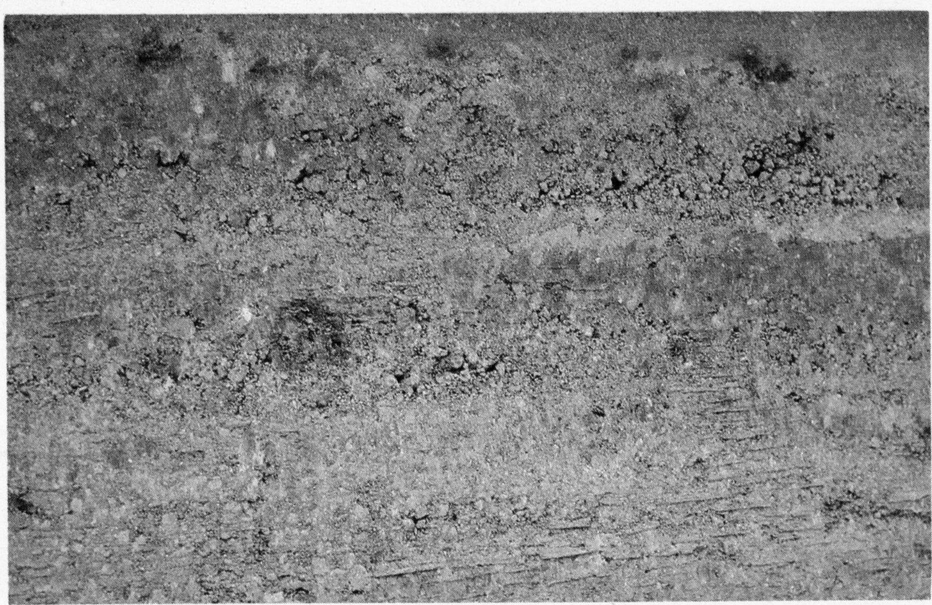

BLOCKS FROM SOIL AND CEMENT

With the aid of a manually operated machine known as the CINVA Ram, the individual owner/builder can fashion ordinary earth into extremely low-cost building blocks that are strong, long lasting, and aesthetically pleasing.

While cement must be added to raw soil as a stabilizing agent to overcome the vulnerability of a dirt-only block to attack by moisture, and fabrication of the bricks is undoubtedly a labor-intensive operation, the resulting product is fireproof, has good insulative qualities, and requires little cash outlay from the builder with more time than money to invest in a new structure.

CINVA is an acronym for the Inter-American Housing and Planning Center of Bogotá, Columbia . . . and Ram is taken from the name of Paul Ramirez, the Chilean engineer who invented this brickmaking device in the mid-fifties.

The CINVA Ram consists of a box, or mold, which is filled with a damp soil/cement mixture, and a lever-actuated piston that compresses the earth/binder mix. Once the mold has been loaded with the proper amount of material, the machine's operator pushes its long handle down with a force of 70 to 100 pounds, exerting approximately 40,000 pounds of pressure on the soil that is being compressed. The brick formed by this procedure is then ejected, set in a cool place, and left to cure for up to three weeks.

Four adults—working in an organized assembly line with the aid of a mechanized cement mixer—can produce only about 50 of the 4″ X 6″ X 12″ bricks an hour. (Since a couple of *thousand* of the blocks are needed for even a small house, it's easy to see why few people ever attempt this construction technique alone!)

THE FIVE BASICS OF BLOCKMAKING

The basic blockmaking process can be broken down into five steps: [1] analyzing the soil, [2] sifting the earth, [3] preparing the mix, [4] manufacturing the blocks, and [5] curing the bricks.

SOIL COMPOSITION

Analysis of the soil that will be transformed into bricks is the first step in the manufacture of pressed-earth blocks. It's necessary to know the composition of the soil intended for use before calculating the amount of cement and missing "native" constituents needed for the final "mix".

All soils are made up of three components: sand, silt, and clay. These components are defined on the basis of particle size (sand being the coarsest of the three, and clay the finest).

Somewhat sandy earth seems to make the best CINVA Ram blocks, and the optimum soil for the bricks is made up of approximately 75% sand and only 25% silt and clay. (The clay alone should never comprise less than 10% or more than 50% of the total.) A good deal of variation is permissible, though. Most earth that is free of vegetable matter will make good compressed-earth blocks.

To make a good estimate of the percentage of each component, use the following procedure: [1] Fill a straight-sided glass jar about one-third full of earth, [2] add an equal volume of water, [3] cover the jar and shake vigorously to suspend all the dirt, and [4] finally, allow the slurry to sit undisturbed about 30 minutes or until the soil has settled into three separate layers with the sand at the bottom.

SIFTING

Whatever the soil's consistency, it must be dried and sieved to remove large lumps, stones, leaves, and other impurities before it can be properly mixed with cement and compressed into blocks.

The soil has the proper moisture content for sifting when [1] a handful can be squeezed without water appearing on its surface, and [2] the ball of earth disintegrates without lumps as it's released. Damp soil of this kind can easily be pushed through a quarter-inch screen.

A sturdy sieve can be built by mounting a piece of hardware cloth on a three-foot-square frame made of 2 X 4's. The important thing is to keep the structure light and small enough to handle easily because an accumulation of stones and other material must be dumped off the screen every now and then.

It's also convenient to make a stand for the sifting tray to rest on while in use. Three sides of the support's base are enclosed to keep the sifted soil neatly confined as it falls through the screen on top . . . and the fourth side is left open so dirt can be shoveled out.

After the Ram is loaded with the proper mixture of soil, cement, and water, the handle is pulled down, exerting the huge pressure needed to form a solid building block.

MAKING THE MIX

Once the soil has been dried and sifted, the mix can be prepared.

The amount of portland cement needed depends upon the composition of the earth to be used: Sandy loams must be fortified—by volume—with from 4.75% to 9.10% cement, desert-like silty dirts need 8.35% to 12.5% of the stabilizer, and clayey soils require 12.5% to 15.4% of the binder. Using more than 15.4% cement is not recommended.

It's actually rather easy to calculate these proportions. For instance, a 10% cement mix consists of one cubic foot of portland cement for every nine cubic feet of sifted, dry soil. This isn't at all difficult to prepare if buckets or containers—preferably with handles—of known volume are available.

All the dry ingredients—cement, sifted dirt, and special additions (such as sand or clay) that may be needed to round out the soil composition—must be thoroughly combined. A cement mixer makes this part of the job easier . . . but the materials can be stirred by hand on any level, hard, and nonabsorbent surface, as long as care is taken to avoid contaminating the mix.

Water—the final ingredient needed to make blocks—must be added a little at a time until the damp soil/cement reaches the right consistency. (Here, it's best to use a garden hose with the nozzle adjusted to produce a fine spray.) There are several ways to tell when to stop adding the liquid. For one thing, if you take a small amount of mix and form it into a ball in your hand, the resulting clod should both hold its shape and not stain your palm. The ball should also pull apart without disintegrating, and when dropped from a height of 1.1 meter (43.3 inches), it should shatter into a loose material that resembles the original (dry) mix.

FROM MIX TO BRICKS

The soil/cement can now be loaded into the CINVA Ram's mold. The only tricky part of this procedure is filling the box with *exactly* the right amount of the mixture each time.

With a little experience, it's easy to tell if the Ram contains as much of the earth-binder mix as it should by the pressure required to depress the block-making machine's long handle. Ideally, *some* resistance should be felt . . . but it shouldn't be necessary to "fight" the lever down.

It's best to make a number of trial bricks—employing carefully measured amounts of soil/cement—to determine the correct loading volume . . . then make an appropriately calibrated scoop. A plastic bleach bottle with the bottom cut away works fine.

Removing the fresh blocks from the Ram calls for a delicate touch, since the bricks are fragile when newly formed. The Ram's instruction booklet suggests placing one's hands "flat at the ends of the block, being careful not to damage the corners or edges, and then gently lift the block from the mold box".

THE CURING PERIOD

The new bricks are placed on a flat, nonabsorbent surface (a board or cement slab covered with sheets of plastic is ideal) in a shady environment to cure. Blocks are stood on edge and spaced far enough apart so that they don't touch. Note that bare ground—which will draw water from the blocks so rapidly that they'll be weakened and may even crack—is not an acceptable surface upon which to age the bricks.

If possible, the curing site should be located directly adjacent to the Ram since it's difficult to carry the freshly molded bricks very far.

The slower the soil/cement blocks dry, the stronger they'll be. During the first four days of their cure the bricks should be kept covered with plastic sheeting. Also, beginning 24 hours after they leave the Ram, the soil/cement blocks should be thoroughly sprinkled three times a day with the fine spray from a garden hose. The bricks can be stacked on the fourth day, but the sprinkling should be continued for another eight days. Finally, three weeks after they've left the mold, the blocks can be used in construction.

USING THE BLOCKS

In building, the same techniques used with concrete blocks can be employed with pressed-earth bricks. Before laying soil/cement blocks it's a good idea to dip them in water to prevent them from absorbing moisture from the mortar (thereby weakening it) used to hold them together.

As usual, courses of the bricks should be laid in such a way that the vertical seams in one row coincide with the center-points of the blocks in the course above. Also, the mortar in all joints should be no more than one centimeter (four-tenths of an inch) thick.

In areas where winters are cold and wet, it is prudent to seal the blocks by applying a good waterproofing such as a clear acrylic masonry sealer to the finished soil/cement walls. Of course, numerous other paint or plaster finishes will do the job as well.

So what if you do live in a part of the country where the winters are frigid and damp? Cold weather or not, pressed earth works beautifully.

HOW TO TEST SOIL/CEMENT FOR STRUCTURAL INTEGRITY

Before thinking about building a house, barn, or other habitable structure out of pressed-earth blocks, you should make sure that the soil/cement mixture you're using is the best one possible. How? Start by creating bricks from four trial mixes: one containing the maximum amount of cement, one with the minimum amount, and two with intermediate concentrations of the binder. Let the blocks cure for 15 days, then test them in each of the following capacities:

TENSILE STRENGTH: Lay a block across two supports spaced eight inches apart, and place weights one by one atop the brick's center until it breaks. The mix producing the strongest block is best.

HARDNESS: A nail driven with the bare hand should penetrate no deeper than five centimeters (about two inches) into the block.

SOUND: When struck lightly with a hammer, the brick should produce a metallic sound.

UNIT WEIGHT: That mix which produces the block having the greatest weight—and therefore the least porosity—should be considered best.

SHRINKAGE: There shouldn't be any. Measurable contraction after curing means that the mix either contains too much clay, too little cement, or both.

Cold, damp weather or not, pressed earth works beautifully.

Removing the freshly made blocks from the Ram requires a delicate touch.

BUILD ON A BURNT-OUT SHELL

The major stumbling block facing couples who want to build their own homes is often simply the bottom-line *cost*. And much of that expense has nothing to do with the ever-increasing prices of lumber and land. Both of those can be bargained for . . . given persistence, prudence, luck, and a lot of legwork. Nor do the rest of the necessary finishing materials—such as windows, doors, paneling, hardware, roofing and cabinets—account for all of those dollars. Such items can frequently be obtained by creative scavenging and the careful combing of junk sales, auctions, flea markets, and salvage yards.

Actually, one of the most expensive components of an owner-built home is simply the hole in the ground that it sits on. After all, that "starting point" includes a costly excavation . . . a foundation . . . and a number of hookups (including electricity, gas, water, sewer or septic tank).

You might also be surprised to hear, as were Jeff Taylor and his wife (who built the house shown here) when *they* set out to build, that the price of concrete has almost doubled in recent years. Worse yet, backhoe operators (who dig the main excavation and trenches) command up to $150 an hour!

Furthermore, the couple found that the utility companies and city services would both have their hands out long before one stick of wood was laid on the foundation. The fees for just setting up the umbilicals (and the meters that attach) seemed high enough to daunt all but the hardiest, most stubborn do-it-yourselfer.

Finally, with building codes being tightened in response to the human tendency to cut corners and save costs—and with local, state, and federal watchdogs mandating new regulations by the minute—the couple was faced with the realization that it's difficult to build a home without such approved "necessities" as electricity and a sewer connection. Just try telling the city or county building inspector—for instance—that your house is going to be strictly solar heated . . . or that it won't require commercial electricity because you're going to wire it to a wind-generator.

Or see what happens when you suggest that you've decided to forgo flush toilets in favor of composting ones. The water-saving commodes are still "experimental", officials will inform you . . . and they intimate that you'd best postpone using that particular innovation until it's been approved by the local, state, and federal regulatory commissions.

The Taylors were able to save the chimney at one end of the building, but new walls were necessary all around the burnt-out home.

You get the picture, and so did the Taylors. To be fair, though, most bureaucrats don't *enjoy* pushing prospective owner/builders through an endless maze of red tape. But, to an individual who has scraped together a down payment for a few acres of bare land or a city lot, the sudden realization that he or she will then have to come up with enough money for sizable permit charges, equipment rentals, architect fees for foundation plans, and other "incidentals" can be staggering . . . and, too often, downright *depressing*!

MOUNTAIN MANIA

Jeff and his wife had decided to move from Oregon to Colorado to build a place of their own in the mountains. They soon discovered, though, that the price of upland property was quite a bit higher than that of equivalent city lots down in the metropolis at the bottom of the pass. And after haunting real estate offices in the pretty little mountain town they'd picked as their first home base, the couple realized that the small nest egg accumulated over seven long years just wasn't enough. Day after day they looked for land/house combinations in town, around town, and beyond town. And each day they were told that a $5,000 to $6,000 down payment was the bare *minimum* for land . . . and with any sort of house on the property, the required "deposit" would be considerably more.

They finally decided that they had enough money either to begin construction from the floor joists up . . . or to remodel an existing structure. So, although they had dreamed of a brand-new house built lovingly with their own labor, they lowered their sights and decided to look for an old cabin that needed a major remodeling job.

The woods—which is where the Taylors hoped to live—were full of old cabins from the 20's and 30's . . . back when the area was little more than a summer retreat for wealthy flatlanders. Realty companies tactfully advertised the sad structures as "rustic handyman specials" . . . but most of them—to be truthful—looked as if the last tenants had sported either fur or feathers. The weary house-hunters soon learned that "fixer-upper" usually meant "bring your own dynamite".

WISHFUL THINKING

After one particularly horrible excursion to a cow-filled house with no well, Jeff and his wife turned the car back in the direction of the smog and looked down toward the gray city that apparently was to be home. They knew that they couldn't even afford to *rent* mountain property.

Before leaving, though, they decided to stop in their mountain community for a farewell lunch . . . and as they ate, they fantasized about the property they *really* wanted to own, even though it wasn't in the cards. All they needed was a *pre-dug* foundation (cured and with all the hookups in place, ready to build upon), a couple of fireplaces (never wish for anything *small* when building castles in the air), a garage or other outbuildings for tool and lumber storage, wood fences, and—what the heck—why not a yard full of trees?

As they got more and more outrageous, Jeff finally stated flatly, "The place would have to have a garden spot and a well before I'd even *consider* buying it. Absolutely."

After lunch, though, their enthusiastic daydreaming subsided to a dull ache as they took one last tour through the sky-capped village, realizing that they'd soon be city mice once again. With calm resignation they drove down a favorite back street . . . one that boasted an incredible view of a panoramic mountain. All the quaint cabins and small homes seemed to be full of friendly people who would never be their neighbors. Wistfully, they stared at each house as they drove by.

EUREKA!

Suddenly Jeff hit the brakes, and their car skidded for several yards. There it was, right on the corner, exactly where it had been the *dozens* of times they'd driven by: a low, wide, squat cabin with a stone foundation . . . a detached garage . . . a tree-filled yard . . . and blackened, gaping windows, where a fire had lapped up and gutted the structure.

In fact, only the foundation and the garage were undamaged by the blaze. One charred but salvageable chimney rose, stone by stone, up one scorched outer wall. Another, at the far end of the house, was half-buried under rubble.

They got out of their car shakily, wondering at their own recent nearsightedness, and looked through the window holes at a blackened, hellish interior: large, charred beams . . . a floor covered with six inches of ash and insulation . . . exploded glass . . . and wooden furniture that was literally ready for the hibachi. This was it!

The job of converting that blackened pit into a home turned out to be exhausting, dirty, and utterly hilarious at times. Not one person they talked to ever thought they could do it alone. Surprisingly enough, though, their greatest support came from the local building inspectors . . . the very folks they'd felt certain would be the toughest to convince. The local authorities encouraged the Taylors' efforts to rebuild, because the property was an eyesore. In fact, the day after the couple looked at it, the city required the owner to board all the openings to prevent trespass.

A brief check through the files at the fire department revealed the owner's name. (By the way, such information is always a matter of public record, and Jeff even went ahead and looked up the names of owners of *other* places that had suffered a similar fate, just in case this deal fell through.) It took only two phone calls to purchase the home-to-be. It had been income rental property, and the fire had followed an explosion from a gas leak only a month previously. The city had given the owner two months to either raze or rebuild the structure, and then the Taylors suddenly showed up . . . two people eager to buy the crispy castle as it stood! The owner accepted their first bid, and even offered (through his attorney) to carry the contract until they could arrange permanent financing!

The day after they closed the deal they visited the city building department and described their plans to remove the existing structure, properly dispose of the debris, and rebuild on the same site . . . using the original foundation. Jeff's confidence must have been contagious, because he soon walked out with a building permit.

AND SO IT BEGINS

The hard part came first. It took a full month just to tear down and haul away the burned building . . . but after that time the edge of their enthusiasm was only a little dulled. They inhaled enough soot to qualify for coal miners' pensions . . . worked from sunup to sundown one day just scraping the floor down to the solid, singed hardwood . . . and discovered that it really *does* help to scream "KREEGAH!" while smashing a wall apart with crowbars. (Adrenalin is truly a miracle drug.)

All the salvageable materials went in one pile and all the trash—a small mountain of it—in another. When they hit the bare foundation and crawl space (they'd forgotten to wish for a basement!), they were overjoyed. For a tiny down payment and a month of sweat, they had a large, intact foundation which had had 60 years to settle . . . two fireplaces (one at each end) . . . a two-year supply of quick-starting firewood . . . about 1,000 board feet of one-inch mill-run boards (which they used as exterior wall sheathing) . . . and ten huge scorched beams. (Those timbers, by the way, had actually been improved by the blaze. The beams simply needed to be wire-brushed down to the hard, undamaged wood . . . and the inspector was so impressed with their fire-hardened strength that he allowed them to be used as the main support beams in the roof.)

Once the frame of the structure was erected, it was easy to obtain a "finishing" construction loan from a bank that was impressed by the Taylors' low investment and large return. (They were prudent enough not to show the bank any "before" pictures. Instead, they accentuated the positive by showing only "after" shots!)

AND NOW IT ENDS

It took two entire years to complete the job, but the house is now fully sided, comfortably warm, and full of designed-in features . . . limited only by the size of the foundation, the Taylors' imagination, and their funds.

The whole construction process was similar to a large—make that *massive*—remodeling job. Yet the house is uniquely their own . . . a two-year-old home worth (at last appraisal) at least *four times* the money they put into it. And the beneficial spinoffs resulting from their project have been incredible, too. Jeff's first carpentry job in Colorado, for example, was clinched when he pulled out pictures of his home building handiwork.

Someone once said that a wish is the lowest form of desire . . . in other words, that it's a fantasy unaccompanied by the willingness to work hard to attain the goal. The Taylors *were* willing to put labor into the bargain, though, and their "shopping list" wish was fulfilled completely, even down to the last two "absolute must" items. Their garden space didn't get tilled right away, it's true—because of the more pressing matters of building a house and working to pay for it—but it was there, just as requested.

And as for the well they had hoped for, even *that* was there, though it wasn't quite as imagined. The original builder had constructed a rustic storybook well . . . but it was merely a landscape decoration. It was, in short, a *wishing* well.

Only the foundation and garage were undamaged by the blaze, though a salvageable stone chimney rose along one scorched wall.

Massive fire-hardened beams, charred but sound, were cleaned up with a lot of sweat and a wire brush and used to support the roof of the Taylors' new home.

HOW TO CHOOSE A HOME FOR RECYCLING

There are now thousands of abandoned farmhouses scattered throughout this country. Although most need modernizing, a good number are available—often with a barn, outbuildings, and a garden patch thrown in—at bargain basement prices.

There are three ways of locating such old houses. The first, and probably easiest, is to contact a real estate company, such as the United Farm Agency (612 West 47th Street, Kansas City, Missouri 64112), Strout Realty (P.O. Box 2757, Springfield, Missouri 65803), or the Safebuy Agency (2405 Gaines Street, Little Rock, Arkansas 72203), all of which deal in farm property from coast to coast . . . and ask for listings in the area of your choice.

The second way to find these old homes is by watching the classified ads in the papers. You'll want to keep your eyes open for offers that say "handyman's delight" or "needs T.L.C.".

The third method of scouting out abandoned farmhouses—and probably the best way to get a good deal—is to make your own discovery. Drive the back roads in the area that interests you, and talk to people.

You'll find the best buys at 60 miles or farther from large cities. Today's commuters don't mind driving that distance daily . . . and most land within (and sometimes even beyond) such a radius is fairly high-priced.

Once you've located an appealing property, you should *determine whether the building is structurally sound*. You may well consider it a good investment to hire a restoration consultant or carpenter to look over the house and advise you on its condition.

If you act as your own inspector, there are several quick checks you'll want to make on the structural integrity of the house.

UNDER THE FLOOR

To begin, look for evidence of termites . . . and look hard. The insects devour beams, joists, and other timbers from within, and their damage is often completely overlooked by people who make a casual walk-through survey of a building. Go down into the basement (or outfit yourself with coveralls and crawl under the house if the structure has no cellar) and stab the joists and sill plates with a sharp knife or ice pick. Undamaged beams will be solid, but your instrument will plunge easily into the timbers that termites have devoured from the inside.

Forget any house that has an understructure badly riddled by the bugs. You'd be buying nothing but trouble. If the insects have made inroads into only small areas of a building, however, you can repair the damaged timbers by "scabbing on" or "nail mating" reinforcing beams across the weakened areas after taking steps to insure that the little woodeaters leave the premises.

Actually, ridding a building of termites without resorting to poisonous chemicals can be relatively easy. The insects do not fly into a house, nor do they reside in its timbers. They require moisture to survive and live underground in colonies, making regular forays from the nest to nearby supplies of wood and other cellulose materials. Termites will attack only wood that is in direct contact with the ground or that to which the colony can build a mud tube. The insects, in short, must have a protected and maintained conduit to the wood they eat. Remove their tunnel, and you've dissuaded the termites.

Termites are controlled most simply and surely, then, by [1] making sure no wooden portions of a building extend down into the ground, [2] removing all wood, paper and other cellulose matter from under the structure and around its foundation, [3] ventilating all damp crawl spaces, and [4] scraping any suspicious mud tubes off the building's masonry or rock foundation.

Your ice pick test may turn up signs of another condition that sometimes damages the timbers of an old house as much or more than termites: dry rot. This is a white, powdery fungus that grows on overly damp wood and spreads most rapidly in warm climates. If the problem isn't widespread, the damaged sections can be removed and/or replaced and the fungus killed by installing ventilators in the trouble spots to reduce the humidity.

After carefully examining the understructure of a house, scrutinize the building's foundation and lower walls for the telltale brown stains of flood marks (which will be more or less horizontal as opposed to the uneven splotches on ceilings and walls caused by a leak).

FROM TOP TO BOTTOM

Check the attic (if you can't find an access opening, make one) by taking a good flashlight and examining the ceiling joists, the rafters, and the roof sheathing. The rule of thumb here is that if only the roof boards need repairs, you're in good shape . . . but if any of the ceiling joists or rafters show signs of weakness, breakage, or rot, you should steer clear of buying the house.

Examine the chimney flue while you're up in the attic . . . is it solid and sound, or is it going to require repair such as pointing (raking out crumbling mortar from the joints and applying fresh)?

Chances are the building will need some new electrical wiring, although, if the leads you trace out are not seriously chewed or deteriorated, you may be able to get by—at least for normal use—with the system already in the house. Then again, if you plan to use modern power equipment and appliances, you might want to completely rewire the structure to prevent overloads.

The walls of most old homes will be finished in plaster over lath, and there's a good chance that the (probably) heavily papered plaster will be falling apart. The situation may not be as bad as it seems, however, as in many cases holes can be patched (joint cement is the easiest method to use), or the walls can be covered with wallboard or paneling.

Most frame homes built before the 1940's were not insulated, although a good percentage of such houses have had insulation added over the years. The addition, obviously, is a plus for any house you might buy . . . so look for it. There's no place to put insulation in a solid brick or stone building, of course, except under the roof or in the attic . . . where it's still a definite asset.

The floors of an old farmhouse may well sag a bit in the middle and slope overall, even though the joists in each room are sound and in good condition. There's a good chance that the flooring itself will be solid oak and in pretty good shape (although some of the earlier country homes do have yellow pine planking that may have deteriorated somewhat more than oak).

Most abandoned houses lose some of their windows to vandals or windstorms sooner or later or, at the very least, need a completely new caulking job around all their glazing. Expect to spend a few dollars here.

THE MATTER OF HEATING

Check the fireplace if the building you're looking at has one. You should be able to see daylight up the flue, and the chimney should be lined with fire brick (or an equivalent) and should draw smoke well. Test the draw by lighting a piece of paper and holding it at the edge of the hearth. The paper should burn quickly and leave no smoke trails in the room.

Many older farmhouses were warmed with room heaters (first a coal stove or a woodburner, and later, possibly, an LP-gas stove). Such an austere heating system means closing off sections of the house in winter, heating only the kitchen and living room and sleeping in a cold bedroom under several blankets. A central furnace (usually in the basement) is better as far as comfort is concerned, though it's more expensive to maintain.

Most really old farm kitchens started out with a woodburning cookstove, which was probably replaced by a gas or electric range sometime along the way. If you look long enough you'll probably discover the old kitchen flue (covered with wallpaper or patched in), and if you unplug the vent, you can even move in a woodburning range again, if you like. Just make sure the flue is not blocked by fallen brick or a collapsed liner, and that the passage is sound all the way up through the roof with metal flashing securely fastened in place and sealed.

PLUMBING

The majority of early farmsteads had hand pumps and outhouses instead of indoor plumbing and toilets . . . and those older homes you find equipped with modern facilities may well have had one or more individual fixtures removed. In any case, plan almost certainly on having to clean the septic tank before being able to use the toilet.

The single most important matter to consider when buying any rustic property is the availability of water. Most old farmhouses have [1] a deep drilled or shallow dug well, [2] a spring, and/or [3] a cistern. Dug wells and cisterns were most favored by the old-timers, although they used springs when they had such a supply of water handy.

Dug wells are generally about 25 to 35—certainly no more than 50—feet deep. They were usually sunk by hand through dirt and clay down to rock or sandstone, then lined to the top with rocks or concrete and topped with a cement or wooden platform on which was placed the familiar old hand pump (or, in rare instances, a roof-covered windlass for letting down a bucket on a rope). Watch out for such a well with a rotten cover and/or sides that have started to cave in . . . it isn't dependable as a water supply, and the danger of further cave-ins makes repairing one hazardous. A good dug well can be made serviceable again by a thorough cleaning and—sometimes—a relining with cement, but unless it's on a really good vein of water, such restoration may not be worth the effort (shallow wells regularly go dry during droughts).

Cisterns or "second wells" are quite commonly found on old farmsteads. They're simply big concrete or stone-lined tanks in the ground and are filled with rainwater piped from the house and barn roofs and strained through a charcoal filter. Such straining doesn't purify the water enough to remove all harmful bacteria and make it safe for drinking purposes, but the soft water stored in a cistern is ideal for such uses as clothes laundering and hair washing.

In some parts of the country, many old houses depended on springs for their water. Any time you run into such a situation, ask around to determine whether the spring in question flows during dry spells and try to learn whether the water comes from far enough underground to remain free of surface contamination.

Although a drilled well is the most dependable farmstead water source, you're not likely to find one on an old farm . . . and you'll probably wind up putting in such a well on any property you buy that lacks one. When you *do* locate an old country place with a driven or drilled deep well, however, you'll often find a genuine windmill and water pump thrown in for good measure.

Before making any commitment to buy such a piece of property, ask the local county extension service or health department to test the water supply.

THE OUTBUILDING BONUS

There's often quite a cluster of woodsheds, chicken coops, barns, garages, and other outbuildings around old country houses, and you should look them over and weigh their value before making a decision whether or not to buy any abandoned farmstead. Most of these extra structures will be reasonably familiar to you . . . but an old storm/fruit cellar half-buried in the back yard can be an agreeable surprise.

When run down, these cellars are usually so full of mud and water and creepy-crawlies that you may tend to completely overlook their usefulness. Once cleaned up, however, the dugout structures are welcome shelters during severe wind storms, and absolutely nothing equals them for the storage of apples, potatoes, and other root crops through a long, cold winter.

If you find yourself discouraged by the points raised here, perhaps you didn't really want to renovate an abandoned farmstead after all. But if you're now more determined than ever to breathe new life into a fine old *real* house, more power to you! There are some great places out there available at reasonable prices, just waiting for you in that fresh country air.

Keep your eyes open for offers that say "handyman's delight", or "needs T.L.C.".

THEY BOUGHT THEIR "DREAM HOUSE" FOR $50!

"You bought a house for $50?"

That's what people always say (in utter disbelief!) when Kathleen and Richard Arens of East Lansing, Michigan tell the story of their three-bedroom, 1,200-square-foot, older home with its fine hardwood floors and mellow oak woodwork.

Of course, there was a catch to the deal: Before they moved into the residence, they had to agree to move *it* from the spot where they'd bought it.

Still, that wasn't such a bad bargain. The total moving cost *plus* the cost of remodeling the home and adding a two-car garage in the basement came to about the same amount of money as the *down payment* on an equivalent modern house! And this total was only about one-fourth of the dwelling's appraised value at the time the Arenses moved in.

PREPARING FOR THE MOVE

Richard and Kathleen looked at—and rejected—dozens of residences before finding the one they finally purchased. Their "dream house" turned out to be a one-story wood-frame bungalow situated on a narrow city lot. Its interior was typical of the older homes in the area: living room, dining room, kitchen, and breakfast area lined up on one side . . . three bedrooms plus an enclosed porch along the other. The furnace was fairly new, the construction was sound, and they did have some ideas about how to modernize the floor plan. So they went ahead.

The next step was to find a suitable neighborhood for the dwelling. To their dismay, they soon learned that many subdividions had prohibitions against bringing in houses that were built somewhere else. Other areas—by virtue of "covenants" contained in the deeds to the land—had restrictions on the minimum number of square feet any house in the area could have. The Arenses were limited, too, by the sheer cost of transporting the building: The mover charged $1,000 just to lift the house off its foundation . . . and an additional $1,000 for each mile it would be moved!

After weeks of searching, they finally found a spacious lot in an older (but well-kept) neighborhood. The mandatory water and sewer hookups weren't too expensive, and the property came with beautiful old gnarled apple trees and raspberry bushes everywhere!

Next, the couple steeled themselves for the confrontation with City Hall. Permits were required for every step in moving a house and locating it on a new site. Happily, they were successful in securing a special "homeowner's permit", which allowed them to complete plumbing and electrical work and to hook up the sewer line themselves . . . thus saving the expense of having to hire professionals to do those jobs.

Meanwhile, at the vacant lot, Richard and Kathleen staked out the perimeter of the home's new foundation. Then they called in an excavator and notified the mover that they were ready to begin.

A HOUSE ON WHEELS

Transporting an entire house from one location to another is a fascinating experience, and the Arenses were anxious to see exactly how it was done. Here—briefly—is what happened:

On the appointed morning, half a dozen workmen arrived at the home's old address and first knocked about four concrete blocks out of the foundation walls at either end of the rectangular house. Through those holes, the workers passed two 50′-long I-beams the length of the building. Next, the men placed a jack under each of the four ends of the beams. Then they raised the whole affair high enough off the ground to slide two short I-beams underneath *at right angles to* the first set of girders. (At this point, the steel underpinnings resembled a giant tic-tac-toe board.)

Then a winch was used to slowly pull the house off its foundation, after which the work crew attached wheels to each end of the long I-beams, and they were ready to roll!

SETTING THE DWELLING DOWN

Once the movers had trundled the building to its new location, they positioned the house over the excavated area. Then they set the ends of the long I-beams on four pillars made by stacking pairs of 8″ X 8″ timbers crosswise. All that remained was to construct the basement walls, remove the wooden pillars, and (with the aid of jacks) gently lower the home onto its new foundation.

During the following summer, Richard dug the footings for the foundation . . . and Kathleen leveled the concrete in the footers with a two-by-four. He put in the sewer line . . . and she painted the house's exterior. They both learned to lay block as they erected the basement walls (with the house hovering rather ominously overhead).

That summer, by the way, they learned one especially important lesson. Namely, *hire a pro to teach you how to do something you've never attempted before*. They found a bricklayer, for instance, who was willing to work part time with them on an hourly basis to construct their home's foundation. As a result, they learned firsthand how to build walls that are level and plumb along their entire 50-foot length . . . how to cut concrete blocks to fit around basement windows . . . and the secret of finishing off a

PHOTOS SUPPLIED BY KATHLEEN ARENS

The new foundation for the residence was built under the structure, which was then lowered into position atop the concrete block walls.

concrete-block wall with those even grooves of [illegible] each row instead of the big pro- [illegible] simply plop one [illegible] frequently [illegible] complish a task. Richard [illegible] fill in around the foundation and do some [illegible] grading . . . and it took him nearly the whole day just to become proficient enough with the controls to avoid swinging the shovel through the basement walls. Later, he found a construction worker with his own backhoe and tractor who agreed to do the work for only a little more than it had cost the couple to rent the first machine.

REMODELING

Improvements the couple devised for the home's floor plan called for placing the building sideways (from its former orientation) on the new lot. They replaced the dining room's bay window with double doors and converted the centrally located room into an entry foyer. Now they can go directly to the living room (on the right) or the kitchen (on the left) when they come in the front door.

Thanks to the way the house sits on its lot, the bedrooms are now along the back of the house instead of being lined up along one side. Also, the large windows that lined the two walls of the former "enclosed porch" currently enclose a sunroom/greenhouse just off the living room. And the outside door to this room (which was once the house's front door) opens out onto a small deck.

TIPS FOR THE WOULD-BE HOUSE-MOVER

Here are a few tips the Arenses came up with as a result of their experience:

[1] Have the building inspector from the area you're moving to inspect the soon-to-be-transported dwelling at its present location before you buy it. He can tell you whether your prospective purchase meets the codes for his area and what structural changes if any will be required before he can issue an occupancy permit. With an older house, you may have to completely redo the wiring or plumbing.

[2] Remember that you can *always* find another house. Don't settle for one that needs [illegible] work.

[3] [illegible] bids from several moving firms. [illegible] Kathleen received estimates rang- [illegible] to $8,000 to transport one [illegible] considered buying.)

[4] If [illegible] ing a lot with the intention of moving a house onto it, by all means make the offer to purchase contingent on your being able to secure all the necessary permits.

[5] Try not to lock yourself into any kind of tight schedule where you must move in by a certain date. Sit down and calculate the amount of time the whole project will take from start to finish . . . then double it! If you try to rush things, delays will be terribly frustrating. The Arenses' house, for example, was stuck in some mud at the edge of their lot for nearly a week due to unusually heavy rains. They spent days, too, tracking down a faulty circuit in the home's outmoded electrical system. And the building inspector returned time after time to ask them to fix "just one more small detail" before he finally issued an occupancy permit.

THE BOTTOM LINE

All told, work on the house took five months from the day the dwelling was moved until the day it was ready to live in. Was it worth the time, the trouble, and—most important of all—the money? Its new owners believe so. Not only did Kathleen and Richard save several thousand dollars cash, but some of the home's features, such as the real plaster walls and the extra-wide oak woodwork, would be difficult to duplicate at any expense.

The thing they like best about their dream house, though, is the happy feeling they get whenever they start to add up all the monthly mortgage payments and interest charges they *haven't* had to pay (*and never will*) over the years, thanks to the fact that they own their "little castle" free and clear.

The real plaster walls and the extra-wide oak woodwork would be difficult to duplicate at any price.

Kathleen and Richard changed the orientation of the house in relation to the street, and they altered the dwelling so the main entrance was on the side of the building rather than on the structure's end.

BUILDING THE GAMBREL ROOF

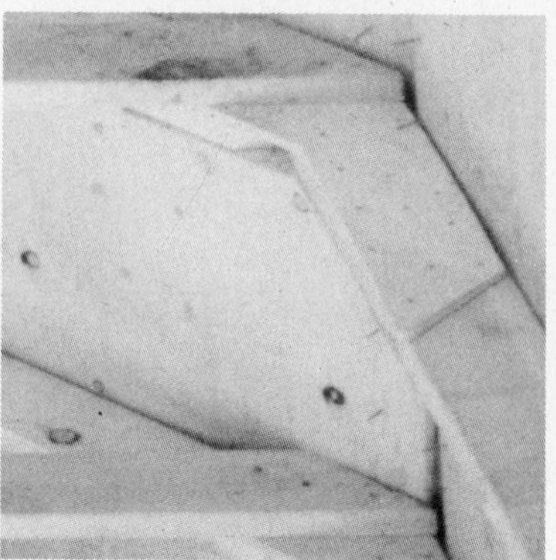

The gambrel roof on Philip Baechler's cabin provides greater living space on the second floor than would a conventional or A-frame roof. Structural integrity for the truss joists is provided by plywood gussets.

The gambrel roof is the hallmark of rural America, for such a structure topping the loft of a barn will hold a considerable amount of hay. There's no reason, though, why the classic gambrel cannot be used on other kinds of buildings . . . such as the log cabin Philip Baechler built in northern Washington.

When Philip was constructing his 15′ X 20′ cabin, he decided to top the residence with a gambrel (rather than a more conventional gable or A-frame) roof. Not only would the gambrel's steep side-pitch give the cabin ample upstairs floor space, he reasoned, but the double-sloping design would make more efficient use of roofing materials than an A-frame ever could. And besides that, he liked the appearance of a gambrel roof.

Philip's background reading had taught him, however, that a conventional barn-sized gambrel is a nightmare of purlin beams, ridge beams, and dovetail joints. What he had in mind, in other words, was a fine project for an army of engineers, but one that was probably beyond the capabilities of two non-professionals (as he and Jim, his building partner, were).

Rather than give up, though, he decided to try to simplify the construction of the roof he wanted. What he ultimately devised was an easy-to-work-with system of lightweight *trusses* that could be built flat on the ground, then erected atop the first story of the cabin and covered with exterior plywood to produce the barn-like roof shown in the accompanying photos. Here, briefly, is how the trusses (and the resulting gambrel roof) were put together.

RESEARCH AND PLANNING

Philip planned to make a dozen or so gambrel-shaped frames or trusses out of 2 X 6 lumber. But, initially, he had no idea how to connect the pieces of each truss so that they'd be held rigidly in the proper configuration.

Then he remembered reading about a system of plywood straps that somebody had used in building a geodesic dome. Actually, the "straps" were wooden gussets nailed to the sides of two connecting sections of a truss to hold the 2 X 6's together. These plywood brackets were just what Jim and Philip needed to give their roofing trusses adequate rigidity and strength.

Next, he and his partner made scale drawings of several gambrel roof designs, with each employing a different combination of slopes. In the end, they settled on a roof plan that looked good, made efficient use of materials, and allowed for porch and eave overhangs.

LAYOUT AND CUTTING

At this point, the partners measured and cut their truss lumber. First, they made a full-size layout of the gambrel design on smooth, level ground and drove stakes into the earth to mark the locations of the four rafters in each truss. Then they laid four 2 X 6 boards out flat in their proper positions and—using a taut string—marked the cutting lines. Next, the pieces of the first truss were sawed to length, set down between the stakes again, and (after their fit was carefully checked) used as patterns with which to mark and cut the rafters for the *remaining* trusses.

TRIANGLES AND DOGLEGS

After all the rafters had been cut, plywood gussets, which—because of their shapes—were dubbed "triangles" and "doglegs", were made by [1] tracing the outlines of the truss joints onto pieces of cardboard, [2] cutting templates from the cardboard with scissors, and [3] using the templates as patterns for sawing the plates out of 1/2″ plywood.

ASSEMBLING THE TRUSSES

To assure uniformity, the pair assembled all the roof trusses on the ground between stakes. The doglegs and triangles were attached with 8d nails, and—as you can see in Figs. 1-A and 1-B—all joints were also tied together with strap metal . . . the kind with which bundles of

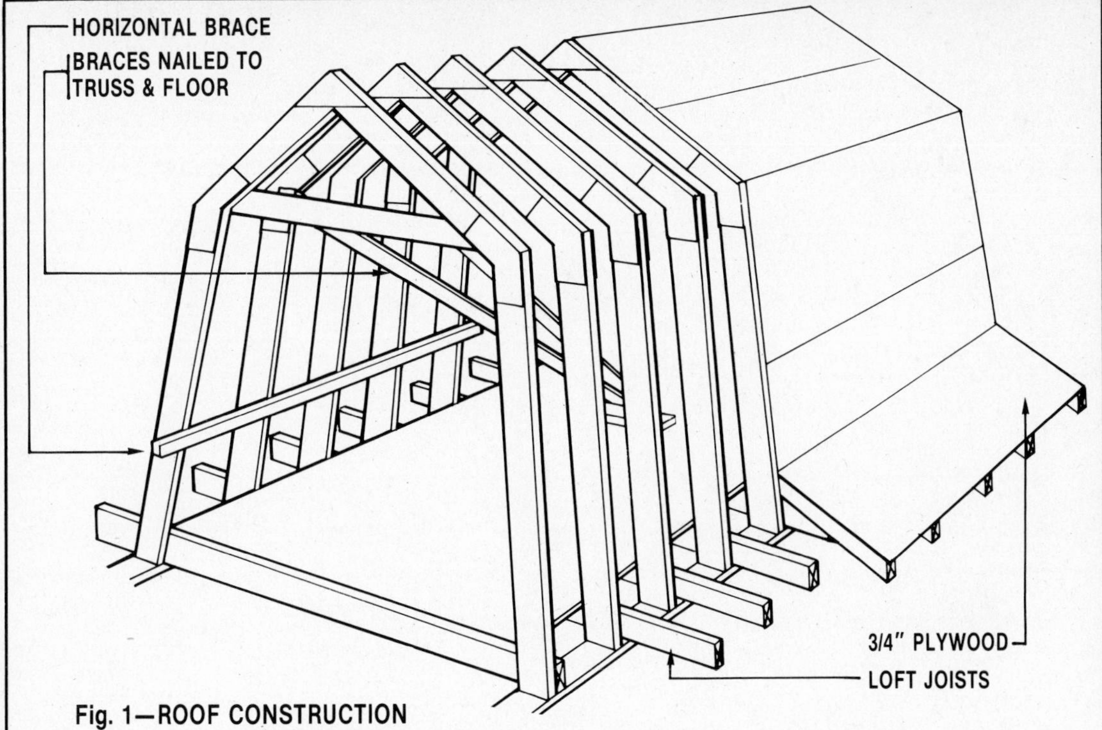

Fig. 1—ROOF CONSTRUCTION

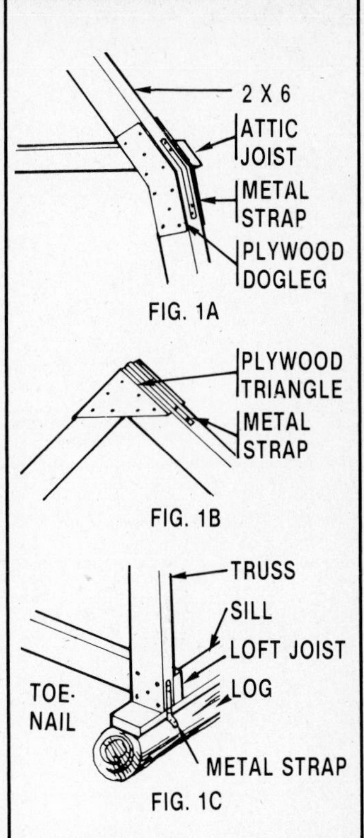

lumber are bound. (You can obtain this metal free at almost any lumberyard. Phil and Jim cut theirs into 8″- to 12″-lengths and used a punch, a mallet, and vise-grip pliers to make nailing holes through each piece.)

After binding the rafter segments together with gussets and metal straps, they then finished each truss by nailing a short length of 2 X 6 between its dogleg joints to act as a stiffener (and to serve—later—as an attic joist).

When they were through prefabbing the gambrel frames, they stacked all the trusses flat on a level surface with spacer blocks placed between them.

RAISING THE RAFTERS

The procedure used to erect the semi-triangular frames on top of the cabin can be summarized as follows: First, they laid one frame flat across the joists with its "feet" butted against one of the joists . . . then they [1] tilted it up part way, [2] nailed a pair of 2 X 4's to the truss's short horizontal crosspiece, [3] pushed the structure upright, and [4] nailed the 2 X 4's to the loft floor to act as temporary braces. (Note: Great pains were taken to ensure that the first truss was absolutely plumb at this point, since they intended to align succeeding trusses on it.) Afterwards, they nailed the frames' feet to the loft joist and bound them to the support sills with metal straps (as depicted in Fig. 1-C).

As successive trusses were erected, they were held upright by horizontal braces, as shown in Fig. 1. These braces were removed after the roofing plywood was nailed in place.

The last couple of frames had to be hoisted into position from the ground, since there was no room to lay them atop the loft before raising them. This, however, was merely a matter of [1] leaning an upside-down frame against the cabin, [2] supporting the frame's peak a few feet off the ground on a stepladder, and then [3] pulling the truss into place by means of a rope and pulley fastened around the crosspiece (attic joist) of an already-standing truss.

ROOFING

Philip and Jim used 3/4″ exterior plywood for roof sheathing. One trick that saved some work while putting the plywood down—and that might come in handy the next time *you* work with plywood siding or roofing—was to drive a nail into each truss at the exact point where the *bottom edge* of the *lowermost sheet of plywood* was to rest. This done, they were able to set the sheathing on the spikes and have both hands free while nailing the piece in place. (The time to make last-minute alterations of truss alignment, by the way, is *before* you apply the roofing . . . *after* is too late.) The men used 10d screwshank nails to anchor the heavy plywood in place.

At this point, the roof was covered with shingles, and any joints vulnerable to moisture were made weathertight with flashing.

THE END WALLS

They finished their cabin's second-story gambrel roof by enclosing its ends. The 2 X 4 studs for these end walls were cut by measuring each one to fit the sloping roof. Then, on opposite sides of each stud, a notch 6 inches long and 1-1/2 inches deep was cut into one end to fit the loft joist and into the other end to fit the truss. (The uppermost notch should, of course, be cut to fit the angle of the roof. See Fig. 2.)

LONG LIVE THE GAMBREL ROOF!

Now that their gambrel roof is finished, Philip and Jim are more than pleased with the good-looking, functional, and easy-on-the-pocketbook cabin. Philip now has a spacious sleeping loft, and he's already planning other ways to use his gambrel concept . . . without an understructure. Some of his ideas are for a chickenhouse, a child's playhouse, a storage shed, and—if covered with clear plastic—a greenhouse.

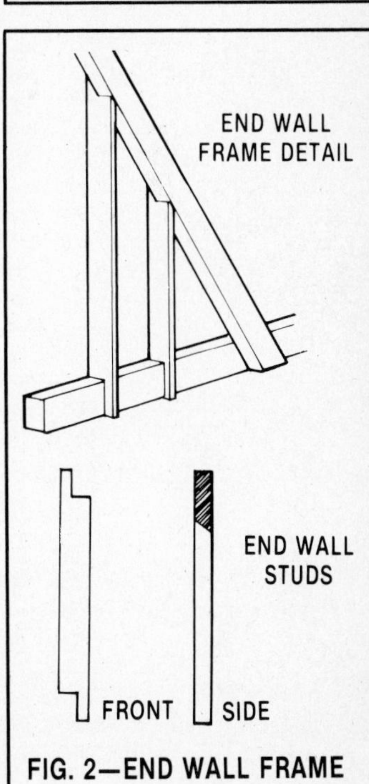

FIG. 2—END WALL FRAME

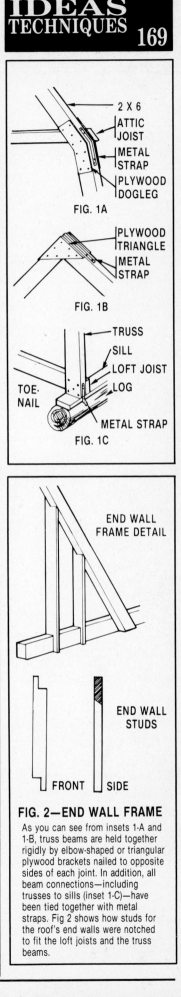

As you can see from insets 1-A and 1-B, truss beams are held together rigidly by elbow-shaped or triangular plywood brackets nailed to opposite sides of each joint. In addition, all beam connections—including trusses to sills (inset 1-C)—have been tied together with metal straps. Fig 2 shows how studs for the roof's end walls were notched to fit the loft joists and the truss beams.

HOW DO THE OPTIONS COMPARE?

There's no simple answer to the question, "Which is best?" It's a problem that's too complicated for a single page, or—for that matter—for a single book.

Every method of energy-efficient construction shown in the pages of this volume has merit, but many could never work alone. For example, as useful as a direct-gain window can be, the house that incorporates it won't be efficient . . . unless it also includes the proper insulation.

Consequently, the appropriate building method for you will probably utilize more than one of the basic energy-saving techniques listed in the chart.

The decision whether or not to *use* each basic energy approach also requires some careful scrutiny. You'll find that the comments listed below the headings won't provide direct answers, but they should suggest areas for more research. Cost of construction, for example, is quite variable . . . both by region and according to the expense of interior and exterior finishing. There are many parts of the country where you'd be hard pressed to buy a new conventional home for the per-square-foot price shown in the chart. And, of course, many of the homes in this book have incorporated important energy features while significantly undercutting that figure.

SYSTEM	COST OF CONSTRUCTION	STANDARD MATERIALS?	SPECIAL ENGINEERING?	EASE OF CONSTRUCTION	SPECIAL SITING?	EXTERIOR MAINTENANCE	REQUIRES ELECTRICITY?	COOLING
ACTIVE AIR	\$10-\$34/ft.² of collector	yes, except collector	collector design; roof structure	collector, moderate	solar exposure	same as conventional	yes	must add venting; no special benefit
ACTIVE LIQUID	\$15-\$34/ft.² of collector	yes, except collector	collector design; roof structure	collector, difficult	solar exposure	liquid changes	yes	no special benefit
DIRECT GAIN	slightly more than conventional for mass and glass	yes, unless special glazing	passive design	more mass	solar exposure	same as or less than conventional	no	ventilation by thermosiphon; mass effect
DOUBLE ENVELOPE	10-25% more than conventional	yes, unless special glazing	envelope and sunspace design and structure	somewhat more difficult than conventional	solar exposure	same as or less than conventional	no	ventilation by thermosiphon; some mass effect
EARTH BERMED	slightly more than conventional	reinforced walls; waterproofing	structure for walls	slightly more difficult than conventional	good drainage	less than conventional	no	some earth tempering
SUNSPACE	slightly more than conventional	yes, unless special glazing	no	about the same as conventional	solar exposure	same as or less than conventional	not usually	can ventilate by thermosiphon
SUPER-INSULATED	5-10% more than conventional	yes	insulation and infiltration detail	somewhat more difficult than conventional	no	same as conventional	no	insulation protection
UNDERGROUND	somewhat more than conventional	reinforced wall and roof; waterproofing	complete structure	somewhat more difficult than conventional	good drainage; no expansive clay; no bedrock	much less than conventional	no	earth tempered
CONVENTIONAL	\$50/ft.² floor space and up	yes	no	simple framing	no	paint and roofing	no	no special benefit

Furthermore, some of the subject areas are so important that major portions of whole articles have been devoted to them.

Ease of construction is very difficult to evaluate. Some people who have had much experience in building earth-sheltered homes feel that such structures are actually easier to erect than more conventional dwellings. Most folks, however, consider underground houses to be somewhat more difficult to build . . . because of both the weight of the structural materials and the care required in waterproofing.

As you can see, it's no easy matter to determine what features to incorporate into an energy-saving home. Only by thoroughly analyzing your climate, your land, and your family's needs will you be able to make the right choice (or combination of choices). Consequently, this chart is—more than anything else—a compilation of some of the lessons learned by people who've already planned and built homes.

As momentous as the necessary decisions may seem, we'd like to leave you with one parting observation. Almost every successful structure has two recurring characteristics. First, the building was well planned. And second, it was built by people who, though not necessarily experts, *cared* . . . and were careful with every detail.

Ease of construction is difficult to evaluate.

PRIVACY	VISIBILITY ON SITE	FLOOR PLAN FLEXIBILITY	HUMIDITY CONTROL	SOUND CONTROL	NATURAL LIGHT	MISCELLANEOUS ADVANTAGES	MISCELLANEOUS DISADVANTAGES
conventional	higher than conventional	conventional	conventional	conventional	conventional	solar storage; easy backup in ductwork; moderate-temperature collector	forced air circulation blower noise
conventional	higher than conventional	conventional	conventional	conventional	conventional	solar storage; easy backup in tank; domestic hot water	high-temperature collector; possibility of leaks
large potential loss	higher than conventional	requires open plan for air circulation	conventional	mass may improve; glass may worsen	thorough daylighting	some solar storage in mass; view; low-temperature collector	possibility of large temperature swings; may require movable insulation; backup arrangement
some potential loss	much higher than conventional	flexible within envelope	some moderation of winter-summer swing	moderate improvement	good daylighting	slightly warmer interior walls; gentle air circulation; can grow some plants; low-temperature collector	backup arrangement
somewhat better than conventional	lower than conventional	limited by egress and daylighting	can be summer problem	moderate improvement	limited, requires careful design	infiltration control; security	limited interior access; backup arrangement; financing; building code
conventional (interior)	slightly higher than conventional	requires connection of rooms for heating	may add moisture in winter	slight improvement (interior)	depends on interior glazing detail	can grow some plants; low-temperature collector	may require movable insulation; backup arrangement
conventional or slightly better	conventional	conventional	can be winter and summer problem	moderate improvement	limited, requires careful design	any appearance possible	limited interior access; backup arrangement; probably requires air-to-air heat exchanger
much better than conventional	much lower than conventional	limited by egress and daylighting	can be summer problem	large improvement	very limited, requires careful design	infiltration control; security	limited interior access; backup arrangement; financing; building code
depends on siting and glazing detail	depends on landscaping	very flexible	humid in summer, dry in winter	minimal protection	some daylighting	readily available and accepted	no need to convince you

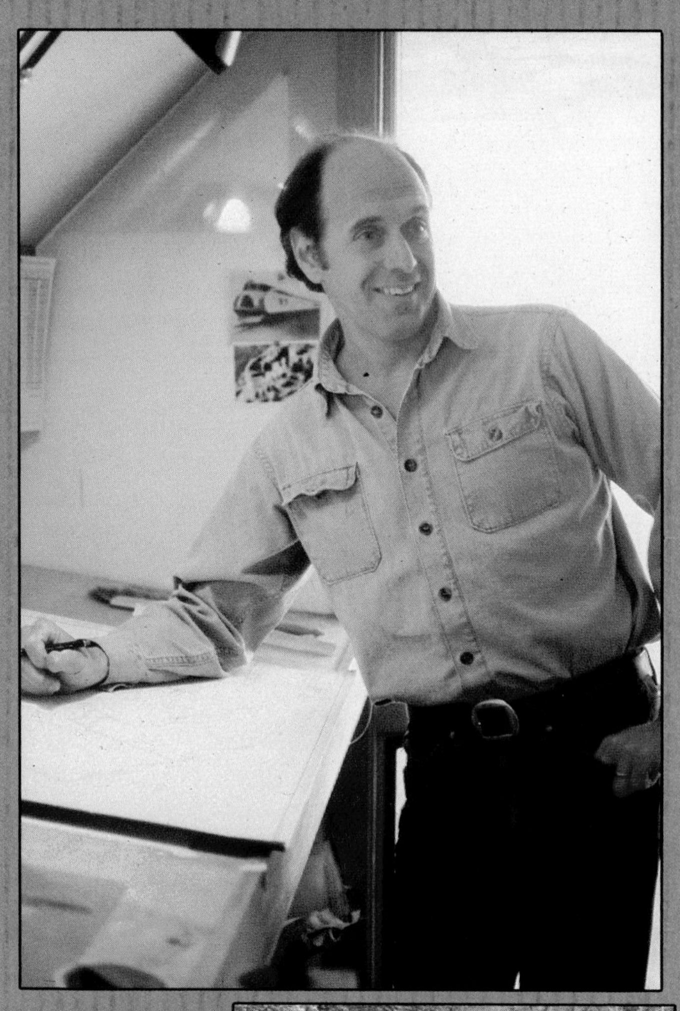

TRENDS, POINTS OF VIEW, PREDICTIONS

As you've found out from the text and the illustrations in the preceding pages, much has been accomplished in the realm of environmentally compatible architecture and in the development of comfortable but affordable housing. But there is still much to be done—and learned—about building houses that enhance living, rather than sap the occupants' strength and resources in their efforts to maintain the dwelling.

Well, this final chapter presents three thought-provoking conversations with men who are interested and experienced in designing and building homes that not only suit the environment but are part of it . . . homes that are built for comfort, economy, and ease of living.

The ideas and ingenuity of these new designers—and others—are vitally important parts of the movement to reduce dependence on nonrenewable resources and to improve the lives we live.

DAVID WRIGHT

Relaxing in the sunlight, which provides the energy to heat and cool the houses he designs, David Wright talks about his belief in the use of solar energy that led him into the field of "natural" architecture.

During the late 1960's a renegade faction of architects began to swing away from the mainstream of their future-thinking (but all too often technology-addicted) brethren. The young designers recognized a fact that wouldn't become apparent to the majority of the population for another ten years: Centralized power systems based on nonrenewable fuels are not in the world's best interest and will eventually fail us. These architects chose to act on their concern about our energy-short future.

Naturally, they turned their attention to benign solar energy approaches ... to which they applied a blend of practical physics and age-old earthen construction methods. By technological-age standards the earth-bermed adobe structures that they began to design seemed regressive, and many so-called "experts" of the time considered architects such as David Wright to be naive. But today there's little scoffing to be heard. From the amalgam of old and new fostered by these "off-beat" designers have come thousands of efficient, attractive, and comfortable structures that set trends in architecture.

The value of construction which works in harmony with the earth and its cycles is both aesthetic and economic. While the homes designed by David Wright—now with SEAgroup (Solar Environmental Architecture group) in Nevada City, California—blend unassumingly into the landscape, instead of towering arrogantly above the land, they also free their owners of 50 to 95% of the utility dependence which is common in conventional houses. Whether you consider the real importance of Wright's work to be measured in beauty or in dollars (or both), bear in mind that the center of each design concept is the sun. In the words of the architect himself, "Solar power, with its democratic distribution throughout the world, is ours for the taking. We can accept the challenge and use it wisely, or we can continue to muddle along, deny the inevitable . . ."

But where does such a man as Wright come from . . . and how does he develop his skills? In the following interview, Wright addresses those questions and traces the steps that led him into the field of "natural" architecture.

INTERVIEWER: I'd like to know, "Why you?" Why have you been able to develop insights into architectural design and the use of solar energy which have eluded more experienced and occasionally much better financed researchers? What is there in your background that has made this possible? What set you on the path you now follow?

WRIGHT: I was born here in California . . . up in the foothills of the Sierra Nevadas—February 13, 1941—and I spent my youth as a boy scout out in the hills gaining an appreciation of nature. I decided at about the age of 12 that I wanted to be an architect, and I received an Associate of Architecture degree from Sierra College in Auburn, California in 1960. After that—in 1964—came a B.S. in Architectural Engineering from California Polytechnic down in San Luis Obispo . . . and after that I joined the Peace Corps.

INTERVIEWER: Why the Peace Corps?

WRIGHT: I wanted to avoid the draft, plus the Corps offered an immediate work opportunity. As a Peace Corps volunteer, I was instantly shipped off to Africa and employed as an architect in the country of Tunisia. I spent a year there and got several interesting projects underway. Then I was transferred to Guinea in West Africa to design a special project—an agricultural junior college—way out in the jungle.

That was where I had my first real taste of working with people on a grassroots level. We trained groups of natives to make CINVA Ram blocks with soil and to use available materials . . . which were practically all we had to work with, except for some Czech, Russian, and Chinese hardware.

INTERVIEWER: What were those locally available materials that you used in Guinea?

WRIGHT: They consisted of beautiful hardwoods, softwoods, and—of course—earth for the CINVA Ram blocks. We had a certain amount of imported cement for concrete, glazing, and things like that . . . but almost all the rest of the main structural materials came from within 15 miles of the school we were building.

I was in Africa from 1964 to 1966 . . . and that's where I got my feeling for earth forms. Almost everything in Tunisia was built out of the earth (when they mixed mud and rocks together to construct walls, they called it "agglomerate"), and I grew to love the idea of taking something right out of the ground and building with it. I had never really seen that done before.

INTERVIEWER: Let's see now. You were in Africa from 1964 to 1966 . . . and then?

WRIGHT: And then I came back to the States and "paid my dues", so to speak, to the architectural profession here. I worked at several different jobs, just gaining experience . . . but all the time trying to put my finger on something that was bothering me . . . trying to figure out what it was that, deep down, I somehow knew had to be done.

This all came to a head about 1970. I was working in Santa Cruz—down below San Francisco—just putting up little redwood jewel-box houses on the California coast . . . and I grew somewhat disenchanted. It was very much a money trip, instead of the people-serving thing I wanted to do. I was also getting really turned off by what I saw happening to the environment down there.

Santa Cruz County, for instance, granted something like 500 building permits in a single week. A very fragile, beautiful area was being jammed with houses and people. And Monterey Bay—a huge body of water—was suddenly closed to all swimmers because of typhoid that had come out of Fort Ord, a military base there on the coast. Then San Francisco Bay area smog started pouring down along Highway 17 and through the pass to Santa Cruz.

That smog was the last straw. I had a friend in Santa Fe, New Mexico I'd been in the Peace Corps with, and I went to visit him. This was Christmas time, and while I was there I met Bill Lumpkins, who is sort of "Mr. Adobe" in the Southwest.

I worked with Bill for three years learning the basics of adobe and I started to understand what a good low-energy material it is, and what good karma and sculptural qualities it has. You can do anything with it. You can punch a window in wherever you want to. You can modify it in almost any way at any time. As a matter of fact, the old traditional adobes were just an ongoing building process. Someone would build an adobe house and then, as the family had more children . . . or the next generation took over . . . or the place was sold, it was *expected* that the home would be expanded or modified to suit the new tenants. The old adobes were really built for change.

Traditional adobe structures—the ones with walls two or three feet thick—were also a lot more comfortable to live in than most of the adobes being put up today. It was the sheer mass of those walls that did it . . . when you put that much adobe around you, you've taken a big step toward regulating the comfort of your living space.

INTERVIEWER: The old adobes worked well *not* because the earth in their walls was a good insulator . . . but simply because there was so *much* earth in those walls that it took a long time for heat—either coming in or going out—to get through them?

WRIGHT: Yes. It's a flywheel effect, and it works well when you use it right . . . when you understand that there's very little but sheer mass working for you . . . and that you must design accordingly.

But what has happened, you see, is that the unit price of an adobe block has gone up eightfold. And as that cost has gone up, people have been putting fewer and fewer of those blocks into the walls of new construction. An adobe block is about 14 inches long and 10 inches wide, and the old walls were built with two or three or even four of them laid side by side. As the price of adobe went up, though, people began turning the blocks lengthwise and building their walls just one brick thick. Well, that made a wall 14 inches thick and it was—thermally—still a pretty fair structure. But then the price kept right on climbing, so the contractors started turning the blocks the *short* way, and that made the walls only ten inches thick . . . and it doesn't take heat very long to go through ten inches of adobe.

INTERVIEWER: You began to learn about adobe once you'd moved to New Mexico. What else happened to you there?

WRIGHT: Well, back in '71 or '72, I got together with Travis Price, a young student at St. Johns College in Santa Fe, and Keith Haggard, a Northwest dropout who'd come to the Southwest looking for something . . . and we decided to attend a solar energy course that Bob Reines was teaching at the University of New Mexico.

"I grew (in Tunisia) to love the idea of taking something right out of the ground and building with it."

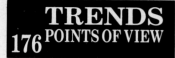

"We began playing around with air collectors and found that, sure enough, air was a good transfer medium."

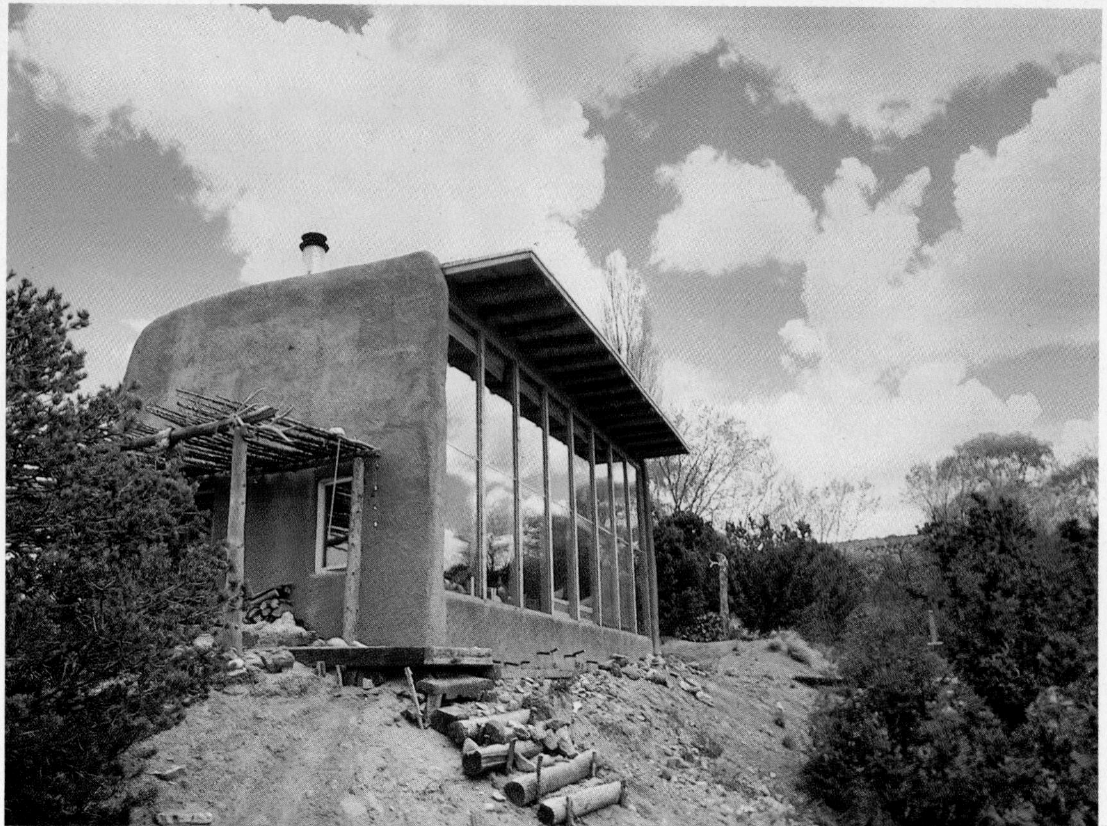

Combining modern materials such as multiple-pane windows with ancient methods such as the use of adobe brick results in a structure that is its own solar collection and storage unit.

Bob's course was enlightening . . . but his whole approach was flat-plate collectors, domes, and wind power . . . and we felt that it was a little too complicated and a little too costly for the common people. So we went out, looked around, and decided that we'd try to take this beautiful old indigenous adobe architecture and fit *it* out with solar collectors.

We played around with that idea awhile—this was before the "energy crisis", you know—and it looked as if it might work. So we asked Bill Lumpkins, the architectural guru I was working with, and Peter Goodwin, a young man with money and an interest in such things, to join us. We also brought a local engineer by the name of Herman Barkman, and Wayne Nichols, a young Harvard graduate who was very much interested in the commercial grassroots application of solar energy, into the group. That made seven of us. We called ourselves Sun Mountain Design, and we were pledged to the development of low-cost, decentralized architecture that—we hoped—would use the so-called "alternative sources of energy" to bring a new kind of reasonably priced housing and other types of shelter to the masses.

Like everybody else, we started off our solar experiments with active fluid systems in which water or some other liquid was pumped through flat-plate collectors to pick up heat, and then stored in big tanks somewhere until we wanted to extract the BTU from the fluid. It was then pumped around again through heat exchangers.

This is an awfully complicated way to use solar energy, and after some study, we found that fluid systems were just too costly and too much trouble for most people to consider. We couldn't even afford to build and test a prototype active hydronic system of our own . . . and we couldn't find any clients who were willing to put up $10,000 to find out if our ideas would work.

Well, we knew that George Lof had used air collectors fairly effectively—he'd achieved about 20% efficiency—in his system up in Denver. So we began playing around with air collectors and found that, sure enough, air was a good transfer medium. It'd pick up heat in a collector panel and then carry those BTU somewhere else if you wanted it to . . . and it would do it a lot less expensively than a hydronic system could. It just wasn't nearly as costly to build and seal a system that pumped air around as it was to build and seal a system that pumped water or some other fluid around.

It was kind of nice, also, to use the traditional Southwest floor—which is just brick on sand or concrete—as the heat sink of an air system. We built some ducting so that we could take hot air off our collectors and then blow it down under one of those traditional floors. We got some good heat retention that way on a very cost-effective basis. Our first couple of air systems were marginal but, eventually, we put two or three together that cost a lot less than hydronic systems and which worked pretty well.

It was just about then that Sun Mountain Design began to have a really hard time of it. We didn't have enough clients to keep all seven of us working, and we were beginning to realize that a bunch of guys can't forge themselves into a design team by just getting together one day and saying, "Hey, we're going to be a team." You have to have the right balance of talent and attitude . . . and we didn't quite have the whole thing. The chemistry just wasn't right.

"Passive heating or cooling or dehumidifying is a way of conditioning a space without using commercial energy."

So we split up at the end of two years and went our separate ways. Bill Lumpkins is still doing solar adobes on his own in Sante Fe, while Herman Barkman is very much involved with active solar systems, heat pumps, and commercial jobs. Wayne Nichols is a self-employed developer building solar homes in the Sante Fe area. Keith Haggard, practically singlehandedly, put together the New Mexico Solar Energy Association . . . which has really been a prime mover in getting the word about solar usage out to people all over the nation. Peter Goodwin is also involved with the NMSEA and other projects of his own. Travis Price went to New York and has made some headlines by helping to put run-down and abandoned tenements into the hands of neighborhood self-help groups, who then completely revitalize the old buildings and sometimes install solar water heaters and windpowered electrical generators on their roofs. And I'm out here in California still doing the same thing I started in New Mexico.

INTERVIEWER: You've told us how you got from active liquid systems to active air systems. But how did you get from there to passive systems? And what's your definition of a passive system anyway?

WRIGHT: I think that the best definition I've heard of passive heating or cooling, humidifying or dehumidifying, or whatever . . . is that it's a way of conditioning a space without using commercial energy.

INTERVIEWER: Without using commercial energy . . . such as electricity?

WRIGHT: Yes. In our modern industrialized society, commercial energy seems to come increasingly in the form of electricity. But it also comes in other forms: natural gas, oil, coal, propane, butane, and so on. So what we're talking about is designing a home, a workshop, an office, or any other space that people will inhabit . . . and designing it in such a way that we really won't need any kind of commercial energy to keep it comfortable. We won't even need a little bit of electricity to circulate water or air through a collector someplace.

We're talking about designing a space so that no matter what goes on outside—no matter how hot or how cold, how wet or how dry the micro-climate surrounding that space might get—the space inside will be a comfortable place in which to live. And it'll be comfortable *just because* of its design. We won't have to pump in any electricity or gas or coal from 1,500 miles away to keep it that way.

A convection-type solar water heater is a nice, simple example of what I'm talking about. Such a unit consists of only two main components—a collector and a storage tank—and enough plumbing to connect them. Actually, it's slightly more complicated than this, since, if we didn't have some way to protect the water in the collector on really cold nights, it'd freeze and tear something up. But we can take care of that easily enough by making our insulated, indoor storage unit a tank-within-a-tank . . . and then circulating a water/antifreeze solution outdoors through the collector and then inside through the heat-exchange part of our storage tank.

Since we know that hot water rises and cold water sinks, it's obvious that we'd be foolish if we set our collector up so that it was higher than our exchanger tank. If we did that, the first water/antifreeze that got up in the collector when we filled the system would start to warm up . . . and the more it warmed, the more it'd want to stay right up there in the top of the collector.

In addition to being energy efficient, a home can be designed to blend into the landscape rather than sit obtrusively on top of it.

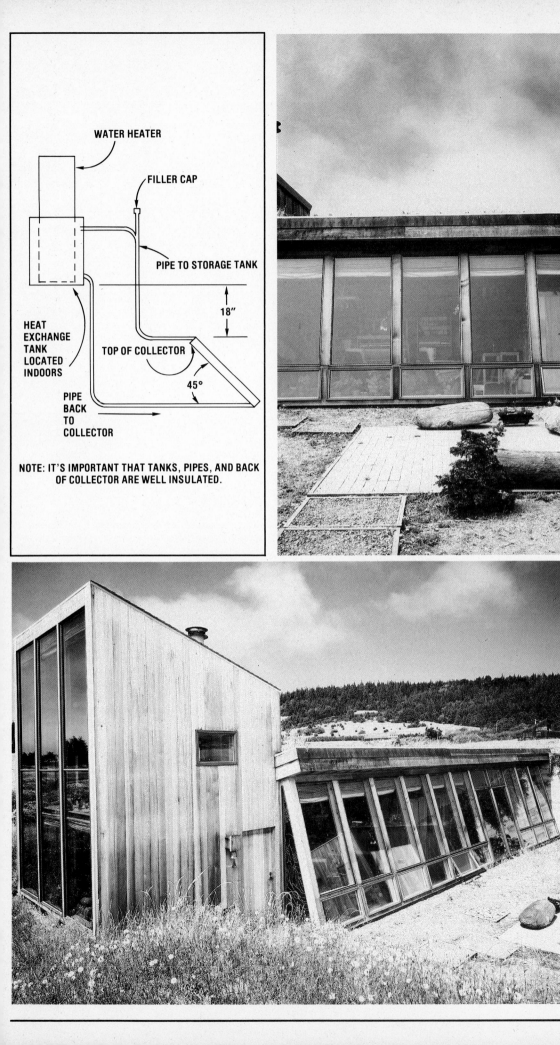

WATER HEATER
FILLER CAP
PIPE TO STORAGE TANK
18″
HEAT EXCHANGE TANK LOCATED INDOORS
TOP OF COLLECTOR
45°
PIPE BACK TO COLLECTOR

NOTE: IT'S IMPORTANT THAT TANKS, PIPES, AND BACK OF COLLECTOR ARE WELL INSULATED.

"Build your house like a thermos bottle, then aim that thermos bottle south."

David's personal office occupies the second floor of the narrow west end of the dwelling he built for himself on the California coast overlooking the Pacific Ocean. Solar energy is collected through the large expanse of south-facing glass in the living area. The glass can be covered at night with insulating curtains, and the panes are protected from cold winds by the building's being sunk into the ground facing a courtyard.

"I began to look around and think about how natives in New Mexico had survived and kept themselves comfortable."

And the only way we'd be able to push that hot water and antifreeze down to our heat exchanger tank would be by adding a pump and bringing in some outside energy—probably electricity—to run the pump. Then we could shove that hot fluid down to the storage tank, but it still wouldn't want to stay there. So we'd just have to keep pumping it back down as fast as it tried to rise . . . we'd have to put something like one-way valves in the system. We'd have to keep pumping in outside energy to make this all work, and we'd wind up with a very active and probably very inefficient water heating system on our hands.

Ah, but there's another—and much simpler—way to do the same job. Simply set the collector up so that its highest point is at least 18 inches *lower* than the lowest point in the exchanger tank.

Now we've got a built-in, automatic thermosiphon working for us. As the water/antifreeze mixture is warmed in the collector, it rises. And as it naturally rises, it flows up into the exchanger tank. And as it does so, the colder mixture of water and antifreeze already up in the tank flows down another pipe into the bottom of the collector . . . where it, in turn, is warmed . . . which, in turn, causes *it* to rise up to the exchanger.

And as long as the collector is hotter than the exchanger tank, this thermosiphon will continue and the water in the whole system will get warmer and warmer until it reaches the maximum temperature that the system is capable of generating. But as soon as the sun goes behind a cloud or the sun goes down and the collector becomes colder than the exchanger tank . . . the automatic siphon will just as automatically shut itself off. The heavier mixture of cold water and antifreeze at the bottom of the collector will stay down there and the lighter hot mixture at the top will stay up at the top and keep the water up there in the heater tank warm.

Here is what the passive conditioning of a living space is all about. It's about the design and construction of a space so that the natural elements—and forces—of the micro-climate surrounding it are all that're ever needed to make that space a comfortable place.

Now this is kind of a revolutionary idea to most modern designers because we've gotten into the lazy habit of just slapping together any kind of structure, putting it up almost any old place, and then pumping in enough commercial energy to run air conditioners, space heaters, humidifiers, and dehumidifiers to make it a comfortable space in which to live. Commercial energy has been cheap, and we've gotten into the habit of letting that fact do our thinking for us.

But this idea of passive systems wasn't revolutionary to the more primitive and traditional cultures of this planet at all. Those people didn't have electricity available at the flip of a switch. They didn't have natural gas piped into their homes or fuel oil delivered regularly to their doors. All they had to work with was their local micro-climate—a certain amount of solar fall, rain, wind, and so on each year—and that was it. If you guessed wrong, nobody came around with a tanker full of OPEC oil—at any price—to bail you out.

INTERVIEWER: So you came up with elegantly simple solutions to your problem instead. Things like the underground dwellings in Tunisia . . . or the very thick-walled adobe structures that were traditional in the Mexican desert and our Southwest.

WRIGHT: That's right. And that's how I finally got into passive systems. The active air systems we were playing around with at Sun Mountain Design made a lot more sense than the active fluid systems we had started out with. But they were still pretty complicated and expensive to build and operate . . . and aesthetically, they didn't add anything to the looks of a building.

So I began to look around and think about how the native peoples in New Mexico had survived and kept themselves comfortable. I especially studied the cave dwellers who had lived at Mesa Verde, Betatakin, Pueblo Bonito, and elsewhere in the Navajo National Monument area. Their south-facing cave dwellings were heated during the winter by the low sun. During the summer, though—when the sun was high—the same dwellings were shaded by the big cliffs that towered up over them.

When you stop and think about it, that's really a very sophisticated use of low-energy materials and natural elements. It's a maximum use of obvious resources with an absolute minimum of high technology. It worked . . . and that impressed me.

I was also greatly inspired by Steve Baer . . . especially his use of 55-gallon drums of water as a passive heat sink in his solar-heated and -cooled house at Corrales, New Mexico. But all of a sudden I saw that while the water-filled drums were fine as a heat sink, that's *all* they were. They were just non-structural heat sinks. I realized that a big mass of adobe could do that job just as well—it could absorb heat from the sun and then radiate that warmth into a living space as those barrels of water did—while, *in addition*, that adobe could be part of a building's structure.

It was as easy as adding one and one and getting two. Once I'd thought about it, I realized just how simple it would be to get a double return on your investment . . . to make an adobe structure work for you in two ways. All you had to do was put those heavy walls up and then isolate them from exterior temperature swings. Build the walls and insulate them on the outside.

INTERVIEWER: Insulate them on the *outside*?

WRIGHT: I know this is just the opposite of the way we've gotten used to doing it, and that's where we've been going wrong for the last 50 or 100 years. We've fallen into the habit of building up an adobe or a cement block or a brick wall, slapping some insulation on the inside, and then putting in enough baseboard heaters to keep ourselves warm.

But this is like building that water heater we talked about and putting the collector on top. When you do it that way, you have to pump an awful lot of commercial energy into the system to make it work. It's the same with a building. When you leave all its thermal mass outside where the summer's heat or the winter's cold can get at it, you're working against yourself. You're just guaranteeing that you're going to have to spend a great deal of money on insulation and commercial energy if you want to stay comfortable inside that structure.

What you really want to do is turn the idea around and put your insulation on the *outside*—just under the weather skin—and keep your thermal mass *inside*. Build your house like a thermos bottle. Insulate it just around its outer surfaces and keep all its heavy masses inside. That way, they can act as thermal flywheels that help you coast right through the seasonal and daily temperature changes that buffet the building's exterior.

Once you've done that, it's a simple matter to take the idea one step further. Now that your thermos bottle is built, you aim it toward the south, and you put a cork in it. That is: You put some large glass surfaces on the south side of your building, and you add some big insulated shutters or other movable panels that you can open or close to uncover or cover those windows.

As you become more sophisticated, you learn to position the homes you build so that the natural terrain around them shelters the structures from winter winds while leaving them open to summer breezes. And you begin to shape the houses to take better advantage of the low winter sun while blocking out the high summer sun. And so on.

INTERVIEWER: Your proposal sounds almost too elementary.

WRIGHT: I know. It sounds too simple to work. I run into that a lot. Every time I explain what I'm doing, someone asks me, "Well, if an idea this simple works so well, why wasn't it used before?"

And that's just the point. It *was* used before in a thousand different ways by almost every example of indigenous architecture that the traditional cultures of the world have ever evolved. They're almost all variations on this same theme.

The cave dwellings in Tunisia . . . the south-facing pueblos here in the U.S. Southwest . . . those traditional old adobes with walls that were three feet thick . . . and so many, many other forms of indigenous architecture illustrate my point. When you really begin to study these structures, you realize that they've all been constructed to take maximum advantage of the micro-climate in which they're located. They were precisely engineered for the prevailing winds, precipitation, and solar fall of the particular regions where they were built.

The first Tunisian cave dwellers didn't have our modern insulations to work with . . . but they got an identical effect by burying their homes 40 feet under the earth's surface. It's the same with those old adobes. Adobe may not be a very good insulation . . . but it starts to work like one when you pile it up in walls that are three or four feet thick. And that goes for the pueblos I've mentioned too . . . especially when you sun-temper them by constructing the dwellings on the side of a south-facing cliff where the winter sun can strike them, but the hottest summer sun can't.

INTERVIEWER: This "brand-new, revolutionary architecture" that you and a few others are currently developing, then, isn't new and isn't revolutionary at all. You're just rediscovering what most traditional cultures learned hundreds or thousands of years ago.

WRIGHT: That's it! Commercial energy has been so inexpensive and easy to use for the past 50 or 100 years that we've slid into the habit of solving all our problems with brute force. We've been putting up the same Cape Cod and ranch houses in California that we build in Maine. Then we just pump in as much air conditioning or as much heat as we need to make them all comfortable.

But the days of low-cost commercial energy are drawing to a close, and we're all becoming more and more energy conscious. As a result, some of us—Steve Baer, Bruce Anderson, and me, to name a few—are rediscovering the philosophy of what I'd call "climatic design" . . . the philosophy that most traditional cultures have followed of designing each building specifically for the region and the climate, and even for the particular site, where it will be located.

The more I dig into this concept, the more I'm amazed by how earlier peoples used it . . . not only in Tunisia or here in our Southwest, but also in Egypt, the Near East, China, India, even Europe. They all used climatic design, passive solar energy, and the other ideas that I'm exploring.

The traditional farmhouses in France, for instance, had big stone arches that faced south to catch the winter sun, and they worked just fine. Then along came the French equivalent of our Rural Electrification Administration with its easy use of fossil fuels, and all that stopped. The French farmers started orienting their houses' arches any way they pleased, and now they've pretty well forgotten what those arches were built for in the first place.

It's been that way all over the world . . . and a lot of good, traditional wisdom has been more or less bypassed and forgotten—blasted away with fossil fuels—during the last 50 or 100 years. Some of us "revolutionary architects" aren't doing anything now but going back and rediscovering little parts of that traditional wisdom.

INTERVIEWER: Is it easier or more difficult now than it was in the first place to make those old ideas work?

WRIGHT: Oh, easier . . . by far! As we learn to swallow our pride and look back and draw from history, it becomes increasingly apparent that the really hard work has already been done. Got a problem positioning your house in this kind of climate? Here's how someone solved it 500 years ago. Having trouble fitting a passive solar system into that set of conditions? Just try this solution from 2,000 years in the past.

Actually, we have a much better chance of making some of those old ideas work now than the people who invented them did. That's because we currently have all these really nice things like glass, insulation and so on that they didn't have. Some of the old

"But the days of low-cost commercial energy are drawing to a close, and we're all becoming more energy conscious."

"Why cut down all the trees and then cool those new houses with air conditioning?"

ideas that were just marginal 1,000 years ago can be made to work really well now with our modern materials. That's what I call a proper use of technology.

INTERVIEWER: The prevailing attitude, though, seems to be that technology isn't any good unless it comes up with a very complicated solution to a problem.

WRIGHT: Yes, I know. And it takes a lot of energy to make complicated, intricate things work the way they're supposed to. That's why I hope our civilization is finally getting to the point where it can start to relax a little.

We've been operating with this insane idea in our heads that, somehow, we must always "fight the elements" . . . that we must use our technology to bludgeon our way through life. But that's simply not true. What we should be doing is just relaxing and *interacting* with the elements.

We've really lost the art of living gracefully in our environment. Look at the way we "develop" a housing tract. First, we go in with bulldozers and knock down all the trees. Then we plop in a bunch of little cracker-box houses—or worse, fiberglass and aluminum mobile homes—so that they're oriented to an arbitrary grid of streets instead of to the natural terrain, solar fall, prevailing winds, etc., of the site. Finally, we use machines—space heaters and air conditioners—and a very large amount of commercial energy to make these dwellings comfortable.

This is all so unnecessary! Everything we need is already at our fingertips. All we have to do is learn to convert these resources to our use, instead of wasting them the way we've been doing. Why cut down all the trees and then cool those new houses with air conditioners? Why pipe in all that commercial energy from 500 miles away when—on the average—there's already something like *3-1/2 times* more solar energy falling on the roof of an energy-efficient, single-family dwelling than is needed for *all* the heating, cooling, and cooking that goes on in that house?

INTERVIEWER: So we're rich . . . but we don't know it.

WRIGHT: Exactly.

INTERVIEWER: Tell me, then, how would you change the way our society develops a tract of land? Or better still, since you've now designed 30 or so houses in seven or eight different states, tell me how you go about designing a residence so that it "cashes in" on its site's available resources . . . whatever those resources may be?

WRIGHT: It doesn't matter whether you're building in British Columbia or Saudi Arabia, Maine or New Mexico. Start off by doing everything you can—given the conditions at hand—to *passively* condition your new living space.

INTERVIEWER: You mean position the house on its site to take maximum advantage of the micro-climate, let the site and that micro-climate help determine the building's shape, build the structure like a thermos bottle with its insulation on the outside—just under the weather skin—and as much of its thermal mass as possible inside, put big panels of double-pane glass on the south side of the residence to admit the low winter sun and construct an overhang over those windows to shade out the high summer sun, use some sort of movable insulated shutters to regulate the amount of solar energy that enters the house on an hour-to-hour basis, and so on, right?

WRIGHT: That's a good beginning. As you get deeper into the climatic-design concept, though, you'll find that all that *is* just the beginning. There are many other ideas you can use. Sometimes it's good to build underground, for instance . . . sometimes it's not. And there are all kinds of things you can do with cross-ventilation ranging from simply putting in a few windows that open and close to mounting a sophisticated flat-plate collector on the south side of the house so that the heated air which rises through it creates a partial vacuum which pulls cooler air into the building through a moistened evaporative wick on the structure's north side.

Anything's fair, you see. The whole idea, first and foremost, is to use every trick you can to condition that new living space passively. Depending on the micro-climate, this first step could take care of 30% to 95% of all your needs. The percentage alone doesn't matter since 30% is still better than nothing . . . and actually, that 30% way up north somewhere in, say, British Columbia might save you more money in a year's time than 95% saves you further south.

Once you've done everything you can passively, you start filling in the gaps with active systems. They'll be more complicated and require more maintenance than your basic passive systems, but they're still the next best thing going. Combined with the passive setups, the right active solar systems—in many climates—can get you up to a 90, 95, or 100% conditioning of your living space. And even if it doesn't do that well, you're still way ahead of the game.

Your third line of defense should be a good little auxiliary stove which will burn wood or some other renewable fuel. And your last choice of all should be commercial energy in any form, preferably as efficient a form as possible. Heat pumps, in other words, are a better choice than electric space heaters or air conditioners.

INTERVIEWER: How do you analyze a site when you're getting ready to design a house, David? What tools do you use?

WRIGHT: Let's say that someone in Oklahoma contacts us—it's happened—and asks us to come and design a house.

All right, the climate in Oklahoma differs considerably from the climate we have here on the coast of northern California. The ocean moderates our seasonal temperature swings, and we have fog in the summer and about three days of clear weather to one of cloudy during our winter months. Oklahoma's summer weather, on the other hand, is much hotter and more humid . . . and its winters can be quite cold and harsh compared to ours. It's obvious that we're going to have some trouble trying to design a house for Oklahoma's climate while living on the coast of California.

So the first thing we do is go right to that specific piece of land in Oklahoma and walk around on it. We see if it has the proper solar exposure and whether or not we can work with the slope on that particular piece of property. If we don't think we can do something effective with what we've been given, we call it quits right there.

But if we can see some real possibilities, we talk to the people who want us to design the house to find out what they're looking for in the way of size, what materials they'd like to build with, what their budget will take, and what their lifestyles are like. We assimilate as much of that personal data as we can.

Then we write to the National Weather Service and get all the available information about the larger design parameters—winter extremes, summer extremes, humidity, etc. —that we'll have to work with. And we pick up the smaller design parameters—which way the wind blows, and how hard, and when and where the tornadoes come from (and how they are combated)—by talking to the old farmers and other people who've lived in that area for a long time.

We can also learn a lot by looking at the indigenous agricultural structures in the region. In Idaho, for instance, there are a number of terrific old potato-storage buildings which are built out of timbers and earth, and constructed halfway down into the ground. They're really inexpensive, and it never freezes inside those storage sheds. All in all, I've found them quite impressive. I'm just waiting to do a house up there so we can imitate one of those structures. It's hard to go wrong when you can look around at regional architecture like that and then copy what the pioneers—who didn't have our sources of commercial energy to draw on—did to survive.

By the time we've gone through this whole process, we have a pretty good idea of what's happening. So we gather up our weather data, photographs of the site, topography maps, soil analyses, and so on, and we come back to our office. Then we start playing around with forms and the usage of materials until we come up with the one structure that we think best uses the indigenous energies—whether they're wind, solar, or water—to solve all the building's external problems while making its internal space function as well as possible.

INTERVIEWER: That sounds simple and straightforward enough.

WRIGHT: It is. On the other hand, when you start working with climatic design, you immediately realize that it's an entirely different ball game than the old sledgehammer approach of just throwing up the same building for almost any part of the country, and then varying the heating and cooling equipment that goes into it.

There are many subtleties that come into play when you're designing one particular house to take maximum advantage of one particular micro-climate . . . a house to operate on just the natural energy sources available.

Every house has a different storage mass, geometry, exterior profile, heat loss factor, amount of window area, and so on. Each house has a different performance curve tailored as precisely as possible to the weather, temperature, and other climatic changes of its particular site . . . and to the preferences of the people who'll live in it. This can be done, and it's a lot of fun doing it . . . but it requires a lot more finesse than just sticking an air conditioner in one of the windows.

You have to learn to give and take. You become much more aware of the weather. You don't just throw a carpet down on the floor if the floor happens to be one of your thermal storage masses . . . because that carpet will act as a piece of insulation between the solar energy coming in the windows and the storage floor. As a result, your living space will heat up too fast during the day and cool off too fast at night.

If you're too lazy or too inflexible to take all this in stride, you're going to hate living in a climatic house. If you can handle these kinds of change, though, you're going to be way ahead of the game as the cost of energy continues to climb. You're going to save yourself a bundle of money and be able to live with a lot more independence and self-determination than the poor souls who still get their daily fix of energy from the utility companies.

We've been living in a petroleum economy for some time, but we're already making the transition to a solar economy. It's only a matter of time until every home and apartment building takes care of its own needs with passive heating and cooling . . . and generates its own electricity with photovoltaic cells or some kind of neighborhood solar-powered generator.

And that's going to free a lot of people from the corporate economics that now control us in a very omniscient and mysterious way. We won't have to spend so much of our time paying off those corporations as we do now . . . and that will elevate the quality of our lives by fostering independence and self-sufficiency.

The change to a solar economy will also change the physical makeup of our world for the better. People can be very sloppy and very tacky . . . not too many of the cities they've built are really beautiful.

Nature, on the other hand, is much more discerning in the way it manifests itself. As we start designing our communities to use the natural sources of energy in each area, you're going to see a big difference.

First, solar collectors will start popping up on a lot of existing buildings. Then subdivisions that are totally oriented towards the sun and contain very energy-efficient structures will begin to appear. They'll be different . . . fitting together and blending into the landscape instead of being individual contradictory little statements which clutter everything up and clash with each other. Eventually, we'll probably evolve megastructures which will be very efficient and serve us better . . . while leaving a great deal more land open for agricultural and recreational uses.

I believe that this is all inevitable and all quite exciting. The Solar Age is just starting to dawn, and I'm very optimistic about it.

"We've been living in a petroleum economy for some time, but we're already making the transition to a solar economy."

DON METZ

Energy . . . thermal efficiency . . . coupling . . . mass . . . these are terms that up until the petroleum crisis of 1973 were used by automotive engineers rather than residential designers. That unforeseen *dilemma, though, sent literally hundreds of people—architects and owner-builders alike—scurrying for the answers that would make their houses more efficient and less dependent on outside energy sources.*

Spurred by rising fuel costs, competition, fear, or any combination of these, housing pioneers of all descriptions set about finding new uses for old technology or developing fresh concepts to meet the demand for new designs.

In addition, there were some who, in effect, stumbled upon energy-saving answers . . . not in a quest for improved efficiency—a variety of experimentation was *going on before 1973 —but in the process of creating new and original designs.*

Don Metz, the subject of this interview, is one such person. Architect, builder, mason, writer, and above all, artisan, Metz has taken a commonsense approach to house construction that combines the matter-of-fact character of a farm boy with the dexterous mind of a Yale-trained designer.

INTERVIEWER: Don, I'm sure I'm not the first visitor who's been taken aback by that climb up your driveway . . . but I have to admit now that the view from Baldtop is well worth the struggle. Would it be foolish to ask if you and your family chose this site for its scenery?

METZ: We were fortunate to find a spot with nearly a 360-degree view . . . but that wasn't the only consideration. Actually, Baldtop has its pros and cons, like any site. On the negative side, for instance, I had to do a little blasting before I could build because the house is partially set in bedrock.

INTERVIEWER: If I'm not mistaken, you designed and built your home here in 1975. Is it true that this was only the second residence you'd constructed?

METZ: The second *earth-sheltered* one, yes . . . the first was the Winston home, over on top of the neighboring hill. That was built "pre-OPEC," in '71 and '72. But I've designed a number of wood-framed houses—and one footbridge—during the past decade and a half. To date, my partner and I have also designed a dozen different earth-sheltered homes throughout the U.S. . . . and a number of our Earthtech 6–style homes have been built.

INTERVIEWER: So your experience as an architect extends to various types of structures. How, then, did you come to be one of today's subterranean design specialists?

METZ: To tell the truth, pretty much by circumstance. When I first began planning the Winston house, I started with a clean slate. My goal wasn't to go underground, but the site was perfect for that concept, and I was eager to try something out of the ordinary. Sometime later I realized that the idea was energy-sensible as well.

When I designed this house—my *own*—I felt a complete freedom to experiment . . . with curves, arches, level-changes, textures, earth loads, building materials, berms, landscaping, and any number of other factors. Again, the outcome was a success, not just aesthetically, but in an energy sense as well . . . only this time, because of the Arab oil embargo, the home was considered big news. And I guess you could say that those two experiences so impressed me with what earth-covered structures could offer—conservation, minimal maintenance, and a Rock-of-Gibraltar sense of substance—that I've been stuck on the concept ever since.

INTERVIEWER: Did your training as an architect help to prepare you for below-grade experimentation?

METZ: Well, not exactly, but I was fortunate to have attended design school at a time—in the early sixties—when there was a new trend afoot toward hands-on *practicality*. In other words, architectural instructors and students were starting to feel the importance of *building* what they'd designed . . . and, as you know, there's nothing quite like some experience under one's belt to establish which ideas really do work.

INTERVIEWER: What made you pursue architecture as a career?

METZ: A desire to create something of beauty. In fact, I actually started out as a sculpture major.

INTERVIEWER: So I take it you place a high premium on aesthetics . . . that's also pretty obvious from seeing what you've done here. But how does beauty relate to energy conservation? There must be situations in which the two are mutually exclusive.

METZ: Absolutely. I got into energy-efficient building simply because conservation is a fact of life these days. The question I ask myself, then, is how can I combine that with my true interest, which is to develop real *architecture*.

A lot of energy-efficient structures, you see, are simply *buildings* . . . they're not pieces of architecture. On the other hand, some architectural delights aren't energy-efficient. I guess I want to do the best job I can of creating graceful *and* efficient buildings.

INTERVIEWER: Are you willing sometimes to sacrifice performance for aesthetics?

METZ: I do it all the time . . . for the sake of what I dare call beauty. If some feature offers a big payoff aesthetically, I'd go with it rather than strive for efficiency to the nth degree. To say it another way, I simply couldn't share my living room with an ugly 55-gallon-drum water wall, even if the containers did save energy. It seems like that's a rather poor compromise of beauty for performance. Ultimately, some of my best design solutions aren't concessions to architecture or to efficiency . . . they're just the right way to do it.

INTERVIEWER: You obviously don't take a *mechanistic* approach to design.

METZ: I don't . . . because I don't relish the idea of living in a machine. We're not robots,

PHOTOS BY ROSS CHAPPLE AND THE MOTHER EARTH NEWS STAFF

"I don't relish the idea of living in a machine. We're not robots, and we shouldn't be forced to live like them."

Metz and a "best friend" enjoy year-round, energy-efficient comfort in his Baldtop Mountain home, which blends well into the seasonal landscape and offers a spectacular view.

"A more compact house means fewer materials and lower fuel bills."

and we shouldn't be forced to live like them. Many contemporary design trends have been too mechanistic. For a while, many designers—particularly those influenced by the Modernist or Bauhaus school—were so enamored of technology that I think they failed to recognize beauty.

INTERVIEWER: And it's high time for a change?

METZ: I'd like to think so. Besides, our architecture is a reflection of ourselves as a nation . . . and it's a shame that we haven't as yet come up with an indigenous American style.

INTERVIEWER: Could you elaborate on that point?

METZ: The overwhelming majority of our architecture has its roots in Europe. It's Neo-Georgian, neoclassical, Romanesque . . . yet we've had some really *original* American architects, artists like Henry Hobson Richardson, Louis Henri Sullivan, and Frank Lloyd Wright. But they—Wright especially—were never recognized by the architectural "powers that be" . . . largely because they were not European. To this day, American designers still maintain an inferiority complex about what we can produce. And really . . . if we're into driving eight-cylinder Cadillacs, what's our architecture going to look like? There's no answer to that unless you truly believe in the Robert Venturi idea that the Vegas strip represents our vital architecture. If that's the case, it's a sad commentary on American design . . . and maybe that's something nobody even wants to admit.

INTERVIEWER: All right, where will we go from here? Are there technical breakthroughs around the corner that are going to have some effect on future designs?

METZ: Well, this is probably very shortsighted, but I feel that—at least from a technical standpoint—the quantum jumps have already been made as a result of OPEC pressures. The building industry adapted very quickly to the energy crunch . . . probably because it's *not* centralized. In the same way, the engineers have done their part in making new structures mechanically functional. Designers can now take those ideas and apply them in a visually pleasing manner.

INTERVIEWER: What about cost?

METZ: There's not a whole lot we can do about that except to use what we've got to the best advantage by allowing single components to serve a number of purposes. Take the walls in this house, for instance. They're curved to break up the rigid, predictable pattern created by conventional walls, but they're also designed that way because an arch—and a curved wall is just an arch turned on its side—can resist pressures more effectively than can a flat surface. Besides that, they can be arranged to satisfy space needs . . . be colored and textured to deal with light and balance in a favorable manner . . . provide a source of thermal mass . . . be insulated . . . and, of course, hold up the roof!

INTERVIEWER: But isn't it more expensive to build the curved walls in the first place?

The exposed walls of the earth-sheltered dwelling feature large windows overlooking the hills and valleys below.

METZ: It's true that setting up forms for a *poured* concrete wall would be a real nightmare, although reinforcing a straight section for lateral loads might be just about as taxing. But you don't have to go that route. The curved walls of this house are made from concrete block, and—though you'd have a hard time finding anyone who'd say block is *better* than reinforced concrete—it *is* less expensive if you lay it yourself . . . and it can be formed into any configuration without difficulty.

INTERVIEWER: What about trends? Do you see American housing design moving in any particular direction today?

METZ: Compacting or miniaturizing our dwellings. Now that our country is populated more and more by smaller families, single heads-of-household, and children living away from their families, I think we'll see houses just getting smaller and smaller.

INTERVIEWER: What's the average floor area of the typical house today?

METZ: I don't know, but I'm sure an awful lot of Americans are walking around in empty rooms . . . and still feel that they "have to" possess such large spaces. But, of course, as the energy situation gets worse, we'll see a change by necessity. After all, a more compact house means fewer materials and lower fuel bills.

INTERVIEWER: But how do residents in small homes achieve a level of comfort comparable with that in larger ones?

METZ: By the creative use of space. Even now, my partner and I are starting to utilize the concept of zone living . . . a fancy-sounding term which boils down to nothing more than arranging the house so that portions of it can be shut off when they're not in use. Some-

times, for example, we'll have to consider the needs of a client who wants a big living room, but realizes it won't be used, save for special occasions. In that case, we isolate that living area—with its cathedral ceiling and huge fireplace—and use the kitchen/dining area as the focal point for everyday activity, adding a hearth to that space to make it more cozy.

INTERVIEWER: This zone-living concept can be applied to small houses?

METZ: Yes indeed . . . and it's as important to aesthetics as any other notion. But the trick in a small home is to *borrow* one space from another—that's a characteristic of open design—so you never feel like you're stuck in a tiny room. Such space flow also increases the *airflow*, which has become a major concern with the increasing popularity of woodstoves.

INTERVIEWER: Aside from—or perhaps I should say together with—minimizing our living spaces, what other conservation methods do you think make sense for the future?

METZ: Let me put it this way. There are a lot of ways to lessen energy consumption, but when all is said and done, the one common denominator in any procedure is the reduction of heat loss. Regardless of what type of house you're dealing with, that can be done in only two ways: either by reducing the Delta T (the temperature difference between the inside and outside environments) through earth sheltering . . . or by insulating heavily. Those two kinds of straightforward approaches could become very common.

INTERVIEWER: What's your opinion of a hybrid house that combines any number of energy-saving features—such as superinsulation, insolation, and earth-sheltered and double-envelope concepts—into one design?

METZ: If it's done sensibly, I think it's a great idea. I'd like to see an end to the belief that houses have to be built with any one of these features exclusively . . . and fortunately, I think designers are waking up to the fact that each one of these approaches offers a number of advantages that can be integrated with other ideas.

Far too often I get hit with the analytical proposal that, because a structure is labeled a double-envelope house, there are only "X" number of features allowed in it . . . and that's just foolish. We need to break down these classifications and simply build a house that makes sense for the site, the climate, and the energy source.

INTERVIEWER: But how could you incorporate everything into one design?

METZ: You probably couldn't . . . but I'd be willing to bet that you wouldn't *need* everything in one design if you built to suit specific requirements.

INTERVIEWER: And figuring out how to best design for a particular site is where *your* talents come in.

METZ: Not necessarily. This may sound strange coming from me, but residential architects are *not* essential to everyday society, simply because there are so many other sources of good information around. Someone who wants to erect an energy-efficient house can just buy a few books and build a really decent dwelling on his or her own.

INTERVIEWER: Who, then, are you designing for?

METZ: I've had all types of clients. Though nobody's ever come in and handed me a blank check, I've done some work for very wealthy people . . . and by the same token I've designed homes for other folks whose cost-consciousness—because of economic necessity—showed through during each and every phase of the operation.

INTERVIEWER: I'd imagine you prefer the former.

METZ: Not necessarily. One advantage to having a financial limitation is that the designer's task is very clear. The person footing the bill has already colored the decision—by eliminating the extravagant—so there's really a form of control present on the architect. Sometimes that's very welcome.

And, looking at it another way, taking on a fixed-budget job allows me to exercise what I might call *practical* creativity . . . making the most of down-to-earth, everyday components.

INTERVIEWER: "Practical creativity" . . . that's a nice concept. I imagine it sums up your whole attitude toward energy-efficient housing and design.

METZ: Well, if I had to put it in ten words or less, yes. For centuries people have been using various aspects of energy conservation in their day-to-day existence, often without realizing all its uses and benefits. Now we've been forced to open our eyes . . . and you know what? The answers are all here. We've just got to use them.

"We need to . . . simply build a house that makes sense for the site, the climate, and the energy source."

Metz's 2,200-square-foot, two-level structure is a study in curves.

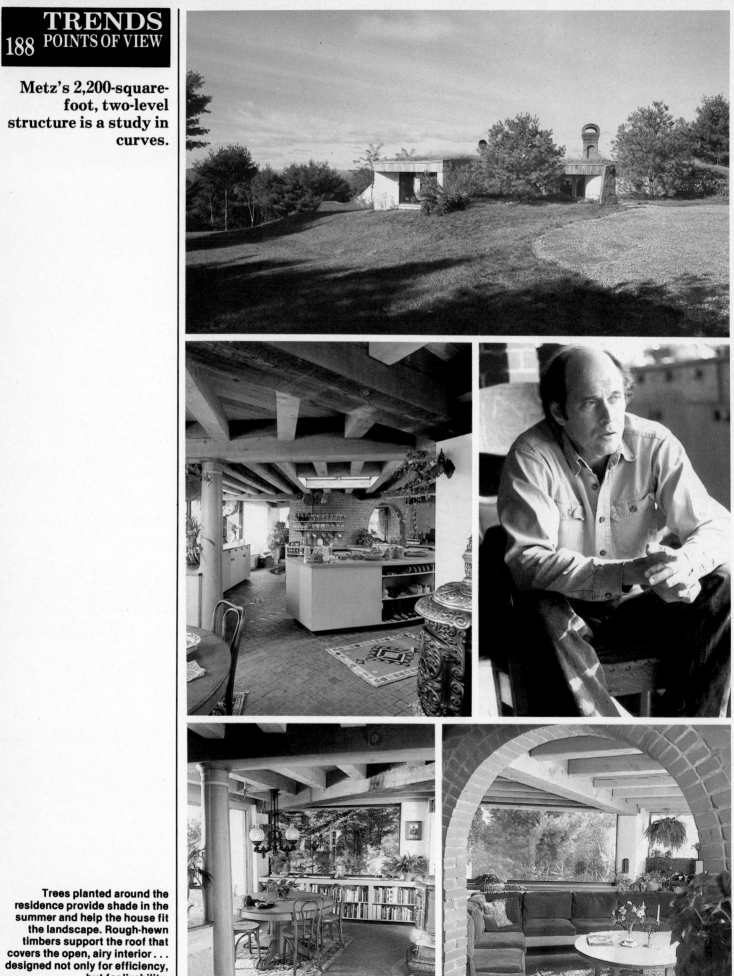

Trees planted around the residence provide shade in the summer and help the house fit the landscape. Rough-hewn timbers support the roof that covers the open, airy interior . . . designed not only for efficiency, but for livability.

True to plan, Baldtop Dugout was made entirely from conventional materials.

A LOOK AT BALDTOP DUGOUT

Baldtop Dugout—Metz's second earth-covered house and the one he built for himself and his family—is a striking example of the freedom that building underground can permit. Rather than resigning himself to the strict, straight-walled, square-cornered arrangement typical of aboveground structures (and often carried through—as if by rote—to the design of subterranean dwellings), Metz cut loose and exercised the notion that "anything goes" belowground . . . within structural limits.

The 2,200-square-foot, two-level structure is a study in curves: Horseshoe-shaped walls, vaulted doorways, and a periphery that defies geometric description all combine to create a feeling that the interior space is somehow vague . . . almost boundless.

An open floor plan (about half the main level is dedicated to the living, dining, kitchen, and entry areas) assures a well-lit, airy atmosphere, yet carefully placed—and shaped—dividers separate these spaces by function . . . and offer needed privacy to the sleeping quarters.

Because Baldtop Dugout is backed into a hilltop knob and is earth-*sheltered* (rather than completely buried in soil), Metz was able to take full advantage of natural light by placing windows not just to the south side—where the lion's share of glazing usually exists—but very nearly all around the structure and even in the roof in the form of large skylights over the foyer and kitchen.

And once the sunlight is in the house, it's put to good use: Light-hued walls and furniture reflect and diffuse brightness, while dark tiles and masonry absorb its energy. By the same token, the natural illumination accents the contrasting surfaces within the dwelling—clay tile here, stucco there, and wood all around—and aids in lending an open feeling to the living room . . . a sensation which is further enhanced by the sunken floor in that area.

Since Metz was interested in relying on traditional methods in the construction of his house (he built and detailed the Dugout himself), he had to strike a delicate balance between maintaining the contoured beauty of the mountain building site and assuring the structural integrity of the dwelling *without* relying on complicated and costly solutions.

His response was admirable: By nestling the basement and much of the main level into the hilltop but leaving the upper sections of the living area walls exposed, Don was able to avoid much of the lateral stress that would be present if the entire two levels were buried, and at the same time provide the dwelling with access to natural light.

Then, by covering the roof with a modest eight inches of soil and encouraging vegetative growth, he was able to use the earth's moderating influence to his advantage while still keeping his roof load far short of extreme . . . and retaining an unscathed appearance on the grassy knob's surface.

True to plan, Baldtop Dugout was made entirely from conventional building materials. The walls are concrete block, insulated with two inches of polyurethane, waterproofed with two layers of asphalt pitch, and drained at the footings. The roof is wooden decking supported on rough-hewn 6 X 8 joists, insulated and waterproofed in the same manner as the walls (but to a higher degree). White windbreaks and retaining walls extending from the structure serve the triple function of supporting roof overhangs, protecting the windows from the effects of wind and unwanted insolation throughout the seasons, and reflecting light inward.

Energy use is, of course, low. Two woodburning stoves provide all the auxiliary heat necessary. Winter fuel consumption amounts to about four cords a year in the harsh New England mountain climate.

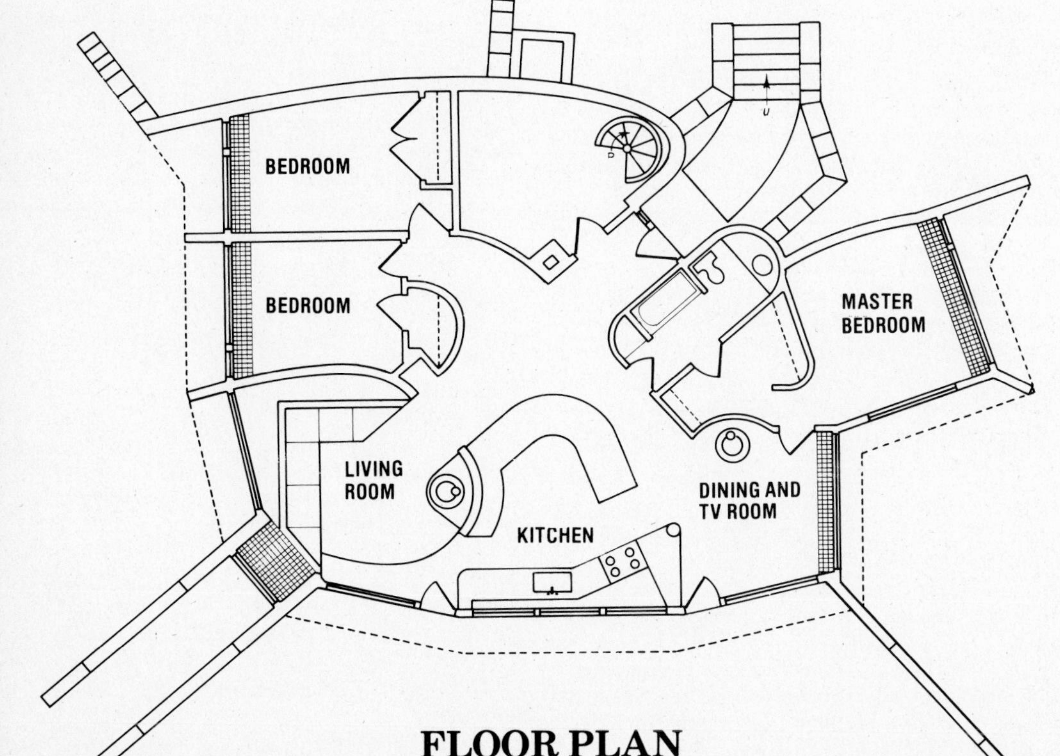

FLOOR PLAN

ANDY DAVIS

The astronomical rise in petroleum prices during the 1970's and the contingent escalation in the cost of other fossil fuels and electricity inspired many individuals across the country to find ingenious—though often unconventional—ways to reduce their dependence on nonrenewable resources and to lessen the impact of increased energy costs on their personal and family budgets.

One of these people is Andy Davis. After recognizing the advantages of using the stable temperature of the earth itself to reduce the heating requirements of a house, Davis—together with his wife, son, and three daughters—built a 1,200-square-foot, three-bedroom "cave", which provides all the amenities of his family's previous conventional dwelling. In addition, the belowground house is quieter, stronger, and less expensive to heat: It cost Davis less than one-hundredth as much to keep his family warm all year than he spent heating their former residence for just one winter month.

In 1977, following the Davises' first winter in their cave home, Andy spoke with a staff member of THE MOTHER EARTH NEWS® magazine about planning, building, and living in the Armington, Illinois dwelling.

INTERVIEWER: Andy, this is really a great house . . . far nicer than I thought it'd be.

DAVIS: That seems to be the general reaction. People come in here expecting one of the old frontier dugouts, maybe. And our visitors wind up using the same words over and over again: "beautiful", "remarkable".

A lot of people have just never thought about covering the walls and ceilings of their homes with something simple like rocks, and they're genuinely amazed at how beautiful it can be.

INTERVIEWER: What gave you the idea to build a place like this?

DAVIS: I got the notion about four years ago when I was down in Arkansas. I was visiting an abandoned mining town on a hot day, and I noticed that the farther back I went into an old mining tunnel . . . why, the cooler it got.

Well, the walls of this old shaft were covered with crystal—big chunks of rock that looked like glass—so I just sat there on a ledge, shining my light around on that rock. It was really beautiful. And I thought to myself, "Boy, this is nice back here . . . and I'll bet this tunnel will be warm in the winter too." And that's what gave me the idea.

INTERVIEWER: So you came back here and built your own cave?

DAVIS: No, not just like that. But I kept the thought in the back of my mind for a while. And then—during a winter that was downright mild compared to last winter—Margaret and I got a heating bill for $167 for one month.

Well, that did it. I was pretty confident I could build an underground house that'd be a lot less expensive to heat than that. So I began turning the idea over in my mind. I must have spent close to three weeks just sitting in this chair thinking through each detail . . . I didn't want to start any actual construction until I was sure I knew what I was doing. And then I just went out and began.

INTERVIEWER: Several architects have been working on and promoting the idea of underground structures for the past several years. There was even a conference on "Alternatives in Energy Conservation: The Use of Earth Covered Buildings" held in Fort Worth, Texas back in the summer of 1975 . . . and I believe some of the folks who attended that conference now publish a newsletter on the subject. Had you heard about any of this activity when you started your house?

DAVIS: No. I didn't even know those people existed. I just saw that old mining tunnel in Arkansas and then, a couple of years later, the bill for $167 for heating a conventional home for a month arrived, and I simply figured I'd build an underground house. That's all there was to it.

INTERVIEWER: And then you just sat there in that chair you're sitting in now until you'd worked out all the details in your mind . . . and then you built this house?

DAVIS: That's right. As far as I knew, there wasn't anybody else who'd done this before, and there wasn't any other place like this that I could look at for reference . . . so I just went ahead and solved all the problems myself.

INTERVIEWER: What kinds of problems?

DAVIS: Weight, for one thing. There's at least three feet of dirt sitting all over the top of this building . . . and it mounds up to four feet deep in the center. At 100 pounds per cubic foot—about 350 pounds for every square foot of the ceiling over our heads—that adds up fast, and I had to allow for it. Also, figure in another 150 pounds per square foot for the weight of the concrete and stone in the roof itself, plus another 100 or so pounds per square foot for "live weight"—say, for when we want to drive the garden tractor or something like that around up there—plus a good margin for error. When you're talking about 1,200 square feet of living space—which this house has—you're talking about a roof that must support 1,200,000 or more pounds.

INTERVIEWER: What about dampness and moisture?

DAVIS: Everybody asks me that question. So many concrete basements are damp inside that most of us have naturally come to expect that any underground structure is going to have a moisture problem. I worried about dampness too in the beginning . . . especially when we hit a small spring as we were digging out the excavation for this place.

Well, when you hit water, and you don't want it, you have to get rid of it. We tiled that little spring up—it wasn't big enough to use for our water supply—and we led it off to a drainage line. And once we poured our concrete floor over it, we never knew it was there anymore.

INTERVIEWER: But what about ordinary seepage through your walls . . . or surface water coming in through the ceiling?

Wood obtained free for the cutting is the primary heat source for the "cave", which because of its thermal mass loses only a few degrees a day when without any heat during the winter.

"As a matter of fact, it's always just about perfect in here."

DAVIS: We tiled the footings, of course, just the way you'd tile the footings for a basement. And we coated the top of the roof and the outside of all the walls that are underground with asphalt. We also laid one inch of Styrofoam insulation across the roof and part way down the sides of all the covered walls. This helps regulate the temperature in the building . . . and it also leaves a space *around* the house that surface water can seep down through—to the drainage tiles under the footings—thereby keeping it from coming into the building through the roof or walls.

That takes care of any water that might want to get into the house from the outside. But, as I'm sure you know, most conventional basements don't get damp because of outside water seeping in anyway. They're damp because the warm, moist air from the rest of the house reaches them and the water condenses. And all you have to do to solve that problem is do away with that warm, moist air in the first place.

That's what we've done. We've taken steps to see that we never get enough of a buildup of heat and humidity in here so that we feel damp, or so that moisture begins to condense out of the air on anything.

INTERVIEWER: What kind of steps?

DAVIS: A good example is my wife's clothes dryer. Its exhaust is both hot and damp. Obviously, we don't want it blowing into the house during the summer when the atmosphere here in Illinois is already warm and frequently laden with moisture. It'd just condense all over everything and make the whole building humid and sticky. Instead, we vent the dryer outside in the summer.

But wait a minute! When you heat a house during the winter, the air inside usually gets too dry anyway . . . so dry that, to feel comfortable, you sometimes have to raise the building's inside temperature up into the high 70's or low 80's. What you want then is to put *both* heat and humidity into your home. So, in the winter, we vent the dryer right into the house. Instead of letting that moisture and warmth just blow outside and go to waste, we use it to regulate the atmosphere here in the house.

That's the idea, you see. If you use just a little common sense, you can take a lot of the things that most of us forget about—the exhaust from a clothes dryer, for example—and, merely by the way you handle them, they can help you live a lot more comfortably the year around.

As a matter of fact, it's always just about perfect in here. The humidity usually hovers around 50%. Once in a while—when it's really damp outside and Margaret is doing a lot of cooking—it may go up to 80%, but I've never seen it over that. Generally, though, it stays around 50% . . . and it's never been below 40% in the winter. We just don't have to overheat our air to stay comfortable during cold weather.

INTERVIEWER: OK. Let's get a few more of the details of your cave's construction. What is this in here . . . about an eight-and-a-half-foot ceiling?

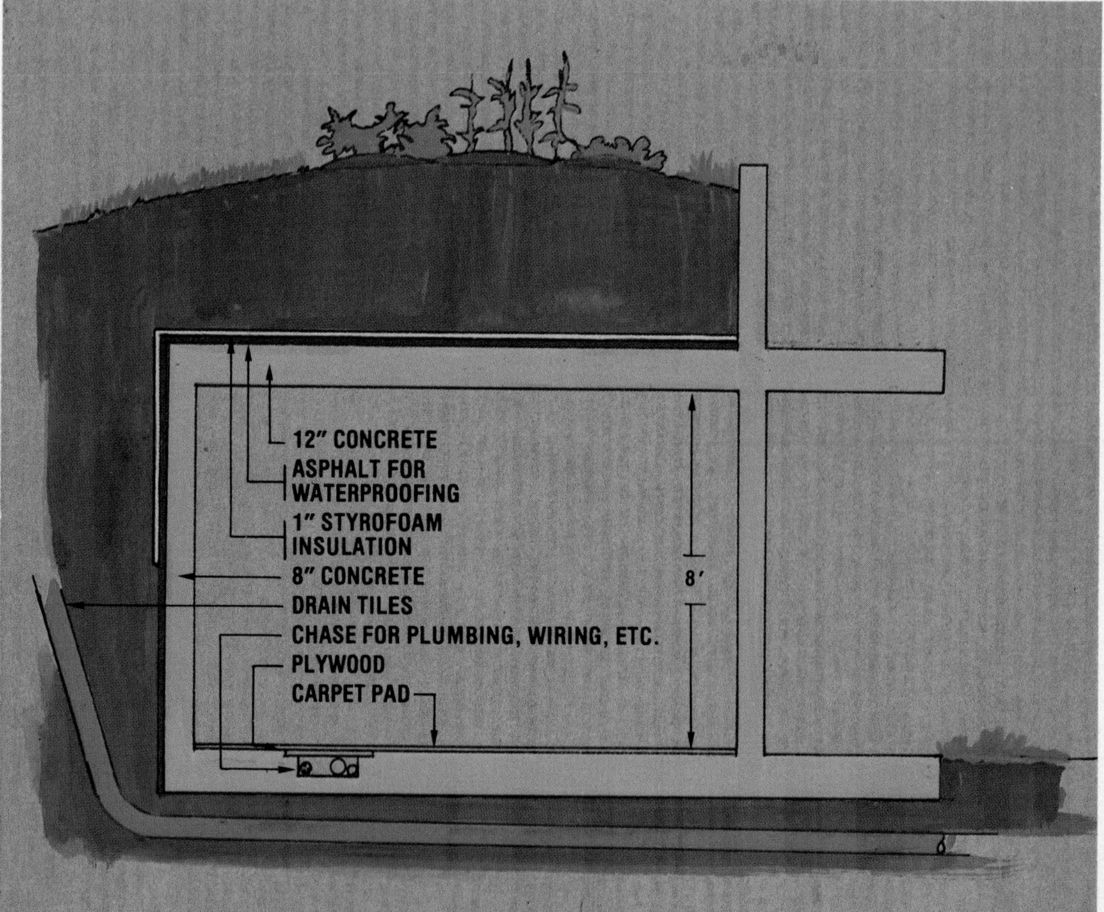

Large circular windows at the front of the dwelling allow natural sunlight into the living area.

DAVIS: A little over eight feet, on the average. It varies some, depending on just how far a few of the rocks stick out of the concrete.

INTERVIEWER: Where did that stone come from, Andy? Did you pick it up yourself?

DAVIS: Right. For the most part my family and I picked it up over at a nearby gravel pit. This is what's called "glacier stone", and the pit where we got it doesn't have a rock crusher. The guys that work there run the stone through a screen before they sell it, and everything that's too big to go through rolls over to the side and just stacks up in the way. So we more or less got all the rocks we used in the house "free for the hauling".

Then—as the word began to get around about what we were doing—people started bringing us special little gifts of rocks from other places. Folks would come in and hand us a rock and say: "Here's one from the ocean," or "Maybe you'd like a rock from a real cave for the cave you're building." We got rocks from all over that way.

INTERVIEWER: How did you embed all the stones in your walls and ceilings? Or, better yet, just go back to the beginning and—step by step—tell us how you built this whole place.

DAVIS: Well, I'm an electrician—not a millionaire—so our *first* step was a visit to the bank for financing.

INTERVIEWER: A lot of bankers have financed conventional housing . . . but not too many have put up money for a cave dwelling.

Did you have any trouble getting the backing you needed?

DAVIS: No. That could have been a problem . . . but our banker was either smarter than the average banker or more willing to take a risk on a new idea. We didn't have any trouble there.

Nor did we have any problem with building inspectors. A lot of the things we've done here are kind of unusual . . . but everything in this house meets or exceeds all the codes. Besides that, I've built some other things in the past, and I guess the local inspectors just assumed that I could do what I said I was going to do.

"We more or less got all the rocks we used 'free for the hauling'."

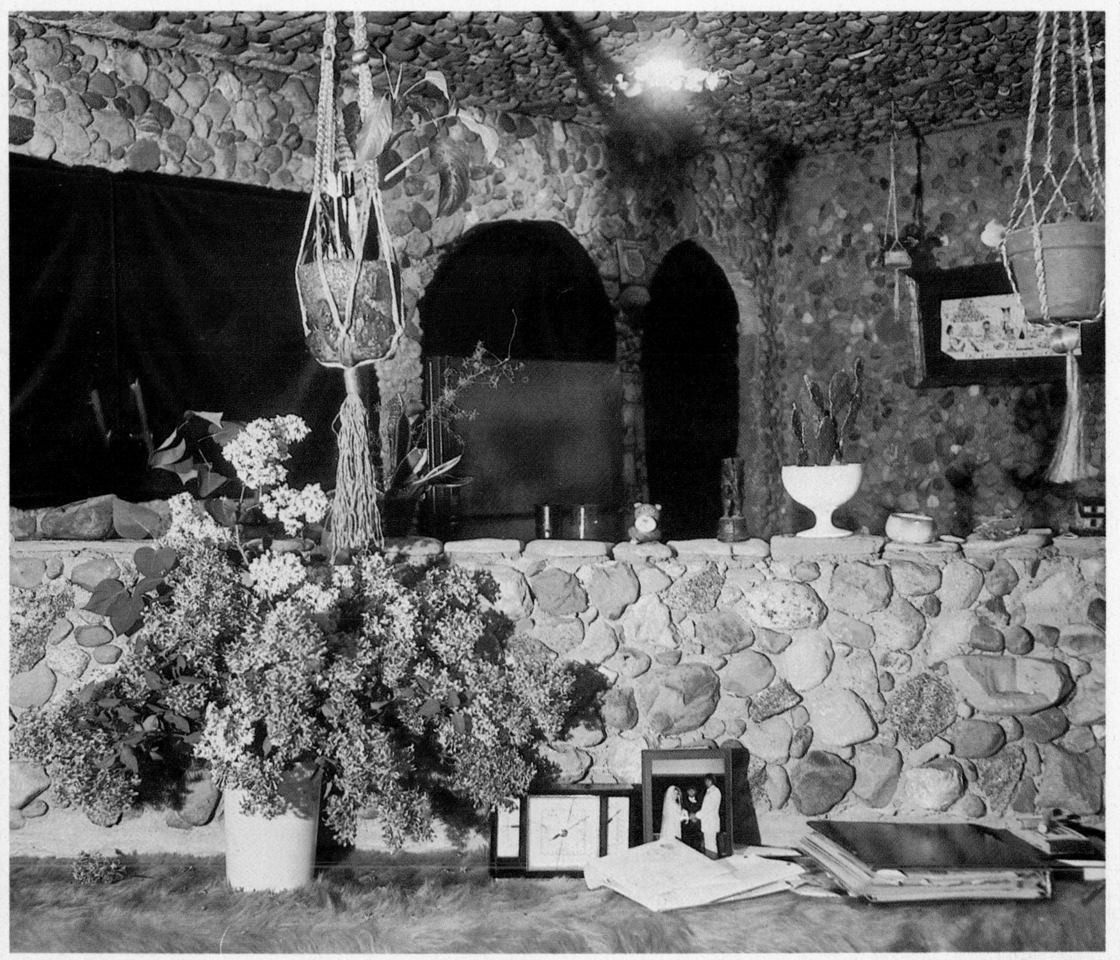

Rocks embedded in the inside of the home's walls and ceiling are not only for decoration, but for permanence.

"Each short wall braces, and is braced by, the ones it joins."

INTERVIEWER: I guess you must have begun your actual construction by digging out an excavation.

DAVIS: Well, we didn't dig *down*, the way some people think. You see, we bought these two lots because they had a hill on them. And then we just brought in a bulldozer and dug straight back into the hill. As it turned out, that was a good idea because the work was easy. We didn't run into any solid stone that would have been tough to pry out or blast loose. But it was a little bad because the original hill was only about ten feet high. And even after we'd finished our house and put all the dirt from the excavation back on top of it, there just wasn't enough earth to spread around and blend into a new slope the way we wanted. We had to haul in 50 truckloads of dirt to landscape the place right.

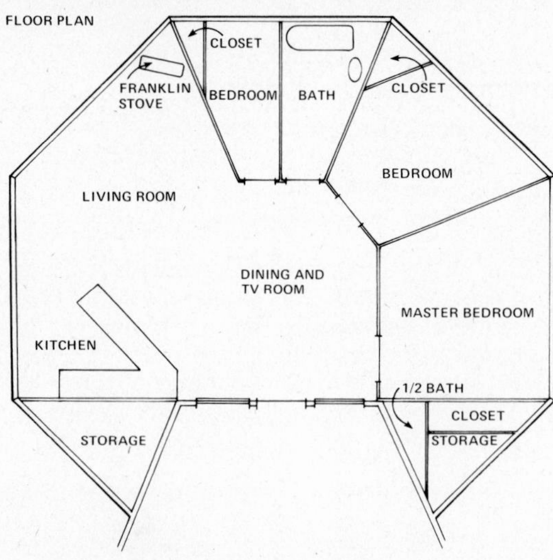

Now you'll notice that the floor plan of our cave isn't square or rectangular. It's an octagon. We did that on purpose. The house is stronger this way. In effect—by using this shape—the building doesn't have long, weak walls tied together by four strong cornerstones the way most buildings do. Instead, each short wall braces, and is braced by, the ones it joins . . . and the structure becomes almost as strong as if the whole thing were one big, rigid cornerstone!

INTERVIEWER: Are the walls poured concrete?

DAVIS: Right. We thought about bricks, but they'd have been too expensive. Cement blocks would have been too weak, and wood would have rotted. So we just built up some forms and then poured the walls out of concrete. The back and side walls are 8 inches thick, and the one across the front—the only exterior wall that's not covered with dirt—is 12 inches thick. The interior partitions measure from 6 to 12 inches through, and the ceiling is a foot thick. We used 127 cubic yards of ready-mix in the walls, the ceiling, and the floor of the house.

INTERVIEWER: You poured the outside walls first and . . .

DAVIS: . . . the ceiling next, the floor after that, and the interior partitions last of all.

INTERVIEWER: Did you use any reinforcing rod in the concrete?

DAVIS: Oh sure, lots of it. We really tied that concrete together. We also embedded pipes in the ceiling and walls so that, later, we could run wires through them for lights and electrical outlets. The floors were done somewhat differently. We made little ditches—or "chases," as they're known in the construction business—in the floor. These are open spaces 16" wide and 6" deep set right down into the surface of the concrete and covered by pieces of plywood that are recessed just the wood's thickness to make the finished floor level and smooth. The chases hold most of the house's plumbing and a lot of its electrical wiring, switches, and plugs. If anything goes wrong, we just roll back the rug, lift a section or two of plywood, and go to work.

INTERVIEWER: What about the rocks?

DAVIS: Well, that's kind of a trade secret, but I can tell you that we put them in by hand. While the concrete in the walls and ceiling was still barely pliable in each pour, we pulled off the forms and then embedded the stones which you see all over the interior of our cave. We're sure they add some strength to the walls and ceiling, but the most important reason the rocks are there is because they really look nice. Lots of modern architecture is built with poured concrete, you know, but we didn't want to live in a "space age" house. We wanted to live in a cave . . . and the stones all over the walls and the ceiling make our home feel like a cave.

The second reason we covered the inside of our house with rocks is so we'll never have to redecorate this place for as long as we live . . . and that's going to save us a lot of time and money.

And the third reason we embedded all those stones in the concrete is because—sooner or later—a concrete wall always seems to crack at least a little bit someplace . . . and we figure that the rocks are going to cover almost any kind of crack that ever appears.

INTERVIEWER: Good enough. I suppose you finished the outside of the building by waiting a while until the concrete had cured . . . and then putting on the coating of asphalt, adding the inch of Styrofoam insulation across the top and down the sides, and covering the whole thing with three to four feet of earth?

DAVIS: Right. That's pretty much the way we did it. Then we smoothed off the dirt and planted grass seed and a few bushes . . . things which have roots that'll never reach all the way down to the roof of our cave where they might someday cause trouble. That's why we didn't plant any large trees on top.

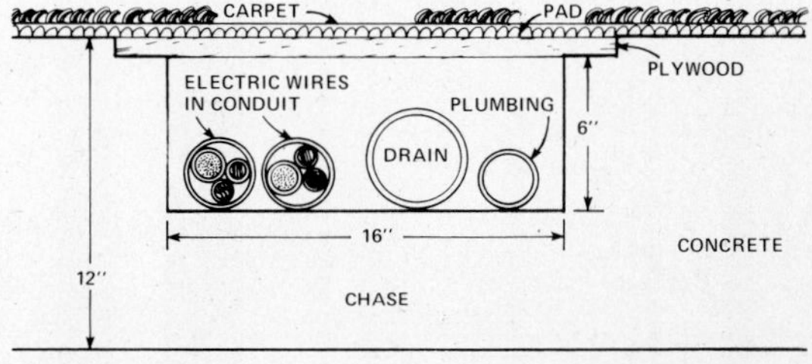

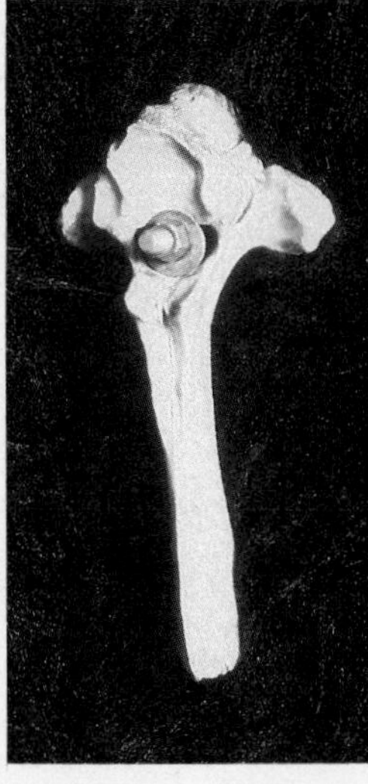

INTERVIEWER: I suppose you get a lot of comments about those two big windows and your rather unusual front door from visitors the first time they walk up to your home?

DAVIS: We sure do. Each one of the windows is six feet across and, as you can see, round. They're also Thermopane, very strong, and quite expensive. The door is framed with 1 X 4's and paneled with particle board. And over the particle board we've stretched a covering of fur . . . which, of course, is what makes the door so unusual.

INTERVIEWER: Why the round windows and the fur on the front door?

DAVIS: For the same reason we've got rocks on the walls and ceiling, fur on all the inside doors, and doorknobs and other hardware in the house made out of cow bones. As soon as we started talking about living in a cave house, the joke began going around town that the Flintstones were going to move into Armington. So we decided to go along with the gag and turn our new home into something that the Flintstone cartoon characters would really enjoy.

INTERVIEWER: And the lights?

DAVIS: We carried the cave motif right on through to our electrical fixtures and wiring, too. There's a total of 48 light fixtures recessed into the ceiling of our home, and we've stuck pieces of colored, broken glass around the edges of all of them. The reflections that come off the glass remind me of the way my flashlight reflected off those chunks of crystal in the walls of that old mining tunnel down in Arkansas.

Here's something else we did that we kind of like. See? There are no switches for the lights on any of the walls. And you don't see any outlets either. They're all out of sight under the rugs. You might have a little trouble finding them at first, but we know where they all are and just where to go whenever we want to plug anything in.

INTERVIEWER: And when you want to turn a light on or off . . . ?

DAVIS: We just walk over and step on one of the floor switches. They're like a dimmer switch in an automobile. Step once, and the light comes on . . . step again, and it goes off.

INTERVIEWER: That's pretty nifty . . . and there's no question about it: Hiding all the outlets, switches, and fixtures this way certainly does make your house seem more like a real cave. How long did it take you to build it?

DAVIS: We figured that we'd finish the place in three and a half months . . . and I still think we could have done it. But as you know, the news media found out what we were doing, and the AP and the UPI ran stories about us in hundreds of newspapers. We were on national TV (11 times, I think it was), and I don't know how many radio broadcasts . . .

"There are no switches for the lights on any of the walls."

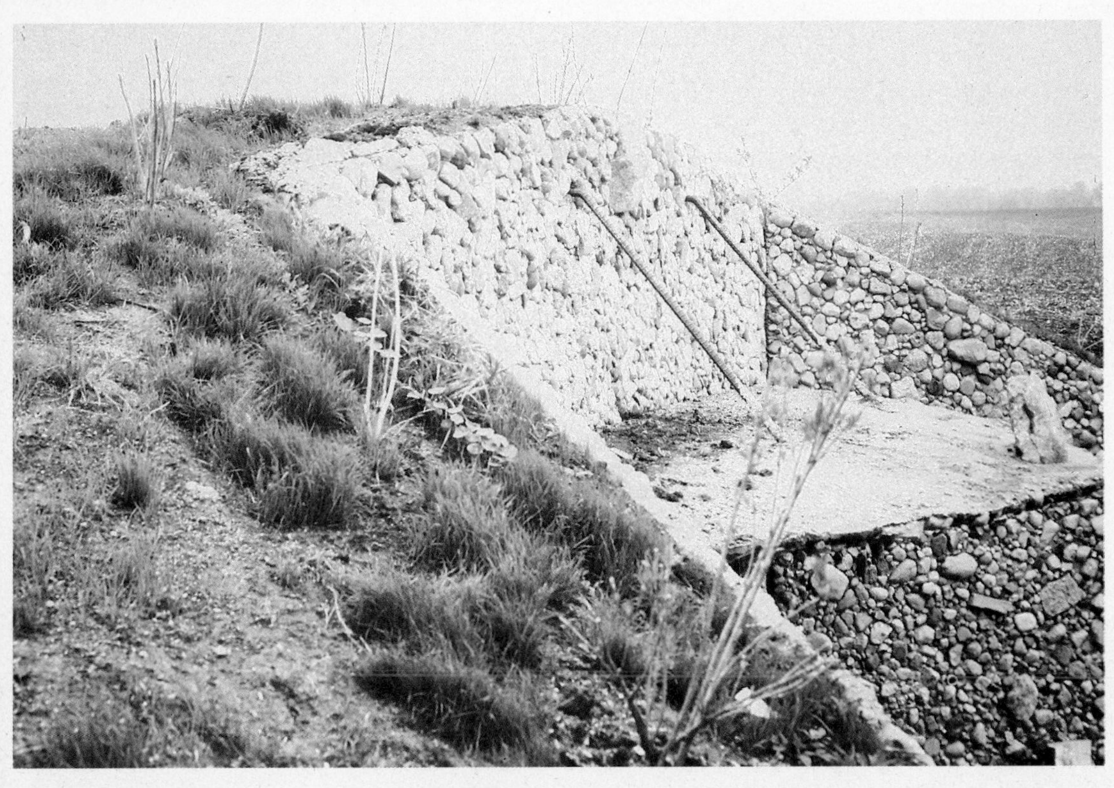

Fur on the interior doors and a bone decoration add to the cave's overall effect. Plants on the earthen "roof" are part of the landscaping.

"The house was far warmer and more snug during that really bad weather than any aboveground house I know of in this part of the country."

The bathroom at the back of the house features built-in fixtures.

and all that exposure brought in just hundreds and hundreds of people who wanted to see what our cave house was all about and learn how it operated.

As it turned out, we spent a total of six and a half months constructing the place . . . and we estimate that three and a half months of that time was used up just talking to people. Thanks to all the publicity and interest, we didn't get moved in here until last December.

Everything worked even better than I'd expected. I was pretty sure my ideas were going to pan out, of course, or I wouldn't have built this cave house to start with. But even I was surprised at how *well* everything has operated. The house was far warmer and more snug during that really bad weather than any aboveground house I know of in this part of the country . . . and we did it on even less fuel than I'd projected.

INTERVIEWER: Can you be more specific about that?

DAVIS: Sure. Let's go all the way back to *why* the house works so well and start from there.

The real secret of this building's performance is *not* the four feet of dirt on its roof. Four feet of dirt, all by itself, doesn't have any more value as insulation than, say, 10 inches of most good insulating materials on the market. So all that earth up there on the roof is all right . . . but it's no big deal.

But the earth *around and underneath* our cave house . . . ahhh, now that's a different story. Dig down eight feet beneath the surface of the ground almost anywhere in this part of Illinois, and you'll find that the temperature of the soil remains at an almost constant 58°F year round. As a matter of fact, since the heat of summer and the cold of winter can penetrate those 96" of earth only just so fast, you'll find something else that's even more interesting: The temperature of the ground 8' down a bit *warmer* than 58°F in *November* and a little *cooler* than 58°F in *May*.

INTERVIEWER: The whole earth, then, is acting like a gigantic thermal flywheel that balances out—at some depth—the seasonal changes of temperature we experience on the planet's surface?

DAVIS: Right. The whole earth works like a big flywheel. It absorbs a certain amount of heat energy during the summer and then slowly releases that energy in the winter.

And that's why we insulated the top and part way—but not *all* the way—down the sides of this underground house. We took that Styrofoam insulation down 8 feet below the ground's surface, and no farther. Why? It's because we wanted to shield our living area from the faster temperature swings near the earth's surface, while leaving it exposed to the much slower temperature variations that take place 8 feet and more beneath the surface of the ground.

Now what does this mean? It means that when the outside air temperature is 10°F and a family living in a conventional house above the ground wants to keep their home at a comfortable 70° . . . they have to burn enough wood or oil or coal or buy enough electricity or gas to maintain that full 80° temperature difference. And that's a lot of fuel.

But under the same conditions—when the outside air temperature is 10°F—the "outside dirt temperature" for our house is still 58°. This means that we have to maintain only a 12° temperature difference to keep our cave home at a comfortable 70°. And it takes a whole lot less fuel for us to maintain that 12° difference than it takes for the other family to maintain its 80° temperature difference.

INTERVIEWER: Besides that, I'll bet you come out even further ahead of the game on windy days. Sheltered under four feet of dirt the way you are, you should have hardly any of the windchill factor to deal with that sometimes seems to actually pull the heat right out of an aboveground house.

DAVIS: Right. That probably translates into an even greater fuel savings for us.

INTERVIEWER: Let's get back to the moderating flywheel effect that all the earth around and under your house has upon the dwelling. Is there anything you can do to make that effect even more pronounced?

DAVIS: Oh sure . . . we've already done it. While all those rocks in the walls and the ceiling are pretty and we like to look at them, they're there also because rocks heat up and cool down slowly . . . in just the same way that the earth does. The sheer mass of the concrete and stone we've put into our residence has very little value as insulation . . . but a great deal of value as a moderator of the temperature in here.

Now, to a certain extent, this works both ways. When we first moved in last December, for instance, we had to run our Franklin stove and an auxiliary electric space heater full blast—both of them—for a whole week until all those rocks and all that concrete in the walls, and a certain amount of the earth around them, slowly came up to 72°F.

Once we finally got everything up to that temperature, though, it all wanted to stay right there. From that point on it didn't take much heat at all to keep everything at a steady temperature in here. We disconnected the space heater, and we cut way back on the amount of wood we burned in the Franklin . . . and everything coasted along as pretty as you please at a constant 72°.

INTERVIEWER: You kept this whole house warm all winter with just that one little Franklin stove?

DAVIS: Right. And we didn't even keep it burning all the time. We'd never, for example, get up at night and stoke the fire. Instead, we'd actually bank the blaze when we went to bed, and—interestingly enough—with the fire banked and all the doors in here closed at night, the temperature would usually *climb* a little before we got up the next morning. It wasn't much—just a half degree or so—but once all these rocks are warmed up it's obvious that, as long as no one is going in and out the way we do during the day, the sheer mass of the heated stones and concrete can keep us warm for a long time.

This is more than just theory, too, by the way . . . as we had graphically demonstrated to us during one of the unexpected big snows that hit Illinois last winter. I had plenty of wood lined up for fuel at the time, but it was all somewhere else waiting for me to cut it. So there we were, snowed in by a blizzard for four full days with nothing to burn.

Well, I went up to a nearby gas station and brought back six old tires. I thought we could at least burn them in the stove and get a little heat that way. But we had to cut the rubber into such small chunks that it wasn't worth the effort . . . so we just let the fire go out.

INTERVIEWER: What happened?

DAVIS: We lost only two degrees a day. It was something like −25°F outside with a windchill factor all the way down to −80°F but, in four days without a fire, the temperature in here slid down from 70° to only 62°. To tell the truth, I could have gotten out and brought wood in a day or two earlier than I finally did . . . but we were all so comfortable that I didn't want to do it. We just didn't have anything to worry about.

At the same time this happened to us, though, they lost their electricity for ten hours in Minier—a little town north of us—and the folks up there suffered tremendously. When the electricity went off for just ten hours there, it left people all over town really up against it. The temperature went right down to below freezing in many homes, and practically every water pipe froze up and burst. Yet here we were without any heat at all for 96 hours . . . and our house never got below 62°F.

INTERVIEWER: What about the rest of the winter?

DAVIS: You know, they claim that this was one of the worst sieges of bad weather the U.S. has had since the government started keeping records of such things. But I never enjoyed a winter so much in my life. We just sat in here and "let 'er blow" outside. We didn't care what happened.

This house is comfortable during the summer too . . . without any need for expensive air conditioning. I can hardly wait until the middle of August. When everyone else around here is rolling and tossing and trying to get some sleep on those hot, sticky nights . . . we'll be peacefully slumbering away—under blankets—in a house that's a cool 58°F. I figure that we may even want to open up some vents during the summer and let in a little of that hot outside air . . . just to keep it from getting *too* cold in here!

INTERVIEWER: Amazing. This house is going to pay for itself in just a few years on what you save on heating and cooling bills alone. But does it have any other advantages? Is there anything else about your underground cave that's different from an aboveground house, and which you like?

DAVIS: Oh, lots of things. It not only wants to help heat itself in the winter and cool itself during the summer, but it does it all so *evenly*. We never get any of that variation that so many houses have every time the furnace kicks on and off. Whatever temperature we want is always just constant in here. Everything works to keep the conditions in here on an even keel. We can change things when we want to, of course, but we know the change will take place gradually with none of the quick fluctuations that can have you broiling one minute and chilled the next. We think that makes this place a lot more healthful to live in.

And then we like the idea that our cave home is fireproof. What happens to the typical aboveground house when a fire breaks out? The people who live there lose everything. What would happen to us under the

"Whatever temperature we want is always just constant in here."

"But, as for feeling nervous in this house because it's underground, we've never had that problem."

same circumstances? Well, in the first place, a fire is sort of unlikely in this cement-and-rock structure sunk four feet under the surface of the earth. But if we *did* have a fire, we'd lose . . . what? . . . some furniture and, maybe, a door or two. That isn't even worth carrying insurance on.

INTERVIEWER: And if you aren't paying fire insurance premiums, that means this cave house of yours is saving you just that much more money every year, year after year, as regular as clockwork.

DAVIS: Right. The same goes for tornadoes and other kinds of storm damage. This part of the country turns into Tornado Alley every spring. And each time one of those twisters comes through, where does everyone head? They move underground, to the storm cellar. Well, guess what? I'm already here . . . and I've got my whole house with me.

INTERVIEWER: How safe are you in the event of an earthquake?

DAVIS: Well, I was talking to a professor from the University of Illinois one day—he's a geologist—and he was telling me this house is a good place to be during an earthquake too. He was saying that the reason buildings fall down when the ground trembles is because they're sitting up above the surface and trying to stand still while the earth moves beneath them, and it's this difference that tears them apart. But this house, which is right down *in* the ground, will just move back and forth a little with the quake and ride the whole thing out. According to the professor, the only way a quake can hurt us is if a fault opens up right under the house and we fall into it. But of course, that's highly unlikely, and nothing else would survive something like that either.

What it boils down to is that our cave home is so far ahead of every aboveground house around here when it comes to surviving any kind of calamity you can name that it isn't even funny. When we lived above the surface, we had an ideal location. Our house sat on a hill overlooking a five-acre lake with oak trees around it, and it was just perfect . . . except for the fact that we were always worried about fire and tornadoes or just ordinary spring storms that could blow a limb through the roof or take the shingles off. Down here, though, we know we're safe from everything but the direct hit of an atomic bomb. This house is a lot more fun to live in.

And quiet! Boy, I'll tell you . . . this is the place to be if you want to get away from noisy neighbors. Once a herd of cattle (there must have been 25 or 30 of them) got loose and stampeded right over this place . . . and Margaret—who was in the house at the time—came out later and didn't know anything had happened.

Another time we were all in here when my son-in-law—who'd just bought one of those really big and really loud snowmobiles—came roaring through the property and up over the roof and right on across our lots. About 20 minutes later he came back and asked us how we liked his new snowmobile, and we said, "*What* snowmobile?" I've even driven crawler tractors over this place, and the people inside never knew it.

INTERVIEWER: Do you ever get claustrophobia living in a cave house?

DAVIS: No. As solid as this place is, we never feel shut in. It's those big windows that do it, I guess. You can see them from almost any spot in the house.

Actually, you know, I *have* claustrophobia. It's awfully easy for me to feel uncomfortable in a tight place. And that's the reason I'd have built two ways in and out of this house even if the building code hadn't called for two entrances. It's important that I always know in my mind that I've got another way out of wherever I happen to be just in case something happens to the way I came in.

But as for feeling nervous in this house because it's underground, we've never had that problem . . . and I don't think anyone else has either. I know we get a lot of visitors who come here to see the place for that very reason. They want to know whether or not being underground will bother them. And the minute they come in and sit down, they feel right at home.

INTERVIEWER: Why does the house face west?

DAVIS: We just took the hill we had to work with as we found it, and that hill faced west a long time before we decided to build a house in it. I don't think it matters much when you're putting in a cave home. Any direction is a good one for a place like this to face, as long as it doesn't look due north. You want the coldest winds in the winter to blow up and over the house . . . not hit it square on.

INTERVIEWER: Have you considered making any changes in your home?

DAVIS: One of these days we may dig on farther back into the hill and put in a root cellar.

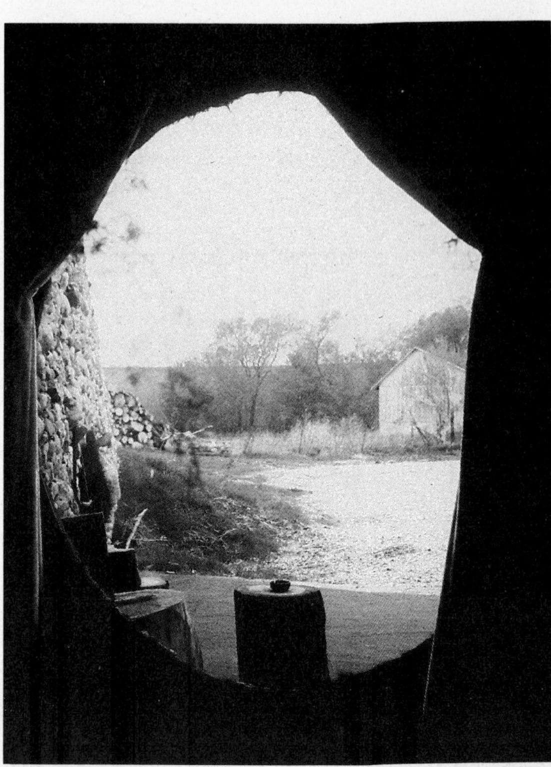

Cut into a hill as the cave is, the large windows at the front afford the family a pleasant view.

And we still haven't decided on the kind of reflectors we want to put over our light fixtures. We need something up there in the ceiling to make the overhead lights look more like sunshine coming down through the roof of a cave . . . but we haven't figured out just what'll do that yet.

We've also played around with the idea of using skylights to put more natural light into the back bedrooms. We've even designed something like a periscope which can pipe sunlight back into the corners, but I don't see any real advantage to it. Some people might think a setup like that is worthwhile, but it's been my experience that, even in aboveground houses, most folks keep their bedrooms sort of dark anyway and just turn the lights on automatically when they go into those rooms. Even without the skylights, I think we get about as much natural light in our bedrooms right now as the average aboveground house gets in a bedroom that has its curtains closed.

INTERVIEWER: All in all, then, you're happy with your cave just the way it is?

DAVIS: Real happy. And you can't beat our maintenance setup. We don't have any! There's nothing to paint or rot out or discolor or fall apart anywhere in the house. We've never used a paintbrush on the place, and we never will. The only thing I have to do to keep our cave looking good is mow its roof once a week in the summer!

INTERVIEWER: OK. Where do you go from here?

DAVIS: Well, we're putting in a garden on top of the house, and I may even decide to build a greenhouse up there. That way we can use what heat goes up the stovepipe from the Franklin stove, and we'll have absolutely no heat loss. Instead, we'll have vegetables—maybe even an orange tree—the year around growing right on top of our home.

We've also talked about adding a greenhouse to the front of the building. It sure would be nice to walk through a garden of flowers and vegetables every time we come into the cave. This construction concept is so adaptable that you can do almost anything with it.

Right now we're in the process of building an underground farrowing house for some pigs . . . and we're mulling over the idea of a cave grain cellar. The more we think about how well our new home is working, the more we get ideas for putting other residential, agricultural, and commercial projects underground. There's just no end to the possibilities! It's all very exciting.

I think we're definitely onto something that will be the wave of the future. And one of the really nice things about building underground this way—besides all the things we've already mentioned—is the fact that the structures we put in should last almost indefinitely . . . thousands of years. Concrete just gets stronger the longer it lasts, and I can't think of any reason one of our caves shouldn't be around from now on . . . unless someone gets tired of it and rips it out.

INTERVIEWER: It sounds as if you're going to make this your life's work.

DAVIS: Well, it didn't start out that way. In the beginning I was just looking for a way to cut my family's living expenses. Most of the people who heard that I planned to build a cave and move in were a little skeptical, you know, of the whole idea. A few of the folks around here probably thought I was nuts.

But then we started getting all that publicity, and for the first time, Armington was on the map. That began to get people in this area enthused about my project. And then we got the house finished and we moved in and, by gosh, it not only worked . . . it worked better than even I'd expected.

"There's no end to the possibilities! It's all very exciting."

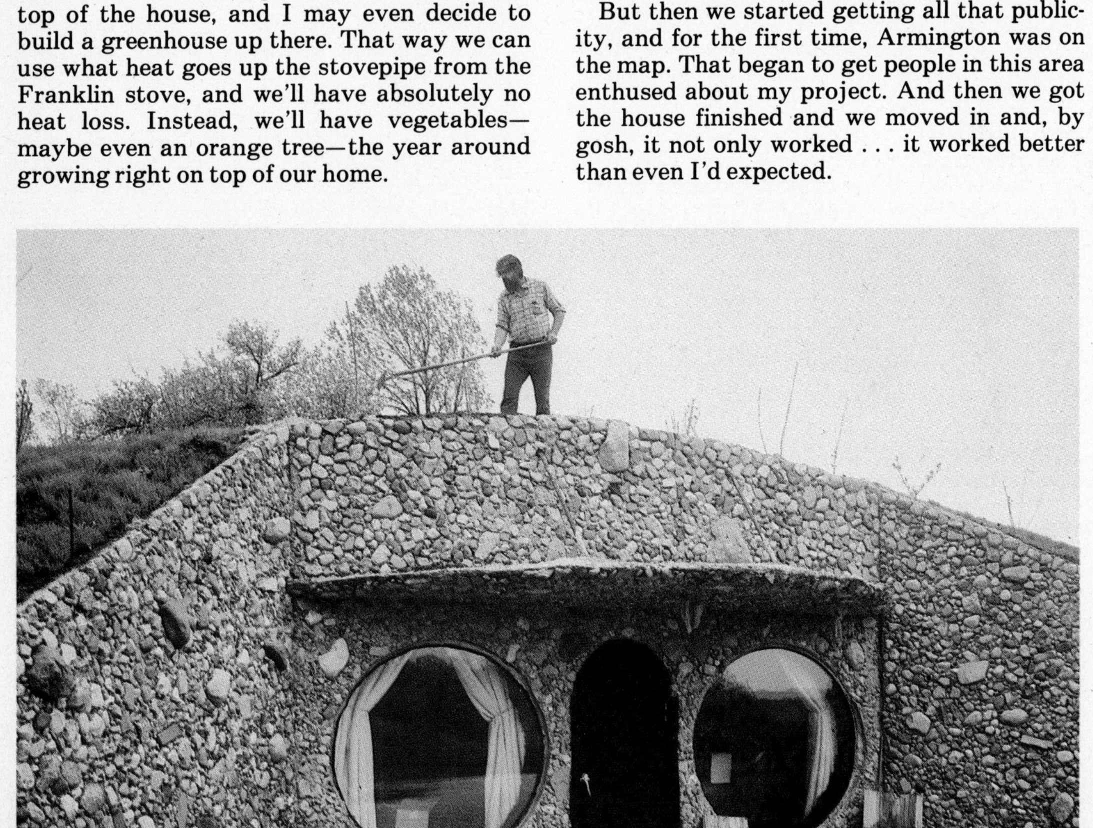

Davis is able to "garden" the roof of his home, and when inside, his family is insulated by the thick earth cover from the noises of the outside world.

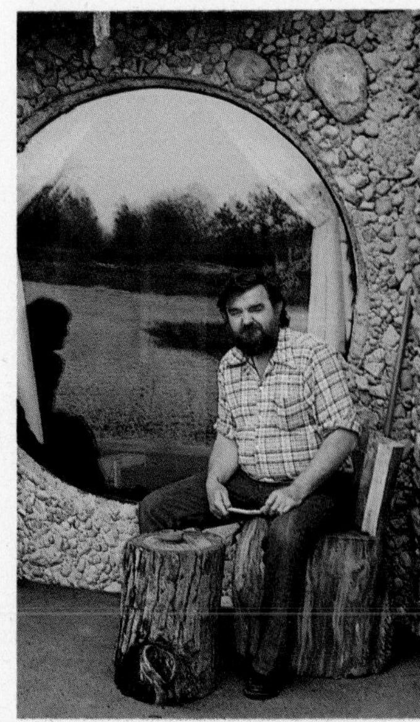

FOR FURTHER READING:

The books listed here provide an in-depth look into some of the alternative, energy-efficient building methods discussed in this publication.

BUILDING SMALL BARNS, SHEDS, & SHELTERS by Monte Burch (Garden Way). This is an indispensable book for the country-property or small-farm owner who needs to extend working, living, and storage areas. Complete, clear, and illustrated directions for building multi-purpose barns, carriage houses, barn-style garages, woodsheds, workshops, and animal housing are given. There are also full details on tools and materials, foundations and floors, framing, sheathing and roofing, windows and doors, and finishing. The step-by-step plans make it easy. 236 pages. Paperback. **64154 $10.95**

BUILDING WITH STONE by Charles McRaven (Lippincott & Crowell). Before you lift the first stone or span the first arch, read this book. It is the beginner's complete guide to using natural stone as a building material, and is richly illustrated with more than 200 drawings and photographs that complement detailed instructions for making stone walls, fireplaces, patios, small dams, and houses. The text is clear, concise, complete, and is written with a love for the beauty of stone and its uses, and with more than an occasional touch of humor. 207 pages. Hard cover. **64152 $15.95**

EARTH SHELTERED HOUSING DESIGN: GUIDELINES, EXAMPLES, AND REFERENCES by Underground Space Center, University of Minnesota (Van Nostrand). A landmark comprehensive handbook on earth-sheltered housing design and construction, this book shows you how to design and build comfortable, energy-efficient homes using soil insulation and passive solar heating. It provides plans, details, and photographs of existing earth-sheltered homes throughout the country. 318 pages. Paperback. **83019 $10.95**

EARTH SHELTERED HOMES: PLANS AND DESIGNS by Underground Space Center, University of Minnesota (Van Nostrand). This is an essential book for those considering the building of energy-efficient earth-sheltered homes. Beautifully illustrated with fine drawings and full-color photographs, it offers detailed construction information, plans, and energy data for twenty-three successful earth-sheltered homes in the United States and Europe. Data on materials for construction, type of earth cover, method of insulation, and waterproofing techniques accompany a full description of each house. 124 pages. Paperback. **83062 $10.95**

THE EARTH SHELTERED OWNER-BUILT HOME by Barbara and Ken Kern and Jane and Otis Mullan (Mullein). Here is a complete and well-illustrated guide to the beauty and efficiency of underground living, complete with full building instructions and details. Underground building can be simple and inexpensive, and the authors present three successful earth-sheltered homes from planning stage to the planting of the roof. An important reference book for anyone considering the benefits of building and living underground. 269 pages. Paperback. **83073 $9.95**

THE $50 & UP UNDERGROUND HOUSE BOOK (fourth edition) by Mike Oehler (Van Nostrand). This is a vital and stimulating book that teaches you how to build comfortable, highly livable underground houses through refreshing, entertaining prose and detailed, practical, and attractive illustrations. This is a how-to-guide to designing, cutting materials costs up to 90%, using solar energy, building into hillsides, solving drainage problems, and much more. A valuable reference book. 115 pages. Paperback. **83024 $8.95**

GETTING A ROOF OVER YOUR HEAD by the editors at Garden Way (Garden Way). Thousands of people are building their own homes these days or are renovating old houses. You may want to follow in their footsteps, break your own ground, raise your own roof beam. This comprehensive book of case histories can help you fulfill that dream. You'll meet in its pages many people who did it themselves, and you'll learn how it was done. It's full of ideas and inspiration . . . it could be just right for you. 168 pages. Paperback. **64153 $9.95**

SALVAGING OLD BARNS AND HOUSES: TEAR IT DOWN AND SAVE THE PIECES by Lawrence and Kathleen Abrams (Sterling). Salvaging old houses and buildings can give you an unlimited source of free or low-cost building materials, a virtual gold mine in decorative accessories, and, possibly, a business of your own that you can start with very little capital. This book, full of expert, technical, step-by-step information and photographs, provides everything you need to know about tools, safety precautions, dismantling procedures, and using salvaged materials. 128 pages. Paperback. **65072 $7.95**

THE SOLAR ELECTRIC HOME: A PHOTOVOLTAICS HOW-TO HANDBOOK by Joel Davidson and Richard Komp (Aatec). Photovoltaics is solar energy . . . electricity produced by sunlight via solar cells. The authors provide all one needs to know to select, build, install, and maintain a complete PV system, whether it be for remote-site, grid-connect, marine, or mobile use. Also described in this well-written and authoritative book are hybrid systems that are able to provide both electricity and hot water. This is an informative and invaluable how-to book on the use of solar energy. 200 pages. Paperback. **83074 $10.00**

UNDERGROUND HOUSES: HOW TO BUILD A LOW-COST HOME by Robert L. Roy (Sterling). An underground house can be practical, efficient, affordable, and bright and airy . . . and it can cost less to build, heat, and cool than a conventional house. Here is a firsthand account on how to build a subterranean home. The book covers, in remarkable detail and through easy-to-follow steps, such topics as site selection, the purchasing of building supplies, home designs, excavation, landscaping, erection of the structure, insulation, heating, and the installation of skylights and windows. Extremely well illustrated. 128 pages. Paperback. **83026 $5.95**

These books are available through most bookstores, directly from their publishers, or from Mother's Bookshelf®, Dept. 332301, 105 Stoney Mountain Road, Hendersonville, North Carolina 28791. When ordering from Mother's Bookshelf, add $1.25 for shipping and handling on 1 or 2 books ($2.00 for 3 or more books). Prices are subject to change.

MOTHER'S BOOKSHELF
105 Stoney Mountain Road, Hendersonville, North Carolina 28791